T0320432

Data Analytics for Business Intelligence

This book studies data, analytics, and intelligence using Boolean structure. Chapters dive into the theories, foundations, technologies, and methods of data, analytics, and intelligence.

The primary aim of this book is to convey the theories and technologies of data, analytics, and intelligence with applications to readers based on systematic generalization and specialization. Sun uses the Boolean structure to deconstruct all books and papers related to data, analytics, and intelligence and to reorganize them to reshape the world of big data, data analytics, analytics intelligence, data science, and artificial intelligence. Multi-industry applications in business, management, and decision-making are provided. Cutting-edge theories, technologies, and applications of data, analytics, and intelligence and their integration are also explored. Overall, this book provides original insights on sharing computing, insight computing, platform computing, a calculus of intelligent analytics and intelligent business analytics, meta computing, data analyticizing, DDPP (descriptive, diagnostic, predictive, and prescriptive) computing, and analytics.

This book is a useful resource with multi-industry applications for scientists, engineers, data analysts, educators, and university students.

Zhaohao Sun is a Full Professor of Information Technology at Papua New Guinea University of Technology. He has held academic positions in China, Germany, and Australia. Dr. Sun is the author of twelve books and numerous academic publications. His current interests include big data, artificial intelligence, and business intelligence. Dr. Sun is a senior member of the Institute of Electrical and Electronic Engineers and the Australian Computer Society.

Data Analytics for Business Intelligence
A Multi-Industry Approach

Zhaohao Sun

CRC Press
Taylor & Francis Group
Boca Raton London New York

CRC Press is an imprint of the
Taylor & Francis Group, an **informa** business

A CHAPMAN & HALL BOOK

Designed Cover Image: Big data technology and data science illustration. Data flow concept. Querying, analyzing, and visualizing complex information. Neural network for artificial intelligence. Data mining. Business analytics. 2236217443. Stock Photo

First edition published 2025
by CRC Press
2385 NW Executive Center Drive, Suite 320, Boca Raton FL 33431

and by CRC Press
4 Park Square, Milton Park, Abingdon, Oxon, OX14 4RN

CRC Press is an imprint of Taylor & Francis Group, LLC

© 2025 Zhaohao Sun

Reasonable efforts have been made to publish reliable data and information, but the author and publisher cannot assume responsibility for the validity of all materials or the consequences of their use. The authors and publishers have attempted to trace the copyright holders of all material reproduced in this publication and apologize to copyright holders if permission to publish in this form has not been obtained. If any copyright material has not been acknowledged please write and let us know so we may rectify in any future reprint.

Except as permitted under U.S. Copyright Law, no part of this book may be reprinted, reproduced, transmitted, or utilized in any form by any electronic, mechanical, or other means, now known or hereafter invented, including photocopying, microfilming, and recording, or in any information storage or retrieval system, without written permission from the publishers.

For permission to photocopy or use material electronically from this work, access www.copyright.com or contact the Copyright Clearance Center, Inc. (CCC), 222 Rosewood Drive, Danvers, MA 01923, 978-750-8400. For works that are not available on CCC please contact mpkbookspermissions@tandf.co.uk

Trademark notice: Product or corporate names may be trademarks or registered trademarks and are used only for identification and explanation without intent to infringe.

Library of Congress Cataloging-in-Publication Data
Names: Sun, Zhaohao, author.
Title: Data analytics for business intelligence : a multi-industry approach / Zhaohao Sun.
Description: First edition. | Boca Raton, FL : CRC Press, [2025] | Includes bibliographical references and index.
Identifiers: LCCN 2024029564 (print) | LCCN 2024029565 (ebook) | ISBN 9781032585338 (hardback) | ISBN 9781032585321 (paperback) | ISBN 9781003450504 (ebook)
Subjects: LCSH: Business--Data processing.
Classification: LCC HF5548.2 .S8395 2025 (print) | LCC HF5548.2 (ebook) | DDC 658/.05--dc23/eng/20240723
LC record available at https://lccn.loc.gov/2024029564
LC ebook record available at https://lccn.loc.gov/2024029565

ISBN: 978-1-032-58533-8 (hbk)
ISBN: 978-1-032-58532-1 (pbk)
ISBN: 978-1-003-45050-4 (ebk)

DOI: 10.1201/9781003450504

Typeset in Minion
by SPi Technologies India Pvt Ltd (Straive)

Dedicated with all my heart

to

My wife Yanxia Huo, son Lizhe (Lee), daughter-in-law Qing Chang, and my twin granddaughters Shannon (Yubing) and Sharon (Yutang) for their lasting support, unforgettable patience, and deep love

To

my motherland, China, and my beloved countries, Australia, Papua New Guinea, Germany, and the United States

Contents

Acknowledgments

THIS BOOK REFLECTS EXPERIENCE, intelligence, wisdom, and persever- ance. First of all, a number of my colleagues and friends in academic settings provided significant suggestions for improving my teaching and research in China, Germany, Australia, Papua New Guinea, the United States, and beyond. For this I am thankful to Prof. Jans-Jürgen Zimmerman, Prof. Ludwig Cromme, Dr. Klaus Weber, Prof. Jianqiang Li, Prof. Shuliang Zhang, Prof. Dong Dong, Prof. Jun Han, Prof. Gavin Finnie, Prof. Sidney Morris, Prof. Andrew Stranieri, Dr. Sally Firmin, Prof. Hepu Deng, Prof. Zhiyou Wu, Prof. Kenneth Strang, Ms. Francisca Pambel, Prof. Narasimha Rao Vajjhala, Prof. Ora Renagi, and Prof. Shamsul Akanda. I owe a debt of gratitude to many people at PNG University of Technology for their sup- port and encouragement throughout the years I worked on this book. A great thanks also goes to Mr. Jordan Dean and Dr. Kulala Mulung of the PNG Science and Technology Secretariat for funding for this book.

I am grateful to the anonymous reviewers of the book proposal for their erudite suggestions for publishing the book and to the executive board for approving the book. I am sincerely grateful to all the members of the edi- torial advisory board for their constructive insights. My sincerest thanks go to my friends, Mr. Gerald Bok, Ms. Patie Peace, Ms. Chelsea Low, Mr. Sreevas Mangattumana, Ms. Petrena Wilbur, and other friends of CRC Press and Taylor & Francis Group for their outstanding and continuous support and patience throughout the book development process.

Last but not least, I would like to express my deepest appreciation to my wife, Dr. Yanxia (Monica) Huo, my son, Lizhe (Lee), daughter-in-law, Qing Chang, and my twin granddaughters, Shannon (Yubing) and Sharon (Yutang), for their understanding, encouragement, and deep love. Without their lasting support and patience, writing this book would not have been possible.

Preface

I INITIALLY UNDERSTOOD ARTIFICIAL INTELLIGENCE (AI) when I attended a national conference held in Taiyuan, China in 1987. The important impact of that understanding was that I started to study AI and logics of computer science, including λ calculus, which was supported by Professor Hongxiang Li of Beihang University. One of my earlier published journal articles is on logics of computer science and expert systems. At that time, I also taught discrete mathematics, AI, expert systems, fuzzy logic, knowledge base systems, knowledge engineering, formal language and automata, software engineering, database management systems, and more. I taught programming languages such as Prolog and LISP as a part of AI. Two AI books were influential at that time. One was the book by Fu and Cai (1987), *Artificial Intelligence* with applications, which mainly include search techniques, problem reduction, knowledge representation methods, and advanced knowledge reasoning in traditional AI. The other one was Nilsson's (1982) book, *Principles of Artificial Intelligence*, Springer 1982; both books guided me to teaching and research in the late 1980s until 1995. These books also affected millions of computer science students in China since then.

In the early 1990s, I studied more articles related to AI (two of them by R. A. Brooks) such as intelligence without reason and intelligence without representation. At the same time, I was teased by a two-year-old child. This motivated me to write an article on intelligence with deception. This article was presented, and well accepted, at a national conference on AI held at Hangzhou, China, 1992. AI deception is important for human's intelligence development. This idea and method have impacted my thinking and research ever since. AI deception has been ubiquitous recently; I just experienced a process-based AI deception.

Reading, learning, thinking, lecturing, discussing, sharing, imagining, associating, and writing have become my academic life since then. For example, I read cybernetics, control theory, information theory, synergetics, dissipative structural theory, the third wave, and what computers can't do: The limits of artificial intelligence (Hubert L. Dreyfus), frames of mind: theory of multiple intelligences (Howard E Gardner), quantum mechanics, to name a few. I have also published several research papers on expert systems, intelligent decision support systems (DSS), AI, logic and a book on discrete mathematics (in Chinese).

I received the national scholarship from the Chinese government in 1995 and studied at Operation Research Institute, RWTH Aachen, Germany with Professor H-J Zimmermann. I studied a lot of fuzzy expert systems and operations research such as dynamic, mathematical, and fuzzy programming. I also loved AI and fuzzy expert systems at that time. Later, I moved to Brandenburg University of Technology Cottbus in 1997 to study numerical mathematics, fuzzy logic, information systems, database systems, AI, and more, I still loved intelligence and updated my reading and thinking of AI including a lot of philosophies and computer sciences including Java and MATLAB.

When studying and working in Germany, I was very impressed by the seminal article of Alan Turing, 1950, Computing Machinery and Intelligence, *published in* Mind. The research and development of AI have been heavily influenced by the mentioned article since then. For example, Turing test, machine learning, machine translation, natural language understanding and processing, and so on. All these can be considered as the imitation, simulation, augmentation, and automation of rational intelligence (Russell & Norvig, 2020). In other words, AI has aimed to imitate, simulate, augment, and automate rational intelligence. However, deception has been mentioned in Turing's article. *Deception is a kind of irrational intelligence.* "Without deception, a child can always be a child", at least in terms of intelligence and mind. The progress of intelligence depends on human's deception. Then I and my colleague (Dr Klaus Weber) published two conference papers: one is Logic with tricks in Baden-Baden. Another is Turing test and Intelligence with Tricks in Belfast. Deception was replaced with trick, because AI deception was not popular at that time.

After receiving the Australian scholarship for PhD research in 1999, I moved to Bond University on the Gold Coast, Australia, to study with Professor Gavin Finnie. My research emphasized intelligent techniques, including case-based reasoning, Knowledge base systems, and multiagent systems. I and Prof Finnie co-authored dozens of papers on them. My PhD thesis is on case-based reasoning and e-commerce. Then we published a book titled *Intelligent Techniques in E-commerce* (Springer, 2004). The intelligent techniques cover fuzzy logic, expert systems, intelligent agents, and multiagent systems. Later, I hoped to publish another book on intelligent techniques in web services. I developed case-based reasoning and transformed it into experience-based reasoning and experience management, both are based on knowledge-based reasoning and knowledge management. This book covers data, information, knowledge, experience, intelligence, and wisdom, all these impacts my thinking and research since then. You will find my exploration in the current book. At the same time, I taught several subjects such as intelligent systems, decision support systems, information systems methodology, logic of computer science, and intelligence computing to my students at the University of Wollongong as lecturer, and then Hebei Normal University as a professor of computer science. My research interests were intelligent techniques in e-commerce and web services. Experience-based reasoning and experience management still filled my head.

Besides rational intelligence, I also developed the theory and technology of irrational intelligence for experience-based reasoning at that time. This research successfully led to 10+ internationally peer-reviewed publications (Sun & Finnie, 2007; Sun, 2019). Mathematics, logic, and AI have played a significant role in my research. Experience-based reasoning is an extension of case-based reasoning. Experience-based reasoning is still an important topic in augmenting human intelligence. Later, I published 3 papers on experience-based reasoning, similarity-based reasoning, and similarity intelligence (Sun, 2023).

Later I was employed at the University of Ballarat as a senior lecturer (which is an associate professor based on the USA's tertiary system, although we could not call us in such a way). I taught business information systems, project management, e-commerce, and management information systems. My research still focuses on e-commerce, web service, and reasoning. In 2012, I read a message from the US government's investment on big data, I forwarded this information to my colleagues at once. I realized that big data would impact individuals and organizations. During that time, I met Professor Paul P Wang of Duke University and Professor Wanlei Zhou of Deakin University. They encouraged me to focus on big data, analytics, and intelligence. My first paper on big data and analytics was accepted by an international conference for publication. I developed my papers and submitted them to international journals for publication. My track of research is data, big data, data analytics, big data analytics, big analytics, intelligent big data analytics, business analytics, AI, and BI. Business Intelligence (BI) has drawn increasing attention in academia and business in the past two decades. I have lectured BI at least for more than two decades in Australia, China, and PNG. At the same time, I was employed as an adjunct professor at the Federation University and worked with my former colleagues to work on intelligent big data analytics and decision support making. I was employed as an associate professor and then promoted to a full professor at PNG University of Technology. I taught database management systems, management information systems, cloud computing, and business intelligence and analytics. My research has been also supported by PNG Science and Technology Secretariat. My research interests focus on data, analytics, intelligence, and their integrations.

We have been in the age of trinity of big data, analytics, and AI since 2012. Data, analytics, and intelligence are dominating all individuals and organizations. This book is dedicated to data, analytics, intelligence, and their applications.

In the process of endeavoring, I organized, edited, and published a special issue on Big Data, Analytics, and AI in *Journal of New Mathematics and Natural Computation* (J NMNC) in 2017 (Sun & Wang, 2017). I published dozens of internationally peer-reviewed, research papers in the area, including a mathematical approach to big data in J NMNC, many research papers in leading international journals like Journal of Computer Information Systems, and international conference proceedings including the paper titled "Big Data Analytics as a Service for Enhancing BI" (Sun, Sun, & Strang, 2018). IGI-Global and I published the quadruplet of data, analytics, and intelligence: *Managerial Perspectives on Intelligent Big Data Analytics* (Sun, 2019) *Intelligent Analytics with Advanced Multi-Industry Applications* (Sun, 2021),, and *Foundations and Applications of Intelligent Business Analytics* (Sun & Wu, 2022), Sun, Z (2022) *Driving Socioeconomic Development with Big Data: Theories, Technologies, and Applications.* Imitating, simulating, augmenting, and automating intelligence based on big data is crucial for these books to realize the goal of AI, analytics, and business analytics.

The following issues and challenges should draw attention:

1. What is the relationship between data, analytics, and intelligence?

2. What is the relationship between Business Intelligence and Analytics?

3. What is the relationship between Business Intelligence and Analytics, as well as data intelligence?

4. How to generalize and specialize data science, big data, BI and AI-based on the research methodology.

This book highlights:

1. The Boolean structure dominating this book.

2. Computing science, engineering, technology, systems, intelligence, services, and intelligence with applications penetrating every chapter of the book.

3. Meta computing, science, engineering, and intelligence. The cycle of business workflow for description, diagnosis, prediction, prescription, which leads to DDPP (Descriptive, diagnostic, predictive, and prescriptive) analytics and computing.

4. Problem-driven computing and analytics.

5. Big data 4.0: = big intelligence.

6. Data analyticizing as a process of creating data analytics.

7. Insight computing and insight science.

8. Data, big data, big information, big knowledge, and big wisdom; and analytics, data analytics, big data analytics, intelligent big data analytics, and intelligent business analytics.

9. A calculus for searching big data, a calculus of intelligent analytics, a calculus of intelligent business analytics, and a calculus of cloud computing have been proposed in this book. These form a calculus paradigm. Then this book can be renamed as a calculus of data, analytics, and intelligence for business.

10. Sharing computing, insight computing, and platform computing have been proposed as the future of intelligent analytics.

Last but not least, not only data, analytics, and intelligence but also information, knowledge, and wisdom are elements of digital economy, technology, and society. Embedding these elements into digital wisdom, networks, products, and services will make the general public, organizations, and communities smarter and more intelligent. Let us embrace it as a new digital citizen in the digital age.

REFERENCES

Brooks, R. A. (1991a, 4). *Intelligence without Reason, A.I. Memo No. 1293.* Retrieved August 31, 2017, from MIT: http://dspace.mit.edu/bitstream/handle/1721.1/6569/AIM-1293.pdf

Brooks, R. A. (1991b). Intelligence without representation. *Artificial Intelligence,* 47(1–3), 139–159.

Fu, J., & Cai, Z. (1987). *Artificial Intelligence with Applications (傅京孙 and 蔡自兴: 人工智能及其应用).* Beijing: 清华大学出版社.

Nilsson, N. J. (1982). *Principles of Artificial Intelligence, ISBN 978-3-540-11340-9.* Springer-Verlag.

Russell, S., & Norvig, P. (2020). *Artificial Intelligence: A Modern Approach* (4th Edition). Upper Saddle River: Prentice Hall.

Sun, Z. (2019). "Intelligent Big Data Analytics: A Managerial Perspective." In Z. Sun, *Managerial Perspectives on Intelligent Big Data Analytics* (pp. 1–19). USA: IGI-Global.

Sun, Z. (2021). *Intelligent Analytics with Advanced Multi-Industry Applications.* USA: IGI-Global.

Sun, Z. (2023). "Similarity Intelligence: Similarity Based Reasoning, Computing, and Analytics." *Journal of Computer Science Research,* 5(3), 1–14.

Sun, Z., & Wang, P. P. (2017). "Big Data, Analytics and Intelligence: An Editorial Perspective." *Journal of New Mathematics and Natural Computation,* 13(2), 75–81.

Sun, Z., & Wu, Z. (Eds.). (2022). *Handbook of Research on Foundations and Applications of Intelligent Business Analytics.* IGI-Global. Retrieved from https://www.igi-global.com/book/handbook-research-foundations-applications-intelligent/275268.

Sun, Z., Sun, L., & Strang, K. (2018). "Big Data Analsytics Services for Enhancing Business Intelligence." *Journal of Computer Information Systems (JCIS),* 58(2), 162–169. doi:10.1080/08874417.2016.1220239.

CHAPTER 1

Introduction

Data, analytics, and intelligence are the elements of every individual and organization to compete and survive in this world.

W E ARE LIVING IN an age of data, analytics, and intelligence. This Chapter will explore data, analytics, and intelligence. This chapter first discusses the heuristics of the Greek philosopher Plato and French mathematician Descartes and reshaping the world. Then, it addresses questions based on a Boolean structure that destructs big data, data analytics, data science, and AI into data, analytics, and intelligence as the Boolean atoms. The data, analytics, and intelligence are reorganized and reassembled, based on the Boolean structure, into data analytics, analytics intelligence, data intelligence, and data analytics intelligence. This chapter presents big data, analytics, and intelligence: A Boolean Structure as the basic structure for this book and lists the characteristics of this book.

Learning objectives of this chapter:

- Identify proper applications of data, analytics, and intelligence.

- Gain familiarity with the impacts of articificial intelligence (AI), business intelligence (BI), big data, and analytics in the real world.

- Distinguish data mining from data analytics.

- Explore data, analytics, and intelligence.

DOI: 10.1201/9781003450504-1

1

- Understand big data, big knowledge, and big intelligence.

- Define big data and big data analytics, with examples.

- Understand BI and data analytics.

- Discuss the relationship among BI, analytics, and data intelligence.

1.1 DATA ANALYTICS AND BI: A MULTI-INDUSTRY APPROACH

Data, analytics, intelligence, and their integration are at the frontier for revolutionizing our work, life, business, management, and organization as well as healthcare, finance, e-commerce, and web services (Henke & Bughin, 2016; Lohr, 2012 February 11; John, 2013; Sun & Huo, 2021; James & Duncan, 2023).

Big data has become one of the most unprecedented and ever-increasing frontiers for innovation, research, and development in the computer industry and business (Chen & Zhang, 2014; Laney & Jain, 2017; Howarth, 2022; Kumar, 2015). Big data has also been a key enabler in exploring business insights, BI, and economics, thus drawing an unprecedented interest in industries, universities, governments, and organizations (Gartner, 2023a; Sharda, Delen, & Turba, 2018). Data analytics has also played a significant role in BI and business activities (3pillarglobal, 2021; Schlegel & Sun, 2023). Market-oriented AI, big data-based AI, and BI (Russell & Norvig, 2020; Laudon & Laudon, 2020), ChatGPT, driverless cars, TikTok, and artificial drones have immersed us in the era of AI.

Big data analytics, advanced analytics, and modern analytics have drawn increasing attention in academia, industry, and government (IDC, 2019). Many vendors in the modern analytics and BI market have double-digit revenue growth (Howson, Richardson, Sallam, & Kronz, 2019). Data analytics can be considered data-driven discoveries of knowledge, intelligence, and communications (Delena & Demirkanb, 2013).

Data science is short for data science, data engineering, data management, data systems, data tools, data services, and data applications. All these topics can be considered as data computing (Sun, 2022a).

AI is becoming a core business with analytic competency to transform business processes, reconfigure workforces, optimize infrastructure, and blend industries (Laney & Jain, 2017). AI, including machine learning, and natural language processing, has promoted the capabilities of BI and analytics software (Kingpin, 2024). BI and analytics as a service enables organizations to automate data analysis, generate predictive insights, and gain a deeper understanding of their business operations.

BI has received increasing attention in academia, business, and management since 1989 (Lim, Chen, & Chen, 2013). BI has become an important technology for improving the business performance of enterprises but also is a marketing brand for developing business, e-commerce, and e-services (Turban & Volonino, 2011). It provides the momentum for developing organization intelligence, enterprise intelligence, management intelligence, and marketing intelligence (Brooks S., 2022). However, what does the intelligence mean in BI? This is still an issue in understanding BI completely. Furthermore, BI is facing new big challenges because of the dramatic development of big data and big data technologies (Fan, Lau, & Zhao, 2015). Thus, how to use big data analytics services to enhance BI becomes a big issue for business, e-commerce, e-services, and information systems (Sun, Sun, & Strang, 2018).

Business analytics is an emerging and fast-growing field (Liebowitz, 2014). It has become a mainstream market adopted broadly across industries, organization sizes, and geographic regions to facilitate data-driven decision-making and is enabled by business analytics solutions (Vesset, McDonough, Schubmehl, & Wardley, 2013). According to Kingpin's research, the global BI and Analytics Software market was valued at US$ 23,22 billion in 2023 and is anticipated to reach US$ 35,76 billion by 2030 with a CAGR (compound annual growth rate) of 5.9% during the forecast period 2024–2030 (Kingpin, 2024). This fact facilitates unprecedented interest and adoption of BI and analytics. SAP, Oracle, IBM, Tableau, SAS, and Microsoft were worldwide top 5 BI and analytics software vendors in 2023.

We are enjoying the analytics service (Delena & Demirkanb, 2013; Sun, 2019; Laney & Jain, 2017) and big data analytics service (Sun, 2018b). For example, Google Analytics provides services like Google maps to billions of people worldwide. Clarivate Analytics is the largest academic quality publication database to provide subscription services to academia and industry. Tableau, Python, and R as software have been widely used to develop big data analytics services (Sun, 2019b; Aroraa, Lele, & Jindal, 2022). Various smartphones provided the health analytics services. Big data and analytics are increasingly critical elements across most industries, business functions, and ICT disciplines. They are creating unlimited business value possibilities, based on the research of Gartner (Laney & Jain, 2017; James & Duncan, 2023).

Intelligent big data analytics as an emerging science and technology based on AI and other big intelligences is becoming a mainstream market adopted broadly across industries, organizations, and geographic regions and among individuals to facilitate decision-making for businesses and individuals to achieve desired business outcomes (James & Duncan, 2023; Sun, Sun, & Strang, 2018; Howson, Richardson, Sallam, & Kronz, 2019).

A Google Scholar search for "data, analytics, and intelligence" found about 11,100,000, 4,860,000, and 4,650,000 results, respectively (retrieved on March 8, 2024). This implies that data, analytics, and intelligence have become significant topics for the research of scholars and researchers. A Google search for "data, analytics, and intelligence" found about 8,530,000,000; 2,650,000,000; and 1,710,000,000 results respectively (retrieved on March 8, 2024). This means that data, analytics, and intelligence have significantly influenced our lives, communities, economies, and societies. Therefore, data, analytics, and intelligence are still topics for us to explore and develop in the digital age.

After the above discussion and reviewing a dozen different books on big data, data analytics, data science, AI, and BI, several issues are still open for comprehending big data, AI, and data science in academia, industries, and governments:

1. What are the fundamentals of data, analytics, and intelligence?

2. How can we understand the relationships between data, analytics, and intelligence?

3. What are the relationships between big data, big knowledge, and big intelligence?

4. How can we understand the relationships among big data and big data analytics?

5. What is the relationship among BI and data analytics?

6. What is the relationship among BI, analytics, and data intelligence?

This book addresses the above research issues based on our motivations, methodologies, and deep investigations. More specifically, this book will first examine data, analytics, and intelligence as the main three atoms for constructing a Boolean structure. Using this Boolean structure, this book will explore the related components of Boolean structure. This chapter first discusses reshaping the world and the heuristics of the Greek philosopher Plato and French mathematician Descartes. Then it addresses these above questions based on a Boolean structure, which destructs big data, data analytics, data science, and AI into data, analytics, and intelligence as the Boolean atoms. The data, analytics, and intelligence are reorganized and reassembled, based on the Boolean structure, to data analytics, analytics intelligence, data intelligence, and data analytics intelligence. The proposed approach in this research might facilitate the research and development of big data, data analytics, AI, and data science.

The rest of this chapter is organized as follows: Section 1.2 looks at the heuristics of Aristotle and Descartes. Section 1.3 discusses how to reshape the world by shaping wood, based on a story. Section 1.4 explores data, analytics, and intelligence using a Boolean structure. Section 1.5 listed the characteristics of this book. The final section ends this chapter with some concluding remarks.

1.2 THE HEURISTICS OF ARISTOTLE AND DESCARTES

The *Republic* was written by the ancient Greek philosopher Plato (Plato & Jowett (Translator), 2022) about justice, order, character, and the man of the republic. A few years ago, my friend told me that he would like to build a republic and become a president. As a scholar, I cannot create a republic. However, I can write an article and publish a book (Sun, 2023b). Writing an article and publishing a book is similar to creating a republic as one must follow a set of rules: writing rules, publishing rules, formatting rules, templating rules, and communicating rules. Some articles and books also are required to have a research methodology consisting of research rules.

Rene Descartes is a great French mathematician. It is he who introduced analytical geometry, which let the author know how to integrate algebra and geometry. It is he who gave the author a better understanding of analytics. Descartes is a great man because of his profound knowledge of analytical geometry and his research methodology (Descartes, 1637). The author does not have a lot of knowledge and skill in data science, AI, and computer sciences although he has been working in these areas for a few decades. However, this research attempts to use a new research methodology and ideas, just like Descartes, to create a new research methodology for a new book.

It should be noted that inspired by the work of Rene Descartes (Descartes, 1637), all science in the digital age is like a tree of which six elements (namely, data, information, knowledge, experience, intelligence, and wisdom) are the root. Mathematics and computing are the trunk, and all the other sciences are the branches that grow out of this trunk.

1.3 RESHAPING THE WORLD

When the author was very young (Sun, 2023b), his dream was to become a carpenter. He bought a very expensive saw, plane, chisel, nail, axe, and ruler to make a table, similar to the existing table around him. His idea was to reshape wood although he could not reshape the world. Yes, he was very happy that he made a table, which made his parents also very happy. His neighbors and villagers helped him to become a master of reshaping wood. However, he did not continue this way. Instead, he continued to study, took the national examination for universities, and changed his way completely.

Then, he became a scholar and drove to an Australian furniture shop to buy a box of a table made in China, from his hometown. After he came back to his home, he opened the box and reassembled the table based on the instructions: how to reassemble the table using a provided screwdriver.

The author asked the boss of the table factory how to make a table. The boss told him that this was a reshaping of wood by:

1. Design a table and draw a table blueprint.

2. Disassemble the table into a table plate, leg, nails, furniture cam lock, and nut.

3. Procure a table plate, table leg, furniture cam lock and nut, nails, and booklet for reassembling the table from different factories, using the Internet, and put them into a box.

4. Advertise the information about the table to the entire world, using the Internet.

5. Sell all the boxes of tables to the world using the Internet.

Therefore, disassembling, procuring, and selling are important tasks of the table factory. The shop only procures and sells the table boxes. The customer can buy the table box and reassemble the table based on the instructions.

This is reshaping wood toward mass production, based on big data and the Internet. In 2023, 40% of the furniture made in China were made by these factories. The Internet and big data have been playing an important role in meeting the furniture requirements of the world.

We cannot destroy the existing world. However, we must smash and reorganize human living conditions and everything such as commodities, organizational structures, design and art, education, and development in the world (Sun, 2023). The rules of the world and new algorithms are about to change the world completely, to reorganize things accordingly based on advanced technologies such as AI, big data, and digital technology. They will overturn the foundation of the whole world that has been established for half a century since the inception of digital computers in 1946. The computer infrastructure is based on chips for CPUs (central processing unit) and AI GCUs of NVIDIA (https://www.wired.co.uk/article/nvidia-ai-chips), and big data as the core of AI computing. This paper aims to smash and reorganize AI, big data, data analytics, and BI into three new atoms of a Boolean structure, and then reorganize the new atoms and internal components of this Boolean structure, using a new algorithm to smash and reorganize computing such as data computing, information computing, knowledge computing, intelligence computing, and wisdom computing.

Data, information, knowledge, experience, intelligence, and wisdom are economic assets of great importance and value to the modern organization; however, it is too often neither recognized nor managed adequately as such. The value of data, information, knowledge, experience, intelligence, and wisdom presents dozens of practical frameworks and methods for the data, information, knowledge, experience, intelligence, and wisdom professionals – and their organizations – to identify, actualize, and maximize the economic value of data, information, knowledge, experience, intelligence, and wisdom (Powell, 2020). This book explores them to serve the people, organizations, and communities.

1.4 BIG DATA, ANALYTICS, AND INTELLIGENCE: A BOOLEAN STRUCTURE

This research will use the Boolean structure (Sun & Finnie, 2004; Judson, 2013) to address each of the issues mentioned in Section 1.1 based on the graduality of data, analytics, and intelligence, as well as a systematic analysis of related books and journal papers and the research methodology such as a meta-processing, systematic generalization, and specialization of existing publications, as illustrated in Figure 1.1.

It will provide multi-industry applications in business, management, and decision-making. All these are treated using an integrated approach. This Boolean structure destructs the existing world of the books

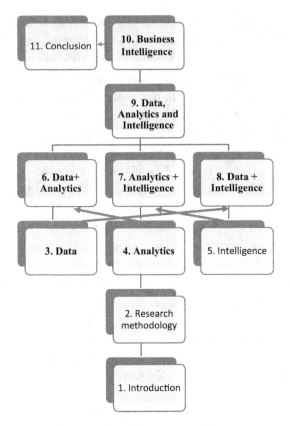

FIGURE 1.1   Data, analytics and intelligence: A Boolean structure.

mentioned in Section 1.3. For example, BI, analytics, and data science (Sharda, Delen, Turban, & King, 2018; Sharda, Delen, & Turba, 2018) are destructed into data, analytics and intelligence at the first atoms of Boolean structure. The data, analytics, and intelligence are reorganized based on the Boolean structure to data analytics, analytics intelligence, and data intelligence, and then data analytics intelligence. In such a way, some of the books mentioned have ignored some of them, for example, analytics intelligence and data analytics intelligence, technologically. Accordingly, big data analytics intelligence has not been discussed in the books mentioned (Sun, 2023).

Based on the Boolean structure, the introduction is the basis. The three atoms of the Boolean structure are data, analytics, and intelligence. Data, analytics, and intelligence will be represented as three composite Boolean expressions, data analytics, analytics intelligence, and data intelligence. Finally, data, analytics, and intelligence have been represented as the Boolean expression: data analytics intelligence. In other words, this book, based on a Boolean structure, is composed of the following chapters (Sun, 2023).

1. Introduction

2. Data

3. Analytics

4. Intelligence

5. Data analytics

6. Analytics intelligence

7. Data intelligence

8. Data, analytics, and intelligence

9. Conclusion

Remarks: this book also uses Chapter 2 to provide research methodology. It will also add business intelligence with applications as in Chapter 10. Therefore, this book consists of 11 chapters.

In what follows, we will explore each chapter topic (except for introduction and conclusion), corresponding to a chapter in the book.

This research uses computing, science, technology, systems, management, services, intelligence, and applications to explore the above terms listed in the Boolean structure. For example, it will explore data computing, data science, data engineering, data technology, data systems, data management, data services, data intelligence, and data applications (Sun, 2022).

1.4.1 Data

All data and big data are important for governing the world. Data has become an important element for the economy (Sun, 2023). One hundred years ago, big companies dominated steel, oil, and manufacturing companies. Recently, big data companies like Apple, Alphabet, Meta (formerly Facebook), Amazon, Microsoft, Tencent, and Alibaba have dominated the whole world. Big data as a disruptive technology is transforming how we live, study, work, and think (Sun, 2023). Therefore, this chapter first looks at data, and then big data. It explores 10 bigs of big data, a service-oriented foundation of big data and the calculus of searching big data. Besides data and big data. This chapter extended the DIKE hierarchy consisting of data, information, knowledge, and experience. This research identifies and examines ten big characteristics of big data, with an example for each: big volume, big velocity, big variety, big veracity, big data technology, big data systems, big infrastructure, big value, big services, and big market. It also explores a service-oriented foundation of big data and calculus of big data. Besides data and big data, this research also explores information, knowledge, and experience (DIKE). It explores DIKE computing, science, engineering, technology, systems, management, and services.

Big data is a foundation of big information, big knowledge, big intelligence, and big analytics.

Big data brings big potential, big market, and big value. All engineering, science, technology, systems, and management are for intelligence. This is why we use data, information, knowledge, experience, and their engineering as a foundation for intelligence. Overall, data in general and big data in particular are foundations of big information, big knowledge, big intelligence, and big analytics.

1.4.2 Analytics

Analytics has been around for about a century (Thompson & Rogers, 2017; Sun, 2019). Analytics is now everywhere, all the time (Thompson & Rogers, 2017, p. 119).

We are in the age of analytics (Thompson & Rogers, 2017, p. 119; Sun, Pambel, & Wu, 2022; Henke & Bughin, 2016). Analytics is vital for running the world. Analytics is the science and technology of using mathematics, AI, computer science, data science, and operations research to provide practical applications to business, management, research and development, economic, and societal problems. After discussing the evolution of analytics, analytics thinking, and the relationship between metrics, analysis, and analytics, this chapter examines mathematical analytics and a system process of analytics. This chapter classifies analytics based on perspectives on organization, discipline, business function, and process. For instance, analytics can be classified into descriptive statistics, diagnostic statistics, predictive statistics, and predictive statistics based on cyclic business operations. This research explores DDPP (Descriptive, diagnostic, predictive, and prescriptive) computing analytics and analytics algorithms, and declares that analytics engineering aims to use analytics science and analytics technology to create and manage analytics systems to provide analytics products and services with analytics intelligence. This chapter also analyzes the leverage analytics for organizations. Finally, this chapter looks at the applications of analytics and discusses three major trends of analytics.

1.4.3 Intelligence

All data, big data, and analytics are for intelligence (Sun, 2023). Intelligence is not only an enduring topic for computer science, AI, intelligence computing, BI, and intelligent analytics, but also an exciting topic for industries, organizations, and businesses (Sun, Sun, & Strang, 2018). AI has facilitated the development of intelligent services, intelligent manufacturing, intelligent systems, and intelligent analytics. BI has promoted the competitiveness of business and marketing performance, supported management decision-making of organizations, and produced trillion-level enterprises such as Google, Amazon, and Meta [3, 36]. However, the current AI is a very mixed intelligence and very market-driven. A lot of companies brand their products as AI products. Many social media brands have found uses for AI products and services. Even so, this chapter looks at the fundamentals of intelligence, including basic intelligence and how can we calculate intelligence. It explores Intelligence 1.0, Intelligence 2.0, and Meta AI, with six levels of intelligence. It examines multi-intelligence and intelligence of the five senses. This research provides a meta-approach to a hierarchy of data and intelligence, including meta (DIKI) and a meta-approach to intelligent systems. This research demonstrates that meta (data) = information; Meta^5 (data) =meta (mind) = wisdom. After reviewing intelligences in AI, this research explores wisdom and mind, from AI to artificial mind, cloud intelligence, data intelligence, and similarity intelligence. It provides an integrated framework of intelligence for a DIKW Intelligence. This research also examines the age of meta-intelligence as competing in the digital world.

1.4.4 Data Analytics

Data analytics might be the oldest of all types of analytics. Data has become the new oil and gold of the 21st century. Data analytics mines the data from data sources, such as data warehouses and data lakes, for new knowledge and meaningful insights (Ghavami, 2020). Data analytics is at the heart of business and decision-making (Sharda, Delen, & Turba, 2018), just as data analysis is at the heart of decision-making in almost all real-world problem solving (Azvine, Nauck, & Ho, 2003). This chapter first discusses the fundamentals of data analytics. Then it explores the classification of data analytics. It explores the fundamentals of big data analytics and advanced analytics platforms. The research examines big analytics covering big information analytics, big knowledge analytics, big wisdom analytics, and big intelligence analytics. Then this research discusses data science, covering database systems, data warehousing, data mining, data computing, and data analytics computing. Finally, this chapter will explore data analytics and big data analytics, with applications in business, management, and decision-making.

1.4.5 Data Intelligence

This chapter introduces data intelligence by addressing the following research questions: What is the fundamental of data intelligence? What are the applications of data intelligence? After reviewing backgrounds and related work, this chapter analyzes data as an element of intelligence and looks at data and knowledge perspective on intelligence, including information intelligence and knowledge intelligence. This chapter examines big intelligence, not only with data, but DIKW intelligence, through proposing an integrated framework of intelligence. This research presents the fundamentals, impacts, challenges, and opportunities of data intelligence in the age of big data, AI, and data science. This research also presents a unified framework for not just data intelligence. This research also looks at the age of meta-intelligence for competing in the digital world. Finally, this chapter explores big data 4.0 as the era of big intelligence we are living in. There are at least two contributions to the academic communities. 1. The research demonstrates that data intelligence is the basis for knowledge intelligence, which is a core of artificial intelligence. 2. Big data 4.0 = big intelligence will play a critical role in our organizations, economies, and societies.

1.4.6 Analytics Intelligence

Analytics intelligence is about how to use analytics to win intelligence (Thompson & Rogers, 2017). Strategically, analytics intelligence is an intelligence that is derived from analytics systems. This chapter looks at analytics intelligence, intelligence analytics, DIKW analytics intelligence, big DIKW analytics intelligence, advanced computing, and quantum computing. This chapter also discusses Google Analytics as a data processing, flow-oriented analytics and presents a unified approach to data processing flow-oriented big data analytics. This chapter discusses responsible big data and big data analytics and proposes applying responsible big data analytics to enhance responsible e-business services. Then this chapter summarizes generative intelligence and explores analytical intelligence as the core of AI and generative intelligence. Analytical intelligence is underpinned by data analytics, big data analytics, and big analytics. The research demonstrates that the earlier analytical intelligence was from logical AI, and then symbolic AI. This period has lasted till the inception of the internet. However, big data has been booming from 2012, onwards. Data analytics and big data analytics have become an important part of business analytics, BI, and intelligent analytics. What is the key to data analytics? It is analytic. How can we use analytic methods and techniques to process data and big data, information and big information, knowledge and big knowledge intelligently? This is the analytical intelligence underpinned by data analytics, big data analytics, and big analytics. Therefore, we can work on intelligent data analytics and intelligent big data analytics, both are used to develop analytical intelligence in terms of business and society.

Mathematically [35],

$$\text{Analytics} = \text{analysis} + \text{SM} + \text{DM} + \text{DW} + \text{ML} + \text{visualization} \quad (1.1)$$

where SM, DM, DW, and ML are abbreviated forms of statistical modeling, data mining, data warehouse, and machine learning. Therefore, using intelligence as a right operation to both sides of the above equation, we have

$$\begin{aligned} \text{Analytics intelligence} = {}&\text{analysis intelligence} + \text{SM intelligence} \\ &+ \text{DM intelligence} + \text{DW intelligence} + \text{ML intelligence} \\ &+ \text{visualization intelligence} \end{aligned} \quad (1.2)$$

The research examines big data analytics intelligence with applications. Finally, the research discusses the spectrum of intelligent analytics.

1.4.7 Data Analytics and Intelligence

This chapter will explore data analytics intelligence and intelligent big data analytics, with applications in business, management, and decision-making. More specifically, this chapter looks at data analytics intelligence and big data analytics intelligence. It explores intelligent big data analytics systems, intelligent big data analytics ecosystems, and intelligent big data analytics as a form of management. It proposes big data 4.0 as the next frontier for revolutionizing the world and presents the calculus of intelligent analytics. This chapter examines intelligent big data analytics for enterprise systems. This chapter also explores insight computing after analyzing CACI computing. The main contributions include: 1. DIKW computing, analytics, and Intelligence will play a significant role in big data 4.0 as the next frontier for revolutionizing the world. 2. The calculus of intelligent analytics is a bridge connecting big data analytics, AI, BI, and other intelligent technologies. 3. Analytics-oriented EIS is an integrated system consisting of SC planning analytics, SC execution analytics, CRM analytics, marketing analytics, sales analytics, service analytics, and big data analytics, supported by the master enterprise warehouse and analytics engine. 4. CACI computing and insight computing are new paradigms in computer science, AI, and data science.

In order to keep the basic structure of this book, we summarize two additional chapters.

1.4.8 Research Methodology

Science and technology are systematic methods for doing any research. For example, mathematics is a method; computer science is a method. This chapter will review and summarize the analytical approach, algebra, logic, statistics, computing, digital computing and digital technologies, and economy. This chapter explores meta computing and discusses systemic generalization and specialization, models, algorithms, equations, and proposes big data derived small data approach.

1.4.9 Business Intelligence

This chapter will explore business intelligence with applications based on data, analytics, intelligence, and their integrations. More specifically, this chapter analyzes BI, business analytics, eSMACS technologies, and intelligent business process analytics. This chapter proposes a calculus of intelligent business analytics and examines techniques for business analytics. This chapter also proposes big data analytics services for enhancing BI and business analytics for enterprise information systems. It explores platform engineering and economics. This chapter will discuss big data driven socioeconomic development, BI analytics, decision analytics, cybersecurity intelligence, and analytics.

1.5 CHARACTERISTICS OF THE BOOK

This book highlights that:

1. The Boolean structure dominates this book.

2. Computing science, engineering, systems, intelligence, services, and intelligence, with applications, penetrate every chapter of the book.

3. Meta computing, science, engineering, technology, systems, and intelligence have been used in the book.

4. The cycle of business workflow for description, diagnosis, prediction, and prescription leads to DDPP analytics and computing.

5. A calculus for searching big data, a calculus of intelligent analytics, a calculus of intelligent business analytics, and a calculus of cloud computing have been proposed in this book. These form a calculus paradigm. Then, this book can be renamed as a calculus of data, analytics, and intelligence for business.

6. Originated from statistics, developed by data mining, big data, and AI, analytics, data analytics, big data analytics, intelligent big data analytics, and intelligent big analytics are the foundations of business analytics and business intelligence.

7. Problem-driven computing and analytics provides the theory, engineering, technology, and systems for this book.

8. Big data 4.0: = big intelligence as a calculus bridges big data and big intelligence.

9. Data analyticizing, as data engineering, is a process of creating data analytics to provide data analytics systems and services with data intelligence.

10. Sharing computing, insight computing, and DDPP computing have been proposed as the future of intelligent analytics.

11. Big data, big information, big knowledge, big intelligence, and big wisdom are not only elements of big analytics but also of big economies.

The book has the following characteristics:

1. The Boolean structure dominates this book.

2. Computing science, engineering, technology, systems, management, services, and intelligence have penetrated each chapter in the book.

3. Computing, science, technology, systems, management, intelligence, services, and applications are used to explore each of the following terms listed in the Boolean structure. For example, this book will explore data computing, data science, data technology, data systems, data management, data services, and data applications. This book also explores the related items in the research. For example, it explores big data computing, big data science, big data technology, big data systems, big data management, big data services, and big data applications. This book is another breakthrough in research methodology, different from the earlier book published by Springer (Sun & Finnie, 2004), which was also based on Boolean structure.

4. Explores data engineering and provides its wild applications.

5. Concept questions and theoretical problems for self-study are at the end of each research description.

6. This book shows readers how to apply concepts using logic methods with various examples.

7. Real-world applications are shown throughout the book.

8. Processes for developing intelligence using science and technology to engineer systems and services are shown.

9. Using natural association and deduction is important to stimulate imagination and curiosity for this book. For example, from prescriptive computing, we have DDPP computing. From business analytics and business intelligence, we have a unified processing of x analytics and intelligence, where x is not only business, but also analytics and intelligence.

10. Finally, all the review questions and problems are from the author's concepts, research plans, and self-motivation towards writing another book.

1.6 SUMMARY

This research began with a review of a dozen books on big data, data analytics, data science, artificial intelligence, and business intelligence, and a discussion of the heuristics of Greek philosopher Plato and French mathematician Descartes and how they reshaped the world (Sun, 2023). The key scientific methodology and tool is the process of destructing, reorganizing, and reassembling to reshape the world of big data, data analytics, data science, artificial intelligence, and business intelligence. This research uses the Boolean structure as a scientific tool to destruct big data, data analytics, data science, and AI into data, analytics, and intelligence, as the three Boolean atoms. The data, analytics, and intelligence are reorganized and reassembled, based on the Boolean structure, to data analytics, analytics intelligence, data intelligence, and data analytics intelligence. The chapter analyzes each of the parts after examining the system intelligence. Corresponding to the above key scientific methodology and tool, this book will use the engineering method to discuss each of the chapters. For example, one of the key contributions of this book is that data (analytics) engineering aims to use data science and data technology to develop and manage data systems to provide data intelligence with data system products and services (Sun, 2023).

1.7 REVIEW QUESTIONS AND PROBLEMS

1. What is the structure of this book?

2. What did Aristotle and Descartes motivate the author of this book to do?

3. How did the author change from reshaping the wood world to an unknown world?

4. What are the characteristics of this book?

5. How can you understand and develop data, analytics, and intelligence?

6. What is the difference between data mining and data analytics?

7. What are the relationships among data, analytics, and intelligence?

8. What are the relationships among big data, big knowledge, and big intelligence?

9. How can we understand the relationships between big data and big data analytics?

10. What is the relationship between BI and data analytics?

11. What is the relation between BI and analytics, as well as data intelligence?

1.8 REFERENCES FOR FURTHER STUDY

1. Russell Dawson, 2023, Fundamentals of Data Analytics: Learn Essential Skills, Embrace the Future, and Catapult Your Career in the Data-Driven World—A Comprehensive Guide to Data Literacy for Beginners, Kindle Edition.

2. Harvard Business Review, 2018, HBR Guide to Data Analytics Basics for Managers (HBR Guide Series), Harvard Business Review Press.

3. Mustafa Ali, 2024, Business Analytics with Excel. Kindle Edition.

4. Elizabeth Clarke, 2022, Data Analytics, Data Visualization & Communicating Data: 3 books in 1: Learn the Processes of Data Analytics and Data Science, Create Engaging Data. Present Data Effectively (All Things Data), Kenneth M Fornari.

5. Gerry Lalonde, 2023, ChatGPT for Beginners - Harness the Power of Artificial Intelligence in Your Daily Life. X-Roads Technology Partners Inc.

6. Max Bennett, 2023, A Brief History of Intelligence: Evolution, AI, and the Five Breakthroughs That Made Our Brains. HarperAudio

CHAPTER 2

Research Methodology

All science and technology are research methods.

As WELL KNOWN, ONE research section at least includes one or a few research methods. One book can include many research methods in the name of a research approach or methodology. Thus, we first look at the research approach or methodology in this book. This chapter will review and summarize the analytical approach, algebra, logic, statistics, computing, digital computing and digital technologies, and economy. This chapter explores meta computing and discusses systemic generalization and specialization, models, algorithms, equations, and proposes a big data-derived small data approach.

Learning objectives of this chapter:

- Gain familiarity with the analytical approach with an example.

- Learn an algebra with two examples.

- Define logic and fuzzy logic.

- Learn basic statistics and practice with Excel.

- Define computing, data computing, and engineering. List a few computing science and technology uses, with examples.

- Understand digital computing, technology, industry, and economy.

DOI: 10.1201/9781003450504-2

- Define meta as an operation, and understand meta computing.

- Gain familiarity with systematic generalization and specialization.

- Define models, algorithms, and equations with an example for each.

- Understand the big data-derived small data approach.

- Research as a search is a method or approach.

2.1 INTRODUCTION

There are many different research methodologies. This book will look at each of them and then explore how each of them will be used in this book.

It is difficult for us to define research methodology and what constitutes research methodology. For example, we will explore systematic generalization and specialization, a research methodology for big data Intelligence.

Some strategies used for this book are: Strategic approaches, tactical approaches, and operational approaches.

The rest of this chapter will be organized as follows. Section 2.2 reviews the analytical approach. Sections 2.3–2.8 review and summarize algebra, logic, statistics, computing, digital computing, digital technologies, and economy. Section 2.9 looks at meta computing. Section 2.10 discusses systemic generalization and specialization. Section 2.11 looks at models, algorithms, and equations. Section 2.12 provides big data-derived small data approach. The final section completes this chapter with a few concluding remarks and related work.

After reading this chapter, you will understand the following question: Science and technology are systematic methods for any research. For example, mathematics is a method, computer science is a method, logic and algebra are methods, and computing is a method.

2.2 ANALYTICAL APPROACH

This book uses a multidisciplinary approach consisting of logical, algebraic, systemic methods, "research as a search," and big data-driven, small data analysis methods to support the multi-industry approach. For example, the principle of "research as a search" and big data-driven small data analysis (Sun & Huo, 2021) underpins statements, claims, and corresponding literature reviews.

This book uses Google to search for relevant publications, which reflect the state-of-the-art development of computing, analytics, and eSMACS computing worldwide. It uses Google Scholar to search for corresponding items, which reflects the state-of-the-art research and development of relevant disciplines and research fields in academia. Both are a complement to each other for understanding state-of-the-art a variety of computing, data, analytics, and intelligence. This book also uses logical and systemic approaches, natural deduction, and natural association as research methods to examine computing, data analytics, BI, and eSMACS computing.

Natural deduction originally is a part of mathematical logic. It is now a practical intelligence. The natural association should have been studied in data mining. However, it is also a kind of advanced intelligence and research intelligence, which has been widely used in many research activities. Hereafter, natural deduction and natural association will be used as research methods in this research.

2.3 ALGEBRA

This section will summarize algebraic systems as follows. Some readers will use algebra to develop an abstract algebraic system to model real-world systems.

Definition 1

Let O be a set of operations, S is a non-empty set, then $\langle S,O \rangle$ is an algebra (Lang, 2002). Algebra is a kind of algebraic system, which can be considered as a mathematical abstraction of systems such as software systems, communication systems, BI, and analytics systems.

Let U be a universe of all data. O is a set of operations. Then $\langle U,O \rangle$ is a data algebra.

Now we elaborate O as a set of operations; each operation is an abstraction of computer processing in general and an ICT technique, an algorithm, and a method in specific. At a relatively lower level, an operation is an abstraction of a "click" or "run", or abstraction of a command related to a model or a program. Based on the above discussion, an algorithm discussed in AI, computer science, data science, and information technology, is an operation sequence (Russell & Norvig, 2020; Kantardzic, 2011).

At a higher level, computer processing includes data processing and management, information processing and management, knowledge processing and management, experience processing and management, and business processing and management.

More generally, if $D \subset U$ is the set of all data, $O_d \sqsubset O$ is the set of operations, then $\langle D, O_d \rangle$ is data algebra, a mathematical abstraction of data processing and management system. For example, when O_d includes select, project, and join, then $\langle D, O_d \rangle$ can be considered as a subsystem of the relational database algebra, an abstraction of relational database management systems (Coronel, Morris, & Rob, 2020; Sun & Huo, 2020).

Definition 2

Let O be a set of operations, S is a non-empty set, $\langle S, O \rangle$ is an algebra (Lang, 2002), then $\langle S, O \rangle$ is a group if and only if

1. For any $a, b, c \in S$, and an operator $o_1 \in O$ if $a o_1 b o_1 c = (a o_1 b) o_1 c$.

2. For any a, there is a reverse of a so that $a o_1 a^{-1} = 1$.

Then, all the reverse matrices form a group in linear algebra.

We use mathematical and computing terms in computer science to process data, information, knowledge, intelligence, mind, and wisdom.

Operation is an ordinary transformation in mathematics (Sun & Wang, 2017b). As well-known, 2+3 = 5, we know that + is an addition operation. We also know business operation, that is, we change one product or service from one place to another, from one state to another.

Therefore, processing, management, and transformation are important for processing any data, information, knowledge, intelligence, and wisdom. "Operations" is a popular term for mathematics, including algebra and discrete mathematics (Johnsonbaugh, 2013). This book prefers to use operations to analyze and abstract the data, including big data, and expose the essence of big data.

A finite Boolean algebra is an algebra if it contains a finite number of atoms as a set. It also consists of two binary relations $\vee$ and $\wedge$ and complement relation (Judson, 2013).

Theorem. The order of any finite Boolean algebra must be 2^n for some positive integer n, where n is the number of the atoms in the Boolean algebra (Judson, 2013).

2.4 LOGIC

Logic is important for mathematics. Logical methods have been used in many disciplines. This book will use a logic method, Boolean structure, to organize its chapters.

Many students and professionals have not known or studied logic, even basic logic such as propositional logic, predicate logic, and fuzzy logic (Zadeh, 1965). A lot of their thinking is chaotic: what to talk about first, what to talk about later, what premise is drawn from, and what inferences will be inferred, all of which have not been seriously considered. The author of this book advises the readers to read some books on logic for computer science, for example, (Reeves & Clarke, 1990).

This book uses the following three reasoning paradigms as a part of logic.

2.4.1 Reasoning and Inference Rules

Reasoning is a process of deriving a conclusion from certain premises, using given rules (Sun, 2017). Deductive reasoning is the most important reasoning form (Johnson-Laird, Khemlani, & Goodwin, 2015; Minsky, 1985). Many other reasoning paradigms can be considered as an extension or revision of deductive reasoning. For example, fuzzy reasoning is an extension of deductive reasoning (Sun & Finnie, 2004). Default reasoning is the revision of deductive reasoning, taking into account discovery of processing exceptions.

Reasoning is a central concept in knowledge-based systems and AI (Nilsson, 1998), where there are a few dozen reasoning paradigms that have been studied, such as non-monotonic reasoning, default reasoning, fuzzy reasoning, probabilistic reasoning, CBR, similarity based reasoning, experience-based reasoning, and human reasoning, to name a few (Sun, 2017).

Reasoning can be used for problem-solving (Johnson-Laird, Khemlani, & Goodwin, 2015). However, one reasoning paradigm, deductive reasoning is not enough to solve all real-world problems (Minsky, 1985). It is better to combine several different reasoning paradigms to solve one real-world problem. For example, deductive reasoning and abductive reasoning can be integrated to solve a class of real problems, such as diagnosis, and treatment encountered in clinical practice (Sun, Finnie, & Weber, 2004). More specifically, abductive reasoning is used to generate an idea or explanation for solving the problem, like diagnosis. Deductive reasoning is used to solve the problem, like treatment in the clinic. Abductive CBR and deductive CBR are proposed and their integration is emphasized to solve some problems (Sun, Finnie, & Weber, 2004). Therefore, one reasoning paradigm can be only used through human reasoning to solve a class of real-world problems. This is why researchers propose abduction, induction, and other reasoning paradigms (Nilsson, 1998).

In mathematical logic, reasoning can be considered as a process of manipulating logical language based on inference rules to infer a new conclusion in logical language (Reeves & Clarke, 1990). The reasoning process for solving a real-world problem makes up a reasoning chain (Minsky, 1985). This reasoning chain consists of several nodes. The reasoning from one node to another is based on one or more inference rules. An inference rule is a scheme for constructing valid inferences (Reeves & Clarke, 1990; Sun, 2017). These schemes establish syntactic relations between a set of formulas called premises and an assertion called a conclusion. These syntactic relations are used in the process of inference, whereby new true assertions are arrived at from other already known ones. Therefore, inference rules are the basis for any reasoning paradigm in human reasoning (Sun, 2017).

There are more than 30 inference rules for natural deduction (Sun, 2017), which constitutes a formalism that models deductive reasoning involved in mathematical proofs, proposed by Prof. Gerhard Gentzen in 1934 (Szabo, 1969, p. 4), who attempted to find a more natural approach to actual reasoning in mathematical proofs.

Furthermore, there is a hierarchy among these existing reasoning paradigms (Sun, 2017). For example, similarity-based reasoning (SBR) is not at the first level in the hierarchy of reasoning paradigms. We can consider SBR as a combination of deduction and similarity, we can also consider SBR as a combination of abduction and similarity (Sun & Finnie, 2007). Inference rules such as modus ponens and modus tollens (see the next subsection) are at the atomic level, because each of them constitutes an edge linking two different nodes in the reasoning chain, and they cannot be further broken down (Sun, 2017).

2.4.2 Modus Ponens

The most common inference rules are the *modus ponens (MP)*, which have played an important role in mathematics and computer science, including AI and fuzzy logic (Nilsson, 1998; Zimmermann, 2001; Zadeh, 1965). These two reasoning paradigms underlie almost every field of science, engineering, technology, business, and management (Johnson-Laird, Khemlani, & Goodwin, 2015).

MP has the following general form (Sun, 2017):

$$\frac{\begin{array}{c} P \\ P \to Q \end{array}}{\therefore Q} \tag{2.1}$$

where P, Q represent any (compound) propositions variables whatsoever such P as "Shanghai is a small city". More specifically, MP (2.1) means that if P is true, and $P \rightarrow Q$ is true, then the conclusion Q is also true. Strictly speaking, (2.1) can be considered as a part of proof theory, while, the explanation of MP (2.1) belongs to model theory, which determines the validity of inferences (Johnson-Laird, Khemlani, & Goodwin, 2015).

MP is an important rule of inference in mathematics because it is the foundation of forward chaining (together with a hypothetical syllogism in problem-solving (Epp, 1995, p. 33). The term *modus ponens* is Latin, meaning "method of affirming" since the conclusion is an affirmation (Epp, 1995). Form (2.1), is a formalized summary and abstraction of experience encountered by many people in the past. For example,

Example 1: *Modus ponens.* We have the knowledge in the knowledge-base:

1. If Socrates is human, then Socrates is mortal

2. Socrates is human

What we wish is to prove "Socrates is mortal". To do so, let

- $P \rightarrow Q$: If Socrates is human, then Socrates is mortal,
- P: Socrates is human
- Q: Socrates is mortal

Therefore, we have Q: Socrates is mortal using *modus ponens* (2.1).

2.4.3 Modus Tollens

Modus tollens (MT) is also one of the most important rules of inference in mathematics because it is the foundation of backward chaining (together with hypothetical syllogism (Epp, 1995, p. 33) in problem-solving.

The general form of MT is as follows (Sun, 2017):

$$\frac{\neg Q}{\begin{array}{c} P \rightarrow Q \\ \hline \therefore \neg P \end{array}} \qquad (2.2)$$

where P, Q represent compound propositions. More specifically, MT (2) means that if Q is false, and $P \rightarrow Q$ is true, then the conclusion P is also false.

The term *modus tollens* is Latin, meaning "the method of denying", since the conclusion is a denial.

> **Example 2:** *Modus tollens.* We have the knowledge in the knowledge-base:
>
> 1. If Peter is healthy, then Peter will fly to Beijing
>
> 2. Peter will not fly to Beijing
>
> What we wish is to prove "Peter is not healthy". To do so, let
>
> - $P \rightarrow Q$: If Peter is healthy, then Peter will fly to Beijing,
>
> - P: Peter is healthy
>
> - Q: Peter will fly to Beijing

Therefore, we have $\neg P$: Peter is not healthy, based on *modus tollens* (2), and the knowledge in the knowledge-base.

Modus ponens and modus tollens are two basic rules of inference related to conditional statements in mathematical logic. In fact, they have also played an important role in problem solving in mathematics and modes of argumentation, as well as in AI. Further, in mathematical reasoning, modus tollens is used almost as often as Modus ponens (Epp, 1995). Based on the above discussion, modus ponens and modus tollens are two basic inference rules for experience-based reasoning (EBR). From a theoretical viewpoint, many knowledge-based systems (KBS) in particular rule-based expert systems (Russell & Norvig, 2020) are also based on these two inference rules.

It should be noted that modus ponens and modus tollens belong to rules of deduction, which are reasoning paradigms in mathematical logic, mathematics, and AI. The reasoning using them can be considered valid; that is, no matter what particular statements are substituted for the statement variables in its premises, if the resulting premises are all true, then the conclusion is also true (Epp, 1995; Johnson-Laird, Khemlani, & Goodwin, 2015).

2.4.4 Abduction

Abduction plays a fundamental role in problem-solving (Baral, 2000; Console, Theseider Dupre, & Torasso, 1991). In particular, abduction seems to be a basic reasoning component in activities such as system explanation (Leake, 1993) and diagnosis (Console, Theseider Dupre, & Torasso, 1991) as well as system analysis (Sun & Finnie, 2007). Abduction is becoming an increasingly popular term in many fields of computer science, such as system diagnosis, planning, natural language processing, and logic programming (Rich & Knight, 1991; Console, Theseider Dupre, & Torasso, 1991). Kindler et al. applied abduction and deduction to the laboratory medicine problem-solving process (Kindler, Densow, Fischer, & Fliedner, 1995). CBR has played an important role in explanatory or abductive reasoning tasks like diagnosis and explanation (Leake, 1993) and abductive CBR (Sun, Finnie, & Weber, 2004). In AI views, explanations are treated as deductive proofs (Sun, Finnie, & Weber, 2004). Abductive reasoning systems build their proofs by non-deductive methods, and additional assumptions may be required for those proofs to apply (Leake, 1993). However, their view is fundamentally the same if the abductive assumptions were shown to be true, the resulting explanation would be considered a deductive proof (Sun, Finnie, & Weber, 2004). Abduction has also drawn increasing attention in philosophy and cognitive science. For example, Magnani integrates philosophical, cognitive, and computational issues on abduction, examines some cases of reasoning in science and medicine, and shows the connections between abduction, induction, and deduction, and argues that abduction is a logic of scientific discovery (Magnani, 2001).

The general model of abduction as a rule of inference is as follows (Rich & Knight, 1991):

$$\frac{\begin{array}{c} Q \\ P \to Q \end{array}}{\therefore P} \qquad (2.3)$$

where P and Q represent any (compound) propositions in a general setting. In clinical diagnosis, $P \to Q$ is a form of general relation: disease $\to$ symptom (Sun, Finnie, & Weber, 2004).

Example 3: Abduction (borrowed from (Magnani, 2001, p. 21) and revised). We begin with the situation: the knowledge (sentences) in the knowledge-base includes (Sun, Finnie, & Weber, 2004):

1. If a patient is affected by pneumonia, his/her level of white blood cells is increased.

2. John's level of white blood cells is increased.

To prove "John is affected by pneumonia" using abduction (2.3). We first represent these facts in a first-order logic, and then show the proof as a sequence of applying abduction (2.3). To this end, let $P(x)$: x is affected by pneumonia, $Q(x)$: x's level of white blood cells is increased, $P(John)$: John is affected by pneumonia, $Q(John)$: John's level of white blood cells is increased. Then the above example can be formalized as:

1: $\forall x (P(x) \rightarrow Q(x))$

2: $Q(John)$

We use the substitution {x/John} (for detail see (Sun, Finnie, & Weber, 2004) or an inference rule (elimination of quantifier; Reeves & Clarke, 1990), and infer:

3: $P(John) \rightarrow Q(John)$

From (2) and (3), and abduction (2.3), we have: $Q(John)$; that is, John is affected by pneumonia.

The above example of diagnostic reasoning is an excellent way to introduce abduction (Magnani, 2001, p. 18). Abduction goes back more than a hundred years. At that time, the American philosopher Charles Sanders Peirce defined "Abduction" as inference that involves the generation and evaluation of an explanatory hypothesis (Magnani, 2001).

Minsky doubts that pure deductive logic plays much of a role in ordinary thinking (Minsky, 1985), although it can help us find the most essential steps, once we find a way to solve a certain problem. However, he has not examined how to find a way at all. We believe that abduction can serve to do so, at least abduction is an important complement to deduction because abduction is a very useful nonmonotonic reasoning, in particular for reasoning towards explanation in (system) diagnosis (Torasso, Console, Portinale, & Theseider, 1995) and analysis in problem solving.

2.4.5 Induction

Induction was already in Ancient Greek philosophy (Russell B., 1967). Induction is still a general method of logic, mathematics, AI, and computer science (Magnani, 2001). Induction is an inference of generalizing a conclusion from particular instances (Merriam-Webster, 2024a). That is, there are instances with property A, that $P(i) = A$, where $i = 1,2,3,\ldots n$, then based on induction, we have $P(n+1) = A$. For example, $P(i) =$ every IT student knows data is vital for data science. Then for all IT students, $A =$ data is vital for data science.

The difference between induction and deduction is that induction is reasoning from detailed facts to general principles, whereas deduction is reasoning from the general to the particular or from cause to effect. Induction is an art form behind machine learning. In other words, the objective of machine learning, coined in 1959 by Arthur Samuel (Wikipedia-Sammuel, 2024), is induction (Siegel, 2016, p. 169). Even so, induction is a kind of common sense, it can be used until other abnormal cases appear.

2.5 STATISTICS

Statistics is the art and science of collecting, analyzing, presenting, and interpreting data based on probability (Sweeney, Williams, & Anderson, 2011, p. 18). Statistics is the collection, presentation, and analysis of data and the use of such data and explanations. It is related to decision-making in the face of uncertainty. If the measures are computed for data from a sample, they are called sample statistics. If the measures are computed for data from a population, they are called population parameters. In statistical inference, a sample statistic is referred to as the point estimator of the corresponding population parameter.

2.5.1 Element and Variable and Measurement of Data

A variable is a characteristic of interest for the elements (Sweeney, Williams, & Anderson, 2011, p. 5). Elements are the entities on which data are collected. The following five variables of a dataset are fund, type, net, asset, and value.

The general goal of data analysis is to acquire knowledge from data (National Research Council, 2013), just as data mining is to discover knowledge from database. Therefore, data mining is a kind of data analysis. However, data mining is an intelligent system, whereas data analysis is a general process. This process can be considered as manual or automatic. In such a way, data analysis is more general than data mining.

2.5.2 Population and Sample, Statistical Inference

A population is the set of all elements of interest in a particular study (Anderson, Sweeney, & Williams, 2011). A sample is a subset of the population. Therefore, the larger group of elements in a particular study is called the population, and the smaller group is called the sample.

Data from a sample make estimates and test hypotheses about the characteristics of a population through a process referred to as statistical inference (Anderson, Sweeney, & Williams, 2011).

2.5.3 Numerical Measures of Location

Numerical measures of location are represented by mean, median, mode, percentile, and quartiles. Mean is the average value for a variable. The median is the value in the middle when the data are arranged in ascending order. The mode is the value that occurs with the greatest frequency. The pth percentile is a value such that at least p percent of the observations are less than or equal to this value and at least (100) percent of the observations are greater than or equal to this value; that is, A percentile provides information about how the data are spread over the interval from the smallest value to the largest value. Quartiles divided data into four parts, with each part containing approximately one-fourth, or 25% of the observations.

2.6 COMPUTING

This section looks at computing.

Merriam-Webster Dictionary defines computing through compute (Merriam-Webster, 2022). Compute is defined as "to determine especially by mathematical means". In other words, compute is to find out something by using mathematics. Compute is also to "determine or calculate using a computer." However, Merriam-Webster Dictionary does not have the term computing. The Oxford Dictionary defines computing as "the fact of using computers" for example, scientific/network, scientific computing, computing power, services, skills/systems (Oxford, 2008).

Computing refers to goal-oriented activities requiring, benefiting from, or associated with computers" (ACM, 2020).

The above three definitions of compute and computing imply that

1. Computing is determined by mathematical means. It is related to compute and calculation.

2. Computing is about computer-centered goal-oriented activities and facts.

In reality, computing is more difficult to define exactly in the digital age. For example, computers should include all related hardware, software, apps, and integrated machinery, devices, and systems. Therefore, computing includes a variety of interpretations. For example, from a software engineering perspective (Pressman & Maxim, 2014), computing includes activities of analyzing, designing, and constructing hardware and software systems for a wide range of scientific, engineering, mathematical, technological, and social purposes. From an information systems viewpoint (Laudon & Laudon, 2020), computing includes activities of processing, structuring, and managing various kinds of data, information, and knowledge. From a mathematics perspective (Johnsonbaugh, 2013), computing includes problem-solving by finding solutions to problems. In the digital age, computing includes all the activities of creating and using communications and entertainment media, finding and gathering information relevant to any particular purpose (ACM, 2020).

Currently, computing refers to computing science, computing technology, computing engineering, computing systems (ACM, 2020), computing intelligence (Cheng & LI, 2020), and more (Sun, 2020). Briefly,

$$
\begin{aligned}
\text{Computing} = \,& \text{computing science} + \text{computing technology} \\
& + \text{computing engineering} + \text{computing systems} \\
& + \text{computing intelligence} + \text{computing management} \\
& + \text{computing X} \quad\quad\quad\quad\quad\quad\quad\quad\quad (2.4)
\end{aligned}
$$

Where X = {x | a keyword together with computing for academia, industry, and society}. For example, X = {tool, service, application, product, industry, society}. Equation (2.4) is a unified representation of computing as a super-discipline, a set of disciplines underpinned by computing (ACM, 2020).

Computing engineering is a process of leveraging computing science and technology to create and manage computing systems to obtain computing intelligence. This definition will be used for a similar definition in this book.

Two disciplines of computing science are computer science and data science (ACM, 2020). Two disciplines of computing engineering are computer engineering and software engineering. One discipline of computing technology is information technology (IT). One discipline of a computing system is information systems (IS). Three courses of computing management offered by many universities around the world are data management, information management, and knowledge management (Sun, 2022a). Three courses or research fields of computing intelligence are AI (Russell & Norvig, 2020), machine intelligence, and BI (Laudon & Laudon, 2020). Furthermore, for computing x, an example of a computing tool is Windows Office Suite. An example of a computing application is TikTok. An example of a computing service is social networking services such as WeChat and WhatsApp. Therefore, based on the Computing Curricula 2020 (CC2020) of ACM (Association for Computing Machinery), computing, as a super-discipline, consists of computer science, data science, computer engineering, software engineering, information technology, information systems, and cybersecurity (ACM, 2020). Briefly, that is,

$$
\begin{aligned}
\text{Computing} = {}& \text{computer science} + \text{data science} + \text{computer engineering} \\
& + \text{software engineering} + \text{software engineering} \\
& + \text{information technology} + \text{information systems} \\
& + \text{cybersecurity}
\end{aligned}
$$

$$(2.5)$$

Computing disciplines in (2.5) have not followed equation (2.4) to develop the computing y in a unified way, where y = {science, engineering, technology, system, intelligence,…}. Instead, its disciplines have not used computing as a part of their names at a discipline level (Sun, 2022). This might have some historical pragmatic reason. For example, in the 1970s, computer science, computer engineering, and IS had become disciplines (ACM, 2020). At that time, computers and information were the greatest expectations of human beings and society. Therefore, ordinary people hoped to study science and engineering behind computers. IS as a discipline promotes the inception of IT as a discipline. Software engineering is the response to the transformation of society and a new vision for the development of computing. Microsoft and other software's business success expedited the inception of software engineering as a discipline.

The mentioned five disciplines except data science have been in the Computing Curricula of the ACM at least since 2005. Data science is the first time to become a discipline of the CC2020, although database management and database systems have been popular since 1970 (Coronel, Morris, & Rob, 2020). In addition, data science as a discipline also covers data engineering, data systems, data management, data service, big data, and data analytics (ACM, 2020). The data system here includes a database system, data mining system, data warehouse system, data analytics system, and data management system (Coronel, Morris, & Rob, 2020; Hurley, 2019).

The web of computing at least consists of a great number of x computing, where x is a keyword that has appealed to several scholars, businessmen, industries, professionals, and others to incorporate it with computing, for example, cognitive computing and enterprise computing, where x = cognitive or enterprise. The web of computing includes ambient computing, business computing, client-server computing, cloud computing, cluster computing, distributed computing, edge computing, green computing, grid computing, internet computing, parallel computing, personal computing, predictive computing, quantum computing, robotic computing, service computing, social computing, ubiquitous computing, and time-sharing computing, to name a few (ACM, 2020). Each of the mentioned computing segments has gathered a number of researchers, scholars, developers, and business persons to develop corresponding knowledge, skills, dispositions, products, and services by addressing corresponding problems, issues, needs, and demands. The openness and inclusiveness of computing have been fostering new x computing emerging in the coming years. The openness and inclusiveness of computing promote a digital economy, digital society, and digital age.

2.7 DIGITAL COMPUTING AND DIGITAL TECHNOLOGIES

Digital technologies have been impacting all areas of our lives, businesses, and society. Digital transformation has been ushering in the digitalized economy and digital society.

We are living in the digital age. eSMACS (electronic, social, mobile, analytics, cloud, security) services have been ubiquitous (Sun & Wu, 2021). In what follows, we will examine eSMACS computing in some detail.

Electronic computing has not been an independent definition. However, it has been used as a part of electronic computing machines since 1947 (Sun & Wu, 2021). Furthermore, Google Scholar focuses on the search for electronic computing + x, where x consists of technique, machine, device, printing, publisher, copying, equipment, and digitalization, based on the search optimization, that is, we use the singular word in the process of search.

Social computing can be defined as "interactive and collaborative behavior between computer users. Personal computing is an individual user activity in that one user generally commands computing" (Techopedia, 2022). Google Scholar focuses on recommending the results based on the user's search for social computing y, where y consists of ACM, online communities, modeling and prediction, behavioral-cultural modeling, cooperative work, and human-computer interaction. In addition, the recommended results include pervasive "social computing".

Mobile computing is "the set of IT technologies, products, services, and operational strategies and procedures that enable mobile end-users to gain access to computation, information, and related resources and capabilities" (Techtarget, 2022). Google Scholar recommends the results based on the user's search for mobile computing z, where z consists of devices, communications, transactions, environments, data management, and security issues. In addition, the search results include searching for "wireless mobile computing" or "pervasive mobile computing".

Analytics computing is a research field about computing-driven analytics science, analytics technology, analytics engineering, analytics system, analytics intelligence, analytics management, and their applications (Sun, 2020).

Security computing can be defined as a research field for computing-driven security science, security technology, security engineering, security systems, security intelligence, and security management (Sun & Wu, 2021). Google Scholar recommends the search results based on the user's search for m security computing, where m consists of cloud, cyber, transaction, cryptography, encryption, vehicular, dependable, and mobile. Google searches demonstrate that security science, security technology, security engineering, security system, security intelligence, and security management have drawn significant attention in academia and industry (Pfleeger & Pfleeger, 2006; ACM, 2020). Therefore, security computing can be briefly articulated as

$$
\begin{aligned}
\text{Security computing} = \ &\text{security science} + \text{security technology} \\
&+ \text{security engineering} + \text{security system} \\
&+ \text{security intelligence} + \text{security management} \quad (2.6)
\end{aligned}
$$

In summary, eSMACS computing should be named digital computing, that is,

$$\text{Digital computing} = \text{eSMACS computing} \qquad (2.7)$$

ICT and digital technologies are computing technology based on equation (2.6). Both have been preferred in many fields such as politics, culture, society, business, and more (PNG Government, 2022). Computing and ICT will be used interchangeably hereafter in this book.

Digital technologies are kinds of digital computing and information and communication technologies (ICT). Digital technologies and ICT have been preferred in many fields, such as politics, culture, society, business, and more (PNG Government, 2022). Digital technologies and ICT will be used interchangeably hereafter in this research. Many governments such as the PNG government, use digital technologies and ICT to achieve sustainable socio-economic development and enhance governance and social integration (PNG Government, 2022). Therefore, we also use digital technology and ICT, and infrastructure to drive a digital government, digital economy, and digital society.

2.8 DIGITAL INDUSTRY, TRADE, AND ECONOMY

This section overviews digital trade and economy and their relationships to provide a basis for this research.

The digital economy is made up of economic activities conducted or facilitated through digital technologies (NZ, 2020). Digital economy has played an important role in the economy through digital technologies. The digital economy is based on digital businesses. A digital business is a process of creating value; creation is based on the use of digital technologies that address (IDC, 2022):

1. Internal and external processes,

2. How organizations engage with customers, citizens, suppliers, and partners?

3. How the business attracts, manages, and retains employees?

4. The mix of products, services, and experiences provided.

That is, a digital business is based on digital transformation, which transforms processes, products, services, and experiences of digital citizens iteratively and cyclically (IDC, 2024). For example, retailers create personalized experiences at scale based on digital platforms (IDC, 2024). The digital processes are based on digital business models that can create, deliver, and capture value based on digital technologies (IDC, 2022). One of the digital business models is dynamic pricing in Financial Services financial services, which is about matching supply and demand to dynamic pricing in near real-time based on current market demands.

Digital trade is a trade that is enabled by digital technologies. Therefore, digital trade is digitally-enabled transactions of trade in goods and services that can either be digitally or physically delivered, involving consumers, firms, and governments (NZ, 2020). For example, China has taken 39.8%, a total 35 trillion YMB; it estimated that the detailed economy will take 51% of the whole economy (Cao, 2022).

Digital economy, coined by Don Tapscott in his book "the Digital Economy" in 1995, referred to the Internet's impact on how companies operate and innovate. Digital economy has covered all things digital, digital technology, digital systems, digital media, digital products, services, and the digital universe (Thompson & Rogers, 2017). Then, we are in the digital age. Digital technology and ICT have played a significant role in the economy and society globally.

Digital Economy Partnership Agreement (DEPA) motivated by Singapore, Chile, and New Zealand, in 2020 to sign the Business and Trade Facilitation module to promote the adoption and use of digital technologies to facilitate trade (NZ, 2020). A new DEPA partnership between New Zealand, Chile, and Singapore will help New Zealand exporters and SMEs take advantage of opportunities from digital trade (NZ, 2020). For example, DEPA strengthens digital trade cooperation between the three countries and establishes relevant norms. The agreement focuses on e-commerce facilitation, data transfer liberalization, personal information security, and improving cooperation in areas such as AI and financial technology (Cao, 2022), that is, DEPA (NZ, 2020).

There are two kinds of economics: those of data and information goods that are made of bits rather than atoms, and those of networks (McAfee & Brynjolfsson, 2017, pp. 135–137). The first 2 important attributes of information goods are free and perfect. Once something has been digitized, it's essentially free to make an additional copy of it. The marginal cost is approaching zero, so, free is a fair approximation. Once a digital original is created, copies are every bit as good as their digital originals. This is perfect. Therefore, the digital economics is free, perfect, and instant in the digital age.

2.9 META COMPUTING

This section will look at meta as an algebra and operation and explore meta operations and strategies.

2.9.1 Introduction

Based on the Merriam-Webster dictionary (Merriam-Webster, 2023c), meta can be defined as

1. a): occurring later than or in succession to

   b): situated behind or beyond.

   c): later or more highly organized or specialized form of.

2. change: transformation.

3. [metaphysics]: more comprehensive: transcending.

Sense 1 covers "later, after, or beyond or more organized and specialized. Sense 2 means change and transformation. Sense 3 means more comprehensive and transcending.

We will use these three senses of meta in this section.

Meta was introduced by a Greek philosopher Aristotle in his metaphysics (related to sense 3; Taylor, 1801) more than 2000 years ago. Metaphysics is one of the greatest philosophical works that has been influencing science, technology, and philosophy. Metaphysics has led to our rationality and systematic thinking in research and development since then (Taylor, 1801; Sun, 2024). Metadata in database systems are data about data (Coronel, Morris, & Rob, 2020).

This section will look at meta as an operation and explore meta operations with its applications.

2.9.2 Meta as an Operation and Processing

An operation is equivalent to a transformation. The transformation is equivalent to processing, that is x is processed to y. Similar to that, x is transformed into y. More generally, all business processing and activities can be abstracted to a meta.

As mentioned above, meta can be defined as a change or transformation. Then meta can be defined as a mathematical operation M, that is,

$$M : U \to U$$

where U is the universe of discourse. For example, $M(\text{data}) = \text{metadata}$. $M(\text{knowledge}) = \text{metaknowledge}$, $M(\text{analysis}) = \text{meta-analysis}$. $M(\text{approach}) = \text{meta-approach}$.

Let

$$M_1 M_2 M_{3,} : U \rightarrow U$$

Be three meta operators. Then we can define the operations concerning these three operators.

1. For any $u \in U$, we have $\left(M_1 + M_2 \right)(u) = M_1\left(u\right) + M_2\left(u\right)$. This is the addition of meta operation. The addition satisfies commutative law.

2. For any $u \in U$, we have $\left(M_1 * M_2 \right)(u) = M_1\left(u\right) * M_2\left(u\right)$. This is the multiplication of meta operation. The multiplication satisfies associative law. The addition and multiplication satisfy the distributive law. Therefore, $<, +>$, and $< U, *>$ is a semi-group from an algebraic perspective.

3. For any $u \in U$, we have $(M_1 . M_2)(u) = M_{1,}(u)(M_2(u))$. This is the composite meta operation.

4. M_I is a meta identity operation, that is, for any $u \in U, (M_I\left(u\right) = u$.

2.9.3 Meta Algebra

It is not enough for Meta to be only an operation. Meta should be considered an algebra, an algebraic system from a mathematical perspective. That is, meta is an algebra consisting of a non-empty set and a set of meta operations. For example, in the competitive data world (Sun, 2021), a non-empty set is a big dataset. The meta has an operation set consisting of meta operations that transform big data into big knowledge. For example, meta operations at least consist of data mining and data warehousing (Aroraa, Lele, & Jindal, 2022). In such a way, data mining and data warehousing are the realization of mathematical meta operations.

Not only data mining and data warehousing, but also expert systems and knowledge-base systems are the realization of mathematical operations, because expert systems and knowledge-base systems are the realization of mathematical logic such as propositional logic and predicate logic (Russell & Norvig, 2020), and they are also the realization of algebraic systems. The equivalence between mathematical logic, algebra, expert systems, and knowledge-base systems (Sun, Li, Liu, & Jie, 2008) is the essence behind the evolution of expert systems and knowledge-base systems. Another essence behind expert systems, knowledge-base systems, information systems, and intelligent systems is meta as an operation and as an algebra.

Therefore, meta is not only an algebraic system but also an intelligent system from a computing viewpoint.

2.9.4 Meta Computing, Science, Engineering, and Intelligence

More generally, meta can be extended to meta computing which includes meta science, meta engineering, meta engineering, meta technology, meta systems, and meta intelligence.

Meta in computing might be influenced by metamathematics, which mainly follow senses 2 and 3. The latter is the study of mathematics itself using mathematical methods. Metamathematics includes many metatheories and metalogics as well as mathematical techniques for investigating a number of foundation problems for mathematics and logic (Kleene, 1952). A metatheory is a mathematical theory about other mathematical theories.

Meta intelligence is intelligence about intelligence, and it is above human intelligences + artificial intelligences. Meta intelligence can be used for understanding, control and interactivity (Sternberg, et al., 2021). Meta intelligence as a processing is composed of understanding, control, and interactivity.

Therefore, meta-intelligence is originally from metaphysics and metamathematics. In computing, metamathematics and metalogic are theoretical and methodological foundations of meta intelligence. Metalanguage is language about languages, metalevel, metalevel state space, meta-reasoning, metarule have been used in AI (Russell & Norvig, 2020). Meta-Dendral as a metasystem has been used to generate rules useful for analytical chemistry (Russell & Norvig, 2020).

2.9.5 Summary

Meta is influencing the competition among academia and industries in the digital world. Meta has become a new rebranding from formerly Facebook. This section considered meta as an operation and discussed meta-processing. It explored meta algebra, intelligent system, and meta computing. If Meta can play a significant role in social media, social services, and social commerce, meta computing will also play a significant role in data science, AI, and computer science.

The popular meta systems are social media, social commerce, and the social networking services of Meta as a company. We will explore meta techniques for big data, analytics, and intelligence in Chapter 5.

2.10 SYSTEMATIC GENERALIZATION AND SPECIALIZATION

Systematic generalization is a meta or induction processing from application to theory. For example, one studied that one apple and 2 apples equal 3 apples, then the theorist developed it into $1+2 = 3$. The practitioners do not care about $1+2 = 3$ but they still apply that one orange and 2 oranges = 3 oranges. This is the application of the theory on apples. This book is about data, analytics, intelligence, and their relationships. Certainly, from a system generalization viewpoint, data, analytics, and intelligence can be generated from AI, data science, and business intelligence. We do not care about data analytics and BI. We should consider the science, engineering, technology, and system of data, analytics, and intelligence. In this way, we can say that data analytics is a kind of data science, engineering, technology, and systems. This book will use the system specification to look at data analytics, and so on.

Systematic specialization is a process from theory via technology, engineering, and system to applications based on deduction, abduction, and the integration of many deductions and abductions. Therefore, the systematic generalization and specialization is the relationship between theory and application, each of them has a tree-like chain.

Question is: What is the meta operation for the systematic generalization?

A meta processing is a kind of systematic generalization. Some books can be generalized as data, analytics, intelligence. More books can be specialized as the applications of data, analytics, and intelligence. Therefore, systematic generalization and specialization are the most general approach for research methodology used in many disciplines and multi-industry, for example, models, algorithms, and equations.

2.11 MODELS, ALGORITHMS, AND EQUATIONS

2.11.1 Models

A model is a representation of complex real-world data structures and their characteristics (Coronel, Morris, & Rob, 2020). Briefly, A model is a description of a real-world entity, usually graphical, number, and equation. For example, 1 is a model of one apple. 1+2 = 3 is the mathematical model of one apple and 2 apples equal 3 apples.

A model is a part of science, engineering, and technology.

A lifecycle is a model. A framework is a model. An architecture is a model. All these can be considered the result of a preliminary design from a systems development viewpoint.

Data modeling is an iterative and progressive process of creating a specific data model for a determined problem domain (Coronel, Morris, & Rob, 2020). Generally, modeling is a process of creating or managing a model to support decision-making. For example, data modeling is a process of creating or managing data models for a business process to support decision-making. An entity-relationship model and relational data model are models for relational database management systems (Coronel, Morris, & Rob, 2020).

2.11.2 Algorithms

An algorithm is a procedure consisting of a set of rules for solving a problem within a finite number of steps (Merriam-Webster, 2023a). The best algorithm for cooking consists of a set of rules to cook a dish with a finite number of steps. Therefore, almost everyone is a cooking algorithm designer, and then almost every person is an algorithm designer and can cook foods excellently.

Algorithm design and analysis are important for realizing a model for computer science, AI, and data science. The best algorithm for a search engine is PageRank, which is the core for the Google search engine. Algorithm design is also important for some ICT companies in the digital age.

2.11.3 Equations

An equation is a description or statement of the equality or equivalence of mathematical or logical expressions (Merriam-Webster, 2024b). For example, the author has used the following equation: $2x^2 - x + 2 = 0$ to check the mathematical skills of many students and staff at universities.

An algorithm is at the level of detailed design from a software engineering viewpoint (Sommerville, 2010). In such a way, models are higher than algorithms in system abstractions. Models, algorithms, and equations can be expressed as a formula, a process, a graph, and an approach. This book will use models, algorithms, and equations to analyze the real-world entities in order to improve our understanding of the world we live and work, and the phenomena we have around us.

2.12 BIG DATA-DERIVED SMALL DATA APPROACH

This section overviews and extends a big data-derived small data approach and big data-derived search (Sun & Huo, 2021), which is the foundation for developing this book. This section presents a dialectic unification between big data and small data by proposing a big data-derived small data approach (Sun & Huo, 2021). As a process, As shown in Figure 2.1, a big data-derived small data approach consists of

1. Big data search;

2. Big data reduction;

3. Big data-derived small data collection;

4. Big data-derived small data analysis;

In what follows, we will look at each of them.

2.12.1 Big Data Search

Big data search is the first step for the big data-derived small data approach. Searching all possible data, if not all existing, is an important task for any research activity. It is also important for literature review, imagination, curiosity, and association. In the big data search process, we can lead to the literature review, imagination, association, and revision of what we have planned and designed. This also implies that research as a search is the first step. In this step, we must identify where is the big data resource for our research.

In this section, we selected Google Scholar as the big data resource because it is the largest scholarly publication base in the digital world,

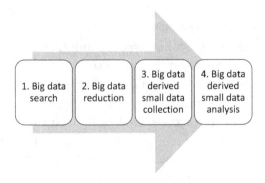

FIGURE 2.1 A big data-derived small data approach.

although EBSCO, Semantic Scholar, ResearchGate are good open-access (free) platforms for locating research. CNKI and Scopus are not free platforms for locating research. Therefore, we use Google Scholar to conduct big data searches. Semantic Scholar and ResearchGate are also free platforms for locating research.

Practitioners across all disciplines are living in the age of big data. However, sometimes, practitioners can only process small data analysis. This is a pragmatic contradiction. It is a challenge to face the relativity between big data and small data (Strang & Sun, 2022).

2.12.2 Big Data Reduction

Big data reduction is the first step for the big data-derived small data approach. Reducing big data is, in essence, a kind of selection. The proper data selection is usually in the name of data reduction (Strang & Sun, 2022).

To address the question, big data should be reduced in the big data search. That is, whenever searching, we must keep in mind that, big data reduction is critical for any big data search, otherwise, big data search would become the search of all the big data, for example, using Google for the entire Web. The heuristic method to address this question is we first analyze the research title and initial proposal or abstract of the research and obtain the important keywords or clauses to narrow the search space. For our search, we should apply the following methodology (Strang & Sun, 2022):

1. Big data,

2. Artificial intelligence, because big data analytics is usually abbreviated as AI, we should also select AI, BI, and data analytics.

This search has revolutionized our tradition that we usually relied on a few sections published in several top journals and so-called important principles and results published in a few classic books or textbooks. The latter is equal to all the data searched from the big data search (Strang & Sun, 2022).

For example, to review big data analytics and classify big data analytics based on research focus, one can search three databases. This is the first step of big data reduction, which uses special databases to collect data, that is, big data-derived small data collection. After the necessary exclusion of invalid sections, one can review the abstracts and titles by focusing on the development, implementation, and discussion of big data analytics and reducing the sections from thousands to less than 100. It can be considered the second step of big data reduction. Then we analyze the 100- publications and classify big data analytics based on research focuses.

2.12.3 Big Data-Derived Small Data Collection

From a statistical modeling perspective, big data-derived small data collection is a special kind of sampling. "Sampling is the process of randomly collecting some data or samples when collecting all or analyzing all is unreasonable" (National Research Council, 2013, p. 120; Conover, 1999). Sampling is also a kind of big data reduction. For example, Google Scholar should be a sampling technique, because Google Scholar cannot collect almost all the data of scholars on the internet. There are two core parts for any sampling toward data analysis based on statistical inference. One is to collect what kind of data. The second is how to collect data. The former refers to what kind of data is important for the designed research. In other words, the importance of data is related to data analysis. The latter has been discussed in terms of statistical sampling. A statistical sampling includes random and non-random sampling (National Research Council, 2013, p. 120).

For the importance of data, not all data needs to be taken for any decision-making and rule-seeking as well as statistical inference (National Research Council, 2013, p. 128). Just as focusing on main problems with main solutions, one can also seek important data for any decision-making and statistical inference. For example, if one likes to research data analysis of social networking services, then one might collect the unstructured data from the Web or online social networking platforms, taking into account the big data-derived small data analysis. Therefore, it is a big issue for a researcher to identify which data set is important to meet the research objectives (Strang & Sun, 2022).

What kind of data is important for this research to examine big data, AI, data analytics, and BI? The possible answers are five types of data, that is, data on 1. big data, 2. AI, 3. data analytics, 4. AI data analytics. 5. BI, from Google Scholar (https://scholar.google.com/). Using this method, this research should collect up to 100×5 data results, that is, if we collect the data on the first 100 scholars' publications in each area with the highest citation, then we can know the state-of-the-art big data, AI, data analytics, BI, and their relationships.

We have still reduced the results using the criteria of citations if the search keywords or clauses are in the publication title or abstract. When we use a

Google Scholar search for a keyword x, there are a lot of search results. This research collects about 100×5 data results. The 100×5 data items are small data, but it is derived from the big data of Google Scholar. Therefore, it is a big data-derived small data collection. This data collection is, in essence, a big data reduction for the proposed research (Strang & Sun, 2022).

2.12.4 Big Data-Derived Small Data Analysis

Big data-derived small data analysis is important for the big data approach and big data analytics as a discipline (Strang & Sun, 2022). First, big data has been controlled by many global data giants such as Meta (formerly Facebook), Google, Tencent, Baidu, and Alibaba, rather than by individual scholars. It is almost impossible for a scholar to use the big data of the mentioned giants to research big data-driven analytics or similar. It is too expensive or unaffordable for a scholar to collect data and analyze the collected data because s/he does not have a platform similar to that of the mentioned giant, like ChatGPT. Sometimes, it is also very expensive for a company like Cambridge Analytica to collect data working together with Facebook, although Cambridge Analytica paid the big price and is bankrupt (Baker, 2018).

Secondly, from a data processing viewpoint, the largest data analyses could be performed in the large data centers of a few global data monopolies running specialized software such as Hadoop over HDFS to leverage thousands of cores to process data distributed throughout the cluster (National Research Council, 2013, p. 55). This means that individuals have to use big data-derived small data analysis to analyze data (Strang & Sun, 2022).

Finally, any research in general, and research publication especially, is, in essence, based on big data-derived small data analysis, because an average research publication consists of about 30 references, which has only up to 30 MB of data from a data volume viewpoint (Strang & Sun, 2022). In the big data world, the data with 30 MB is relatively small. In comparison, Amazon (AWS) and Google have processed 500 exabytes (EB) and 62 petabytes (PB) of big data in 2021 respectively (Clissa, 2022) where 1 EB = 1024 PB = 1024 x 1024 TB.

2.13 SUMMARY

Every science and technology is a method for undertaking any research. This chapter reviewed analytical approach, statistics, algebra, computing, digital computing, meta computing, logic, system generalization and speciation, big data-derived small data approach, and research as a search as the research methodology for our thinking and developing this book. This is also what we used to understand data, analytics, and intelligence in the past three decades.

Engineering aims to use science and technology to develop and manage systems to obtain intelligence. One of these systems is our book, which will be developed in the next research. That is, using computing, science, technology, systems, intelligent analytics, management, services, and applications to explore each of the following terms listed in the Boolean structure. For example, we will explore data computing, data science, data technology, data systems, data management, data services, and data applications. We also explore the related items in the research. For example, we explore big data computing, big data analytics, big data science, big data technology, big data systems, big data management, big data services, and big data applications.

2.14 REVIEW QUESTIONS AND PROBLEMS

For each of the definitions below, an example for each of them is necessary.

1. What is the relationship between meta and operation?

2. What is the difference between data mining and data analytics?

3. What is a digital technology? What is digital computing?

4. What is statistics?

5. What is data engineering?

6. What is the relationship between data engineering, data science, data technology, data systems, and data intelligence?

7. What is computing?

8. What are systematic generalization and specialization?

9. What is a model, algorithm, and equation?

10. What is the big data-derived small data approach?

11. How can we look at computing and its relationship with problems?

2.15 REFERENCES FOR FURTHER STUDY

1. Howard Kahane, Alan Hausman, & Frank Boardman, 2021, Logic and Philosophy: A Modern Introduction Thirteenth Edition, Hackett Publishing Company, Inc.

2. Herbert Bruderer, 2020, Milestones in Analog and Digital Computing 3rd ed., Springer.

3. Thomas Erl, & Eric Monroy, 2023, Cloud Computing: Concepts, Technology, Security, and Architecture, 2nd Edition, Pearson

4. Lefteri Tsoukalas, 2023, Fuzzy Logic: Applications in Artificial Intelligence, Big Data, and Machine Learning, McGraw Hill.

5. Charles Henry, Brase Corrinne, Pellillo Brase, 2018, Understanding Basic Statistics 8th Edition, Cengage Learning.

6. John W. Creswell & J. David Creswell, 2022, Research Design: Qualitative, Quantitative, and Mixed Methods Approaches 6 Sixth Edition, SAGE Publications, Inc.

CHAPTER 3

Data

All data are important for ruling the world.

THIS CHAPTER FIRST LOOKS at data and then big data. It identifies and examines ten big characteristics of big data. It looks at data engineering, science, systems, and technology. It explores a service-oriented foundation of big data and the calculus of big data. Besides data and big data, this chapter explores not only data, but also information, knowledge, intelligence and experience (DIKE). Then it explores DIKE computing, science, engineering, technology, systems, management, intelligence, and services. This chapter discusses data science and data engineering.

Learning objectives of this chapter:

- Define data and big data, with examples.

- Distinguish data from crude oil.

- Define data science, data systems, data warehousing, data mining, and OLAP.

- Understand E-R modeling and optimization.

- Understand 10 big characteristics of big data.

- Explore a service-oriented foundation of big data at three different levels.

 DOI: 10.1201/9781003450504-3

- Understand not only data and big data.

- Define information, knowledge, and experience with three examples.

- Examine information, knowledge, and experience using a meta as a mathematical operation.

- Gain familiarity with DIKI computing, science, engineering, technology, systems, management, intelligence, and services with examples.

- Analyze data and big data and their impacts on information, knowledge, and experience.

- Gain familiarity with the calculus of searching big data.

- Understand DIKE engineering, technology, systems, and intelligence.

- Understand big data analytics.

3.1 INTRODUCTION

Data is abundant and ubiquitous. Data becomes increasingly prominent in any individual, business process, and organization (Thompson & Rogers, 2017). Furthermore, data has become an important element of the economy (Sun, 2023). One hundred years ago, big companies dominated steel, oil, and manufacturing companies. Recently, big data companies like Apple, Alphabet, Meta (formerly Facebook), Amazon, Microsoft, Tencent, and Alibaba have dominated the world. Big data as a disruptive technology is transforming how we live, study, work, and think (Sun, 2023). Therefore, this chapter first looks at data, and then big data. It identifies and examines ten big characteristics of big data, with an example for each (Sun, Strang, & Li, 2018). It also explores a service-oriented foundation of big data and calculus of big data. Besides data and big data, this research also explores information, knowledge, and intelligence (DIKI). Then it explores DIKI computing, science, engineering, technology, systems, management, intelligence, and services (Sun, 2022). Finally, this chapter provides big trends in the era of big data. These six big trends will bring about big industries, smarter cities, smarter societies, and smarter countries.

3.2 FUNDAMENTALS OF DATA

3.2.1 What Is Data?

There are many books or research sections on defining data throughout history. This book will explore three definitions and critically review each of them. Finally, this research will provide a unifying definition for data.

Based on https://www.merriam-webster.com/, data can be defined as

1: Factual information (such as measurements or statistics) used as a basis for reasoning, discussion, or calculation. The data is plentiful and easily available

2: Information in digital form that can be transmitted or processed

3: Information output by a sensing device or organ that includes both useful and irrelevant or redundant information and must be processed to be meaningful

Data is defined as information. However, data and information are different in computer science and information systems (Laudon & Laudon, 2020).

Data are streams of raw facts representing events occurring in organizations or the physical environment before they have been organized (arranged) into a form that people can understand and use (Laudon & Laudon, 2020). These facts will be organized and arranged into a form for computerized systems to process. The form can be understood and used by people. Briefly speaking, data are streams of raw facts for computerized systems processing through organizing and arranging to become information.

The example of data is that it consists of 0 and 1, which are the fundamentals of computer science and data science.

Data are "the facts and figures collected, analyzed, and summarized for presentation and interpretation" (Sweeney, Williams, & Anderson, 2011, p. 5). All the data collected in a particular study are referred to as the data set for the study. Data are all the input of computerized systems (Laudon & Laudon, 2020). For example, data are first an input of database management systems (Coronel, Morris, & Rob, 2020).

For example, raw data from a supermarket checkout counter can be processed and organized by an organization or a company to produce meaningful information, such as the total unit sales of dish detergent or the total sales revenue from dish detergent for a specific store or sales territory (Laudon & Laudon, 2020).

3.2.2 The Characteristics of Data

There are many different characteristics of data from different disciplinary perspectives. In what follows, we only look at SACIDS. SACIDS is an acronym that refers to the set of 4 key properties that define a transaction: serializability, atomicity, consistency, isolation, durability, and big sociality (Coronel, Morris, & Rob, 2020). A transaction is a logical unit of a program consisting of related operations and activities. ACIDS are four important properties of transactions (Coronel, Morris, & Rob, 2020; Aroraa, Lele, & Jindal, 2022).

3.2.2.1 Serializability

Serializability is important for concurrent control, multiuser, and distributed databases to realize the macro concurrence from a customer viewpoint, through micro Serializability of events from a system development viewpoint (Coronel, Morris, & Rob, 2020). Both realize the concurrent execution of transactions yields consistent results.

3.2.2.2 Atomicity

All parts of a transaction must be completed (Coronel, Morris, & Rob, 2020).

3.2.2.3 Consistency

Consistency is the permanence of the database's consistent state. The data should remain consistent even after the execution of an operation (Aroraa, Lele, & Jindal, 2022, p. 173).

3.2.2.4 Isolation

Data used during one transaction cannot be used for a second until the first is completed (Aroraa, Lele, & Jindal, 2022, p. 8).

3.2.2.5 Durability

Durability ensures that once transactions are committed, they cannot be undone or lost (Coronel, Morris, & Rob, 2020).

TABLE 3.1   Unit of Measuring Data

Items	For Short	Meaning
gigabyte	GB	2^{30}
terabyte	TB	2^{40}
Petabyte	PB	2^{50}
exabyte	EB	2^{60}
Zettebyte	ZB	2^{70}
yettebyte	YB	2^{80}

3.2.2.6 Sociality

Data is everywhere (Hu & Kaabouch, 2014). Sociality is big people's engagement with data such as social media and social networking services.

3.2.3 How to Calculate Big Data and Data Sources

How can we calculate data? Table 3.1 lists and measures data.

Human beings, machines, systems, and sensors are the main data sources. The big data contributors include 1. The CERN community is one of the most prominent players concerning big data production, generating roughly 40k EB of raw data (Clissa, 2022). 2. over 100 trillion objects were reportedly stored in Amazon's simple storage service (S3). Google and Meta are also two big data contributors.

Everyone is a selfless contributor to data. Whenever one clicks, one can be instructed to click next. The click has been tracked (Laudon & Laudon, 2020). More and more robots and bots are around you, helping you more and more, tracking you more and more, making you smart more and more, although you are concerned about your privacy and security sometimes.

3.3 DATA ENGINEERING, TECHNOLOGY, AND SYSTEMS

Strategically, data engineering aims to use data science and data technology to develop and manage data systems to obtain data services and applications with data intelligence.

Specifically, data engineering consists of three different worlds: objective world, logical world, and physical world. The data preprocessing steps from objective world to logical world 1. Data sources from real world 2. Data consolidation, 3. Data cleaning, 4, data transformation, and 5. Data reduction. Then it will be changed into well-formed data in the logical world. In the logical world, we use conceptual data modeling to create data models to formalize data. For example, data models include the E-R model and normalization model. All these can change the data into a relational database schema. Then we normalized the relational database schema based on database management systems. All these databases can be saved into a physical world in the name of databases, data warehouses, data marts, data lakes and cloud databases.

This section looks at data modeling, data warehousing, data mining, and online analytical processing as parts of data engineering. Data modeling leads to data systems. Data warehousing leads to data warehouses. Data mining leads to data mines, and online analytical processing leads to OLAP systems.

3.3.1 Data Systems

A data system is a process of converting data into data, based on data technology, " (Coronel, Morris, & Rob, 2020). Data models, data collection, storage, and retrieval are used for the data system.

A model is an abstraction of a real-world entity or event. Data models are representations of complex real-world data structures and their characteristics. Entity-relationship (E-R) model and object-oriented model are models for relational database management systems (Coronel, Morris, & Rob, 2020).

Data modeling is an iterative and progressive process of creating a specific data model for a determined problem domain (Coronel, Morris, & Rob, 2020).

Since the 1950s, data management has focused on processing the transaction of many businesses, with perfect reliability and with ever-increasing numbers of transactions per second (Betser & Belanger, 2013), for example, transaction processing systems such as airline reservation systems and credit card systems. The size of databases involved in these systems has been increased from megabytes in the 1970s through terabytes in the 1990s and petabytes in the 2000s. The basic data models of the databases have also evolved from network and hierarchical in the 1970s to relational in the past few decades (Codd, 1970). The classic data systems are relational database systems, developed by E.F. Codd in 1970–1973 (Codd, 1970), the early design of database systems is also based on entity-relationship modeling (Chen, 1976). At a strategic level, SQL = search engine, just like Chrome as a search engine online. At an operational level, SQL= DDL+DML for data definition language and data manipulation language (Coronel, Morris, & Rob, 2020). SQL becomes the dominant tool for accessing, managing, and manipulating data in any databases involving in the above-mentioned transaction processing systems (TPS) and information systems (such as enterprise resources planning and other enterprise systems), because relational databases have dominated the market since then (Krishnamurthi & Fisler, 2020).

Currently, Oracle, Alibaba cloud database, and Microsoft SQL server are the most popular database systems in the market. Database systems have also been integrated into data warehouses and data lakes.

3.3.2 Removed Data Warehousing

Data warehousing (DW) plays a role in analytics as an input of data (Thompson & Rogers, 2017, p. 8). The concept of data warehousing dates back to the late 1980s, when IBM researchers Barry Devlin and Paul Murphy developed the "business data warehouse" in 1988. Bill Inmon's Building the Data Warehouse (Inmon, 2005) has played an important role in promoting data warehouses since then.

Briefly, A data warehouse is a collection of integrated databases (Coronel, Morris, & Rob, 2020). More specifically, a data warehouse is a subject-oriented, integrated, non-volatile, time variant dataset to support management decision-making (Inmon, 1992, 2005; Coronel, Morris, & Rob, 2020; Sharda, Delen, & Turba, 2018).

Data warehousing is a progress of creating or managing data warehouses to support decision-making using intelligent data techniques. Data warehousing is a kind of data engineering. Data warehousing is the action. data warehouse is the goal. The goal of data warehousing is to change data from data sources into the data warehouse. Data warehousing is also used to capture, store, and maintain the data in the data warehouse (Sweeney, Williams, & Anderson, 2011, p. 17).

Data warehousing systems are analytical tools designed to assist reporting users across multiple departments to make decisions for businesses in an organization (Ingle, 2023). Advanced data warehousing has been incorporated within BI and advanced business analytics (Richardson, Schlegel, Sallam, Kronz, & Sun, 2021). Data Warehousing is the consolidation and aggregation of masses of data from multiple sources into a reconciled format for reporting. DW extracts and obtains the data from operational databases and external open sources, providing a more comprehensive data pool (Coronel, Morris, & Rob, 2020).

The current leading DW providers include Amazon Redshift, Snowflake, Google BigQuery, Microsoft Azure, Teradata, Amazon DynamoDB, PostgreSQL, and so on (EM360 Tech, 2020; Ingle, 2023; Sharda, Delen, & Turba, 2018). We only briefly introduce three of the above-mentioned.

Amazon Redshift: A cloud-based data warehousing tool for businesses is called Redshift. The fully managed platform can provide a petabyte-scale data warehouse service in the cloud. Redshift is appropriate for high-speed data analytics because of quick processing of petabytes of data (Ingle, 2023).

Microsoft Azure: Microsoft's Azure SQL Data Warehouse is a relational database hosted in the cloud (Ingle, 2023). It can be optimized for real-time reporting and petabyte-scale data loading and processing. The platform's machine-learning technologies can be used to create clever apps.

Google BigQuery. BigQuery is a data warehousing platform with built-in machine learning capabilities (Ingle, 2023). Combining TensorFlow and Cloud ML, BigQuery can be used to build effective AI models. For real-time analytics, BigQuery can run queries on petabytes of data quickly.

A data mart is a small, single-subject data warehouse subset to provide decision support to a small group of people at a division or department in an organization. (Coronel, Morris, & Rob, 2020). The benefits of the data mart over data warehouses are lower cost and shorter implementation time.

A data lake is a centralized repository designed to store, process, and secure large amounts of data (Google, 2024). It can store data in its native format and process any variety, ignoring size limits. Data lakes also include clickstream user information, and business and external data (Blatt, 2017).

3.3.3 Data Mining
This section looks at data mines and data mining.

3.3.3.1 Introduction
Data mining (DM), coined by Mike Lovell in 1973 (Hardin, 2013), is defined by Dr. Kurt Thearling as "the automated extraction of predictive information from large databases and data warehouses (Sweeney, Williams, & Anderson, 2011, p. 17). Data mining has been important for data science, data engineering, big data, and big data analytics. Traditionally, data mining is knowledge discovery from a large database (Laudon & Laudon, 2020). DM employs advanced statistical and

analytical tools to analyze the big data available through DWs and other sources to identify possible relationships, patterns, and anomalies and discover information or knowledge for business decision-making. Currently, advanced data mining aims to discover and generate insights, intelligence, and wisdom to support decision-making (Richardson, Schlegel, Sallam, Kronz, & Sun, 2021). DM is one of the top intelligent technologies for business analytics, big data analytics, and intelligent business analytics. Not only is mining data a future trend in the age of big analytics and AI, but DIKIW mining is future-oriented mining technology for intelligent business analytics. For example, knowledge mining, intelligence mining, and wisdom mining as a part of DIKIW mining have become a social demand for business people and analytics professionals.

3.3.3.2 Data Mining as a Process

There are many definitions for data mining.

Data mining is a process that uses statistical, mathematical, AI, and machine-learning techniques to extract and identify useful information from large databases (Coronel, Morris, & Rob, 2020).

Data mining is a process of mining data in databases. The goal is a data mine.

Data mining is a process for mining databases and the data warehouses using statistics, mathematics, and computer science, and for analysts in the warehouse to convert the data into useful knowledge and insight.

Data mining is a process of discovering various models, novel patterns summaries, derived values, and knowledge from a large database or data warehouse, or the web to support intelligent business analytics and managerial decision-making (Strang & Sun, 2022; Ghavami, 2020).

Data mining is a process of discovering information and knowledge from a large database or warehouse. This implies that data mining is a kind of information discovery, and knowledge discovery (Sharda, Delen, Turban, & King, 2018, p. 278).

The subject of data mining deals with methods for developing useful decision-making information from large databases (Sweeney, Williams, & Anderson, 2011, p. 17).

Data mining is a technology that relies heavily on statistical methodology such as multiple regression, logistic regression, and correlation (Sweeney, Williams, & Anderson, 2011, p. 17).

Association, rule learning, clustering analysis, classification analysis, and regression analysis are the main functions of data mining (Van Rijmenam, 2020, pp. 145–149).

3.3.3.3 Web Mining and Text Mining
Web mining and text mining are applied data mining.

Web mining aims to analyze massive amounts of data on customer behavior, evaluate a Web site's effectiveness, and quantify the success of a marketing campaign (Coronel, Morris, & Rob, 2020):

1. Uncover hidden trends, patterns, and association relationships.

2. Form computer models to stimulate and explain the findings.

3. Use the models to support business decision-making.

4. Run in two modes: Guided and Automated.

Text mining is the process of extracting patterns and knowledge from big unstructured data sources (Sharda, Delen, Turban, & King, 2018, p. 278). Big unstructured data sources include Word files, PDF files, text files, and XML files.

3.3.3.4 Clustering and Classification
Data mining includes descriptive data mining and predictive data mining (Aroraa, Lele, & Jindal, 2022; Kantardzic, 2011). The former produces new nontrivial patterns and knowledge, while the latter produces models and roles of the systems. The primary tasks of descriptive data mining include clustering, summarization, association, and dependency modeling (Fan, Lau, & Zhao, 2015). The primary tasks of predictive data mining include classification, regression, change, and deviation detection (Aroraa, Lele, & Jindal, 2022; Kantardzic, 2011; Fan, Lau, & Zhao, 2015). Therefore, DM has four functions as a service for organizations and customers: regression, classification, clustering, and association rules.

Clustering and classification organize the input data into k-groups (Tsai, Lai, Chao, & Vasilakos, 2015). Clustering can be used to understand the new input data. The essence of clustering is to separate a set of unlabeled input data into k different groups, using k-means. Classification can be considered the opposite of clustering because it uses a set of already labeled input data to construct a set of classifiers or classes. The decision tree-based algorithm, naïve Bayesian classification, and support vector machine are widely used for classification (Tsai, Lai, Chao, & Vasilakos, 2015).

Association rules and sequential patterns focus on revealing the "relationships" between the input data (Tsai, Lai, Chao, & Vasilakos, 2015). More specifically, association rules aim to find all the co-occurrence relationships between the input data. The *a priori* algorithm is one of the most popular methods to discover the association rules between objects. Sequential patterns aim to mine the sequences or time series of the input data; it can also be considered as a sequential patterns mining problem, which can be solved using several *a priori*-like algorithms.

3.3.3.5 Data Mining and Statistics

Data mining has roots in classical data analysis (Kantardzic, 2011). Data mining has its origins in statistics and machine learning (Sharda, Delen, Turban, & King, 2018). Statistics has its roots in mathematics. Machine learning has its origins in computer science and AI (Russell & Norvig, 2020). Model Statistics is almost entirely driven by the notion of the model (Kantardzic, 2011, p. 4). Modern machine learning and statistics are based on data (Sharda, Delen, Turban, & King, 2018). Machine learning emphasizes algorithms while statistics emphasizes models because learning contains the notion of a process.

Data visualization plays the same role in statistics and data mining. Therefore, data mining is inherited from statistics. Even so, data mining has extended statistics because data organization, and algorithms from machine learning have played more roles in data mining. Therefore, data mining realizes the integration of models and process, an implicit algorithm.

3.3.3.6 Data Mining as a Data Engineering

There are many models for data mining. For example, data mining as a process consists of data preparation phase, data analysis phase, and knowledge acquisition phase, and prognosis phase (Coronel, Morris, & Rob, 2020). Basically, data mining as a process consists of the following phases. We added visualization and reporting phase in this data mining process.

1. Data preparation phase. This phase identifies, cleans, and stores the dataset in a database or data warehouse. This is the reason that database and data warehouse are data preparation for any data mining.

2. Data analysis phase: This phase can use many data analyses, such as classification, clustering, and deviation analysis, to analysis data.

3. Knowledge acquisition phase: This phase can use data mining algorithms and AI-driven algorithms, including neuro networks and machine learning, to discover knowledge from the database and data warehouse.

4. Prognosis phase. This phase provides a prognosis for what will happen next.

5. Visualization and reporting phase: This phase uses visualization techniques to visualize acquired knowledge and prognosed recommendations in a visual form.

3.3.3.7 Summary

Data mining is a progress of creating data mines from a large database to support decision-making, where data mines consist of knowledge patterns, association relationships, and insights. Therefore, data mining discovers the knowledge and intelligence from a large database.

3.3.4 NoSQL database

NoSQL is a set of databases based on not only a database model (Blatt, 2017). It is loosely defined as being a data store that provides fewer consistency guarantees than a conventional data and/or a database that store non-relational data (National Research Council, 2013). Non-ArangoDB is a NoSQL product with graph database capacity, which provides a faster and more direct access to the network of relationships between sales personnel and customers (Blatt, 2017).

3.3.5 Online Analytical Processing (OLAP)

Online Analytical Processing or OLAP is an analytical tool, technology, and technique, directly for data/business analytics. It is an advanced data analysis environment that supports decision-making, business modeling, and operations research (Coronel, Morris, & Rob, 2020).

Characteristics of OLAP are:

- Multidimensional data analysis techniques.

- Advanced database support.

- Easy-to-use end-user interfaces.

- Multidimensional data analysis techniques.

- Data are processed and viewed as part of a multidimensional structure.

- Augmenting functions.

- Advanced data presentation functions.

- Advanced data aggregation, consolidation, and classification functions.

- Advanced computational functions.

- Advanced data-modeling functions.

3.4 DATA SCIENCE

Although data science has existed for 50 years (Donoho, 2017), data management and database systems have been around us at least since 1970. Data warehousing and data mining have been around since the 1980s. Data science has been developing rapidly thanks to big data since 2019 and AI's resurgence.

In what follows, this section highlights data science as a kind of science and profession (Mike & Hazzan, 2023; Stodden, 2020).

3.4.1 Data Science as a Science

Data Science is a science that brings together domain data, computer science, and statistical tools for interrogating the data and extracting useful information, knowledge, and intelligence (Danyluk & Leidig, 2021, p. 10). In this definition, domain, statistics and mathematics, and computer science are the disciplinary elements. The domain provides the data; statistics and mathematics are used for analysis, modeling, and inference; and computer science is used for data access, management, protection, and effective processing in modern computer architectures. Data science focuses on understanding data and developing data systems, tools, and methods to perform research on data (Mike & Hazzan, 2023). Data science promises new insights, helping transform data into information, knowledge, and intelligence that can drive science, engineering, technology, and industry. This disciplinary relationship is illustrated below based on a Venn diagram (Mike & Hazzan, 2023), as illustrated in Figure 3.1.

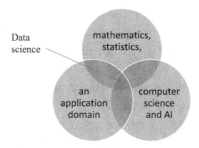

FIGURE 3.1   Data science as an interdisciplinary science.

Data science refers to the science of data and relationships. It is a continuation of data mining, analytical analysis, data systems, and data technology (Weber, 2020, p. 80). Data science emphasizes the universal approaches to business and management problems (Weber, 2020, p. 84). The data science process involves solving problems related to data science. There is a framework of data science that is followed during the project life cycle (Weber, 2020, pp. 90–94):

1. Consider the problem.

2. Gather the data (obtain data sources using MySQL or Excel, etc., based on data models, algorithms, and programs).

3. Scrub the data (clean and strain the data, it is required to have skills in Hadoop and Spark).

4. Explore the data (using association to explore the data).

5. Model the data (make useful and meaningful models).

6. Understand the data (using project analytics and prescriptive analytics, to have a business area understanding to show the results of providing answers to the business questions).

More generally, data science is a part of data computing. Data computing consists of data science, data engineering, data technology, data management, data systems, data services, and data intelligence.

3.4.2 Data Science as a Profession

The definition of data science can be derived from the description of the profession. This profession includes data scientists.

Data scientists can use specific data science knowledge, skills, and dispositions to find the meaning of data and answer questions using data (Danyluk & Leidig, 2021). They can use (extremely powerful) algorithms (e.g., machine learning, NN) to discover knowledge, many reliable patterns. BI analysts use business domain knowledge, dashboard to provide informative decisions to the mangers.

Data scientists are not programmers (e.g., Python programmers with technical skills), but data scientists should have a deep understanding of programming. A data scientist can do three tasks: data analysis, data modeling, data engineering, and prototyping processes (Weber, 2020, p. 81). Understanding the discovered knowledge and intelligence requires more mathematics, AI, business, and analytics.

Data scientists need sound theoretical and technical skills and domain skills to provide data-driven decision-making. Some data scientists possess the three key roles: deep analytical talent, data savvy professionals, and technology and data enablers.

Data scientists aim to invent data intelligence-driven engineering, technologies, and machines to represent, learn, simulate, reinforce, and transfer human-like intuition, imagination, curiosity, and creative thinking through human-data interaction and cooperation.

Finally, data scientist should have a passion for excellence in data intelligence and big data intelligence.

3.5 DATA ENGINEERING FOR E-R MODELING

As mentioned in the previous section, data engineering is a part of data computing. Data engineering is a process, including all aspects of data gathering, cleaning, organizing, analyzing, interpreting, and visualizing the facts represented by the raw data. Data science is indeed commonly presented as an iterative and incremental workflow for generating value and data-driven actions from the above data processing (Mike & Hazzan, 2023).

This section will look at business case mining and E-R modeling optimization.

3.5.1 Introduction

Data science, big data analytics, and business intelligence have drawn increasing attention in academia and industries (Sun, 2023; Ghavami, 2020). Entity relationship (E-R) modeling is an important technique for converting the physical world to a logical world through modeling entity relationships (Chen, 1976; Hu, Liu, & Wang, 2020). E-R modeling is a foundational technology of data science, big data analytics, business intelligence, and database systems (Thalheim, 2000). Business rules are fundamental for E-R modeling, database design, and big data analytics (Ghavami, 2020, p. 13). Many books on data management systems and big data analytics such as (Coronel, Morris, & Rob, 2020) and (Ghavami, 2020, p. 13) have mentioned business rules and discussed how to discover business rules. However, none have examined them in depth. Therefore, how to transform business cases through business rule discovery into E-R models is still a fundamental issue for a database design, although many database management systems provide the built-in development tool of E-R diagram.

Without business rules as a basis for comprehending business cases, there would be neither data science and big data analytics nor business intelligence. Business case mining is business rule discovery from a business case. Identifying, analyzing, and refining the business rules are the first important tasks for designing relational database systems in particular and information systems and big data analytics in general (Ghavami, 2020). However, there are not many research publications in this direction, based on our Google Scholar search. Therefore, a big issue for designing database systems, big data analytics, and business intelligence is identified as:

1. How can we discover business rules from mining business cases?

Moreover, when we undertake E-R modeling, we assume that the business rules are already there or that business rules automatically exist. This is, however, not a reality in many instances. Even though one has rich experience in undertaking E-R modeling, one still does not have a unified method for dealing with business rules. There is also no automated method for business rule discovery from mining business cases, although data mining has been developed for a few decades (Kantardzic, 2011; Sharda, Delen, & Turba, 2018). Therefore, the second big issue for database design is identified below.

2. How can we mine business cases for business rule discovery?

E-R modeling optimization aims to improve the E-R modeling process to get better E-R diagrams that understand and translate business cases properly. This implies that the third big issue for database design is:

3. How can we optimize E-R modeling?

This section will address these three issues by exploring business case mining and E-R modeling optimization. Addressing the first two issues, this section explores business case-based reasoning and presents a unified approach to business case mining for business rule discovery. Addressing the third issue, this section proposes a unified optimal method for E-R modeling.

The remainder of this section is organized as follows: Subsection 3.5.2 explore business case-based reasoning. Subsection 3.5.3 provides a unified process of business case mining for business rule discovery. Subsection 3.5.4 looks at business rule discovery from business case mining. Subsection 3.5.5 examines E-R modeling optimization. The final sub section ends this research with concluding remarks and future work.

3.5.2 Business Case Based Reasoning

This subsection explores business case and business case-based reasoning.

3.5.2.1 A Business Case

There are many definitions for a business case. Different disciplines have different definitions. For example,

1. Oxford defines a business case as "a justification for a proposed project or undertaking based on its expected commercial benefit."

2. a business case can be defined as a description of a business scenario, including a set of business activities and associated stakeholders. The following is a business case (Sun, Han, & Dong, 2008).

The Beem (a fictional name) Medical Center (for short, BMC) will design a database system to manage their patient appointments and billing system, based on the following basic description of the system.

BMC has employed many doctors. A doctor may be scheduled for many appointments. However, each appointment is only with a single doctor. BMC records the details of every doctor's ID, first name, and surname.

A patient may have many appointments on the same day. The patient's details include her or his first name, surname, date of birth, the policy, and identification number of any insurance. BMC records the details and addresses of every patient on their system. Every patient may have multiple phone numbers including home, mobile, and work phone.

BMC records the details of every insurance company on its system, including the name of every insurance company, its postal address, a single phone number, and a webpage address. Every insurance company can have many different policy types. Each policy type includes a description of the policy and the percentage rebate amount that the insurance company will pay for each appointment.

FIGURE 3.2   A model for business case mining driven E-R modeling optimization.

A bill is generated after each appointment. For patients who have medical insurance, referred to as private patients, the insurance company may pay a certain percentage of a bill depending on the type of coverage that the patient holds. The patient and the insurance company may make multiple payments on a single bill. When a payment is made, a payment receipt number is recorded, along with the amount that has been paid, the date/time of the payment, the method of payment, and who has made the payment. The system records the available payment methods, including cash, credit card, check, and direct debit.

When a bill for an appointment is generated and if the patient has insurance, the amount of the bill that is covered by the insurance company is stored, along with an amount not covered by insurance. The status of each bill is also stored; these being: outstanding or paid in full.

The above business case leads to a model for business case mining-driven E-R modeling optimization, illustrated in Figure 3.2. We will look at this model by exploring business case-based reasoning, business case mining, and E-R modeling optimization in the following sections.

3.5.2.2 Business Case Mining for Business Rule Discovery

Business case mining is fundamental for discovering detailed information on entities and their attributes as well as their relationships, the latter are the foundations for E-R modeling and database systems design.

Discovering business rules is a complex task for which many approaches have been proposed, including analysis and extraction from code and data mining (Gailly & Geerts, 2013). For example, Gao, at al., look at business rule discovery through data mining methods (Gao, Koronios, Kennett, & Scott, 2010). Bajić-Bizumić, et al., proposed an interactive, simulation-driven approach for discovering business rules with an Alloy Analyzer tool (http://alloy.mit.edu/alloy/). Alloy Analyzer is used as a platform for rule simulation and discovery (Bajić-Bizumić, Rychkova, & Wegmann, 2013).

Business case mining aims to mine the business case to discover business rules for E-R modeling and database design.

3.5.2.3 Entities and Relationships

Entities, attributes, and relationships are the three main components of an E-R model (Coronel, Morris, & Rob, 2020).

An entity is a "thing" that can be distinctly identified (Chen, 1976). A doctor, a patient, or a bill are examples of an entity. An entity at the E-R modeling level refers to an entity set, denoted by capitated letters. For example, entity DOCTOR is an entity set corresponding to a table that consists of a number of doctor's records, that is, DOCTOR = $\{x \mid x = a$ doctor working at BMC$\}$.

A relationship is an association among entities (Chen, 1976). For instance, an appointment is a relationship between two entities, DOCTOR and PATIENT. Generally speaking, n entities have a relationship, where n is a natural number. However, we only consider binary relationships between two entities. At the E-R modeling level, we mainly consider three kinds of connectivity or relationship classification: one-to-one (1:1), one-to-many (1:M), and many-to-many (M:N) relationships (Coronel, Morris, & Rob, 2020).

Have a look at the following excerpt from the above-mentioned business case:

> A doctor may be scheduled for many appointments. However, each appointment is only with a single doctor. BMC also stores details of every doctor's ID number, first name, and surname.

In this business case, doctor, appointment, and patient correspond to three entities, DOCTOR, APPOINTMENT, and PATIENT. A doctor may be scheduled for many appointments, which is a kind of 1:M relationship between DOCTOR and APPOINTMENT. *A patient may have many appointments on the same day*, which is a 1:M relationship between PATIENT and APPOINTMENT.

The above discussion implies the following findings:

- Every relationship between entities is bidirectional. It is better to use one verb to represent these two bidirectional relationships. One is used with the active voice while another is with the passive voice.

- In the business case, a doctor may be scheduled for many appointments with patients whereas a patient may be scheduled for many appointments with doctors. Therefore, the relationship between DOCTOR and PATIENT is M:N.

- An entity is a noun while a relationship is usually represented by a verb associated with a noun, for example, the appoint is associated with the appointment.

Therefore, different verbs in the business case may lead to different relationships. The question is: how many verbs are related to business, business management, and business decision-making. All these related verbs are useful for discovering business rules from mining the business case to developing business rule-driven E-R diagrams.

Furthermore, intransitive verbs are not used for creating relationships between entities. Therefore, if all the business and management-related verbs are denoted as V, then, intransitive verbs are not in V.

Based on the above analysis, in order to develop business rules-driven E-R modeling, it is necessary to extract triple elements from mining a business case, that is, the nouns that are related to persons, objects, things, etc. Each of these nouns may be an entity, and all these entities are aggregated as a set, denoted as E, consisting of business entities. Every element in E is a candidate element of a business rule as a pre-condition or a sequence of the business rule. They are also the candidate entity for E-R diagrams through E-R modeling.

The business-associated verbs extracted from the business case are aggregated as a set of business verbs, denoted as V.

The numbers related to quantity and restraints are aggregated to be a set of cardinality and restraints, donated by C.

Formally, we have

$$E = \{x \,|\, x = \text{an entity}\} \tag{3.1}$$

$$V = \{v \,|\, v = a\,\text{business} - \text{associated activity}\} \tag{3.2}$$

The above-mentioned business case is mined and the following candidate entities and business-associated activities are discovered:

E = {*doctor, ID, first name and surname, appointment, patient, address, phone, insurance company, system, policy, description, percentage, amount, bill, coverage, payment, method, cash, credit card, cheque, direct debit, insurance, status, home, mobile and work, name, surname, date of birth, policy identification number*}.

V = {*manage, billing, store, schedule, include, have, generate, hold, make, pay, record, cover*}.

Named entity recognition (or Name's entity recognition) is a procedure to identify entities of interest such as persons, locations, organizations, and products (Ghavami, 2020, p. 73). Its input is a text, its output is entities of interest. Apache OpenNLP (https://opennlp.apache.org/, accessed on June 3, 2021) is a platform that supports not only named entity extraction but also the most common natural language processing tasks such as tokenization, sentence segmentation, part-of-speech tagging, and parsing. One can use OpenNLP to get the above-mentioned E. However, the above results are blind mining because only nouns and most business-associated activities are discovered. In other words, every element in E is only a candidate entity. Every element in V can be a candidate relationship. We should mine the business case based on people-centered entity discovery, and function-centered entity discovery to find the entities. People-centered entity discovery is to extract the people or organization elements from E. Function-centered entity discovery is to extract the business activity-centered elements from V.

Using people-centered entity discovery, we have E = {DOCTOR, PATIENT, INSURANCE COMPANY}.

The mentioned business case aims to "design a database to manage their patient appointments and billing system". This implies that the system has mainly two functions or business activities: appointment management and billing system. The billing system is related to payment and bill directly. That is, using function-centered entity discovery, we have E = {APPOINTMENT, PAYMENT, BILL}.

Combining people-centered entity discovery and function-centered entity discovery, we have six entities from the business case mining.

$$E = \begin{cases} \text{DOCTOR, PATIENT, INSURANCE COMPANY,} \\ \text{APPOINTMENT, PAYMENT, BILL} \end{cases}.$$

Similarly, we have V = {appoint, bill, schedule, have, generate, hold, make, pay, record, cover}

It should be noted that the business activity *appointment* is related to *schedule*, while the *payment* is related to *generate, make and cover*. All these will be discussed in the business rule discovery.

3.5.2.4 Business Rules

Business rules have been studied from various perspectives, such as an IS perspective (Bajec & Krisper, 2001) and an ontology perspective (Gailly & Geerts, 2013). Automated business rule management systems have been available in the market (Bajec & Krisper, 2001). In what follows, we discuss business rules from the perspective of E-R modeling and database design (Coronel, Morris, & Rob, 2020).

Generally speaking, a business rule is a statement that specifies policies, conditions, and knowledge in business (Bajec & Krisper, 2001). More specifically, a business rule is a brief, precise, and unambiguous description of a policy, procedure, or principle within a business organization (Coronel, Morris, & Rob, 2020, p. 37–39). For E-R modeling and database design, business rules are the basis for defining entities and relationships, as well as constraints for organizations' operations. Business rules are statements that specify entities and their relationships in the form of 1:1, 1:M, and M:N (Chen, 1976; Coronel, Morris, & Rob, 2020). That is, a business rule mainly consists of four elements below:

- Entities;
- Relationships (1:1, 1:M, M:N, expressed through connectivity and cardinalities);
- Attributes;
- Constraints.

The business rules can enable the designer to fully understand how the business works and what role data plays within company operations. Business rules are derived not only from the practice of business organizations but also from a business description of organizations' operations. In our research, business rules are hidden in the business case. Business rules are discovered from the business case mining. Therefore, business case mining aims to discover business rules with 1:1, 1:M, and M:N relationships between entities under either an optional or mandatory condition from the business case.

For example, in our business case,

A doctor may be scheduled for many appointments

is a business rule, which is a summarized principle based on the business practice of many medical centers. This business rule reveals that a relationship between doctor and appointment is one to many (1:M). Hence, DOCTOR is an entity and APPOINTMENT is another. The sentence from our business case below:

each appointment is only with a single doctor

is another business rule that is an unambiguous description of the relationship between DOCTOR and APPOINTMENT. This relationship is one-to-one (1:1).

Business rules can establish entities, relationships, and constraints (Coronel, Morris, & Rob, 2020). For example, the above-mentioned first business rule describes the relationship between DOCTOR and APPOINTMENT. The second business rule describes the constraint of the appointment at the medical center.

3.5.3 A Unified Process of Mining Business Cases for Business Rule Discovery

A unified process of mining business cases for business rule discovery consists of six steps (Sun, Pinjik, & Pambel, 2021).

Step 1. Identify and construct the set of entities E, using people-centered entity discovery, and function-centered entity discovery from mining the business case.

Step 2. Identify and construct the set of relationships V, and the set of constraints C from mining the business case, using people-centered relationship discovery, and function-centered relationship discovery.

Step 3. Build mapping between elements of E taking into account the element of V.

These steps are an iterative process (Pressman & Maxim, 2014).

All the mappings over E together constitute a set of business relationships, donated as R, that is,

$$R = \{r \mid r = (e_i, v_k, e_j), \text{ei, ej} \in E, v_k \in V \} \tag{3.3}$$

Note that any verb describing a business relationship can exist independently and must associate with at least one entity.

Now we look at these three steps using an example. If doctor and appointment are in E, and schedule in V, then there is a candidate relationship between doctor and appointment. This candidate relationship might be *schedule*, that is,

$$r = (\text{doctor}, \text{schedule}, \text{appointment})$$

Furthermore, taking into account the connectivity of association relationship 1:1, 1:M, and M:N (Coronel, Morris, & Rob, 2020), we can represent the above formula in (3), r = (e$_i$, v$_k$, e$_j$, connectivity), for example, r = (doctor, *schedule*, appointment, 1:M).

> Step 4. Traverse the business case iteratively and look at which elements r = (e$_i$, v$_k$, e$_j$) of R most fit the business case. Then select these most fitting elements to form a set of R. We still use R as the business relationships of the business case.

This step is related to optimization because it is related to "most fitting".

> Step 5. Attach the connectivity and cardinality (Coronel, Morris, & Rob, 2020) to the element of R taking into account the business case in the form r = (e$_i$, v$_k$, e$_j$, connectivity, cardinality).

> Step 6. Use the business rule definition language to translate (e$_i$, v$_k$, e$_j$, connectivity, cardinality) into a natural language description or in semi-structured language.

Finally, we have the following set of business rules concerning the business case,

$$\left(e_i, v_k, e_j, \text{connectivity}, \text{cardinality}\right).$$

3.5.4 Business Rule Discovery from Business Case Mining

Business rule discovery aims to analyze information about organization units (Bajec & Krisper, 2001). Bajec and Krisper stated that the entire business rule life cycle consists of six stages: business rule discovery, analyses, classification, articulation, formalization, and documentation. Each of the stages is related to E-R modeling and database design. Business rule discovery in this research consists of people-centered, function-centered, and people and function combined entity/relationship/business rule discovery. In other words, when the business case is mined, people-centered, function-centered entities, relationships, and business rules will be discovered. Then they will be combined to obtain the business rules for developing E-R diagrams. Based on this principle, the business case is mined and all possible corresponding business rules are discovered sequentially as follows:

> Based on people-centered entity discovery, DOCTOR and PATIENT are the most important entities in the business case.

"*A doctor may be scheduled for many appointments, however, each appointment is only with a* single doctor" is extracted from the business case. Then the relationship between doctor and appointment is 1:M optionally, that is:

Business rule 1. *A doctor may be scheduled for many appointments.* The relationship between DOCTOR and APPOINTMENT is 1:M optionally.

Note that doctor belongs to people, therefore, this business rule discovery belongs to people-centered business rule discovery.

"*A patient may have many appointments*" is extracted from the business case. Then we have

Business rule 2. *A patient may have many appointments.* The relationship between PATIENT and APPOINTMENT is 1:M optionally.

Business rule 1 and Business rule 2 imply that

Business rule 3. The relationship between DOCTOR and PATIENT is M:N optionally.

In other words, one doctor might see many patients via appointments. One patient might see many doctors via appointments. APPOINTMENT (corresponding to APPOINT) is a composite entity that decomposes Business rule 3 into Business rules 1 and 2.

"*BMC records basic details of each insurance company on their system, including the name of the insurance company, their postal address, a single phone number, and a webpage address.*" is extracted from the business case. This implies that INSURANCE COMPANY is an entity, which directly associates with the patient as an entity. That is, a patient might associate with many insurance companies.

Business rule 4. A patient may associate with many insurance companies. The relationship between PATIENT and INSURANCE COMPANY is 1: M optionally.

"*Each insurance company can have several different policy types. Each policy type includes a description of the policy and the percentage rebate amount that the insurance company will pay for each appointment*" is extracted from the business case. This implies that

Business rule 5. *The insurance company will pay for each appointment.* The relationship between INSURANCE COMPANY and APPOINTMENT is 1:M optionally.

In reality, an insurance company has no direct relationship with appointments but with the bill and payment of an associated patient. Therefore, this business rule should be removed in the stage of the E-R Modeling optimization.

"*The patient's details including her or his ... policy identification number of any insurance are stored within the database*" is extracted from the business case. This implies that the policy identification number of any insurance is an attribute of PATIENT and:

Business rule 6. *A patient may have many insurances.* The relationship between PATIENT and INSURANCE COMPANY is 1:M optionally.

"*The patient and the insurance company may make multiple payments on a single bill*" is extracted from the business case. This implies:

Business rule 7. *Multiple payments on a single bill.* The relationship between BILL and PAYMENT is 1:M optionally.

Business rule 8. *The patient may make multiple payments.* The relationship between PATIENT and PAYMENT is 1:M optionally.

Business rules 7 and 8 imply that the relationship between the BILL and PATIENT is M:N, which leads to a new composite entity PAYMENT (Coronel, Morris, & Rob, 2020). This is true in theory. However, in our business case, we use Business rule 12 (see below).

Business rule 9. *The insurance company may make multiple payments.* The relationship between INSURANCE COMPANY and PAYMENT is 1:M optionally.

Business rule 8 and Business rule 9 implies that (Coronel, Morris, & Rob, 2020)

Business rule 10. The relationship between PATIENT and INSURANCE COMPANY is M:N optionally.

That is, one patient can have many insurance (Company) policies, and an insurance company can provide many patients with insurance policies.

"*After each appointment, a single bill is generated*" is extracted from the business case. This implies that

Business rule 11. *Each appointment generates a single bill.* The relationship between APPOINTMENT and BILL is 1:1.

Business rule 12. One bill is generated for one patient. The relationship between PATIENT and BILL is 1:1

Business rule 13. One patient can have many insurance (company) policies, and an insurance company can provide many patients with insurance policies. Therefore, the relationship between BILL (PATIENT) and INSURANCE COMPANY (insurance policy) is M:N, which leads to a new composite entity PAYMENT.

Therefore, the discovered all possible business rules from the above business case mining can be summarized in Table 3.2.

TABLE 3.2   The Brief Representation of Discovered Business Rules

Business Rule No.	Entity	Relationship	Connectivity	Entity
1	DOCTOR	schedule	1:M	APPOINTMENT
2	PATIENT	schedule	1:M	APPOINTMENT
3	DOCTOR	see	M:N	PATIENT
4	PATIENT	associate	1:M	INSURANCE COMPANY
5	INSURANCE COMPANY	pay	1:M	APPOINTMENT
6	PATIENT	have	1:M	INSURANCE COMPANY
7	BILL	have	1:M	PAYMENT
8	PATIENT	make	1:M	PAYMENT
9	INSURANCE COMPANY	make	1:M	PAYMENT
10	PATIENT	have	M:N	INSURANCE COMPANY
11	APPOINTMENT	generate	1:1	BILL
12	BILL	pay	1:1	PATIENT
13	INSURANCE COMPANY	make	M:N	BILL

Noted that APPOINTMENT, BILL, and PAYMENT are three composite entities from the business case mining. They are the core functions of the database system designed by BMC, corresponding to appoint, bill, and pay in the form of verbs or business activities.

From a viewpoint of people-centered business rule discovery, the primary relationships are between people, not between people and things. For example, DOCTOR and PATIENT have a primary relationship, whereas DOCTOR and APPOINTMENT have a secondary relationship because APPOINTMENT is a composite entity. However, from a viewpoint of function-centered business rule discovery, DOCTOR and APPOINTMENT have a primary relationship. Therefore, people-centered business rule discovery and function-centered business rule discovery must be combined to discover business rules from the business case mining.

3.5.5 E-R Modeling Optimization

There are many methods for developing an E-R diagram from business rules. For example, Coronel, Morris, & Rob suggested the following method for developing an E-R diagram (Coronel, Morris, & Rob, 2020):

- Develop the initial E-R diagram;

- Revise and review E-R diagram;

- E-R to relational mapping for database design the initial E-R diagram.

The drawback of the above-mentioned method is how to develop the initial E-R diagram. This section addresses this issue by presenting a unified optimal method for E-R modeling. The unified optimal method includes people-centered E-R modeling, function-centered E-R modeling, and hierarchical E-R modeling.

3.5.5.1 People-Centered E-R Modeling

People-centered modeling means that the initial E-R diagram starts from a people-related entity or two. DOCTOR and PATIENT are two people-related entities discovered from our business case mining. Our initial E-R diagram includes DOCTOR and PATIENT and their M:N relationship (see Business rule 3 in Section 3.5.4). This M:N relationship has been converted into two 1:M relationships (see business rule 1 and business rule 2 in Section 3.5.4), which has been realized by the first E-R diagram, illustrated in Figure 3.3.

Furthermore, INSURANCE COMPANY is a people-related entity, therefore, the next step is to add the INSURANCE COMPANY-related

FIGURE 3.3　The first E-R diagram.

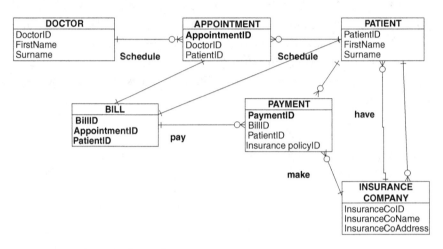

FIGURE 3.4　An initial E-R diagram-2.

business rules to the first E-R diagram, taking into account Table 3.2. This implies that business rules 6 and 8 are added to the initial E-R diagram, as illustrated in Figure 3.4.

Similarly, we can continue the development of the E-R diagram using people-centered E-R modeling. We will now turn our focus on function-centered E-R modeling.

3.5.5.2 Function-Centered E-R Modeling

Function-centered E-R diagram starts from a functioning entity such as APPOINTMENT, BILL, or PAYMENT. We will continue our development of the initial E-R diagram by first adding BILL and then adding PAYMENT, as illustrated in Figure 3.5. Consequently, we have developed the initial E-R diagram based on the discovered 13 business rules.

3.5.5.3 Hierarchical ER Modeling

From the discovered business rules in Section 3.5.4, the relationship between DOCTOR and PATIENT is M:N. We introduce a new composite entity: APPOINTMENT, which leads to two relationships: the relationship between DOCTOR and APPOINTMENT is 1:M; the relationship between PATIENT and APPOINTMENT is 1:M. This implies that hierarchical E-R

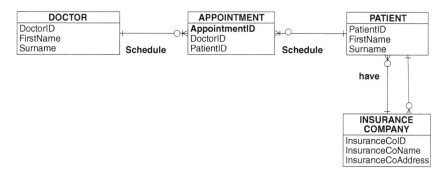

FIGURE 3.5   Initial E-R diagram-3.

modeling should be introduced (Pressman & Maxim, 2014). A hierarchical E-R modeling aims to develop first-level E-R diagrams, second-level E-R diagrams, and a detailed E-R diagram that includes the attributes of the entities (Coronel, Morris, & Rob, 2020). This research will not cover detailed E-R modeling (Sun, Pinjik, & Pambel, 2021).

3.5.5.4 First Level E-R Diagram

The first level E-R diagram can be considered as a primary entities-based E-R diagram. At this level, we only focus on the primary entities and their relationships. Primary entities are only people-associated entities and people-related organization-associated entities. Therefore, the first level E-R diagram is people-centered. Based on the discovered business rules from the business case mining, DOCTOR, PATIENT, and INSURANCE COMPANY are three primary entities. Therefore, we have the first level E-R diagram illustrated in Figure 3.6, based on business rules 3 and 10 discovered in Section 3.4.

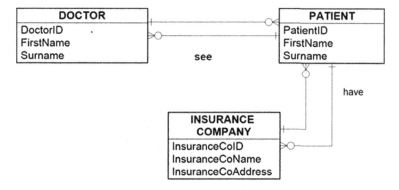

FIGURE 3.6   A segment of the first level E-R diagram.

A key idea behind developing a first-level E-R diagram is to realize the principle of top-down, stepwise refinement used in software engineering (Pressman & Maxim, 2014). Therefore, the second level E-R diagram can be considered as a refinement of the first level E-R diagram.

3.5.5.5 Second Level E-R Diagram

At the second level, we must first decompose the M:N relationship between primary entities by creating a composite entity and corresponding two 1:M relationships between primary entities and the composite entity. For example, we find that the M:N relationship between DOCTOR and PATIENT is to "schedule an appointment". APPOINTMENT is then created to be a composite entity to decompose the M:N relationship into two 1:M relationships that occurred in business rules 1 and 2. Similarly, PAYMENT is created as a composite entity to decompose the M:N relationship between PATIENT and INSURANCE COMPANY into two 1:M relationships that occurred in business rules 8 and 9. The results are illustrated in Figure 3.7.

Figure 3.6 can be considered as a people-centered E-R diagram. Similarly, based on business rules 7, 9, and 13 discovered in Section 3.5.4, the relationship between INSURANCE COMPANY and BILL is M:N. This M:N

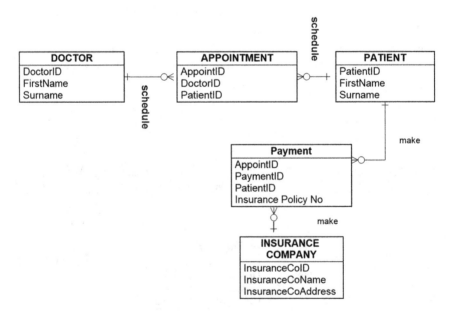

FIGURE 3.7   A second level E-R diagram.

relationship can be decomposed by creating the PAYMENT entity. Furthermore, BILL is a primary entity from a function-centered development of an E-R diagram. This has been illustrated in Figures 3.9 and 3.10.

3.5.5.6 Finalizing E-R Diagram

After these two-level developments of the E-R diagram, we further consider business rule 12, discovered from "After each appointment, a single bill is generated" and add entity BILL to the latest updated E-R diagram. This entity is associated with business rules 7, 11, 12, and 13 in order. From the viewpoint of function-centered development of an E-R diagram, we first add entity BILL to link entity APPOINTMENT. Then we add the relationship between APPOINTMENT and BILL. Finally, we have an E-R diagram, illustrated in Figure 3.8.

It should be noted that the 1:1 relationship between BILL and PATIENT can be eliminated by adding BillID as an attribute in the entity PAYMENT (Coronel, Morris, & Rob, 2020). We leave it there in order to keep the nature of business case-based reasoning.

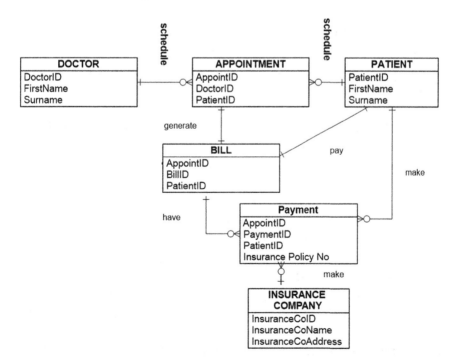

FIGURE 3.8 A final E-R diagram based on the discovered 13 business rules from BMC.

3.5.6 Summary

Business case mining and business rule discovery center entity-relationship (E-R) modeling and database design to obtain entity relationship models. How to transform business cases through business rules into E-R models is a fundamental issue for database design. This section addresses this issue by exploring business case mining and E-R modeling optimization. Business case mining is business rule discovery from a business case. This section also explores business case-based reasoning and presents a unified approach to business case mining for business rule discovery. The approach includes people-centered entity/business rule discovery and function-centered entity/business rule discovery. This section proposes a unified optimal method for E-R modeling, including people-centered E-R modeling, function-centered E-R modeling, and hierarchical E-R modeling.

In future work, we will delve into E-R modeling optimization.

3.6 FUNDAMENTALS OF BIG DATA

This section will look at what is big data, where is big data from.

3.6.1 Introduction

Data is originally based on simple 1s and 0s from a computer science viewpoint. Big data has been considered a frontier for research and development in many disciplines since 2012 (Strang & Sun, 2022). Big data is a transforming science that has impacted engineering, technology, medicine, healthcare, finance, business and management, education, and ultimately society – due to the emergence of big data analytics. Big data is becoming a mainstream focus in academic research and operational deployments. Big data is also a strategic asset for an individual, organization, and nation.

Big data has been studied for about 12 years since its inception in 2012 (Sun & Huo, 2021; Sharda, Delen, & Turba, 2018). Big data is a rapidly expanding research area spanning the fields of computer science and information management and has become a ubiquitous term in understanding and solving complex problems in different disciplinary fields such as engineering, mathematics, medicine, computational biology, healthcare, social networks, finance, business, government, education, transportation, and telecommunications. This section looks at big data and crude oil, analyzes definitions of big data, where is big data from? It examines big nature for big data, and an evolutionary perspective on characteristics of big data.

3.6.2 Big Data and Crude Oil

Some consider big data as crude oil. Some consider big data as the black gold of the 20th century. For example, a former Chief Data Scientist at Amazon, Andreas Weigand, suggests that big data is like crude oil (Patil, 2014). Certainly, crude oil and big data have commonalities. For example, both have been revolutionizing our lives and societies. However, there are at least five differences between oil and data.

First, the biggest volume of oil is deposited only in a few countries including Iran, Russia, and Saudi Arabia, to name a few. Data are mainly deposited on the web or cloud. It is said that a few big companies such as Meta, Google, Amazon, Microsoft, Baidu, Tencent, and Alibaba collect about 80% of the data (Clissa, 2022).

Second, crude oil changed our work, lives, and society in the 20th century because of the exploration, refinement, and processing of crude oil. Oil from oil fields is the lifeblood of most people in the world, if not all. Without crude oil, there would be no paved roads, auto highways. Without crude oil, there would be no beautiful clothes, or cosmetics to make us attractive, beautiful, and decent; there would be no plastic products for our smartphones, laptops, and houses.

Third, crude oil is originally very dark. It needs to be refined by the giant companies of the petrochemical industry, following a workflow; for example, it is refined into petrol, diesel, etc. Crude oil is only a very primary material for the petrochemical industry. Then the products of the petrochemical industry become the materials of the textile industry, pharmaceutical industry, and other industries. All these industries consist of chains of industry, which underpin the social and economic prosperity of the 20th and 21st century. Big data are the lifeblood of more than half of the people in the world. Everyone inputs it to computers, laptops, and smartphones, for a purpose. A variety of smart sensors (billions of them) collect data directly for a purpose. Most data are available on the cloud. The development of the Internet of Things (IoT) makes almost all data available on the cloud. Without big data, there would be no social networking platforms, such as Meta, YouTube, and WeChat, TikTok, WhatsApp. Almost all will lose patience with staying at home. Data needs to be processed by various individuals and organizations, as well as giant companies of data such as Google and Meta, Amazon, and Baidu. Google and Baidu use search as a service to make big money. Meta and Wechat use social networking as a service to make big money. The data also leads to a chain of industry, first the data industry, then the security industry, the service industry, and the network industry. The emerging data processing industry consists of the e-commerce industry, e-services industry, big data analytics industry, big data trade industry, healthcare industry, to name a few. The top 10 companies based on market value in the world are data companies rather than oil companies.

Fourth, crude oil is a one-time-consumed material. One can refine crude oil to petrol for a family car. However, it cannot reverse petrol oil to crude oil anymore. Data can be transformed into information; information can be transformed into data. Therefore, the reusability of data is the biggest difference between data and crude oil. If one hopes to use one directional usage of crude oil to think about data, then one can reuse data easily, one can trade data easily. One can change data to information, information to knowledge, knowledge to experience, experience to intelligence, and intelligence to wisdom.

Fifth, we ask ourselves where is oil from? And where is the data from? For the first question, we must explore crude oil from below the ground, using physical exploration technology. It is not easy for us to find a new oil field with billions of tons of oil through the existing physical exploration technology. For data, we also have mining technology to explore where data is and to easily find one of the biggest databases, similar to a new oil field, with a big amount of data in the web or the cloud. However, it is not easy for us to discover knowledge from the Web. This is why Google or alphabet became one of the most market-valuable companies. Further, we ask if some petrochemical industries will become less important for social development shortly, because oil will be used up at the end of the decades or centuries. big data industry will become more and more important in the future: big data industry, big data trade industry, big information industry, big knowledge industry, big intelligence industry, and big wisdom industry are booming, complementing each other. They can lead to the real revolution for our lives and societies in the near future.

3.6.3 Analysis of Defining Big Data

Big data is "a collection of very huge data sets with a great diversity of types so that it becomes difficult to process by using state of art data processing approaches or traditional data processing platforms" (Chen & Zhang, 2014). Let's analyze this definition of big data in some detail. This definition consists of three parts: Part 1. big data is "a collection of very huge data sets with a great diversity of types" Therefore, this latter part can be put into the characteristics of big data rather than in the definition of big data. From here, we can define "big data" as "a collection of very huge data sets". Part 2. big data "becomes difficult to process by using the state of art data processing approaches or traditional data processing platforms." It seems that this part is not related to the definition of big data, this is related to how to process the big data. How do "huge data sets" belong to big data? For example, only petabytes and zettabytes of data sets belong to big data. Thus, the majority of people will not care about big data anymore; it is too big for us, at least this is true for children. Therefore, the definition for "big" can be exactly defined, because big should be fuzzy, the fuzzier the better, the fuzziest definition can attract more and more people to pursue its development.

Gartner defines big data as "high-volume, high-velocity and/or high-variety information assets that demand cost-effective, innovative forms of information processing that enable enhanced insight, decision-making, and process automation" (Gardner, 2024) and this definition has been most frequently used in both analyst communities and academia communities.

Gartner's definition consists of three parts mentioned above:

Part 1. big data are high-volume, high-velocity and/or high-variety information assets,

Part 2. that demand cost-effective, innovative forms of information processing,

Part 3. that enable enhanced insight, decision-making, and process automation.

Part 1 is problematic because it is related to three highs, therefore, we should call big data as high data, because high has been emphasized here. In fact, high-volume, high-velocity, and/or high-variety are similar to the representation of big volume, big velocity, and/or big variety. Big is better than high, because we discuss "big data" rather than "high data." Big data is data with high-volume, high-velocity, and high-variety, where the three highs can be considered three characteristics (or attributes) of data or big data. This infers that big data can be defined as data with n characteristics, where n is an integer. At the moment, Gartner uses $n = 3$ (as above); IBM uses $n = 4$ workflow (Sathi, 2013). In this section, we will use $n = 10$. Furthermore, big data is "information assets". Big data is the basis for any information. Therefore, data is at a lower level from a viewpoint of abstraction. From a perspective of definition, we cannot use information to define data; reversely, we can use data to define information, which has been done by many textbooks (Laudon & Laudon, 2020).

Part 2, related to the means for achieving the desired outcome, is "demand cost-effective, innovative forms of information processing," which can be used to define other concepts in ICT because almost all real-world problem-solving demands cost-effective, innovative forms of information processing. Information processing is not a good choice because of using information, maybe innovative forms of data processing are better than information processing.

Part 3 is also problematic because it only mentions some purposes or goals, it includes more because not only data, but also information and knowledge are the basis for enabling enhanced insight, decision-making, and process automation. This can also be used to define a significant number of other concepts in ICT. For example. data mining is also for enhancing decision-making (Aroraa, Lele, & Jindal, 2022).

Therefore, Gartner's definition of big data is still an open definition requiring more elaboration. More generally, big data can be defined as data that 1. is big in many dimensions, 2. demands cost-effective, innovative processing, 3. is for decision-making. This definition covers Gartner's definition.

McKinsey defines big data as "the datasets whose size is beyond the ability of typical database software tools to capture, store, manage, and analyze." (Manyika, Chui, & Bughin, 2011). This definition consists of two parts: the first part is the basic attributes of big data, and big data is the datasets (with a special size). Part 2, the datasets have a big size that is beyond the ability of typical database software tools to process. The definition of McKinsey has not mentioned part 3. This definition mainly emphasizes the big size of big data, although it implies that big data requires sophisticated technology to process it.

3.6.4 Where Is Big Data From?

Big data is generated from various instruments, billions of calls, texts, tweets, phones, payment systems, cameras, sensors, Internet transactions, emails, videos, clickstreams, social networking services, and other sources (Henke & Bughin, 2016). Big data has become one of the most important research frontiers for innovation, research, and development (Chen & Zhang, 2014; Sun & Huo, 2021).

CERN community [15], AWS (Amazon Web Service), YouTube, Instagram, Meta, and Google are the most prominent players concerning big data production in 2021 (Clissa, 2022)

3.6.5 Big Data and Its 'Big' Nature

It is only "big" data that makes everyone draw much attention to data, big data, because everyone can engage in data and big data, and everyone can understand "big" based on his or her background knowledge. For example, Fuzzy logic tells others that big is "fuzzy." Probability theory tells others that big is "probabilistic." USA government tells others that big (data) is strategic, then it officially invested a big amount of money to "big data" in 2012. For size of big data, because different people have different understanding of big, there are different impacts on different people and organizations. For example, a 2 year old child believes that 10,000 is a big data (number), whereas an undergraduate student of mathematics at Stanford University considers that 10^{50} is big data.

However, the following two important issues have not drawn significant attention in the scholarly peer-reviewed literature:

- What are the big trends in the era of big data?

- How do these big trends impact our society?

This section will address these two issues.

Over the past decades, we have used many different concepts to measure the ever-increasing volume or size of data because of significant progress of ICT. For example, large-scale data (Halevy, Norvig, & Pereira, 2009); vast amounts of data, very large data (in very large database), huge volume of big data, far larger quantities of data, huge amount of data, etc., are used in various media, such as conferences, books, and new sections. All these have affected us so we pay attention to the increasing data and their impacts on our life, and work, for example, database management systems. However, all these concepts, such as very large, vast amount, huge volume, etc., always try to have a professional feature or scholarly flavor, to attract researchers to explore new and sophisticated methods and techniques. This is an obvious weakness for such a research trend that is far removed from ordinary people.

However, "big" is the greatest common divisor of all these above-mentioned concepts. From a semantic viewpoint, all the above mentioned have the semantics of "big" as a basis for them. This big as the greatest common divisor makes big data available and accessible to different communities of interests, ignoring the age of the people, in the world and facilitating to develop big data as a technology, and as a discipline, as a service, and as an industry. Therefore, everyone can well understand big, big data. Understanding is the first step in supporting. Then everyone can support big, big data and their development. For example, a small child likes to eat a "big" apple and then read pictures from the Internet, and then support the development of big data.

3.6.6 Characteristics of Big Data: An Evolutionary Perspective

From an evolutionary perspective, Doug Laney of the META Group (now Gartner) used 3 Ds: data volume, data velocity, and data variety to represent the characteristics of data in e-commerce in 2001. These 3 Ds should be controlled in data management using novel techniques (Laney, 2001). Later, Laney wrote a blog post that concentrated on the 3 Ds as 3 Vs (volume, velocity, and variety) as three characteristics of big data (Thompson & Rogers, 2017, p. 40). These 3 Vs have been extended first to 4 Vs as four characteristics of big data by adding veracity, big data could be characterized by any or all of three "V" words, as suggested by IBM (Sun, Strang, & Li, 2018). 5 Vs are then five characteristics of big data (volume, variety, velocity, veracity, value; Teradata, 2023), and finally to 56 Vs (Hussein, 2020). With the advancement of big data research, more Vs might be proposed to extend these 56Vs. These researches are a kind of linear thinking and reasoning, because from 3V we can have 4V. Thus, mathematically speaking, we can have infinite Vs (at least a big number) for understanding data, rather than big data because all the mentioned Vs are used to characterize data rather than big data.

The above discussion motivates us to change 3 Ds (Laney D., 2001) to 3 Bigs rather than 3 Vs (McAfee & Brynjolfsson, 2012) for big volume, big variety, and big velocity as the three "big" characteristics of big data. Then, this section extends 3 Bigs to 10 Bigs to examine ten big characteristics of big data and their interrelationships.

3.7 TEN BIG CHARACTERISTICS OF BIG DATA

This section identifies and examines ten big characteristics of big data, with an example for each (Sun, Strang, & Li, 2018).

3.7.1 Big Volume

The big volume of big data reflects the size of the data set, which is typically in exabytes (EB) or zettabytes (ZB) (Teradata, 2023). Data volume is so big that the size of data are terabytes, petabytes (PB), and ZB level and beyond available on the Web and other data sources (Betser & Belanger, 2013). Now, many data-driven companies are working with a PB level of data daily. For example, Google processes over 20 PB of data daily (Clissa, 2022). The volume of big data has been increased at EB or ZB (Clissa, 2022).

Big data has a variety of representations (Erickson & Rothberg, 2013). Different professionals have different understandings of big data. These phenomena make big data available and accessible to different communities of interest in the world and facilitate the development of big data as a technology and as an industry.

Big data are not only from various databases employed in enterprise information systems but also from all the accessible or non-accessible information online. Big data has become a new form of strategic natural resource (Liebowitz, 2013, p. 133).

3.7.2 Big Veracity

Big veracity refers to the accuracy, truth, and truthfulness of big data. Big data has the features of big ambiguity, incompleteness, and uncertainty (Teradata, 2023; Sun, 2018a). This might be the reason why veracity has been considered as one of ten challenges of big data (Borne, 2014). Accuracy and reliability are less controllable for many forms of big data, for example, in the case of Twitter (now X) posts with hashtags, abbreviations, typos, and colloquial speech. Big veracity is a big characteristic of big data; this is particularly true in big data analytics for business decision-making (Sun & Wu, 2021).

3.7.3 Big Variety

Variety means the diversity of sources from which it arrived and the types of data available to nearly everyone (Betser & Belanger, 2013). Big variety means the big diversity or big different types of data sources with different structures from which it arrived, and the types of data available to nearly everyone (Kumar, 2015). Big data can be classified into three types at a higher level: structured, semi-structured, and unstructured. The data stored in relational database systems like Oracle are structured. The data available on the web are unstructured. 80% of the world's data is unstructured (Sathi, 2013). In the WeChat world (https://web.wechat.com/), one can interact with his/her friends anywhere in the world using a variety of media, with unstructured media such as text, Word and PDF files, photos, audio, and videos (Sun, Strang, & Li, 2018).

3.7.4 Big Velocity

Big velocity is related to throughput and latency of data workflow (Sathi, 2013). For big throughput, big velocity means that data in and out from the networked systems are at a big speed in real-time (Chen & Zhang, 2014). The big velocity of big data is more important than the big volume for many real-world applications (McAfee & Brynjolfsson, 2012; Sun, Strang, & Li, 2018).

3.7.5 Big Data Technologies

Another 3 Bigs (i.e., big technologies, big systems, and big infrastructure) are technological characteristics of big data. Big data technologies consist of ICT (information and communication technology), digital technology, and computing technology.

3.7.6 Big Data Systems

Big data systems are made up of enterprise systems such as Oracle and Alibaba cloud (https://www.alibabacloud.com/).

3.7.7 Big Data Infrastructure

Big infrastructure, abbreviated from big data infrastructure, refers to all the structures, technologies, systems, platforms, facilities, governance, and controls that serve the big data management and processing in a country, city, or area (Goes, 2014; Sun & Wu, 2021). Big infrastructure is a decisive factor for the utility of big data, big data technology with applications, reflecting the level of national big data research and development, just as traffic infrastructure and network infrastructure are the criteria for the standards of social advancement (Sun & Wu, 2021). Big data processing includes ingesting, storing, analyzing, modeling, mining big data, and discovering, visualizing, simulating, reporting knowledge, and generating insights and reporting knowledge workflow (Sathi, 2013; Sun & Wu, 2021).

Although the price of the elements of computing machinery, such as storage, memory, processing, and bandwidth, has been declining (McAfee & Brynjolfsson, 2012), big infrastructure is still a big characteristic to differentiate developing countries from developed ones.

The cloud infrastructure is a kind of big infrastructure (Erl, Mahmood, & Puttini, 2013). 6G wireless network infrastructure (for short, 6G) is also a big infrastructure in the big data world, facing fierce competition in the international communication and networking market.

Big data infrastructure is composed of SpaceX's Starlink, GPS, and BeiDou. Currently, Apache Hadoop ecosystem has been considered as a part of big infrastructure for processing big data (Kumar, 2015; Goes, 2014).

3.7.8 Big Services

Services have played a pivotal role in individuals, businesses, organizations, nations, service computing, and cloud computing (Erl, Mahmood, & Puttini, 2013).

Big services include big data services, big data driven services, big data-based services, big data as a service, and big data analytics services (Sun, Strang, & Li, 2018). They also cover all the Internet of Services (IoS) for all the Internet of People (IOP). Therefore, the Internet of Everything (IoE) covers IoT, IoP, and IoS. (Sun & Wu, 2021). That is, IoE = IoP + IoT + IoS. There are well over 14.76 billion connected IoT devices around the globe. It's expected that there will be 25.44 billion IoT devices by 2030 (Howarth, 2023).

The bigness of big service implies that it can provide big data-based services to hundreds of millions of people, if not billions. for example, big data infrastructure services, cloud services, mobile services, big analytics services (Sun, Sun, & Strang, 2018). Social networking services provided by Meta and WeChat are examples of big services for billions of people in the world.

In the big data age, everyone enjoys big services in terms of living, studying, working, moving, and socializing. For example, the automation of driving and the GPS navigation services (Vardi, 2016) based on big data will make everyone enjoy wonderful driving service from one place to a corner of another city easily, safely, and optimally even if s/he can sleep in the car, enjoy the chat using WeChat (www.wechat.com) in the car, watch movies in the car until her/his car arrives at the destination and tells him/her "You have reached your destination, my darling".

Big services are an emerging frontier for innovations, competencies, and improving business performance of governments, organizations, and enterprises (Sun, Strang, & Li, 2018). AWS and Alibaba are examples of big services online and offline. Pinduoduo and JD.com are also examples in China and the world.

3.7.9 Big Value

Oracle introduced value as a defining characteristic of big data (Gandomi & Haider, 2015). Big value indicates the importance and context of the big data (Sun & Wu, 2021). The big business value can transform an organization to have more competitiveness in the global platform (Borne, 2014). Big data has extremely big value for increasing productivity, efficiency, and revenues, lowering costs, and reducing risk in businesses and management (Loshin, 2013). For example, big data has brought big value to Facebook, Google, Amazon, and Tencent and made them become the top companies in the world, based on market cap (Desjardins, 2019; Sun & Wu, 2021). Organizations are utilizing the big data technology platform to gain big value from big data to grow faster than their competitors and seize new opportunities in the global market of big data and big data technologies (Kumara et al., 2015; Howson, Richardson, Sallam, & Kronz, 2019). For example, governments use big data technologies to gain insight into citizen activities and requirements (Koorn et al., 2015).

Big value implies that big data brings big social value and big cultural value. The big social value means that big data has been revolutionizing society in terms of working, living, and thinking (Mayer-Schoenberger & Cukier, 2013). For example, learning heavily relied on teachings, books, libraries, schools, and so on in the past centuries, whereas in the digital age, learning could be based on search online, online learning, learning as a search (LaaS). One can learn using LaaS whenever and wherever s/he is.

Big cultural value means that big data has significantly impacted the cultural activities of human beings. For example, X (formerly Twitter), Meta, and WeChat have made it possible for everyone to know what happens at every corner of the globe instantly. They also allow everyone to share the different cultures globally, due to semi-automated translation from one language to another through translators such as Google translator and Baidu translator.

Big data has extreme value for bringing productivity and efficiency to businesses and management (Chen & Zhang, 2014). It also has extreme value for scientific breakthroughs in science and technology. Both have given and will give us a big number of opportunities to make great progress in many fields. Additionally, the big value of big data will be exposed with the enthusiasm over big data.

3.7.10 Big Market

A big market refers to a big data-driven market (Sun & Wu, 2021). The big market includes the market of big data technologies, systems, tools, and services. For example, IDC predicted that 40% of the total revenue for G2000 organizations will be generated by digital products, services, and experiences by 2026 (IDC, 2022).

Data trade is a big part of the big market to monetize big data. Data trade as a company has been blossoming in China. Several industries have established data-sharing agreements for a long-term strategy. Data-sharing agreements include advertising, merchandising, and sales in the customer-packaged goods industry (Thompson & Rogers, 2017).

The big market of big data attracts the CEOs of big companies to make big decisions for developing big data and related technologies, systems, tools, and services. For example, more and more executives put big data and advanced big data technologies and systems as the strategic priorities in both strategy and spending to compete in the era of big data and their technologies and systems (Howson, Richardson, Sallam, & Kronz, 2019; Brown, Gandhi, & Herring, 2019).

For example, the researcher forecasts that the global big data market will generate $103 billion in revenue by 2027 (Howarth, 12, 2022). Similarly, according to Research And Markets, the worldwide big data & analytics industry is expected to reach $146 Billion by 2027 (ResearchAndMarkets, 2022). Big data are bringing big analytics, big intelligence, big markets, and big value to our industry and society.

3.7.11 Summary

Based on the 10 bigs of big data examined earlier, the definition of big data provided by Gartner (Gardner, 2024) can be referred to as "the data assets with at least one of 10 bigs that demand cost-effective, innovative forms of data processing for enhanced hindsight, insight, foresight, and decision-making, where 10 Bigs consist of big volume, big velocity, big variety, big veracity, big technologies, big systems, big infrastructure, big service, big value, and big market". These 10 bigs of big data form the foundation of big data as a service (Techopedia, 2018).

The data industry is the sum of industries, manufacturers, and enterprises that use data science, technology, and systems to transform data into data assets, information assets, and knowledge assets, process data assets into data/information/knowledge products and services, and empower related industries with data products and services (Lu, 2023). The global giant manufacturers and enterprises are Alphabet (including Google), Meta, Amazon, Microsoft, Baidu, Tencent, Alibaba, TikTok, Samsung, TSMC, Nvidia, and Huawei. Each of them has played a significant role in the data industry, all these have played a vital role in the big market, big industry with big values.

The fundamental characteristics, technological characteristics, and socioeconomic characteristics of big data have either directly or indirectly significant implications for socio-economic development, which will be examined in the next sections.

3.8 A SERVICE-ORIENTED FOUNDATION FOR BIG DATA

This section provides a service-oriented foundation for big data with presenting a service-oriented framework for big data. It looks at each level of the proposed framework from a service-oriented perspective (Papazoglou & Georgakopoulos, 2003).

3.8.1 Big Data as a Service

Big data as a Service (BDaaS) has drawn increasing attention in academia and industries. For example, Xinhua, et al, define BDaaS, and propose a user experience-oriented BDaaS architecture (Xinhua & Han, 2013). This architecture supports unstructured data and provides a wide variety of services such as analysis and visualization services, different from the existing data services architectures. Swami and Sahoo propose a service delivery model for BDaaS and claim that their model achieves quicker deployment than other models (Swami & Sahoo, 2016). However, a service-oriented framework of big data proposed in this research is the first attempt to delve into BDaaS, which emphasizes that BDaaS will play a central role in big value and big market. Also, big analytics as a service, big intelligence as a service, big infrastructure as a service will play a significant role in the age of big data and big data analytics, taking into account service providers, brokers, and requestors at fundamental, technological and socio-economic level.

3.8.2 A Service-Oriented Framework Based on 10 Bigs

The service-oriented framework is illustrated in Figure 3.9. This framework covers the 10 Bigs, along with their interrelationships to one another. The framework consists of three levels: a fundamental,

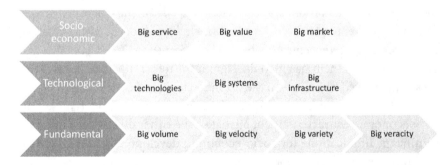

FIGURE 3.9   A service-oriented framework based on 10 Bigs.

technological, and socio-economical level. At the fundamental level, there are 4 Bigs: Big volume, big velocity, big variety, and big veracity (Sun, Sun, & Strang, 2018). These are four fundamental characteristics of big data (Sun, Sun, & Strang, 2018).

This redefinition of big data covers the four fundamental characteristics of big data.

The main service providers on this level include data scientists, and cloud services providers, including Amazon, Google, Meta, and Tableau (http://www.tableau.com/) (Howson, Richardson, Sallam, & Kronz, 2019). The main service requestors on this level include everyone who can access the Internet. The main service brokers on this level include big consulting groups like McKinsey, Gartner, and IDC, as well as public media (Sun, Strang, & Li, 2018).

Computing scientists are working on big technologies, big systems, and big infrastructure to meet the challenges of big data with these four fundamental characteristics using ICT technologies, systems, and tools. This requires transforming from the fundamental level to the technological level.

At the technological level, there are three (3) Bigs: big technologies, big systems, and big infrastructure. They are three technological characteristics of big data. These 3 Bigs provide smart solutions to meet the challenges arising from the 4 Bigs at the fundamental level. The smart solutions and technologies include MapReduce, NoSQL technology, MPP (Massively Parallel Processing), In-Memory database technologies (Tableau, 2020; Coronel, Morris, & Rob, 2020), augmented analytics (Howson, Richardson, Sallam, & Kronz, 2019), and intelligent analytics (Sun, 2019a), to name a few. Apache Spark is a popular big data analytics platform for several enterprises (Tableau, 2020; Reddy, 2014). Spark provides dramatically increased large-scale data processing compared to Hadoop, and a NoSQL database for big data management (Coronel, Morris, & Rob, 2020). Apache Spark has provided Goldman Sachs with excellent big data analytics services (Tableau, 2020).

The main service providers on this level include Google, Amazon, Microsoft, and Salesforce (Howson, Richardson, Sallam, & Kronz, 2019) and other digital technology-driven companies and computing scientists. Big analytics service providers include developers, vendors, systems or software, and other intermediaries that can provide big analytics services (Sun, Sun, & Strang, 2018). For example, Tableau as a software developer has been provisioning decentralized analytics and agile, centralized BI services (Tableau, 2020; Howson, Richardson, Sallam, & Kronz, 2019). Amazon, Google, Microsoft, and Baidu are examples of big analytics services providers on the cloud (Sun, Strang, & Li, 2018).

The main service requestors on this level include everyone who can access the Internet. Big data service requestors include organizations, governments, and all-level business decision-makers such as CEOs, CIOs, CFOs and other managers. More generally, big data requestors include people who like to acquire information based on analytical reports provided by big data service providers (Sun, Strang, & Firmin, 2017). Therefore, a person with a smartphone receives big data services such as GPS information, Google map, and Gaode map (Sun, Strang, & Li, 2018).

The main service brokers on this level are all the entities that facilitate the development of big technologies, big systems, and big infrastructure, which include popular presses, traditional media and social media, consulting companies, scholars, university students, and so on (Sun, 2023). Big consulting groups like McKinsey, Gartner, IDC, and all the big data intermediaries (Mayer-Schoenberger & Cukier, 2013) have played an important role as brokers on this level (Sun, Strang, & Li, 2018).

At the socioeconomic level, there are 3 Bigs: Big service, big value, and big market, which are three big socioeconomic characteristics of big data. The socioeconomic consequence of the dramatic development of big technologies, big systems, and big infrastructure brings big service, big value (Manyika, Chui, & Bughin, 2011), and big market (Howarth, 12, 2022) to the society in a big data world.

Big service, big value, and big market are interdependent on and complementary to each other closely. Big value from big data brings big market (Kumar, 2019), big market from big data brings about big services, and big services bring about big value and big market, and vice versa. All these statements have been proven and will be justified repeatedly in the big data world (Manyika, Chui, & Bughin, 2011; Kumar, 2019). The main service providers on this level include big industries such as manufacturing, healthcare, finance and insurance, social networking, and all the companies related to Industry 4.0 (GTAI, 2014; Howarth, 2022), China Manufacturing 2025 (State Council, China, 2016) and so on. The main service requestors on this level include everyone in the big data age. The main service brokers on this level include big consulting groups like McKinsey, Gartner, IDC, public media and other big data intermediaries (Mayer-Schoenberger & Cukier, 2013).

3.9 A CALCULUS FOR SEARCHING BIG DATA

This section proposes a calculus for searching big data.

Let $u \in U$ be a document on the Web. u may be a Microsoft Word file in .docx or a report in PDF Let $v \in V$ be an attribute value. v may be a word such as "big" or "data" or "analytics" or "intelligence."

Definition 1. A search function, denoted as $s : V \to U$, is defined as

$$s(v) = u, \text{if } v \in u \tag{3.1}$$

For example, if we use Google to search "analytics," denoted as v, then we searched a file on business analytics services, denoted as u including v. More generally,

Definition 2. A search function s can be defined as

$$s(v) = F(v) \tag{3.2}$$

where $F(v) = \{u_i|$, if $v \in u_i$, $u_i \in U$, $i = \{0, 1, 2, \cdots, m\}$. This is valid for search practice using Google, Baidu, and other search engines online: One keyword search corresponds to at least a picture/document or a set of pictures/documents as the search results. When searching "big data," one might receive over 60,500,000/318,000,000 results (https://www.google.com.au/, retrieved on 07 Sept 2016/05 January 2024). Therefore, $F(v) \subseteq U$. For $i = 0$, we receive no researched results.

We use equation (3.2) as the definition of the most general search function in what follows. Now we have a look at the property of search function as an operation because searching on the Web using Google or Baidu search engine is an operation.

Let $v_1, v_2, v_3 \in V$, then using equation (3.2), $s(v_1) = F(v_1)$, $s(v_2) = F(v_2)$, $s(v_3) = F(v_3)$. Then the following properties of search functions hold:

$$s(v_1 \vee v_2) = s(v_1) \cap s(v_2) = F(v_1) \cap F(v_2) \tag{3.3}$$

where $\vee$ is a space operation between v_1 and v_2 to reflect the search using Google. $\vee$ as an operator has the property of association, that is, $v_1 \vee (v_2 \vee v_3) = (v_1 \vee v_2) \vee v_3$. This operation is similar to concatenation between data items in linguistics or formal language (Johnsonbaugh, 2013).

Now given an attribute value sequence v_i, $i = \{1, 2, 3, \ldots, n, \cdots\}$, then $s(v_1) = F(v_1)$, $s(v_2) = F(v_2), \ldots, s(v_n) = F(v_n)$, $\ldots$, we have

Theorem 1. In the infinite world of big data, the search results with respect to operation $\vee$ are

$$s\left(v_1 \vee v_2 \vee \cdots \vee v_n\right) = \prod_1^n F\left(v_i\right) = F\left(v_1\right) \cap F\left(v_2\right) \cap \cdots \cap F\left(v_n\right) \quad (3.4)$$

Theorem 2. When $n \to \infty$, the following property of search as an operation $\vee$ in the Web search holds.

$$s\left(v_1 \vee v_2 \vee \cdots \vee v_n \vee \cdots\right) = \prod_1^\infty F\left(v_i\right) \quad (3.5)$$

Many people have the experience of searching on the Web using equation (3.4) and (3.5), although each of us has not experienced searching the Web based on the equation (3.5). This is because an individual's search on the Web is finite (in terms of attribute value) whereas all the human beings' search on the Web should be infinite.

Let's look at the following example: Paul just searched "big data analytics" using Google. However, he has not searched what he expected, so he had to extend his search space by using "big data". From a mathematical viewpoint, we can denote "big data analytics" as v_1, and "big data" as v_2. Then Paul's extending search space means that he uses $v_1 \wedge v_2$ (a kind of intersection in set theory (Jech, 2003)) to search for what he expects on the Web. Then we have the following dual results corresponding to equations (3.4) and (3.5), based on a dual principle in discrete mathematics.

Theorem 3. In the infinite world of big data, the search results with respect to operation are $\wedge$

$$s\left(v_1 \wedge v_2 \wedge \cdots \wedge v_n\right) = \coprod_1^n F\left(v_i\right) = F\left(v_1\right) \cup F\left(v_2\right) \cup \cdots \cup F\left(v_n\right) \quad (3.6)$$

And

Theorem 4. When $n \to \infty$, the following property of search as an operation $\wedge$ in the Web search holds:

$$s\left(v_1 \wedge v_2 \wedge \cdots \wedge v_n \wedge \cdots\right) = \coprod_1^\infty F\left(v_i\right) \quad (3.7)$$

Equations (3.4), (3.5), (3.6) and (3.7) are a mathematical basis for searching big data on the Web.

3.10 BIG DATA STATISTICS

The most notable big data statistics were introduced at least in 2010. The following data are from big data statistics based on the prediction (Howarth, 2022)

1. The global big data and analytics market is worth $274 billion.

2. Around 2.5 quintillion bytes worth of data are generated each day.

3. Big data analytics for the healthcare industry could reach $79.23 billion by 2028.

(Clissa, 2022) big data statistics is also based on infinitesimal analysis. For example, 5.4k PB/year is based on 71k Billion e-mails sent from 2020–10 to 2021–09 with an average size is 75 KB per email (Clissa, 2022).

Another method for big data statistics is based on the search of search machines, such as Google and Baidu. For example, we Google "big data" and find 318,000,000 results. However, the Google results can be a simple number for our research; it cannot be exhaustive. For example, we Baidu and find 620 results.

3.11 INFORMATION, KNOWLEDGE, AND EXPERIENCE

This section looks at data, information, knowledge, experience, and their relationships.

3.11.1 Introduction

In the big data world, it seems that all digital things online are data, big data, but much of it is not really "data" outside the big data world (Williams, 2016). This section examines not only data and big data but also information, knowledge, and experience that have played a significant role in computer science and AI, as well as impacts on economy, and society. It argues that big data must incorporate information, knowledge, and experience to serve science, engineering, technology, systems, management, and the world. We also use Q-A-R (Question-Answer-Remark; Sun & Finnie, 2005a) to differentiate data, information, and knowledge from experience, as follows.

Information, knowledge, and experience are more popular than data and big data in computer science, business, and management, market, even AI, and many other fields. This section will review them and explore DIKE (data, information, knowledge, and experience) using an integrated framework and their impacts on industry, economy, and society (we do not look at experience for most cases in this book). This research demonstrates that data are mainly for computers and computerized systems, while information, knowledge, experience are all for both humans and computers. The research questions are:

1. Why Data ≠ information ≠ knowledge ≠ experience?

2. Why can data and information be used interchangeably?

3. Can data and information and knowledge and experience be used interchangeably?

The remainder of this section is organized as follows:
Subsections 3.11.2–3.11.4 explore DIKE and its relationships. Subsection 3.11.5 presents an integrated framework of DIKE. Section 3.12 explores DIKE engineering, technology, systems, and management. Section 3.13 ends this research with some concluding remarks.

3.11.2 Information

Information is defined in terms of data (Rowley, 2007). Information is the processed data, a set of data, with the usefulness, content, relevance, purpose, and value (Ackoff, 1992; Sabherwal & Becerra-Fernandez, 2011). For example, the manipulation of raw data for a company, as data processing, is to obtain more meaningful information on the trend for daily sales (Sabherwal & Becerra-Fernandez, 2011).

Information is data that have been processed, so that it is meaningful and useful to human beings for a purpose (Laudon & Laudon, 2020). Two important points should be discussed from these definitions of data and information. First, generally, information is the processed data. More specifically, information is the data processed by ICT, that is, the input for ICT processing is data, and the output of the ICT processing is information. In relational databases, data processing consists of data definition and data manipulation. Data manipulation has 6 basic commands: SELECT, INSERT, UPDATE, DELETE, COMMIT, and ROLLBACK (Coronel, Morris, & Rob, 2020). It should be noted that in databases, the processed data are still data, we do not consider the processed data as information.

Second, different from data, information, in the majority of the cases, is visible, for example, we can see the picture on the Internet; we can read the story displaying on the screen of either a laptop or smartphone. Therefore, we should use visibility as a feature for information rather than for data. Roughly speaking, information is visible, meaningful, and useful data that is easily understood by human beings.

One example of the relationship between data and information is that the supermarket checkout counters scan millions of pieces of data from bar codes or 2D codes, and process what a customer bought from this supermarket via bar codes, and then produce the invoice or bill for the customer and ask the customer to pay the bill. The customer can check the items that he or she bought and pay the bill using a credit card or savings card. In the example, the bar code digits are data, an ordinary customer cannot understand what the bar code digits mean. However, after scan and computer processing (scan is a processing of ICT), the data of bar codes are converted into the information on the bill or invoice. The customer can easily understand what the invoice or bill means. At the same time, the computer or transaction processor has calculated how much the customer should pay. Here calculation is also a process!

Now we differentiate information from data as follows.

Q2: Do you know data about PA5510898?

A2: I believe that this is an Australia passport number.

R2: Few say "Do you know information about PA5510898". The answer A2 has been based on the knowledge or experience of the person. Maybe s/he has a friend with an Australian passport.

The answer A2 is correct. After computer processing, one finds that Dr. Peter Davison (an artificial name) is the holder of the Australian passport with the No. PA5510898. Peter is a millionaire in real estate and lives in Melbourne. The information is processed based on the data PA5510898, using computer software.

The dramatic development of the Internet and WWW since the late 1990s has made huge amounts of information available to everyone. The significant development of social media or social networking services, such as Facebook, Tweeters, and QQ, have produced not only big data but also big information because everyone has been contributing to this big data, big information through online shopping, email communication, online communication, social networking, etc. In developed countries, everyone has been working online for a few hours on the Web using the Internet. Just as everyone consumes electricity, they also contribute data and information.

3.11.3 Knowledge

Knowledge is defined in terms of information and data (Sabherwal & Becerra-Fernandez, 2011). Knowledge is processed, organized, or structured information with the insight of experts (Laudon & Laudon, 2020; Liew, 2013). Knowledge is a central concept in intelligent systems and cognitive systems (Wang, 2015; Russell & Norvig, 2020; Sun, 2023). In computer science and information science, knowledge is usually defined as the beliefs, objects, concepts, and relationships that are assumed to exist in some areas of interest (Sabherwal & Becerra-Fernandez, 2011).

Knowledge is processed information (Turban & Volonino, 2011). Knowledge also includes data because information is the processed data. In other words, knowledge is the processed data and/or information.

We use Q-A-R (Question-Answer-Remark) to differentiate knowledge from data and information (Sun & Finnie, 2005b).

Q3: What do you study at university?

A3: I study the knowledge of data science.

R3: Few said that they study the data on data science.

Therefore, data science theory can be considered as knowledge rather than data. The above discussion also implies that the students at a university mainly study knowledge rather than data.

Further, Lisa has enjoyed drawing pictures since childhood. Later, she became a famous artist.

We use Q-A-R to differentiate information from knowledge

Q1: What are you learning in your school?

A1: I am learning knowledge.

R1: Few say that "I am learning information."

Knowledge has also played a pivotal role in business management and information management (Laudon & Laudon, 2020). How to find useful knowledge from a large database or from the WWW to assist business decision-making has become one of the most important issues in data mining and business management.

3.11.4 Experience

Knowledge and experience are both intelligent assets of human beings. experience can be taken as previous knowledge or skill one obtained in everyday life. For example, Peter avoided a traffic tragedy on Pacific highway yesterday because he drove carefully and focused on the drive. This is a typical experience for driving. In other words, experience is previous knowledge which consists of problems one has met and the successful solution to the problems. Therefore, experience can be taken as a specialization of knowledge. On the other side, knowledge can usually be considered as a generalization of experience that human beings have encountered.

we use Q-A-R (Question-Answer-Remark) method to differentiate them with some comments.

Q1: What are you going to study in your school?

A1: I am going to study to gain knowledge.

R1: Few say that "I am going to study to gain experience."

Q2: Why did you visit that old doctor?

A2: Because he has rich experience in diagnosing and treating the disease that I suffered from.

R2: In this case, the knowledge of the doctor in diagnosing and treating the mentioned disease is not sufficient to attract the customer to see the doctor. This is common sense. That is, experience is a more important asset than knowledge in some fields. Therefore, in diagnosis, a doctor's experience can be considered the kernel of his possessed knowledge.

Experience management is experience-based reasoning that has been studied in CBR (Sun, Han, & Dong, 2008). How to manage experience is still important for online customer behaviors in e-commerce and web services (Sun, Meredith, & Stranieri, 2012; Sun & Finnie, 2005b).

3.11.5 An Integrated Framework of DIKE

DIKE consists of data, information, knowledge, and experience, as illustrated in Figure 3.10. We have the following inclusion relationships for DIKE:

$$\text{data} \subset \text{information} \subset \text{knowledge} \subset \text{experience} \qquad (3.8)$$

This leads to an integrated framework of DIKE as a pyramid, as shown in Figure 3.10.

We have proven this equation (3.8) in Section 3.11.

Data, information, knowledge, and experience (DIKE) have played a significant role in computing and ICT in the past few decades. They have led to the development of data computing, information computing, knowledge computing, and experience computing (for short, DIKE computing).

$$\text{DIKE computing} = \text{data computing} + \text{information computing} \\ + \text{knowledge computing} + \text{experience computing} \\ (3.9)$$

For example, knowledge computing encompasses knowledge science, engineering, technology, systems, intelligence, and management, and so on (Sun & Huo, 2020; Sun, 2022). That is,

$$\text{Knowledge computing} = \text{knowledge science} + \text{knowledge engineering} \\ + \text{knowledge technology} + \text{knowledge systems} \\ + \text{knowledge management} \\ + \text{knowledge intelligence} \qquad (3.10)$$

DIKE computing covers almost all the aspects of current ICT and digital technology, with applications. Therefore, data, information, knowledge, and experience are elements for the digital age (Sun & Stranieri, 2021).

FIGURE 3.10   DIKE Pyramid: An integrated framework

3.12 DIKE ENGINEERING, TECHNOLOGY, SYSTEMS, AND MANAGEMENT

From this structure of thinking, we should look at DIKE information engineering, technology, systems, and management. However, this section only briefly looks at information engineering, technology, systems, and management, and knowledge engineering, technology, systems, and management.

3.12.1 Information Engineering, Technology, Systems, and Management

Information engineering aims to use information science and technology to create and manage information systems to provide information services and applications with information intelligence.

An information system is a process of converting data into information, based on information technology (Laudon & Laudon, 2020).

3.12.2 Knowledge Engineering, Technology, Systems, and Management

Knowledge engineering is a set of intensive activities encompassing the acquisition of knowledge from human experts (and other information sources) and converting this knowledge into a repository (commonly called a knowledge base) (Sharda, Delen, & Turba, 2018; Laudon & Laudon, 2020). The primary goal of knowledge engineering is to help experts articulate how they do, what they do, and to document this knowledge in a reusable form (Laudon & Laudon, 2020). More generally, knowledge engineering aims to use knowledge science and technology to create and manage knowledge systems to provide knowledge services and applications with knowledge intelligence.

The knowledge engineering process has been provided in a feedback-driven form, illustrated by Figure 3.11 (Sharda, Delen, & Turba, 2018). Every step has been detailed by them.

3.12.3 Knowledge Management and Knowledge Systems

Knowledge management means to manage knowledge. Knowledge management is a process of defining, retrieving, capturing, planning, organizing, classifying, structuring, generating, disseminating, retaining, identifying, using, storing, and sharing an organization's knowledge (Taherdoost & Madanchian, 2023).

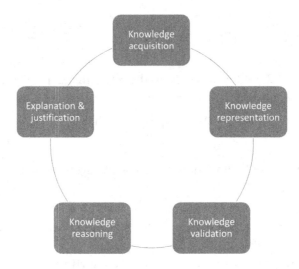

FIGURE 3.11   A model for knowledge engineering.

Knowledge systems is a system that can transform data and information into knowledge. Therefore, knowledge systems focus on knowledge creation, while KM focuses on management.

A knowledge system is a process of converting information into knowledge, based on knowledge technology (Laudon & Laudon, 2020).

3.13 SUMMARY

This chapter first looks at data, and then big data. This chapter identifies and examines ten big characteristics of big data, with an example for each: Big volume, big velocity, big variety, big veracity, big data technology, big data systems, big infrastructure, big value, big services, and big market. It also explores a service-oriented foundation of big data and calculus of searching big data. It looks at data engineering, science, systems, and technology. Besides data and big data, this research also explores information, knowledge, and experience (DIKE). This chapter explores DIKE computing, science, engineering, technology, systems, intelligence, management, and services.

Big data brings big potential, big market, and big value. All engineering, science, technology, systems, and management is for intelligence. This is why we use data, information, knowledge, experience, and their engineering as a foundation for intelligence.

Overall, data in general and big data in particular are a foundation of big information, big knowledge, big intelligence, and big analytics. Therefore, we are still at the foundational stage and enter the emerging age of big information, big knowledge, big intelligence, and big analytics.

3.14 REVIEW QUESTIONS AND PROBLEMS

1. What are the five steps for processing oil and data, respectively? Can you create a correspondence between them?

2. What is the difference between data mining and data analytics?

3. Now a fundamental question arises: Why big is important in a big data world?

4. Is ChatGPT an AI product?
   No, it is the first NLP product using reinforcement learning from human feedback (RLHF) (OpenAI, 2023), but NLP and reinforcement learning are parts of AI. We can see ChatGPT is a later part of AI. ChatGPT is a large language model (OpenAI, 2023), ChatGPT and GPT-3.5 with 1.5 billion parameters were trained on an Azure AI supercomputing infrastructure.

5. How can you optimize data modeling and data reasoning?

6. Can you discuss the idea, "Data, information, and knowledge are rich; however, intelligence and wisdom are poor."

7. What is data science?

8. What is data engineering? Gave three examples of data engineering.

3.15 REFERENCES FOR FURTHER STUDY

1. George V. Neville-Neil, 2020, Numbers Are for Computers, Strings Are for Humans, Vol. 63, No. 2, pp 29–30.

2. Berman, Jules J. 2013, Principles of big data: preparing, sharing, and analyzing complex information. Morgan Kaufmann Publishers Inc., Waltham, MA.

3. Sathiyamoorthi Velayutham, 2021, Challenges and Opportunities for the Convergence of IoT, Big Data, and Cloud Computing.

4. Dream Sky, 2024, Data Engineering in the Age of Big Data 2024: Data Engineering in the Age of Big Data 2024, Kindle Edition.

5. Philip M. Parker, 2022, The 2023–2028 Outlook for Big Data in China. ICON Group International, Inc.

CHAPTER 4

Analytics

Analytics originated from statistics, developed through data mining, boomed in big data.

ANALYTICS IS THE SCIENCE and technology of using mathematics, AI, computer science, data science, and operations research to provide practical applications to business, management, research and development, and economic and societal problems. Analytics can be defined as a process of understanding and exploring data by creating meaningful patterns and insights [19, p. 25]. Data visualization is one of the most important parts of analytics [Blatt, 2017, p. 25] (Aroraa, Lele, & Jindal, 2022). After discussing the evolution of analytics, this chapter looks at analysis ≠ Analytics, and examines mathematical analytics. This chapter classifies analytics based on a few perspectives. One of them is that analytics can be classified into descriptive statistics, diagnostic statistics, predictive statistics, and predictive statistics (DDPP analytics) based on cyclic business operations. This chapter explores analytics algorithms, and DDPP analytics and computing. Analytics engineering aims to use analytics science and technology to create and manage analytics systems to provide analytics services with analytics intelligence [Sun Z., 2022a]. This chapter also analyzes the leverage analytics for organizations. Finally, this chapter looks at the applications of analytics and discusses three major trends of analytics.

DOI: 10.1201/9781003450504-4

Learning objectives of this chapter:

- Analyze metrics ≠ analytics.

- Understand Analysis ≠ Analytics.

- Understand analytics thinking.

- Understand types of analytics.

- Understand computing and analytics.

- Define DDPP analytics and computing.

- Define statistical analytics.

- Define analytics as a rule-based system.

- Describe two examples for analytics applications.

- Analyze analytics and organizations.

- Search major trends of analytics online and gain familiarity with its development.

4.1 INTRODUCTION

Analytics relies on algorithms to produce a number of outcomes (Thompson & Rogers, 2017, p. 13).

Analytics can be defined as a process of understanding data by creating meaningful patterns (Blatt, 2017, p. 25).

The bigger big data become, the more complicated to address the foregoing problems. This requires more sophisticated and new techniques to deal with. Mathematics, optimization, machine learning, data mining, cloud computing, statistical modeling, as well as visualization technology, underpin the research and development of big data and big analytics. There is significant need for better understanding of big data and big analytics through an in-depth investigation of mathematics, optimization, statistical modeling and machine learning for big data, and analytics with intelligent applications (Sun, Sun, & Strang, 2018; Chen & Zhang, 2014).

Google search found about 4,300,000,000 items of analytics (on October 18, 2023). Data analytics might be the oldest among all these analytics (Kauffman, Srivastava, & Vayghan, 2012; Delena & Demirkanb, 2013). Business analytics consists of descriptive, diagnostic, prescriptive, and predicative analytics (Delena & Demirkanb, 2013).

Analytics is a system for augmenting human capabilities (Thompson & Rogers, 2017). Analytics is a tool to support human intelligence and decision-making (Thompson & Rogers, 2017).

After discussing the evolution of analytics, this chapter looks at analysis ≠ Analytics, and examines mathematical analytics, a system process of analytics. This chapter provides types of analytics based on a few perspectives, one of them is that analytics can be classified into descriptive statistics, diagnostic statistics, predictive statistics, and predictive statistics based on cyclic business operations. This chapter explores analytics algorithms and models, and analytics computing. Analytics engineering aims to use analytics science and analytics technology to create and manage analytics systems to provide analytics services with analytics intelligence (Sun, 2022a). Finally, this research analyzes three major trends of analytics. The rise of analytics scientists, algorithms, and still algorithms become more and more important for the algorithm industry and the blossoming analytics industry. Then, all analytics, including the analytical approach, analytical modeling, analytical analysis, analytical metrics are central for running the world.

The remainder of this chapter is organized as follows. Section 4.2 looks at the evolution of analytics. Section 4.3 explores analytics thinking and analytical thinking. Sections 4.4 and 4.5 analyzes the relationship among metrics, analysis, and analytics. Section 4.6 studies statistical analytics. Section 4.7 looks at analytics and rule-based systems. Section 4.8 classifies analytics based on organizations, disciplines, business functions, and processes. Sections 4.9 and 4.10 explores DDPP computing, analytics, and algorithms. Section 4.11 discusses applications of analytics. Section 4.12 analyzes the leverage analytics for organizations. Section 4.13 provides three major trends of analytics. The final section ends this chapter with concluding remarks and possible future work.

4.2 EVOLUTION OF ANALYTICS

Analytics was first mentioned in 1936 (Thompson & Rogers, 2017; Sun, 2019b). Analytics can date back to operations research that blossomed in the 1950s. Analytics has already been used in business science for many decades. However, analytics has gained popularity more rapidly than any other business and managerial paradigms, including BI (Delena & Demirkanb, 2013, p. 66). In history, the schools of business have considered analytics as an application of mathematical and statistical techniques under the titles of operations research/management science, simulation analysis, econometrics, and financial analysis (Holsapple, Lee-Post, & Pakath, 2014)

Analytics = operations research (OR) + management science
+ simulation analysis + econometrics + financial analysis.

However, analytics was not a focus until the blossoming of big data in 2012. Since then, analytics, big data analytics, and intelligent analytics have drawn increasing attention in academia, industry, and government (IDC, 2019; Howson, Richardson, Sallam, & Kronz, 2019). We are now in the age of analytics (Sun, 2019b). Analytics is a science and technology of using mathematics, AI, computer science, data science, and operations research to provide practical applications to business, management, research and development, economic, and societal problems. Analytics is one area that requires complex algorithms (Thompson & Rogers, 2017; Russell & Norvig, 2020). Data visualization is one of the most important parts of analytics (Blatt, 2017, p. 25; Aroraa, Lele, & Jindal, 2022).

4.3 ANALYTICS THINKING AND ANALYTICAL THINKING

Computing has underpinned research and development of ICT and digital technology over the past half century. Computing thinking has drawn attention in computing fields since 1996 (Sun, 2020b). Just as computing thinking has played a significant role in computing, analytics thinking will play a critical role in the research and development of analytics and intelligent analytics. However, what is analytics thinking? How can analytics thinking influence research and development of analytics with applications? These are big issues.

Rene Descartes found a way to study geometric problems using algebraic methods, called analytic geometry (Descartes, 1637). This implies that analytical thinking originated in 1637. The key behind analytical thinking is that it is based on two different disciplinary methods and their combination. The essence behind analytical thinking is that one method is not enough for solving complex problems.

Similarly, analytics thinking uses different thinking to analyze complex problems and solve the complex problems using different system paradigms to develop an integrated system, an analytics system.

Analytics thinking includes two levels of thinking: horizontal level and vertical level:

At the horizontal level, analytics thinking includes descriptive thinking, diagnostic thinking, predictive thinking, prescriptive thinking, and business process thinking. This analytics thinking will lead to research and development of descriptive analytics, diagnostic analytics, predictive analytics, prescriptive analytics, and business process analytics.

At the vertical level, analytics thinking is composed of strategic thinking, tactic thinking, and operational thinking for organizations and management decision-thinking. This analytics thinking will lead to research and development of strategic analytics, tactic analytics, operational analytics, organizational analytics, and decision analytics.

In summary, old analytical thinking is algebraic, geometric, and logical thinking. Current analytical thinking is computing, mathematics, data science, and AI (Sun, 2020b). Big data analytics thinking is a thinking process for developing big data analytics based on analytical thinking, analytical tools, and analytical modeling (Sun, 2020b).

4.4 METRICS ≠ ANALYTICS

Metrics and analytics have been discussed in big data, data science, and cybersecurity (Weber, 2020, pp. 132–146). Metrics and analytics are important for any business processing performance. Metrics provides an answer to the "what" kind of questions, while analytics answers the "so what" kind of questions (Weber, 2020). Therefore, analytics with metrics is important for managerial work. From a mathematical perspective, metrics are a set of metric formulas, while analytics is a set of integrated systems consisting of many different subsystems. The basic principle between metrics and analytics is that metrics is the basis for analytics (Weber, 2020, pp. 132–135). In other words, any analytics is determined by a set of metrics. Or we have

$$Analytics = metrics + analysis + visualization.$$

This formula will dominate this book.

4.5 ANALYSIS ≠ ANALYTICS

This section explores the relationship between analysis and analytics because both are used in a very confusing way sometimes. In some countries, they are misused interchangeably.

Based on Merriam-Webster Dictionary (Merriam-Webster, 2023b), analysis can be defined as 1. "a detailed examination of anything complex to understand its nature or to determine its essential features, 2. "separation of a whole into its component parts". Analysis was first used in 1581 in the meaning defined in sense 2. Analysis at sense 1 is a thorough study in every field at any level of research graduality. Analysis has become a most popular term for not only academia and industry but also every level of society, even for a child of 3 years old who might say, I am doing an analysis on foods. Can she say, I am doing analytics on foods? Certainly No (Sun, Strang, & Wu, 2022).

Analysis has been used since the early stage of human civilization, at least 2000 years ago, since ancient Greek times. However, analytics has been used in academia and industry very recently, only in the last century, thanks to the power of specification since the industrial revolution (Sun, Strang, & Wu, 2022).

Based on the Merriam-Webster Dictionary (Merriam-Webster, 2023b), analytics is "the method of logical analysis." It was first used circa 1590, borrowed from Late Latin Analytica.

In contrast to analysis, analytics cannot be found in this mentioned dictionary (Oxford, 2008), but we can use analytic or analytical to infer the meaning of analytics. According to the dictionary, analytic refers to "using scientific analysis to find out about something" or "using a logical method of thinking about something to understand it". The most general concept for analytics is the "using scientific analysis and method to discover and communicate meaningful patterns in something.". The scientific analysis includes logical method. Briefly,

$$\text{Analytics} = \text{scientific analysis} + \text{logical method} \rightarrow \text{understand} \\ + \text{discover} + \text{communicate} \qquad (4.1)$$

Therefore, analytics is a method incorporating one analysis within another analysis. It is also the essence of analytics differentiating from analysis. In other words, analytics is a method of incorporating one analysis method within another analysis method, or a set of analyses. More generally, analytics is a science and technology of incorporating at least one scientific paradigm within another scientific paradigm. This fits the state-of-the-art usage of analytics in many disciplines, such as big data analytics, business analytics, mathematical analytics, intelligent analytics, market analytics, Google Analytics, and cybersecurity analytics, to name a few (Sharda, Delen, & Turba, 2018; Sun, Pambel, & Wu, 2022; Weber, 2020).

The difference between analytics and analysis is that the former is a science and technology, whereas the latter is a method. Analysis is a basic part of any research and development, scientific investigation. Overall, analytics is a science and technology on analytical analyses, that is

$$\text{Analytics} = \text{science and technology on analytical analyses} \quad (4.2)$$

The first question is more general than the second. The second is more important than the first in the digital. Both are fundamental for analytics.

Based on the above exploration, we find that analytics is a special form of analysis. It can be defined as using scientific analysis and logical method to understand, discover, and communicate the meaningful patterns in something. In other words,

$$\text{analytics} \subseteq \text{analysis} \quad (4.3)$$

The relationship of (4.3) technologically ignores data and its role in analytics and analysis. This is the most general consideration of the relationship between analytics and analysis. Turban, et al. claim that the difference between analysis and analytics is that analysis is a more general term than analytics as a process (Turban & Volonino, 2011), which is same as that of (4.2) and (4.3).

Analytics is about "the scientific process of transforming data into insight for making better decisions" (Wang, 2012). More generally, analytics is a science and technology about analyzing, examining, summarizing, acquiring intelligence, and drawing conclusions to learn, describe, and predict something. Data analytics is an application of analytics to data, data science. Data analytics can be also considered as data-driven discoveries of knowledge, intelligence, and communications (Delena & Demirkanb, 2013). More generally, data analytics is a science and technology about analyzing, examining data, summarizing, acquiring intelligence, and drawing conclusions to learn, describe, and predict something (Sun, 2019b; Gandomi & Haider, 2015).

Applying data as an operation to both sides of (4.4), we have

$$\text{Data analytics} \subseteq \text{Data analysis} \quad (4.4)$$

The relationship between data analysis and data analytics is that the general goal of data analysis is to acquire knowledge from data (National Research Council, 2013). We will turn to data analytics in Chapter Seven.

4.6 STATISTICAL ANALYTICS

Analytics is the practical use of mathematical approaches-formulas, rules, and laws to either describe the world or work and live in to predict phenomena (Thompson & Rogers, 2017, p. 24). Descriptive analytics and predictive analytics are directly from descriptive statistics and predictive statistics. Therefore, this section will first look at descriptive statistics, diagnostic analytics, predictive statistics, and prescriptive analytics.

4.6.1 Descriptive Statistics

Descriptive statistics can be defined as methods of descriptively modeling data in the data set or in tabular, graphical, or numerical form (Sweeney, Williams, & Anderson, 2011; Hurley, 2019, p. 133). Tabular and graphical summaries can be found in annual reports, news articles, and research studies. We begin with tabular and graphical methods for summarizing data concerning a single variable (Sharda, Delen, Turban, & King, 2018).

Descriptive statistics are used to transform data to information and help organizations accelerate conversions and maintain business continuity.

Descriptive Statistics can be based on numerical measures of location, dispersion, shape, and association (Sweeney, Williams, & Anderson, 2011, p. 88). Descriptive analytics describes data and its phenomena (Blatt, 2017). Descriptive analytics uses averages, clusters, categories, and other statistical features to describe data. This also implies that descriptive analytics is from descriptive statistics.

Modern statistical software packages provide extensive capabilities for summarizing data and preparing graphical presentations. Minitab, SPSS, and Excel are three widely available packages (Sweeney, Williams, & Anderson, 2011, p. 33).

Finally, descriptive analytics is originally from descriptive statistics, which underpins descriptive mining, a part of data mining.

4.6.2 Diagnostic Analytics

Diagnostic analytics is a form of analytics that examines data or content to answer the question, "Why did it happen?" It is characterized by techniques such as drill-down, data discovery, data mining, and correlations

(Gardner, 2024). The result of diagnostic analytics is also a kind of diagnostic statistics with visualized reports. For example, the report of a medical checkup for a patient covers the result of testing blood and urine. The GP (General practitioner) will use this report to analyze a patient's symptoms, predict the possible situation, and prescribe medication for the patient.

Diagnostic analytics is about why something happened. A good example is Microsoft diagnostic analytics. For example, IBM Watson can provide diagnostic support for doctors (Thompson & Rogers, 2017, pp. 14–15).

Descriptive and diagnostic analytics are all about the past and the present. Descriptive analytics is about what happened. Diagnostic analytics is about why something happened. They enable organizations to sense, filter, shape, learn, and calibrate opportunities by providing insights into what has happened in their internal and external environment to know their strength and weakness (SW). A well-known example is Google Analytics.

Finally, diagnostic analytics is originally from clinic practice, based on the diagnostic analysis and measurement, as well as visual report.

4.6.3 Predictive Statistics

Descriptive data mining is from descriptive statistics (Sweeney, Williams, & Anderson, 2011). Predictive analytics is referred to as application of long-established statistical and or operation research methods to historical business information to predict, model, or simulate future business and/or economic performance and potentially prescribe a favored course of action for the future. (Williams, 2016, p. 52).

Predictive analytics predict what could happen given certain conditions based on the algorithms, which review past cases and learn, or they create examples to compare current datasets to predict the probability of what might be (or will be) happening. These algorithms include that from neural networks, machine learning, AI, cognitive computing, and so on.

Prediction is power (Siegel, 2016, p. 3). Prediction is very difficult because it's about the future (Siegel, 2016, p. 13). There are many predictive technologies (Siegel, 2016, p. 15). Predictive analytics (PA) is a predictive technology that learns from experience (data) to predict the future behavior of individuals in order to drive better decisions (Siegel, 2016, p. 15). ML is a kind of predictive technology based on predictive modeling to find patterns of experience (data) to predict the future behavior of individuals to drive better decisions (Siegel, 2016, p. 36). Siegel looks at predictive analytics as the power to predict who will click, buy, lie, or die using the following strategy (Siegel, 2016, p. 26):

1. PA application: targeting direct marketing,

2. What is predicted: which customers will respond to marketing contact.

3. What's done about it, contract customers are more likely to respond.

All these examples and case studies demonstrate the following five effects of prediction (Siegel, 2016, p. 294):

4. The prediction effect: a little prediction goes a long way.

5. The data effect: data is always predictive.

6. The induction effect: art drives machine learning, when followed by computer programs, strategies designed in part by informal human creativity succeed in developing predictive models that perform well on a new case.

7. The ensemble effect: when joined in an ensemble, predictive models compensate for one another's limitations so the ensemble as a whole is more likely to predict correctly than its component models are.

8. The persuasion affect: although imperceptible, the persuasion of an individual can be predicted by lift modeling, predictively modeling access to two distinct training data sets that record, respectively, the outcomes of two competing treatments.

Finally, predictive analytics are originally from data mining, because one of the important applications of data mining is prediction. Therefore, we can say that data mining is a science of prediction.

4.6.4 Prescriptive Analytics

Prescriptive analytics prescribes the best results to be used in decision-making. It refers to optimization systems and cognitive computing. Prescriptive analytics is about what to do (now) and why to do it, given a complex set of requirements, objectives, and constraints. It can offer recommendations on how an organization and individual can do it, but it can also make decisions autonomously based on these recommendations.

Prescriptive analytics has been used by General Electronics (GE) to develop customized applications for asset performance management.

Predictive analytics and Prescriptive analytics are all about the future and predicting what will happen. It uses ML and algorithms to find patterns and capture relationships in multiple unstructured and structured data sources to create foresights. Predictive analytics solutions allow one to make future projections based on historical and present data. Sisense offers predictive analytics solutions. Prescriptive analytics will further facilitate analytical development for automated analytics to replace the need for human DM with automated DM. (Van Rijmenam, 2020, pp. 31–36)

Finally, prescriptive analytics is originally from prescription of the GP in the clinic practice. The prescription is in the form of visual report, and business report or in the form or formula.

4.7 ANALYTICS ARE RULE-BASED SYSTEMS

Analytics are rule-based systems. Rule-based systems have been used for many decades as a part of expert systems and knowledge-base systems (Russell & Norvig, 2020). They have been used in numerous business applications (Laudon & Laudon, 2020; Thompson & Rogers, 2017). Rule-based systems can be used to capture and codify knowledge in the knowledge base (Thompson & Rogers, 2017). More general, Analytics is an AI-based system; it can help companies to move and adapt customer's behavior changes (Thompson & Rogers, 2017; Sun & Huo, 2021).

4.8 TYPES OF ANALYTICS

This section classifies analytics into: company-based analytics, discipline analytics, business function analytics, and business process analytics.

4.8.1 Introduction

There are many different types of analytics. For example, Blatt classifies analytics into descriptive analytics, diagnostic analytics, predictive analytics, and prescriptive analytics (Blatt, 2017, pp. 31–26). The analysis of mathematical analytics will lead to the classification of analytics. However, this classification is based on either purpose or question. Hurley classifies analytics into descriptive analytics, diagnostic analytics, predictive analytics, and prescriptive analytics (Hurley, 2019, pp. 25–26). He believed that most data scientists favor this classification. Thompson and Rogers classify analytics into descriptive analytics, predictive analytics, and prescriptive analytics (Thompson & Rogers, 2017, pp. 14–15). In fact, they focus analytics to address three different problems, that is, descriptive, predictive, and prescriptive problems (Sun, 2022a). Each of these problems requires analytics to address. This classification has been used as three levels of analytics (Sharda, Delen, Turban, & King, 2018).

Analytics can be classified based on companies, business processes, and disciplines.

Prescriptive computing was introduced in IBM from an industry application (Thompson & Rogers, 2017, pp. 25–26) which led to DDPP computing in this section (Sun, 2022a). Prescriptive analytics as a software provides optimal recommendations around achieving business objectives like customer satisfaction, profits, and cost savings for organizations (IBM, 2023). IBM uses prescriptive analytics to provide solutions based on optimization technology to solve complex decisions with millions of decision variables, constraints, and tradeoffs. Then, prescriptive analytics has led to DDPP analytics (Sun, 2022a).

4.8.2 Organizational Analytics

From a company viewpoint, more and more companies and organizations have used analytics as their brand name, product name, and service name. For example, Cambridge Analytica was a famous company in the UK; now it has collapsed. Google Analytics is a product for services from Google and Alphabet. Baidu Analytics is also a product of Baidu.

Diagnostic analytics is a part of system analytics from Microsoft. For example, in Windows 11: Go to Start, then select Settings > Privacy & security > Diagnostics & feedback. Make sure that the View Diagnostic Data setting is turned On, and then select Open Diagnostic Data Viewer (https://support.microsoft.com/en-us/windows/). Microsoft uses diagnostic data to keep Windows secure and up to date, troubleshoot problems, and make product improvements as described in more detail below. In fact, all other software systems use this similarly.

4.8.3 Discipline Analytics

From a discipline viewpoint, mathematics has its analytics, mathematical analytics. Business science has business analytics, data science has data analytics, and knowledge science has its knowledge analytics. Big data has its big data analytics. Information science has its information analytics. Behavior science has its behavioral analytics. Intelligence science has its intelligence analytics.

We have mentioned information analytics. In fact, we also have DDPP information analytics, big information analytics, and intelligent big information analytics.

We have also mentioned knowledge analytics. In fact, we also have DDPP knowledge analytics, big knowledge analytics, and intelligent big knowledge analytics.

Visualization has become a computing-level research field in computer science and cloud computing. Visual analytics is playing an important role in visualization.

Visual analytics integrates reporting, data preparation, visual exploration, and dashboards into a single product; it also provides the underpinnings of SAS solutions (prebuilt analytical applications). Visual analytics is also a component of data science, visual data mining, and Machine Learning (Howson, Richardson, Sallam, & Kronz, 2019). Data can be manipulated while visualizing — such as when creating groups, bins, and new hierarchies. Dashboards are basic, without rich mapping, visual-based data discovery. Business users would like to scale and share visual explorations with more users.

For example, TIBCO Software was an early visual-based data discovery disruptor with Spotfire, which helped shift the market from traditional reporting to modern analytics and BI. Yellowfin was one of the first to bring augmented analytics capabilities to market in 2017.

Embedding technology is also important for computer science. For example, embedded analytics remains an important use case because customers want to create extranet applications, monetize data, and provide analytics as a part of overall business applications.

4.8.4 Business Function Analytics

Business functions are the activities with the purpose of the business performed by a business organization or company (Vaidya, 2023). Well-structured business functions enable a company to be successful in communicating with its customers, employees, investors, and other stakeholders. Normally, an organization or company has business functions, such as production, marketing, sales, customer services, general management, HR (human resources), accounts and finance, and public relations. Therefore, business function-based analytics encompass production analytics, marketing analytics, sales analytics, retail analytics, supply chain analytics (SCM analytics), customer services analytics (CRM analytics), HR analytics, accounting and finance analytics (Brooks, 2022).

4.8.5 Business Process Analytics

A business process consists of many different functions; every function has its analytics, for example, supply chain analytics, marketing analytics, HR analytics, customer analytics, and so on (Brooks, 2022). A cyclic business process in clinic and system diagnosis and maintenance consists of descriptive activities, diagnostic activities, prescriptive activities, and predictive activities. Therefore, such a cyclic business process consists of descriptive analytics, diagnostic analytics, prescriptive analytics, and predictive analytics. Some of them are based on descriptive statistics, diagnostic analytics, prescriptive analytics, and predictive analytics, as well as decisive analytics (see the next section).

Decisive analytics is the analytics for supporting human decisions with visual analytics. The user models are set to reflect reasoning.

4.9 DDPP COMPUTING AND ANALYTICS

Analytics is a cognitive, autonomic, and prescriptive computing (Thompson & Rogers, 2017, p. 25). This is one of the motivations to develop DDPP computing and analytics. Descriptive, diagnostic, predictive, and prescriptive can be abbreviated as DDPP. Then all these classified problems can be abbreviated as DDPP problems (Hurley, 2019, pp. 25–26). DDPP problems have been addressed by a great number of professionals and academia in the past centuries (Hurley, 2019). Therefore, the problem-driven computing to address these four categories of problems are descriptive computing, diagnostic computing, predictive computing, and prescriptive computing. All these four types of computing are emerging research fields for competing for competitive advantages in the world. Then, the following holds.

$$\text{DDPP computing} = \text{descriptive computing} + \text{diagnostic computing} \\ + \text{predictive computing} + \text{prescriptive computing} \tag{4.5}$$

Equation (4.5) implies that computing as an operation satisfies the right distributive law.

The following also holds (Sun, 2022a):

$$\text{DDPP Computing} = \text{DDPP science} + \text{DDPP engineering} \\ + \text{DDPP technology} + \text{DDPP systems} \\ + \text{DDPP intelligence} + \text{DDPP management} \tag{4.6}$$

Equation (4.6) theoretically shows that DDPP science, that is, descriptive science, diagnostic science, predictive science, and prescriptive science should draw much attention in academia and industry.

It should be noted that on the right side of equation (4.6), computing has been ignored from each item like DDPP science; that is, DDPP science is simplified from DDPP computing science. In fact, computing plays a foundational and underpinning role in developing each item on the right side of the equation (4.6), but in an invisible way. If emphasizing the importance of computing, each of them can be represented computing driven DDPP science, technology, systems, intelligence, and management. This representation and treatment of computing reflects the corresponding research fields more closely with computing.

Descriptive analytics, diagnostic analytics, predictive analytics, and prescriptive analytics are a classification of analytics, abbreviated as DDPP analytics (Sun, Pambel, & Wu, 2022; Ghavami, 2020). This classification can be obtained by replacing computing in equation (4.5) with analytics (Hurley, 2019), taking into account the right distributive law, as follows:

$$
\begin{aligned}
\text{DDPP analytics} = {}& \text{descriptive analytics} + \text{diagnostic analytics} \\
& + \text{predictive analytics} + \text{prescriptive analytics} \quad (4.7)
\end{aligned}
$$

More generally, based on equation (4.6), DDPP analytics can be represented as

$$
\begin{aligned}
\text{DDPP analytics} = {}& \text{DDPP analytics science} + \text{DDPP analytics engineering} \\
& + \text{DDPP analytics technology} + \text{DDPP analytics systems} \\
& + \text{DDPP analytics intelligence} \\
& + \text{DDPP analytics management} + \text{DDPP systems} \\
& + \text{DDPP services and DDPP intelligence.} \quad (4.8)
\end{aligned}
$$

This is because analytics science, analytics engineering, analytics technology, analytics systems, analytics management, analytics services, analytics systems, and analytics intelligence have been mentioned in many research publications (Sun, 2019b; Thompson & Rogers, 2017).

In summary, problems are first classified into DDPP problems, then DDPP analytics addresses DDPP problems to produce DDPP intelligence. From a systemic viewpoint, DDPP problems should be the input of the DDPP analytics. DDPP analytics is the process of the system. DDPP intelligence is

FIGURE 4.1   DDPP problems, analytics, and intelligence.

output of the DDPP analytics, as illustrated in Figure 4.1. DDPP intelligence is the aim of using DDPP analytics to address DDPP problems.

It should be noted that in the business setting, DDPP problems can be considered operation problems. Therefore, DDPP computing and DDPP analytics can be operation computing and operation analytics. We will focus on intelligence in Chapter 6 and DDPP problems in Chapter 7.

4.10 ANALYTICS ALGORITHMS

Analytical techniques and algorithms can be applied to solve data- and math-oriented problems (Thompson & Rogers, 2017, p. 82). The analytics algorithms are used to convert data into information, information into insights, and knowledge into intelligence on a regular and repeatable basis (Thompson & Rogers, 2017, p. 76).

The algorithms are also used for data-intensive systems, advanced computing, advanced computing programs, data-driven science along with simulation, large-scale simulations and/or data analytics, numerically-intensive computing, software infrastructure, science portfolio, simulation science, and data-driven science, (National Academies of Sciences, 2016). Advanced computing hardware acquisition, computing services, data services, expertise, algorithms, and software have been processed in a unified way (National Academies of Sciences, 2016).

Data is inherently dumb, but algorithms know where the real value lies because algorithms can define an action for mining data from a large database using analytics. The big payoff will come from this action (Thompson & Rogers, 2017).

Companies and organizations have been using and managing algorithms for decades. However, algorithms have created an algorithm industry and the economy is a matter of over 3 decades. Algorithms are not only for big data and AI. So far, no search algorithms can defeat Google. This is why Google is still a search company in the world. Problem reduction is second for big data and AI (Russell & Norvig, 2020). Amazon, Alibaba, and Jd.com have used problem reduction for intelligent supply chain and logistics to deliver products and services to customers efficiently.

A specific algorithm can create a company and build an industry. An algorithm can develop an algorithm economy. Therefore, we are in the age of the algorithm economy (Thompson & Rogers, 2017). Each person, organization, and company is consuming myriad algorithms embedded in analytics, systems, machines, and apps daily.

4.11 APPLICATIONS OF ANALYTICS

When having the right datasets, an organization or company should determine which analytics are necessary to improve its business performance (Blatt, 2017, p. 40). For example, data analytics can be used for basic data analysis; retail analytics can be used for pricing optimization and customer demand; people analytics can be used to assess turnover risk management or recruitment studies; and operations analytics can be used for new product planning studies. This section will overview analytics systems and platforms for a range of business function areas: marketing, customer relationship management, sales, financial services, logistics, supply chain management, manufacturing, security, and HR (Thompson & Rogers, 2017). Each of them has been considered as business analytics and intelligence for the corresponding function (Brooks, 2022). For example, manufacturing intelligence and analytics each aim to help business functions acquire, manage, integrate, and exploit data, information, knowledge, and intelligence to get better business performance.

Analytics is a unique book name published in the past few years by Thompson & Rogers (Thompson & Rogers, 2017). They focus on analytics, based on their understandings of how to win with Intelligence. They first provided the competitive advantage stemming from analytics (Chapter 1) and understanding advanced analytics (Chapter 2), the age of the algorithm economy (Chapter 3), the modern data systems (Chapter 4), and then provided a few business cases. Their discussion on analytics continues with the subjects "takes a village" (Chapter 5), operational analytics (Chapter 7), and analytics everywhere, all the time (Chapter 8). However, they have not investigated analytics itself. For example, what is analytics. In what follows, we review the applications of analytics in some detail. The following also implies that we are in the age of analytics ubiquity. Analytics is everywhere, all the time, around us, because metrics and measurement and visualization are everywhere, all the time, around us in the digital age.

4.11.1 Analytics and Amazon

Amazon has deployed analytics to optimize virtually every aspect of its marketing and customers, and those endeavors have produced invaluable insights (Thompson & Rogers, 2017, p. 105).

4.11.2 Logistics and Supply Chain

Supply chain analytics uses data intelligence to resolve supply chain planning and execution (or operation) problems at the strategic, tactical, and operational levels (Brooks, 1991, p. 124). The issues of the supply chain industry are 1. Managing demand volatility, 2, supply chain and logistics transparency, and 3. cost fluctuation.

UPS uses ORION (On-Road Integrated Optimization and Navigation) analytics to crunch data from sources to optimize a driver's route concerning distance, fuel consumption, and time (Thompson & Rogers, 2017, p. 108).

Supply chain analytics is a kind of supply chain technology. Gartner predicts that over 50% of companies deploying intralogistics robots will have a multiagent orchestration platform By 2026, and over 65% of short-term decisions within supply chain planning will be automated or autonomous (James & Duncan, 2023). We will discuss supply chain analytics in Chapter 10.

4.11.3 Manufacturing Analytics

Manufacturing can be classified into process and discrete. Process manufacturing is about the distilling and refining of batch flows, like the pharmaceutical industry, which uses analytics to replicate the best production runs. Process manufacturers can use analytics to ensure that the parts being supplied to them for the assembly of their products are effective and efficient. Discrete manufacturing is more about the assembling of pieces and parts. The current home furniture manufacturing company mentioned in Chapter 1 of this book is an example of discrete manufacturing.

Manufacturing companies use analytics to improve the quality of their outputs (Thompson & Rogers, 2017, p. 111).

4.11.4 CRM Analytics

Customer relationship management analytics is behavioral analytics. Behavioral analytics examines the "whats" and "hows" of customer behavioral data to inform the "whys" of customer behavior (Brooks, 2022). The customer behavioral data can be based on a collection of customer page views, email sign-ups, surveys, and other actions, such as checkouts.

The departure of customers is called customer attrition, churn, or defection (Siegel, 2016, p. 166). The CRM analytics can be used to know "whys" of customer departure behavior. Predictive analytics can use predictive models and algorithms to monitor customer activity and behavior (Thompson & Rogers, 2017, pp. 124-27).

CRM analytics should prepare their customers and employees to use technology in new and unconventional ways because 30% of customer service reps will automate portions of their workflows and tasks by 2026 (James & Duncan, 2023). We will discuss CRM analytics in Chapter 10.

4.11.5 Security Analytics

Most companies suffer from fraud and theft (Thompson & Rogers, 2017, p. 115). Security analytics looks at various transactional and behavioral patterns to detect and stop fraud and loss to acquire security intelligence.

4.11.6 Analytics and Starbucks

Starbucks has used analytics to extend its new brand into the new market (Thompson & Rogers, 2017). By analyzing customer data and post of sale (POS) information using the analytics, the company has created a new line of grocery-store products to attract customers inside their homes.

4.11.7 General Electronics and Analytics

General Electronics has created its industrial data and analytics, Predix, which is directed at the customers in aviation, healthcare, energy, and transportation (Thompson & Rogers, 2017).

All of them are optimizing their operations and developing new innovative solutions by combining data with analytics.

4.12 LEVERAGE ANALYTICS FOR ORGANIZATIONS

Leverage analytics for organizations can be useful for any organizations and companies. The next steps are important (Thompson & Rogers, 2017; Sun & Stranieri, 2021).

1. Look at the problems strategically, tactically, and operationally.

2. At the operational level, analyze whether the problem is descriptive, diagnostic, predictive, or prescriptive, and address these problems using descriptive analytics, diagnostic analytics, predictive analytics, and prescriptive analytics.

3. Big data is useful with a great value. Please use the 10 bigs of big data and analyze which is most important. Maybe, having a variety of data can be valuable.

4. Most traditional analytical systems have the traditional method of analyzing data. Use the traditional method of analyzing data as much as possible.

5. Look at the crucial issue encountered in real-world problems and find if there are new systems, methods, and algorithms, as well as models, to address it and try to find new valuable insights to solve it.

4.13 THREE MAJOR TRENDS OF ANALYTICS

There are many organizations that report the major trends of analytics, for example, Gartner, IDC, and MaKinsey. Many articles and books also have similar predictions (Thompson & Rogers, 2017). This section will provide three major trends of analytics.

4.13.1 The Rise of Analytics Scientists

Organizations and companies have a shortage of analytics professionals or scientists with data modeling and analyticizing. They are also difficult to find and expensive to retain (Thompson & Rogers, 2017). Then, the rise of analytics scientists is still vital for the development of any organizations and companies.

4.13.2 Algorithms and Still Algorithms

Analytics relies heavily on models and algorithms to produce a wide range of outcomes (Thompson & Rogers, 2017). These models and algorithms are based on mathematics, statistics, and computing. These models and algorithms include data organization and storage, data analysis and mining, data and discovered knowledge's reporting. Each of those models and algorithms requires input data in a requisite format and sequence. A model and algorithm can create a trillion-level industry (like Google has done). Algorithms engineers have become an ever-important position of analytics and AI for organizations and companies.

4.13.3 From BI to Analytics

BI and business analytics should be subsumed into analytics to smooth the continuous development of data-driven decision-making by emphasizing the connection of analytics to generic knowledge and analytical techniques and reducing the use of business jargon (Holmstedt & Dahlin, 2021). This may be why analytics is sometimes used for business analytics (Davenport, December 2013). In fact, analytics is not only on data but also on DIKI (data, information, knowledge, and intelligence). Further, analytics is not only on business and management organizations and governments. Analytics is from mathematics and computing. DIKI analytics certainly will become an enabler for any individuals, organizations, and companies.

4.14 SUMMARY

We are in the age of analytics (Thompson & Rogers, 2017; Sun, 2019b; Henke & Bughin, 2016). Analytics is vital for ruling the world (Sun, 2022a). Analytics is a science and technology of using mathematics, AI, computer science, data science, and operations research to provide practical applications to business, management, research and development, and economic and societal problems. After discussing the evolution of analytics, analytics thinking, and the relationship among metrics, analysis, and analytics. This chapter classifies analytics based on perspectives on organization, discipline, business function, and process. One of them is that analytics can be classified into descriptive statistics, diagnostic statistics, predictive statistics, and predictive statistics based on cyclic business operations. This chapter explores DDPP computing, analytics, and analytics algorithms, and highlights that analytics engineering aims to use analytics science and analytics technology to create and manage analytics systems to provide analytics products and services with analytics intelligence. This chapter also analyses the leverage analytics for organizations. Finally, this chapter looks at the applications of analytics and presents three major trends of analytics.

Chapter 6 will demonstrate that data analytics is a science and technology about data analyticizing. Data analyticizing is a new complement to data modeling, data warehousing, and data mining. Data modeling, data warehousing, data mining, and data analyticizing are techniques of data engineering which can be used to develop and manage data systems.

4.15 REVIEW QUESTIONS AND PROBLEMS

1. What is the difference between data mining and data analytics?

2. How can we develop a spectrum of analytics?

3. How can we develop a calculus of intelligent analytics with corresponding technological components?

4. How can we create analytics algebra?

5. List 5 innovative algorithms in smart, effective, and seamless ways in the market.

6. List 5 technology-oriented topics for building the analytics platform or system.

7. What is the enterprise-wide analytics?

8. What is algorithm computing?

9. What are data-oriented insights? Who, when, and where will you use data-oriented insights?

10. What problems you encounter could be addressed by data analytics?

11. How can you develop meta strategies for your business?

4.16 REFERENCES FOR FURTHER STUDY

1. Wu J., Coggeshall S. Chapman & Hall, 2012. Foundations of predictive analytics, CRC, Boca Raton, FL.

2. Brian McBreen, John Silson, et al. 2022, Organizational Intelligence and Knowledge Analytics (Working Methods for Knowledge Management) Emerald Publishing Limited.

3. Mert Damlapinar, 2022, Agile Analytics For Startups: The Step-by-Step Guide for Building an Agile Startup with Data Analytics, Kindle Edition.

4. Philip M. Parker, 2022, The 2023–2028 World Outlook for Big Data and Data Engineering Services. ICON Group International, Inc.

5. Philip M. Parker, 2022, The 2023–2028 Outlook for Patent Analytics Services in China. ICON Group International, Inc.

CHAPTER 5

Intelligence

Intelligence is still a preferred benefit and requirement of human beings.

THIS CHAPTER WILL FOCUS on basic intelligence and explore intelligences. More specifically, it explores intelligence 1.0, intelligence 2.0, and meta, AI with six levels of intelligence. It examines multi-intelligence and intelligence of five senses and discusses artificial feet to artificial heads. It looks at system intelligence, hyperintelligence, data intelligence, knowledge intelligence, wisdom, and mind. This chapter provides a meta-approach to a hierarchy of data and intelligence, including meta (DIKIMW) and a meta-approach to intelligent systems. This research demonstrates that meta^4 (data) =meta (intelligence) = mind, Meta^5 (data) =meta (mind) = wisdom. After viewing intelligences in AI, this chapter explores wisdom and mind, from AI to artificial mind, cloud intelligence, and similarity intelligence. It provides an integrated framework of intelligence to a DIKIM. This chapter also examines the age of meta-intelligence and inspects the applications of AI.

Learning objectives of this chapter:

1. Define AI using two different perspectives.

2. Understand neurons in your head.

3. Understand intelligence of five senses and our bodies.

DOI: 10.1201/9781003450504-5

4. Analyze artificial feet to AI.

5. Understand system intelligence.

6. Define hyperintelligence.

7. Differ data intelligence from knowledge intelligence.

8. Understand intelligence, mind, and wisdom, with examples.

9. Analyze a hierarchy of data and intelligence from a meta viewpoint.

10. Define cloud intelligence.

11. Define similarity intelligence.

12. Understand unlearnability and its impacts on the society.

13. List three examples of AI applications.

5.1 INTRODUCTION

Intelligence is not only a lasting topic for computer science, AI, intelligence computing, BI, and intelligent analytics, but also an exciting topic for industries, organizations, and businesses (Sun, Sun, & Strang, 2018). AI has facilitated the development of intelligent services, intelligent manufacturing, intelligent systems (Russell & Norvig, 2020), intelligent chips, and intelligent analytics (Sun, 2019). BI has improved competitive business and marketing performance, supported management decision-making of organizations, and produced trillion-level enterprises, such as Google, Amazon, and Meta (Sabherwal & Becerra-Fernandez, 2011; Howarth, 2022). However, the current AI is very mixed and very market-driven. A lot of companies brand their products as AI products. Many social media brands do things as AI products and services. Even so, this chapter looks at the fundamentals of intelligence, including basic intelligence, and how can we calculate intelligence. Then it explores intelligence 1.0, intelligence 2.0, and meta, AI with six levels of intelligence. It examines multi-intelligence and intelligence of the five senses, and discusses artificial feet and artificial heads. This research provides a meta-approach to a hierarchy of data and intelligence, including meta (DIKI) and a meta-approach to intelligent systems. This research demonstrates that meta^4 (data) =meta (intelligence) = mind, Meta^5 (data) =meta (mind) = wisdom. After reviewing intelligences in AI, this chapter explores wisdom and mind, from AI to artificial mind, cloud intelligence, and similarity intelligence. It provides an integrated framework of intelligence to a DIKW Intelligence, DIKW is the abbreviated form of data, information, knowledge, and wisdom. This chapter also examines the age of meta-intelligence and applications of AI.

The remainder of this chapter is organized as follows. Section 5.2 looks at the fundamentals of intelligence. Section 5.3 explores intelligence of the five senses and our body. Section 5.4 examines artificial feet and artificial hard. Sections 5.5 and 5.6 examines intelligence 1.0 and 2.0. Section 5.7 discusses artificial intelligence. Section 5.8 explores wisdom and mind. Section 5.9 analyzes a hierarchy of data and intelligence based on a meta approach. Section 5.10 explores unlearnability. Section 5.11 inspects the applications of AI including machine learning, deep learning, and cloud intelligence. The final section ends this chapter with some concluding remarks and future work

5.2 FUNDAMENTALS OF INTELLIGENCE

5.2.1 Intelligent and Intelligence

The term "intelligent" has been popular, not only in academia but also in the wider community, due to a longtime, ongoing research and development of AI and intelligent systems (IS) since 1955 (Russell & Norvig, 2020). In academia, the term "intelligent" appears in the titles of a great number of books, book researches, sections, and international conferences, as well as other media or products. In the wider community, the term "intelligent" often appears in home appliances and consumer electronics, including televisions, cameras, vacuum cleaners, washing machines, and mobile phones, to name a few.

According to the Macmillan Dictionary (2007, p. 787), intelligence means "the ability to understand and think about things, and to gain and use knowledge". Similarly, the term intelligence has been defined in IS as "the ability to learn and understand, solve problems, and make decisions" (Negnevitsky, 2005, p. 18). The term intelligent means to be able to perceive, understand, think, learn, predict, and manipulate a system (Russell & Norvig, 2020). All these definitions of intelligence are mainly human intelligence, which has impacted the development of AI (Russell & Norvig, 2020). AI has been focusing on intelligence of machines or machine intelligence. In other words, AI is the science and engineering of making intelligent machines to imitate and augment human intelligence (Wang, 2012). However, a system may not be considered intelligent, even if it has these abilities associated with human intelligence, because the term intelligent implies some expectations from human beings or society. Practically, an intelligent system contains a set of functions that jointly make the system easy to use (Astrom & McAvoy, 1992), because "easy" is a term related to human intelligence. More generally, a system or a product is intelligent if and only if it contains a set of functions that jointly make the system either easier or faster and friendlier, more efficient and satisfactory to use than an existing cognate system, taking into account the time. Easier, faster, friendlier, or more efficient, or more satisfactory are all the expectations of humans and society for the performance of a system or product. For example, a high-speed train running in China is intelligent, because it is faster and friendlier than the existing ones; these are what the Chinese expect.

The above discussion leads to three perspectives on system intelligence, which consists of temporality, expectability, relativity, and connectivity of intelligence. See the later section.

5.2.2 Basic Intelligence

Intelligence is the ability of "learning, thinking, and understanding" (Oxford, 2008). These three abilities are the core of basic human intelligence. Machine learning, including deep learning, aims to automate the ability of human learning by "improving the performance on future tasks after making observations about the world" (Russell & Norvig, 2020) and then improve the ability of learning of humans, machines, and systems. One of the first digital machines is the perceptron, a US Navy-funded attempt at building a thinking and learning machine, led by Frank Rosenblatt (McAfee & Brynjolfsson, 2017, p. 72). The goal of the perceptron, which debuted in 1957, could classify things that it saw. However, persistence with perceptrons paid off because of the success of AlphaGo in 2016. AI has finally fulfilled at least some of its early promise. However, only learning, thinking, and understanding are not enough in modern society. Connecting and sharing should be other components of human intelligence.

Connecting is an intelligence of human beings; human beings need to connect in families, communities, in a country, and then in the world. Normally, a human connects others in the world to improve his knowledge, intelligence, and wisdom. This is why global vision will bring wisdom for individuals and organizations. In the current society, the connection between human beings is not enough. The connecting of human beings and machines becomes popular, that is, human-to-human (H2H) connecting, human-to-machine (H2M) connecting, and machine-to-machine

(M2M) connecting have become popular. Therefore, the connecting intelligence of human beings has been improved in these three forms: H2H, H2M, and M2M through the stream of data, information, knowledge, intelligence, and wisdom. Therefore, one's connecting intelligence depends on H2H connecting, H2M connecting, and M2M connecting. That is:

$$
\begin{aligned}
\text{Connecting intelligence} = &\ H2H \text{ connecting intelligence} \\
&+ H2M \text{ connecting intelligence} \\
&+ M2M \text{ connecting intelligence}
\end{aligned}
$$

$$(5.1)$$

Connecting is the infrastructure of sharing. Sharing is an intelligence of human beings. Human beings have a long history of sharing in the form of story-telling and speech-telling. Later, human beings have developed a history of sharing in the form of words, articles, books, signals, and then media. This is our civilization's evolution.

Recently, sharing has been conducted by human beings (H), machines, and systems (M), that is, H2H sharing, H2M sharing, and M2M sharing. In H2H sharing, we still share data, information, knowledge, experience, intelligence, and some wisdom with others through story-telling and book sharing. Who the sharing object is plays a critical role in deciding the future. One's future will be decided by a sharing. Question-answer-remark (or QAR) is a good method for sharing (also see Section 3.11). One uses QAR to share with others to optimize the sharing intelligence. Normally, we have a lot of people who do not share with others. Rejecting sharing is similar to rejecting learning (see Section 5.10). Both might affect one's career in the future.

In H2M sharing, we have to share data and information with machines and systems. We have to click passwords based on the requirements of our laptops and smartphones. We must provide a lot of important data and information required from machines and systems, although we do not tell this information to our loved one (because we do not trust them). If you reject sharing with machines and systems, your businesses cannot be processed. Crying becomes useless today. This is why we must love machines and systems. The first condition is that we must love rules.

In M2M sharing, as soon as you share data and information with machines and systems, the data and information will be shared with other machines and systems many times. Finally, you might receive some information from the machines and systems.

Therefore, one's sharing intelligence depends on H2H sharing, H2M sharing, and M2M sharing. That is,

$$\text{Sharing intelligence} = s_1 \times \text{H2H sharing intelligence} +$$
$$s_2 \times \text{H2M sharing intelligence} +$$
$$s_3 \times \text{M2M sharing intelligence.} \qquad (5.2)$$

Where s_1, s_2, and s_3 are coefficients of general sharing intelligence, maybe decided by decades. If we do not look at the coefficients, Equation (5.2) reflects the general performance of one's sharing intelligence. If one only shares data and information in H2H, one is weak at sharing in H2M and M2M. finally, one will become a loser in the digital age.

Advanced communication technologies and tools such as mail, telephone, email, social media, and sharing tools on the Web aim to develop the skill of connecting (communication) and sharing as intelligences. For example, the current advanced ICT technology and system (Laudon & Laudon, 2020) have brought about social networking services such as Facebook, LinkedIn, and WeChat. All these have developed the skill of connecting and sharing as intelligences (e.g., human intelligence). In what follows, we will use WeChat and TikTok to further analyze sharing intelligence. WeChat and TikTok are important social media or social networking services in the world.

Let p be a person, p is living in a friend cycle, p likes to share data, information, knowledge, video, audio, in his friend cycle. p's sharing intelligence is decided by p's friend cycle.

WeChat and TikTok's sharing intelligence are decided by the more powerful machines and systems such as WhatsApp and Facebook. Some believe that TikTok has the most powerful push ability or recommendation ability to attract customers to use their services. This means that TikTok sharing intelligence is powerful. This is why everybody loves TikTok. Some believe that if one rejects TikTok, then one will reject the digital age we are living in.

Therefore, intelligence consists of the intelligence of learning, thinking, understanding, connecting, and sharing. The first three are traditional intelligences: learning intelligence, thinking intelligence, and understanding intelligence. The latter is modern intelligence: connecting intelligence and sharing intelligence.

The state-of-the-art connecting intelligence and sharing intelligence have been summarized in Table 5.1 based on the search of Google Scholar (on April 20, 2024).

In Table 5.1, 450 and 7,460 are the searched results based on Google Scholar, respectively. Table 5.1 implies that

TABLE 5.1   Connecting Intelligence and Sharing Intelligence

intelligence	Google Scholar (m)
Connecting intelligence	450
Sharing intelligence	7,460

1. Connecting intelligence has drawn attention in academia, in particular, in computing. Sharing intelligence covers more general topics, such as sharing intelligence community, police, terrorism, agencies, law enforcement, threat, gathering, counter, failures, and multi-agency.

2. Compared with connecting intelligence, sharing intelligence has drawn more attention in academia. However, connecting is related to communication, so connecting has been a lasting topic for scholar's publication.

More generally, sharing intelligence should be extended into sharing computing because of the sharing economy based on natural association and deduction, that is,

$$
\begin{aligned}
\text{Sharing computing} = {} & \text{sharing science} + \text{sharing engineering} \\
& + \text{sharing technology} + \text{sharing systems} \\
& + \text{sharing services} + \text{sharing intelligence} \quad (5.3)
\end{aligned}
$$

As the engineering in computing (see Section 2.6) sharing engineering aims to use sharing science and sharing technology to create and manage sharing systems to provide sharing services with sharing intelligence. The popular examples for equation (5.3) and sharing engineering are TikTok, WeChat, Facebook, and WhatsApp.

5.2.3 How Can We Calculate Intelligence?

There are a few methods for calculating intelligence, for example, intelligence quotient (IQ). However, how to calculate AI and analytics intelligence is still a big issue.

In AI, we use neural networks to characterize our brains and then decide the learning from ML. In what follows, we first look at the neural networks of our brain. Then we still believe that we have not found a DNA-like physical element from our brain to characterize our intelligence. Even so, we have computerized systems to characterize system intelligence, machine intelligence, web intelligence, Internet intelligence, and cloud intelligence.

There are 10^9 neurons in our own head (Sharda, Delen, & Turba, 2018). Then from a system viewpoint, the connecting neurons (outputs and inputs) should be 2×10^9 neurons.

Furthermore, there will be 25.44 billion IoT devices by 2030 in the connected world (Howarth J., 2023), and then we have 5×10^{19} ($= 2 \times 10^9 \times 25.44$ billion) intelligences that reflect the quality of neurons in your head. This is the answer to what is the quality of neurons in your head? Therefore, the quality of neurons is important for us to study our head and brain from an intelligence viewpoint.

5.2.4 Multi-Intelligence

Gardner developed the theory of multiple intelligences, which consists of nine human intelligences of human beings (Howard, 1983). These nine human intelligences can be only considered as basic (atomic) human intelligences, although Prof. Gardner Howard has not defined what is intelligence.

Later thought concluded that multi-intelligence means that human beings have at least 10 intelligences (Howard, 1983; Howard, 1999): musical intelligence, visual-spatial intelligence, verbal-linguistic intelligence, logical-mathematical intelligence, bodily-kinesthetic intelligence/ physical intelligence, interpersonal intelligence, intrapersonal intelligence, naturalistic intelligence, spiritual (existential) intelligence, and pedagogical intelligence. Verbal-linguistic intelligence typically means being good at reading, writing, telling stories, and memorizing words. Logical-mathematical intelligence deals with logic, abstractions, reasoning, numbers, and critical thinking. Logical-mathematical intelligence also deals with introspective and self-reflective capacities. Physical intelligence is also known as bodily-kinesthetic intelligence. Bodily- kinesthetic intelligence is reflected in a person's movements and how they use their physical body. Interpersonal intelligence is characterized by individual sensitivity to others' moods, feelings, temperaments, motivations, and the ability to cooperate to work as part of a group; therefore, interpersonal intelligence is social intelligence.

There are more compound intelligences based on these basic intelligences. How many compound intelligences are there in the world? It is at least 2^{10} compound intelligences based on Boolean algebra.

The multi-intelligence theory leads to the following thinking.

1. Multi-intelligence has been reflected by AI and its development.

2. Many facets of a human cannot be characterized by one intelligence.

3. The multi-intelligence implies that human intelligence should be classified into multiple intelligences, 10 intelligences (Howard, 1999).

4. AI should be also characterized into multiple intelligences, that is, only AI is not enough, multiple intelligences can reflect the state of the art of AI.

5. Similarly, BI should also be characterized into multiple intelligences (see Chapter 10).

6. Digital intelligence is a kind of intelligence of human beings understanding and using ICT and digital machines, systems, apps, and tools. Digital intelligence should be a part of multiple intelligences for human beings.

5.2.5 How Many Intelligences Are Related to AI?

Now the questions: How many intelligences are related to AI?

From a system viewpoint, logical-mathematical intelligence has been realized by AI systems since the founding of AI in 1956, from expert systems to knowledge-based systems, from intelligent agents to current advanced intelligent systems (Russell & Norvig, 2020). This means that each of them creates a logical-mathematical intelligence that emulates, simulates, and augments the logical-mathematical intelligence of humans or super humans if using humanoids. If you calculate them as a m, then we have intelligences of 11 m × 80 billion humans for the existing worlds. At least, we can see there are many more artificial intelligences related to AI, that is, we must use artificial intelligences to replace the current AI.

Further, there are many more BIs related to BI, including financial intelligence, marketing intelligence, supply chain intelligence, HR intelligence, manufacturing intelligence, product intelligence, and more. Brooks listed at least 15 intelligences of BI. That is, we have intelligences of 15 × n humanoids for the existing worlds, where n = developed and planned developed machines, apps, and tools of BI, covering 15 intelligences. We must use business intelligences to replace the current BI.

In the next chapters, one can see artificial intelligences and BIs in this book.

5.3 INTELLIGENCE OF FIVE SENSES AND OUR BODY

We have five senses: see, hear, smell, taste, and feel (Krippendorff, 2019). We can speak, read, learn, think, write, and move. AI has imitated,

TABLE 5.2   Intelligence of Our Body

Human Body Parts and Functions	The State of Art AI for Human Body Parts and Functions	Remarks
Hear and listen	Speech recognition, speaker recognition, machine translation	Hearing intelligence
Smell	1. Artificial networks learn to smell like the brain. 2. How AI can detect and identify smell	1. MIT News 2. https://nttdata-solutions.com/ Smelling intelligence
Taste	Best Taste Intelligence Companies	https://www.cbinsights.com/esp/ consumer-&-retail/digital-engagement Tasting intelligence
Feel	As a part of emotional intelligence	Feeling intelligence
See	Image recognition, text recognition, license plate recognition	Seeing intelligence
Speak	Speech synthesis voice synthesis, dialogue between human and machine	Speaking intelligence
Read	Loudspeaker (reader), computer speaker (reader), mobile phone speaker (reader), radio and TV (reader)	Reading intelligence
Think	Human-computer chess, theorem proving, medical diagnosis	Thinking intelligence
Learn	Machine learning, knowledge representation	Learning intelligence
Write	ChatGPT, Natural language understanding	Writing intelligence
Move	Robots, EV car, driverless car, drone airplane, highspeed train,	Moving intelligence or Mobility intelligence

simulated, and augmented each of them, and generated five intelligences, seeing intelligence, hearing intelligence, smelling intelligence, tasting intelligence, and feeling intelligence (Tan, 2018). For example, there is a representation form of AI for these five intelligences, in particular, intelligences of our body, including speaking intelligence, reading intelligence, thinking intelligence, learning intelligence,, writing intelligence, and moving intelligence (Tan, 2018). All of them are listed in Table 5.2.

This implies that AI has impacted every part of our body and imitated, simulated, and augmented it. In fact, basic kills and intelligences of human beings have been mimicked, simulated, and augmented since 1956. AI first focused on human-centered intelligences, and then human-centered intelligence for her/his activities.

AI research aims to imitate, augment, extend, and surpass the intelligence of human beings. The form for showing intelligences of human beings is that it can see, listen, talk, read, move, think, learn, write, and speak, which humans can. All the intelligent systems like to say "I can too. I can do it much better than the human beings" (Tan, 2018). From a human viewpoint, AI has been promoted towards human-centered intelligence development since 1956.

AI can see, based on image recognition, literal or letter recognition, label (car) recognition.

AI can hear based on voice recognition, dialogue recognition, machine translation.

AI can speak based on voice synthesis, and dialogue between humans and machines.

AI can read Loudspeaker (reader), computer speaker (reader), mobile phone speaker (reader), radio and TV (reader).

AI can move based on driverless cars and drones.

AI can think based on games between humans and machines, theorem proving, and medical diagnosis.

AI can learn based on machine learning, and knowledge representation.

AI can write based on many handwriting methods, for example, we can use Word to write, we can use Grammarly to review what we have written and remove type-setting errors.

Recently, ChatGPT can help us to think, learn, and write towards the completeness of academic reports, papers, and theses. Some have used ChatGPT to write academic reports, theses, and books. However, there is a long way to go towards imagination and association-driven reports, papers, and theses.

This is why "only AI" is not enough. In fact, we need more intelligences to augment basic skills and intelligences of our feet.

5.4 ARTIFICIAL FEET AND ARTIFICIAL HEAD

AI is becoming a core business, governance, and analytic competency to transform business processes, reconfigure workforces, optimize infrastructure, blend industries, and bring about digital leadership, and 3D print digital leaders to lead the world in the near future (Laney & Jain, 2017). Artificial feet are used to represent the scientific inquiry into imitating, augmenting, and automating human feet and their functions throughout this research, different from the current usage of artificial feet for medical services. This section explores the age of AI, examines artificial feet, and looks at evolution from artificial feet to artificial brain. The research reveals that artificial feet are one of the origins of the industrial revolution and a real foundation of AI. The research demonstrates that AI will play a critical role in making artificial feet, artificial hand, artificial mouth, artificial eye, artificial ear, and artificial brain more intelligent.

5.4.1 Introduction

Intelligence in AI is not important, because human beings have discussed intelligence in the past 2000+ years. Artificial is new for human beings, thanks to the advanced technology. Therefore, the importance of AI comes from the artificial and its combination with intelligence in 1955 by John McCarthy (Russell & Norvig, 2020). Further, when we deeply think about AI, we might first ask

- What are artificial feet?

- What is the relationship between artificial feet and AI?

This section will address these three problems and have three key contributions. The first key contribution is to reveal that artificial feet are one of the origins of the Industrial Revolution. The second key contribution is the evolution of artificial feet provides a new way for current AI. The third key contribution is that artificial feet are the real foundation of AI.

The remainder of this paper is organized as follows: Subsection 5.4.2. explores the age of AI. Subsection 5.4.3 looks at artificial feet. Subsection 5.4.4 discusses the evolution from artificial hand to artificial brain based on the principle of "liberation from bottom to top and control from top to bottom of a human body". Subsection 5.5.5 discusses how to apply AI to artificial feet and brains. The final subsection ends this section with concluding remarks and future research work.

5.4.2 The Age of Artificial intelligence

The age of AI goes back to 1950 when Alan Turing published his seminal paper titled 'Computing Machinery and Intelligence' (Turing, 1950). AI was first coined by John McCarthy in 1955, defined as the "science and engineering of making intelligent machines" (Wang, 2012). It aims to imitate, extend, augment, and automate intelligent behaviors of human beings using computing machinery (Russell & Norvig, 2020; Sun & Wang, 2021). In the past seven decades, researchers and developers have been working on the intelligence of machines (Wang, 2012), neural networks, machine learning and translation (Laney & Jain, 2017), natural language processing, machine translation, expert systems, knowledge base systems, fuzzy logic and systems, genetic algorithms and so on under the flagship of AI (Russell & Norvig, 2020; Schalkoff, 2011).

The age of AI has officially arrived in 2013 (John, 2013). The significant success and global concern of market-driven AI are other reasons for the coming of the age of AI. Autonomous vehicles, advanced vision systems, virtual customer assistants, smart personal agents, and natural language processing, including ChatGPT, are all advanced technologies of market-driven AI (Laney & Jain, 2017; Sun, 2023, 2024). Google and Baidu driverless cars running on the road in the USA and China symbolize the significant progress of market-driven AI. Smartphones as intelligent products provide health analytics, weather, shopping, and travel services to wherever and whenever one is.

However, have you found an artificial leader who is leading a country? In fact, artificial leadership is the eventual goal of AI, robots, intelligent agents, digital workforces, and robotic process automation. Therefore, the biggest change for these research fields is how to create an artificial leader to win the national election in a state to become the national president. This creation requires first knowing artificial feet, because the journey of manufacturing artificial leaders begins with a single step of artificial feet, just as "a journey of a thousand miles begins with a single step of feet", a Chinese proverb said.

5.4.3 Artificial Feet

According to an English Dictionary, the foot is the lowest part of the leg, below the ankle, on which a person or an animal stands, walks, runs, and flies. In other words, the feet are the most important part of the human being as an animal. Without a foot a few hundred years ago, for example, 500 hundred years ago, one could only stay at home within a village. This is why someone wrote a poem at that time and dreamed that, "I hope to have a pair of wings to fly to where I like." Late, a Chinese writer Wu Chengen published the novel, "Journey to the West" (Xiyou ji) in the 16th century. (https://en.wikipedia.org/wiki/Journey_to_the_West, retrieved on 39 March 2014). The novel is a comic adventure story, a humorous satire of Chinese bureaucracy, a spring of spiritual insight, and an extended allegory in which the group of pilgrims journey toward enlightenment by the power and virtue of cooperation. For example, it describes that the Master Sun could fly tens of thousands of miles within seconds. Master Sun was the representation of light because light can travel about 300,000 km per second. This story implies that the human being had a dream to fly in the sky at least in the 16th century. In other words, human beings like to have artificial feet and legs or intelligent feet and legs to fly for at least 500 years.

Different from the current usage of artificial feet for medical services, artificial feet are used to represent the scientific inquiry into imitating, augmenting, and automating human feet and their functions hereafter. The main function of artificial feet is to move from one place to another. In what follows, we only discusses the development of artificial feet since the Industrial Revolution.

Bicycles were introduced in the late 19th century in Europe (Wikipedia-Bicycle, 2024) and are popular artificial feet for recreation and transportation.

The car was introduced in 1886 and became popular in the early 20th century. Now it is necessary artificial feet in modern society (Wikipedia-Car, 2024). It not only mimics, and automates but also augments the human feet successfully. Currently, a person can use his feet to walk 5 km per hour, whereas, s/he can drive the car on the highway with a speed of 120 km per hour. Therefore, cars dramatically increase the speed of human feet.

The train is another artificial foot invented in 1784. Now, it is an important transportation system (Wikipedia, 2024). If one goes to Shanghai from Beijing on foot, one needs to take a few months. But now, one takes a high-speed train, which takes 4 and a half hours to get there. Therefore, trains have mimicked, augmented, and automated human feet. From an AI viewpoint, trains are not only artificial feet but also intelligent feet, although no researchers consider trains in such a way. They intentionally leave space for AI to use intelligent transportation systems.

The airplane is an artificial foot. It not only mimics, augments, and automates the jump function but also the fly function of human feet. The airplane is the first step for realizing what Master Sun did in the mentioned Chinese novel.

The rocket is another artificial foot. It not only mimics, augments, and automates the jump function but also the fly function of human feet. It can jump and fly into outer space. For example, the astronauts took the rocket

TABLE 5.3   Various Kinds of Artificial Feet

Artificial Feet	Invention Time	Current Speed km/h	Remarks
Bicycle	1847	15.5	A transportation tool
Car	1886	120	Excellent artificial feet
Train	1784	350	It becomes an enjoyment tool
Airplane	1903	955	Learn from Master Sun
Rocket	1200's	7.9 km per second	Did like Master Sun
Light	N/A	299 792 458 m / s	Did as Master Sun
Digital signal	N/A	N/A	Faster artificial feet

as an artificial foot to visit the moon in the 1960s. The rocket played the same role as the feet of the astronauts so that they could fly from the Earth to the Moon and come back to the Earth. Therefore, the rocket has realized what Master Sun did in the mentioned Chinese novel.

Most generally, digital signals based on light are the most powerful artificial feet. A digital signal is a signal that is being used to represent data as a sequence of discrete values; at any given time it can only take on one of a finite number of values (Wikipedia-Digital signal, 2024). Have an imagination. We can go to the USA from China on our feet, then visit the Amazon company and buy a book on artificial feet. The CEO of Amazon tells us that it is not necessary to come here, please go home, and receive the digital book on your computer at your home in China. You say "Really?". This means that the digital signal of the Internet has replaced your feet and augmented the function of your feet: movement. The light signal transmission has completely realized what Master Sun did in the mentioned Chinese novel.

The various kinds of artificial feet have been listed in Table 5.3.

The above discussion leads to the following:

1. The mentioned artificial feet and their evolution are the results of the Industrial Revolution in the past four centuries.

2. If bicycles, cars, trains, airplanes, rockets, and light digital signals are artificial feet, then each of them is also intelligent feet based on the principle of AI.

3. If every artificial foot mentioned above is an intelligent foot, then research and development of artificial feet and intelligent feet are much earlier and wider in scope than AI.

4. The current advance of AI in driverless cars should have been the further step of artificial feet (Laney & Jain, 2017), although no people promote driverless cars to the market in such a way.

The above discussion raises a research problem: How can we change our research direction of AI based on the development of artificial feet? In other words, what lessons learned from the above intelligent feet can be used to further develop current market-oriented AI.

5.4.4 From Artificial Hand to Artificial Brain

This section looks at the evolution from artificial feet, via artificial hands, artificial mouths, artificial eyes, and artificial ears, to artificial brains since the Industrial Revolution. This evolution follows the principle of liberation from the bottom to the top of the human body, illustrated in Figure 5.1. Reversely, artificial development follows the principle of "control from top to bottom" of a human body. The evolution of the Industrial Revolution always focuses on the human-centered artificial development to liberate the human being from the feet to the brain, and then at the same time, to control the human being from the brain to the feet, not only artificial brain and feet but also physical brain and feet. AI, artificial mind, and artificial wisdom are only a further continuous development based on the updated principle: intelligent liberation from bottom to top, and intelligent control from top to bottom, as shown in Figure 5.1, which led the author to the journey of AI from nothing.

In what follows, we will delve into each of them using the method of the previous section.

5.4.4.1 Artificial Hands

Artificial hands refer to the scientific inquiry into imitating, augmenting, and automating the human hand and its functions hereafter.

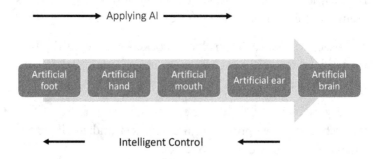

FIGURE 5.1 From artificial feet to artificial brain.

The main function of an artificial hand is to carry things from one place to another. Therefore, any transportation tool is a realization of "imitating, augmenting, and automating the human hand," because transport is to move humans, animals, and goods from one location to another using various tools. (Wikipedia-Transport, 2024). The modes of transport include air, land (rail and road), water, cable, pipeline, and space. The transportation tools for each mode include

Air: airplanes, rockets, drones, helicopters.

Land (rail and road): trains, trucks, buses, cars, and bicycles.

Water: watercraft, ships, and aircraft carriers.

Cable: electronic communication cable transmits the voice message, computer data, and visual images via electronic signals to telephones, wired radios, TV and cable TV, computing machines such as laptops, desktops, and smartphones.

Digital: Computers, mobile phones, smartphones, radio, and interactive TV.

Pipeline: Oil pipeline, and water pipeline.

Space: Spacecraft.

In fact, all the kinds of artificial feet mentioned in the previous section are also working together artificial hands to carry things from one place to another. All the mentioned artificial hands have improved the intelligence of human beings since the Industrial Revolution and liberated human hands from heavy carrying. Some of them, such as trains and ships, can carry thousands of millions pounds more than a human can. Therefore, they are not only artificial hands but also intelligent hands. However, nobody recognized the current high-speed train as an artificial hand and an achievement of AI. This is the tragedy of the history of AI. This also shows that the research and development of artificial hands and intelligent hands happened much earlier than that of AI. The former started in the early stage of the industrial revolution.

5.4.4.2 Artificial Mouths

Artificial mouth refers to the scientific inquiry into imitating, augmenting, and automating the human mouth and its functions.

The main function of an artificial mouth is to speak to others as far as possible and get what one has said understood as much as possible.

The artificial mouth includes a loudspeaker, which converts an electrical audio signal into a corresponding sound (Wikipedia-speaker, 2024). Another is a computer speaker. The smartphone has a special speaker installed. Therefore, we can consider the smartphone speaker as an artificial mouth.

The loudspeaker can augment the function of the human mouth significantly. The computer speaker, mobile phone speaker, radio, and TV enable everyone in one corner of the world speak to others in another corner of the world. The author can use a smartphone in Australia to chat with his family members in China and the USA. These artificial mouths ignore the limitations of distance and time. Therefore, we can consider loudspeakers, computer speakers, and mobile phone speakers as an intelligent mouth. AI has helped artificial speakers with the intelligent technique of natural language understanding (Russell & Norvig, 2020).

5.4.4.3 Artificial Ears

Artificial ear refers to the scientific inquiry into imitating, augmenting, and automating the human ear and its functions hereafter. The main function of an artificial ear is to listen to what others speak as far as possible. The artificial ear is a telephone and microphone. Both are a transducer that converts sound into an electrical signal. Voice recorders are also artificial ears. One can listen to the voice from TV sets, radios, and other digital devices. The voice might have been recorded many decades ago from any corner of the world. Therefore, artificial ears are really intelligent ears in the digital world.

5.4.4.4 Artificial Eyes

Artificial eye refers to the scientific inquiry into imitating, augmenting, and automating the human eye and its functions hereafter. The main function of the artificial eye is to see things clearly as far as possible.

Cameras, camera recorders, and CCTV systems are all artificial eyes. Now, one can see what happens anywhere and at any time through TV, smartphones, and computers. Therefore, TVs, smartphones, and computers are also artificial eyes. Artificial eyes are really intelligent eyes.

5.4.4.5 Artificial Brains

Artificial brain refers to the scientific inquiry into imitating, augmenting, and automating the human brain and its functions hereafter. The main

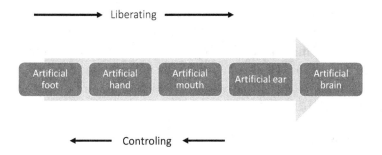

FIGURE 5.2   An intelligent model for artificial feet to artificial brain.

function of an artificial brain is to control all the parts, in general, and feet, hands, mouths, eyes, and ears and their functions of the human body as a human.

The digital computer was named the electronic brain. It is an artificial brain. Now computers, laptops, and smartphones are all the artificial brains for augmenting the human brain.

5.4.5 Applying AI to Artificial Feet and Artificial Brain

The previous sections have discussed artificial feet, artificial hands, artificial mouths, artificial eyes, artificial ears, artificial brains, with examples. In fact, we can find that smartphones are not only artificial feet, but also artificial mouths, artificial eyes, artificial ears and artificial brains. This is the reason why a smartphone has become an organic part of our brain, work, and life.

Furthermore, we find that two issues arise from the above discussion.

How to make the existing artificial feet, artificial hands, artificial mouths, artificial eyes, artificial ears, and artificial brains more intelligent is a topic for the current AI research and development, as illustrated in Figure 5.2. For example, the remarkable progress of driverless car is really a part of making artificial feet more intelligent (Henke & Bughin, 2016) (Laney & Jain, 2017). Market-oriented AI will play a critical role in making artificial feet, artificial hands, artificial mouths, artificial eyes, artificial ears, and artificial brains more intelligent. The evolution of artificial feet, artificial hands, artificial mouths, artificial eyes, artificial ears, and artificial brains has dominated the core of the Industrial Revolution. Market-oriented AI will usher in the coming of an intelligent society by applying AI to make artificial feet, artificial hands, artificial mouths, artificial eyes, artificial ears, and artificial brains more intelligent.

Another topic for the current AI research and development is how to get heuristics from the evolution of the mentioned artificial feet, artificial hands, artificial mouths, artificial eyes, artificial ears, and artificial brains, so as to develop artificial mind and artificial wisdom to create 3A: AI, artificial mind, and artificial wisdom, which underpin a trinity for the intelligent society.

5.4.6 Summary

Artificial feet, hands, mouths, eyes, ears, and brains have been developed as medical devices to aid a patient in replacing a natural foot, mouth, eye, ear, and brain. However, few researchers provide a wider vision of artificial feet, hands, mouths, eyes, ears, and brains. Few consider a train to look like feet. This myopia limits our vision concerning artificial feet, hand, mouth, eye, ear, and brain and their significant impacts on the history of the modern Industrial Revolution. This section presents a novel perspective on human-centered social development, starting with artificial feet. This section explores the age of AI and artificial feet, hands, mouths, eyes, ears, and brains. It also discusses applying AI to artificial feet and artificial brains. The research reveals that artificial feet are one of the origins of the Industrial Revolution and a real foundation of AI. The research demonstrates that AI will optimize artificial feet, hands, mouths, eyes, ears, and brains in the digital age.

In future work, we will examine the evolution from artificial feet, via artificial hands, mouths, eyes, ears, to artificial brains, taking into account the history of the Industrial Revolution, and look at how to apply AI to make artificial feet, hands, mouths, eyes, ears, and brains more intelligent from a system perspective.

5.5 SYSTEM INTELLIGENCE

The existing systems lead to a new question: how can we calculate system intelligence? This research explores temporality, expectability, relativity, and connectivity of intelligence as four system intelligences (Sun, Sun, & Strang, 2018).

5.5.1 Temporality of Intelligence

There are two meanings for temporal intelligence. 1. Temporal intelligence is the ability to adapt to change. This has motivated development of temporal logic and evolutionary computing, including genetic algorithms (Russell & Norvig, 2020). 2. Temporality of intelligence means that intelligence is related or limited to a time interval [35]. For example, at the time of writing this section, few people consider floppy disks as intelligent storage devices. However, a few decades ago, floppy disks were considered intelligent in comparison to paper tape for data storage. Only two decades ago, the author bought a Nokia mobile phone for communicating with others. However, later he bought Huawei smartphones, Apple phones, and now Huawei Mate 60 Pro in order to get smarter and smarter at communicating via social networking services and connecting to the cloud computing and IoT.

In what follows, we limit ourselves to the meaning of item 2.

5.5.2 Expectability of Intelligence

Intelligence can be referred to as a substitution for easier, or faster, smarter or friendlier, or more efficient, or more satisfactory. This is expectability of intelligence. We denote them using the degree of satisfaction. All these related concepts are a set of expectations of humans, as parts of human intelligence. Some aim to become billionaires. Some would like to become the president of a country to provide services to the people of the county. Others aim to become a CEO of a top company in the world. Different people have really different expectations. We denote these expectations for a system or product P, as $E_P = \{e_i \mid e_i$ is an expected performance for function$_i$ of a product$\}$ $= \{ei \mid i \in \{1,2,\ldots,n-1,n\}$, where n is a given integer. For every $i \in \{1,2,\ldots,n-1,n\}$, there is a perceived performance of the customer for function$_i$, p_i, then a product P is intelligent if and only if there exists at least one $i \in \{1,2,\ldots,n-1,n\}$ such that (Sun, Sun, & Strang, 2018)

$$s_i = \frac{p_i}{e_i} \geq 0 \tag{5.4}$$

where s_i is the satisfaction degree of the customer to the ith function of system P.

For example, a Huawei Mate 60 pro smartphone, cost CN¥ 6,599 ($923.99) as a Launch price in August 2023, with BDS satellite calling and message and 5 G telecommunication is smarter. "smarter" is what the customer perceived, $p_1 = 1.5$, while "smart" is an expected performance, $e_1 = 1$, for Huawei Mate 60 pro from a customer, based on Equation (5.4), we have the satisfaction degree of the customer $s_i = 1.5 > 0$. Then a Huawei Mate 60 pro smartphone is intelligent.

Intelligence is the future of humans. Some expect a smarter smartphone because the existing smartphone is out of date. Some expect a smarter car because the existing car is out of date. Some expect a smarter house because the existing house is out of date. All of these are smarter. Pursuing all these is the basic intelligence of human beings and the motives of society and the world.

5.5.3 Relativity of Intelligence

If one lives in the data world, one will find information = metadata (i.e., meta (data)) is a result of meta-intelligence. However, if one lives in the information world, one cannot have such knowledge. Furthermore, if one lives in the information world, one will find knowledge = meta(information) (i.e., meta (information)) is a result of meta-intelligence. However, if one lives in the knowledge world, one cannot have such a vision. Therefore, one has relativity of intelligence and relativity of meta-intelligence. This also means that meta is relative.

Generally speaking, let X and Y be two systems. X is intelligent if X is better than Y with respect to E, where E is a set of human expectations. "Better" is a relativity concept. For example, a new microwave is intelligent because it displays the temperature when microwaving food. A user believes that displaying the temperature is better than not displaying it. This example reflects the relativity of intelligence. Displaying temperature belongs to the set of expectations E. The set of human expectations can be considered as a set of demands. The expectation of human beings and society promotes intelligence and social development. Therefore, it is significant to define the intelligence of Systems with respect to the set of human expectations or demands.

In summary, system intelligence can be measured through three dimensions: temporality, expectability, relativity, and connectivity. In other words, there are four characteristics of system intelligence: temporality, expectability, relativity, and connectivity. The degree of intelligence of a system or product or service can be measured using these dimensions, that is:

$$\text{Degree of system intelligence} = \text{temporality} + \text{expectability} \\ + \text{relativity} + \text{connectivity} \quad (5.5)$$

In Section 5.2, we mentioned connecting is a component of human intelligence. In fact, our examples there also imply that connecting is an intelligence of machines and systems. Therefore, temporality, expectability, relativity, and connectivity of system intelligence can be considered as fundamental for all the systems mentioned in this book. They are also important for the understanding of BI, including organization intelligence, enterprise intelligence, marketing intelligence, big data intelligence, analytics intelligence, and data analytics intelligence (Brooks, 2022) and its systems. We will explore them in the next chapters.

5.6 INTELLIGENCE 1.0 AND 2.0

This section looks at intelligence 1.0 and 2.0.

5.6.1 Intelligence 1.0

Early AI focuses on the simulation and automation of human intelligence 1.0. That is, the ability to "learn, think, understand, and connect." For example, learning in AI is data learning, machine learning in AI is a kind of data learning.

Machine learning is about how to predict from data using knowledge, rules, and patterns (Siegel, 2016, p. 15). Machine learning (ML), introduced by IBM in 1958 (Hurley, 2019), aims to automate the ability to learn and to discover patterns hidden in the data (Hurley, 2019; Russell & Norvig, 2020). Deep learning improves the automation of the ability to learn using neuro networks. Natural language processing automates the ability to understand the natural language. ChatGPT is the latest product of deep learning and natural language processing.

5.6.2 Intelligence 2.0

Intelligence 2.0 is an augmented intelligence from human intelligence. Intelligence 2 is a kind of intelligence towards knowledge creation or creative intelligence. All of them have been used in teaching and research. Meta (intelligence) belongs to intelligence 2.0. Intelligence 2.0 at least consists of curiosity, association, imagination, and originality. In other words, intelligence 2.0 is advanced. The best examples of intelligence 2.0 include BI, emotional intelligence (EI), marketing intelligence (MI), service intelligence (SI), analytics intelligence, organizational intelligence (OI), and so on. Collaboration, cooperation, and coordination as collective intelligence belongs to intelligence 2.0. System intelligence, platform intelligence, and intelligence of machines are also intelligence 2.0. Finally, intelligence 2.0 is an integrated intelligence.

Currently, AI also focuses on intelligence 2.0, for example, IoE intelligence, collective intelligence, system intelligence, platform intelligence, and integrated intelligence.

In fact, like knowledge has six different hierarchies, intelligence should be classified into 6 different levels, intelligence 1.0, intelligence 2.0, intelligence 3.0, intelligence 4.0, intelligence 5.0, and intelligence 6.0. Then we use meta as an operation such that meta (intelligence 1.0) = intelligence 2.0, meta (intelligence 2.0) = intelligence 3.0, meta (intelligence 3.0) = intelligence 4.0, meta (intelligence 4.0) = intelligence 5.0, meta (intelligence 5.0) = intelligence 6.0, we leave them as future work. Therefore, we only look at intelligence 1.0 and intelligence 2.0 hereafter.

5.6.3 Hyperintelligence

Hyperintelligence is important in the digital age. We have hypertext, implies that hyper knowledge is meaningful. Then hyperintelligence is motivated from hypertext, hypertext drives hyperconnecting. Hyperconnecting is the key for developing Hyperintelligence.

MicroStrategy has hyperintelligence capability, which embeds insights, suggestions, and actions directly into enterprise applications. Hyperintelligence is a kind of Tableau's expectation to offer wisdom analytics (Richardson, Schlegel, Sallam, Kronz, & Sun, 2021).

Based on the above analysis, hyperintelligence should be a part of intelligence 2.0 to 6.0. we will examine it as future work.

5.7 ARTIFICIAL INTELLIGENCE

This section views AI and explores machine learning, and AIs for next-generation intelligences.

5.7.1 Introduction

Alain Turing published his seminal paper in 1950 (Turing, 1950). John McCarthy, a math professor at Dartmouth defined AI as the "science and engineering of making intelligent machines", in 1955 (McAfee & Brynjolfsson, 2017, p. 67). His definition can be updated as "science, engineering, and technology of making and managing intelligent machines and systems." From that time on, AI has become one of the most important forces affecting our human beings, machines, and systems. AI is one of the most rapidly developing fields in the last decade. Now, we are immersed in the age of AI. AI directly focuses on intelligence and wisdom. However, since the later 1950s, AI researchers have found that knowledge-driven intelligence is important because of expert systems' development. In the past decade, data intelligence has become more important because of machine learning's resurgence and deep learning development.

Briefly, AI is a subfield of computer science and data science, concerned with symbolic reasoning and problem-solving (Sharda, Delen, & Turba, 2018). Technically, AI is concerned with imitating, extending, augmenting, amplifying, and automating the intelligent behaviors of human beings (Russell & Norvig, 2020). AI attempts not only to understand how humans think, understand, write, learn, and act rationally and smartly, but also to build intelligent entities that can think, write, perceive, understand, predict, and manipulate a world.

Jenkins, et al., state that "the history of AI has included several "waves" of ideas" (Jenkins, Lopresti, & Mitchell, 2020). The first wave, from the 1950s to the 1980s, focused on logic and symbolic hand-encoded representations of knowledge, the foundations of so-called "expert systems." The second wave, starting in the 1990s, focused on statistics and machine learning, in which, instead of hand-programming rules for behavior, programmers constructed "statistical learning algorithms" that could be trained on large datasets. In the wave of the last decade, AI research has largely focused on deep learning. AI has seen a resurgence recently, mainly because of the increasing computing power and algorithms becoming increasingly refined (Mueller, 2016). Other reasons include data-driven and market-oriented AI becoming popular products around us; AI on social media has blossomed in these communities (Chowdhary, 2020). The current wave is that AI has been ubiquitous in the market. Market-driven AI is aimed at machines, systems, apps, and tools. Most people have been immersed in AI.

5.7.2 ML ≠ AI

Machine learning (ML) is one of the most popular techniques used for the analysis of big data (Strang & Sun, 2022; Ghavami, 2020, p. 25). ML is concerned about how computers can adapt to new circumstances, and detect and extrapolate patterns. The essence of ML is that it is an automatic process of pattern recognition by a learning machine. Machine learning mainly aims to build systems that can perform at or exceed human-level competence in handling several complex tasks or problems. Decision trees, including tree pruning and tree induction are a part of ML (Weber, 2020, p. 26). Case-based reasoning is also a part of ML (Laudon & Laudon, 2020)

Deep learning is a class of ML methods (Weber, 2020, p. 26). Classifications are a form of supervised ML (Weber, 2020, p. 25). Associations are also a form of unsupervised ML (Weber, 2020, p. 26).

The relations among deep learning, machine learning, and AI are mathematically represented as follows: deep learning ⊏ machine learning ⊏ AI (Strang & Sun, 2022). In other words, deep learning is a subset of machine learning, and machine learning is a subset of AI.

5.7.3 Intelligences

Why is intelligence a singular word in the world? It is not right. For all of neuroscience's advances, we've made little progress on its biggest question: How do simple cells in the brain create intelligence? Hawkins and his team discovered that the brain uses map-like structures to build a model of the world - not just one model, but hundreds of thousands of models of everything we know. This discovery allows Hawkins to answer important questions about how we perceive the world, why we have a sense of self and the origin of high-level thought. A thousand brains herald a revolution in the understanding of intelligence. We have multi-intelligence. Therefore, we should have many intelligences, in such a way, we can develop intelligences from a thousand brains (Hawkins, 2021). In fact, this book also uses artificial intelligences to replace the recent AI, we cannot use a singular intelligence to cover all the intelligences of human beings, machines, and systems (Howard, 1999). Therefore, this book has used intelligence and intelligences.

5.7.4 Next AI

Robustness and trustworthiness are the basic characteristics of the next generation of AI systems, which will be robust, explainable, fast, mostly accurate, and adaptable to new circumstances (Jenkins, Lopresti, & Mitchell, 2020). The Next Wave of AI includes:

1. This new wave will coalesce the speed and recall power of today's data-driven AI with the robustness and explainability of traditional symbolic, logic-based AI, along with new ideas related to human commonsense reasoning, analogy-making, conceptual abstraction, and developmental learning.

2. Integrating existing knowledge with machine learning.

3. Going beyond supervised learning, that is, "self-supervised learning," "reinforcement learning," and "active learning."

4. Integrating probabilistic and causal Models with deep learning.

5. Incentivizing Ethical AI.

6. Policies for accountability and liability.

7. Special AI has made breakthroughs: robots, ML, translation, and generative AI, including ChatGPT.

8. Statistical learning is the theoretical foundation of AI applications. For example, deep learning and reinforcement learning are the basis for ChatGPT.

9. Industrial AI or market-oriented AI: intelligent technology, intelligence + x, and AI chips.

10. Wisdom is still more important than intelligence.

However, intelligence is still a dream; we are still pursuing intelligences to make things more reasonable and optimistic. In fact, how to reduce the items from our tasks is still a vital job of human beings, machines, and systems. This is more important for human wisdom, see the later section.

5.8 WISDOM AND MIND

This section looks at wisdom and mind.

5.8.1 Introduction

The greatness of human wisdom lies in the ability to summarize the connotation of the essence of the observed object only from a small amount of data (Da, 2023). This is the creativity of human wisdom. In the process of human evolution, it is not good for the survival and development of human beings to spend a lot of time on large-scale sampling to learn, just like what machine learning is doing. Human beings must acquire knowledge as quickly as possible in the shortest time and make decisions quickly, even if it is wrong knowledge or decision-making. Therefore, the ability of human beings is to "guess." That is, the brain quickly associates different things. Even if the association is proved to be wrong afterward, the ability to correct it later has been developed unprecedentedly and finally formed the great infinite creativity of human beings. This is the pinnacle of wisdom. AI has only touched the tip of the iceberg of human wisdom, and there is still a long way to go for us. Looking at the essence through the phenomenon of things is also a feature of human wisdom. Another human wisdom is how to relinquish the most important things that others are enjoying. This is why we introduce Meta (intelligence) = wisdom.

DeepMind is a software of machine learning, which has been particularly effective in combining deep learning with reinforcement learning (McAfee & Brynjolfsson, 2017, p. 77). In other words, a hundred intelligences can produce a wisdom. Similarly, we know a lot of birds can fly, then we infer that all the birds are flying although a few birds cannot fly. This solution is the wisdom of human beings in history (Sun & Wang, 2021).

5.8.2 Wisdom

Wisdom is defined as "the ability to make sensible decisions and give good advice because of experience and knowledge that you have" (Oxford, 2008). Wisdom can be defined as the ability to increase effectiveness through processing experience, knowledge, information, and data, all together (Ackoff, 1992). Wisdom adds value through appropriate judgments and creative ideas (Rowley, 2007). For example, the key idea in PageRank of Google is a wisdom. The business model of Uber is also a business wisdom. Wisdom usually consists of revolutionary ideas that can bring big decisions and value for an organization. A question for wisdom is as follows. Why has only Peter pointed out such a wisdom in our big organization? Therefore, wisdom is closest to innovation, creativity, and ingenuity, comparing with experience, knowledge, information, and data, although the latter can be used for producing wisdom.

5.8.3 From Data to Wisdom

Some friends told me that if you are young, intelligence is important; if you are an elder, wisdom is important; this implies that intelligence and wisdom are different. Therefore, now we have big data industry with big data trade. In the near future, we will have big information industry, big knowledge industry, big intelligence industry, and big wisdom industry. All those can provide wisdom from mining data, knowledge, and intelligence.

5.8.4 From Data to Mind

Data, information, knowledge, intelligence, wisdom, and mind are six elements and resources of computer science, AI (Russell & Norvig, 2020) and data science (Sharda, Delen, & Turba, 2018). The first three, data, information, knowledge can be considered as resources in the real world, while the last three are usually in the mental world of human beings. Therefore, we can consider data, information, and knowledge as raw resources of computer science, AI, and data science. We consider intelligence, wisdom, and mind as artificial resources. The raw resources are similar to raw oil, whereas the artificial resources can be considered as processed resources by human beings or computing machinery.

5.8.5 Summary

This section looks at wisdom and mind and distinguishes wisdom and mind from data. In the past, the scientific and technological revolution was basically driven by knowledge. The future trend is not only driven by knowledge but also driven by wisdom and data (Ma, 2016). In fact, AI has also followed this trace. AI was knowledge-based intelligence, where the trend is that AI is wisdom-based AI, and data-based AI, not only knowledge-based AI.

5.9 A HIERARCHY OF DATA AND INTELLIGENCE: A META-APPROACH

This section proposes a novel meta-approach, using it to look into the hierarchy of data, intelligence, and wisdom.

5.9.1 Introduction

Data, intelligence, and meta have become a future-oriented frontier for academia and industry (Sun, 2022c). Meta is replacing Facebook means that the latter company has selected meta as an intelligent brand to face the challenges and opportunities of social commerce, big data, and AI. However, many fundamental issues for them and their integration are still in an unknown stage. Meta-intelligence is an emerging area for data science, big data, and AI. The challenge is that most searched research publications lack the theoretical analysis and formalization of the hierarchy of data. For example,

1. What is the hierarchy of data and intelligence from a meta-perspective?

2. What are the impacts of the research on meta-analytics, meta-intelligence, and metaverse?

This section will address these issues by proposing, then using, a novel meta-approach to look into the hierarchy of data and intelligence. More specifically, this section looks at meta as an intelligent system. This research also examines information systems, knowledge systems, and intelligent systems as meta systems.

FIGURE 5.3   A pyramid model of DIKIMW.

5.9.2 Meta (Intelligence) = Wisdom

Meta has significance when it, as an operation, transforms an object on the x level to another object on the x +1 level. This is motivated by the above discussion, because data, information, knowledge, intelligence, mind, and wisdom form a reverse pyramid, as illustrated in Figure 5.3. This can also be considered as the DIKIMW pyramid (Sun & Huo, 2020).

Overall, this section looks at DIKIMW. It then examines data, information, knowledge, intelligence, mind, and wisdom that have played a significant role in computer science and AI. It argues that data should incorporate information, knowledge, and intelligence to serve science, engineering, technology, systems, management, and the world (Russell & Norvig, 2020; Brooks, 2022).

Meta is an approach, a research approach. This approach includes many multi-disciplinary methods to realize the more comprehensive and transcending goal when exploring a research issue. The multi-disciplinary method aims to realize a more comprehensive goal, not only the transcending goal. The essence of meta as an approach is also to realize from level x to level x+1, which is a kind of transcending from level x to level x +1. For example, in database systems, metadata is at a higher level than the data level because metadata is data about data (Coronel, Morris, & Rob, 2020). Meta as an operation can realize the hierarchy of data as follows (Sun, 2024):

1. Meta (data) = information.

2. Meta^2 (data) = meta (information) = knowledge.

3. Meta^3 (data) = meta^2 (information) = meta (knowledge) = intelligence.

In such a way, meta forms a series of operations, including power operations. These operations can be analyzed in a setting of mathematics and algebra, as discussed in an earlier chapter. From an AI perspective, the hierarchy of data consists of four levels: The first level is data, the second level is information, the third level is knowledge, and the fourth level is intelligence. we can consider meta as a transformation, although meta is a special transformation with hierarchical characteristics.

We are in the age of meta, which has become a new frontier for competing for meta-intelligence in the digital world. This section explores the hierarchy of data and intelligence based on the metal approach and looks at meta-analytics, meta-intelligence, and metaverse.

Meta-analytics and metaverse aim to discover meta-intelligence through competing for meta-intelligence in the digital world.

However, as we know in data science or database systems (Coronel, Morris, & Rob, 2020), metadata is data about data. Based on the idea behind it, meta-intelligence can be defined as intelligence about intelligence. Therefore, from a hierarchical viewpoint, intelligence is at level x, then meta-intelligence is at level $x + 1$, a higher level. In such a way, meta-intelligence is not a kind of knowledge, but it is a kind of wisdom, a higher-level intelligence. Briefly, meta-intelligence can be considered as intelligence about intelligence, that is,

$$\text{Meta} - \text{intelligence} = \text{intelligence about intelligences} \qquad (5.6)$$

Therefore, the hierarchy of intelligence consists of three levels. the first level is intelligence. The second level is mind, and the third level is wisdom. In other words, mind and wisdom are meta-intelligence (Sun, 2021).

The interrelationships between mind, intelligence, and wisdom are that (Sun & Wang, 2021).

$$\text{mind} = \text{meta}(\text{intelligence}), \text{and wisdom} = \text{meta}(\text{mind}).$$
$$\text{Then wisdom} = \text{meta}^2(\text{intelligence}).$$

In summary, the hierarchy of data consists of six levels. the fifth level is mind, and the sixth level is wisdom.

$$\text{meta}^4(\text{data}) = \text{meta}(\text{intelligence}) = \text{mind}, \text{Meta}^5(\text{data})$$
$$= \text{meta}(\text{mind}) = \text{wisdom}.$$

These have been used to transform data into intelligence and wisdom (Sun & Finnie, 2003). For example,

1. Extract and transform of ETL correspond to meta operations. Or they are the realization of meta as an operation and technique.

2. Data mining is a meta^2 technique.

3. Machine learning is a meta^3 technique.

5.9.3 A Meta Approach to Intelligent Systems

This section will look at information systems, knowledge systems, intelligent systems, and analytics systems from a meta-perspective.

Frist of all, information systems, knowledge systems, intelligent systems, and analytics systems are meta-mathematical systems, because each of them is the practical use of a mathematical approach (Thompson & Rogers, 2017, p. 24). The mathematical approach includes models, formulas, rule laws, equations, algorithms, mathematical methods, and so on. This extends the original thought of metamathematics (Kleene, 1952) to the application of metamathematics to computer science, data science, and AI. They cover all these mentioned systems. Therefore, computing as a super-discipline, including computer science, data science, and AI, can be considered as a further development of metamathematics with applications.

Generally speaking, knowledge systems and expert systems, including rule-based systems, are the practical realizations of mathematical logic, including propositional logic, predicate logic, and algebraic systems (Sun, 2023). Intelligent systems, including rule-based systems, are practical realization of common-sense reasoning, default logic, and monotonic logic. This is why logic and fuzzy logic are the foundations of AI.

Furthermore, meta can be considered as transformation with two variables, that is.

Meta (x, y). x can be a world, where y is multiple worlds, as illustrated in Figure 5.4.

For example, meta (x, y), where is y = data, we have meta (x, data) = information, and then we have information world, based on the above discussion. Now we use this meta approach to give a discovery for computing, strategically:

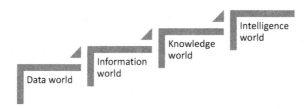

FIGURE 5.4   A meta world for DIKI.

1. Data management and database systems are only in the data world
(Coronel, Morris, & Rob, 2020). Thus, it is not related to meta-
operation. However, information systems aim to transform data into
information (Laudon & Laudon, 2020). Therefore, it is transiting
from the data world to the information world. Therefore, an information system is a meta system. This evinces that information systems include a set of meta operations that transform data into
information. SAP R/3 is an example of information systems.

2. Information management is only in the information world. Knowledge
management is only in the knowledge world Therefore, information
management and Knowledge management not related to meta-
operation. However, knowledge systems aim to transform data and
information into knowledge. Thus, they are transiting from data
worlds and information worlds into a knowledge world. Therefore, a
knowledge system is a meta system. This further demonstrates that
knowledge systems include a set of meta operations that transform
data and information into knowledge. HR knowledge management
systems are examples of knowledge management. MYCIN is an
expert system, which is a knowledge system.

3. Intelligence management is only in the intelligence world. Thus, it is
not related to meta-operation. However, intelligence systems aim to
transform data, information, and knowledge into intelligence (Sun,
2024). They are transiting from the data world, information world,
and knowledge world into the intelligence world. Therefore, an intelligence system is a meta system. This also demonstrates that intelligence systems include a set of meta operations that transform data,
information, and knowledge into intelligence.

An analytics system is a rule-based system and, then, an intelligence system (Thompson & Rogers, 2017, p. 24). MYCIN as an analytics system is

an intelligence system. An analytics system is also a practical realization of mathematic logic.

Finally, metaverse refers to the all the above-mentioned and their corresponding systems in the digital world.

5.9.4 Summary

This section provides a meta-Approach to a hierarchy of data and intelligence including meta (DIKI) and a meta-approach to intelligent systems. This research demonstrates that meta^4 (data) =meta (intelligence) = mind, Meta^5 (data) =meta (mind) = wisdom. This section also demonstrates that 1. Meta-analytics and metaverse aim to discover meta-intelligence from competing in the digital world. 2. the hierarchy of data and intelligence based on the meta-approach is a fundamental solution for meta-analytics, meta-intelligence, and metaverse. The unified framework for information systems, knowledge systems, and intelligent systems as meta systems is presented in this section. The research demonstrates that data management, information management, knowledge management, and intelligence management are in the corresponding worlds: data world, information world, knowledge world, and intelligence world respectively. However, metasystems include an information system, a knowledge system, and an intelligence system; each of them will at least include one Meta operation from one world to a higher world. Meta operations are necessary for these transformations and transitions. The proposed approach in this section might facilitate research and development of meta-analytics, meta-intelligence and metaverse, artificial intelligence, and data science.

In future work, we will delve into meta-analytics and meta-intelligence from a data-driven intelligence.

5.10 UNLEARNABILITY

What is unlearnable? How to define unlearnable and unlearnability? How does ML consider the unlearnable problem? These questions are motivated by unsolvable problems or solutionless problems. This section addresses these issues through corresponding mathematical approaches, taking into account machine learning. To address the first issue, this section proposes stories on bounded learnability To address the second issue, this section looks at unsolvability and unlearnability and presents a mathematical approach to the learnability space of all human beings with a spectrum of unlearnability. To address the third issue, this section explores unlearnable intelligence by discussing intelligence of data, information, knowledge, experience and wisdom. The research demonstrates that the learnability space is limited or bounded. This is also why we introduce the concept of bounded learnability. It also reveals that bounded learnability is a characteristic of human learning and decision-making.

The remainder of this section is organized as follows. Section 5.10.1 proposes a theory of bounded learnability. Section 5.10.2 looks at unsolvability and unlearnability. Section 5.10.3 discusses Axioms of learnability and unlearnability. Section 5.10.4 analyzes unlearnable intelligence. The final subsection ends this section with some concluding remarks and future work.

5.10.1 A Theory of Bounded Learnability

We use unlearnability as our research.

For one person, learnability is limited: s/he can only learn what s/he can. Basically speaking, s/he cannot learn what is unlearnable for him/herself. For example, the author has a friend who studied mathematics at a university and graduated with a Bachelor of Mathematics. A few years later he changed his major and studied philosophy in a Master's program and PhD program and later became a famous professor of philosophy. This means that philosophy is learnable for his friend with a mathematics background. The author has another friend, who studied English at university and graduated with a Bachelor of English. The author advised him to study mathematics because he told the author that he loves mathematics. He tried many times in order to make a mathematician's dream come true. However, he told the author that mathematics is not learnable for him. The author thinks that one has more stories related to learnable and unlearnable.

This is the limit of learnability. We can define it as bounded learnability, similar to bounded rationality introduced by H.A. Simons, a Nobel Winner in Economics. Herbert A. Simon proposed bounded rationality as an alternative basis for the mathematical modeling of decision-making (https://en.wikipedia.org/wiki/Bounded_rationality). We propose bounded learnability as an alternative basis for the mathematical modeling of decision-making in the spectrum of learnability and unlearnability.

An organization can only learn what it can, as it cannot learn what is unlearnable. This is very traditional, not revolutionary. One university likes to learn or has no interest in what is far ahead of its own (the reverse direction of far behind). If we use university ranking to illustrate this fact, that is, a 500th-ranked university cannot learn anything that works for a 1st or 2nd-ranked university, although the former does not want to confess it. However, it can learn something from a university ranked 489th. The former case is unlearnable, the latter case is learnable. Therefore, for one, s/he has a learnable space or cycle, beyond which is the unlearnable space or cycle. Only a few or a few percentages of people like or can enter the unlearnable space. The majority of the rest can only stay in their learnable cycle and do not care about what happens in the unlearnable cycle. From a statistical viewpoint, the function of any education lies in people staying in the learnable cycle or world rather than in the unlearnable world. Therefore, identifying the learnable cycle is important for one's development. How to dynamically extend the learnable cycle is more important for any education. Changing the unlearnable cycle into a learnable cycle is important for the extraordinary one.

Bounded learnability covers learnability, most possible learnability, and possible learnability in the spectrum of unlearnability in the next sub-section.

It should be noted that we understand that bounded learnability and unlearnability are also important for education, philosophy, and decision science. We do not focus on their impacts in these areas.

5.10.2 Unsolvability and Unlearnability

It is well-known that all the problems for learning in primary and middle school are solvable. Unsolvable problems are encountered often for study at a university. However, as soon as we start to work in organizations after graduating from a university, we meet more and more unsolvable problems from society.

Similar to solvability, we meet always learnable things at a university. We are very intelligent because we have learned a lot of learnable topics, knowledge, and values there. However, as soon as we start to work in an organization after graduating from a university, we meet a lot of unlearnable problems, topics, and things.

Solvable is the first topic in software development. Therefore, we use a feasibility study to examine if the problem is solvable. As soon as the problem for software development is solvable, we start to use system analysis and system design to develop this software (Pressman & Maxim, 2014).

We have not met unlearnable things, topics, and knowledge at primary, middle school, and university because the knowledge learned there has been selected based on national or international standards. Unlearnable problems have become more important as soon as we face the challenges met in society.

5.10.3 Axioms of Learnability and Unlearnability

Assume that P is the set of all the human beings and intelligent machinery, p is an element of P.; E is all the entities, e, of the world, visible or invisible, tangible or intangible; $Learn(p,e)$ is a binary predicate, denotes: p can learn e, where $p \in P, e \in E$.

It should be noted that the entity here is the most general concept related to objects existing in the world. It can be referred to as things.

For an $e \in E$, if there exists a $p \in P$ such that $Learn(p,e)$, that is, $\exists p Learn(p,e)$, we call $e \in E$ is learnable. We define L as a learnable set, then $L \subset E$. L includes all the existing data, knowledge, information, and wisdom, each of them can be learnable.

For an $e \in E$, if for all $p \in P$ such that $\neg Learn(p,e)$, that is, $\forall \neg Learn(p,e)$, then we call $e \in E$ is unlearnable. We define L_n as a un learnable set, then $L_n \subset E$.

Therefore, $E = L \cup L_n$ and $L \cap L_n = \varnothing$.

For an $e \in E$, if for all $p \in P$ in 20 years ahead such that $\neg Learn(p,e)$, that is, $\forall \neg Learn(p,e)$, then we call $e \in E$ is hard unlearnable.

Therefore, we define learnable, unlearnable, and hard learnable. The hard unlearnability provides a limitation for machine learning. That is, some hard unlearnable things can be studied by machine learning in 20 years.

The spectrum of learnability, bounded learnability, and unlearnability is illustrated in Figure 5.5.

In Figure 5.5, learnable space is the space for anyone who can learn in this world. The most possible learnable space is the space for someone who can learn in this world. The possibly learnable space is the space for someone who might learn in this world. Bounded learnability covers learnable space, most possible learnable space, and possibly learnable space. The unlearnable space is the space for anyone and machines that can't learn in this world.

5.10.4 Unlearnable Intelligence

Wisdom is at the highest level of intelligence (human intelligence). The second highest level of human intelligence is experience. The lowest level of human intelligence is data. The second lowest level of human intelligence is information. Knowledge is at the middle level of human intelligence (Sun & Finnie, 2004). Therefore, wisdom, experience, knowledge, information and data form a hierarchical structure of intelligence (human intelligence). This

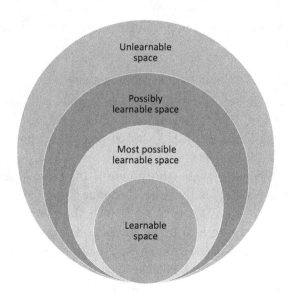

FIGURE 5.5   A spectrum of unlearnability.

can be considered as a dimension. Another dimension of intelligence (human intelligence) is learn, think, understand, and connect.

The above discussion presents a theoretical or integrated framework for intelligence: From top to bottom (dimension 1): data, information, knowledge, experience, and wisdom. From left to right (dimension 2): learning, thinking, understanding and connecting, as illustrated in Table 5.4.

At the data row, we have data-based learning, data-based thinking, data-based understanding, and data-based connecting. All these we call data-based intelligence, which is also called data intelligence.

At the information row, we have information-based learning, thinking, understanding, and connecting, All these we call information-based intelligence, which is also called information intelligence.

At the knowledge row, we have knowledge-based learning, thinking, understanding, and connecting. All these we call knowledge-based intelligence, which is also called knowledge intelligence.

At the experience row, we have experience-based learning, thinking, understanding, and connecting. All these we call experience-based intelligence, which is also called experience intelligence.

At the wisdom row, we have wisdom-based learning, thinking, understanding, and connecting. All these we call wisdom-based intelligence, which is also called wisdom intelligence.

TABLE 5.4 DIKEM Intelligence

DIKEM	Learning	Thinking	Understanding	Connecting
Data	Data-based learning	Data-based thinking	Data-based understanding	Data-based connecting
Information	Information-based learning	Information-based thinking	Information-based understanding	Information-based connecting
Knowledge	Knowledge-based learning	Knowledge-based thinking	Knowledge-based understanding	Knowledge-based connecting
Experience	Experience-based learning	Experience-based thinking	Experience-based	Experience-based connecting
Wisdom	Wisdom-based learning	Wisdom-based	Wisdom-based understanding	Wisdom-based connecting

Machine learning (ML) is data-based learning. It is a part of machine intelligence (MI) because, from Table 5.4, we have machine thinking (MT), machine understanding (MU), and machine connecting (MC). ML, MT, MU, and MC are all part of MI. Therefore, we have

$$ML \cup MT \cup MU \cup MC \subseteq MI \subset AI \qquad (5.7)$$

And

$$ML \cap MT \cap MU \cap MC = MI \qquad (5.8)$$

It is interesting to extend this discussion to unlearnable intelligence (UI), which is part of unlearnability. From Equation 5.7, we have ML $\subseteq$ MI, then

$$UMI = MI - ML \qquad (5.9)$$

That is, unlearnable machine intelligence (UMI) is all that belongs to machine intelligence but not to machine learning. More generally,

$$UI = I - L \qquad (5.10)$$

That is, unlearnable intelligence (UI) belongs to intelligence but not to a learnable set.

Data intelligence, knowledge intelligence, experience intelligence, and wisdom intelligence can be integrated into a hybrid intelligence.

5.10.5 Summary

This section provides a theory of bounded learnability and unlearnability. This section proposes stories on bounded learnability and presents a mathematical approach to the learnability space of all human beings. This section also presents axioms on learnability and unlearnability with a spectrum of unlearnability, and explores the relationship between learnability and unlearnability. The research demonstrates that the learnability space is limited or bounded based on the spectrum of unlearnability. It also reveals that bounded learnability is a characteristic of human learning and decision-making because learning is fundamental for any decision-making.

Finally, for data, knowledge, experience, and wisdom, any data, knowledge, and experience can be learned. Some wisdom might not be learned.

5.11 APPLICATIONS OF AI

This section looks at AI and its applications.

5.11.1 Foundations of AI

Fundamental concepts in AI include data, information, knowledge, experience, intelligence, mind, wisdom, classifications, associations, and recommendation (Weber, 2020, pp. 22–27). AI's foundations cover search, problem reduction, human reasoning, deep learning, robot, and so on. Intelligent and smart are key for any applications in the market. Behind them is computer science, data science, mathematics, philosophy, psychology, statistics, and logic (Russell & Norvig, 2020).

The goal for data science is for AI and computer science to combine intelligence and big data analytics. Even so, based on the report on AI development (Tsinghua University & CAAI, 2019), AI includes the following 13 main fields: machine learning, computer vision, knowledge engineering, natural language processing, voice (speech) recognition, computer graphics, multimedia, human-machine interaction, robotics, databases, visualization, data mining, information retrieval, and recommendation. We only focus on natural language processing, Machine learning, knowledge Engineering, visualization, and data mining.

5.11.2 Natural Language Processing

Natural language processing, or NLP, combines computational linguistics—rule-based modeling of human language—with statistical and machine learning models and algorithms to enable computers and digital devices to recognize, understand, and generate text and speech (IBM, 2024a). NLP can be applied to big data to derive a well-fitting logical representation called small data (Sharda, Delen, & Turba, 2018).

NLP combines data mining with pattern associations to identify relationships between adjacent keywords in large, big data sources (Strang & Sun, 2022). For example, NLP may read languages other than English. NLP can understand human language in spoken or written format, by having the grammatical rules and comparing against those as words are processed from the big data. NLP may search any type of readable structured or unstructured data, including social media sites, job posting databases, or profiles stored anywhere on the internet. NLP makes judgments of phrase association strength based on distances between keywords the same data and in the context and other words surrounding those of interest.

NLP: = voice cognition+ text analytics+ translation and generation, statistical modeling, ML, NN and deep learning are current AI hotspots.

5.11.3 Machine Learning

Machine learning (ML) was introduced by Mr. Arthur Samuel of IBM in 1957. ML has been developing for about 70 years. It mainly consists of supervised learning, unsupervised learning, and reinforcement learning.

Machine learning has become vital for big data analytics (Weber, 2020, p. 33). Recently, advanced machine learning includes deep learning based on artificial neural networks (Ghavami, 2020, p. 97). Deep learning involves multiple hidden layers of non-linear processing for extraction, transformation, pattern recognition, and classification (Weber, 2020, pp. 26–33; Ghavami, 2020). Machine learning, including deep learning, aims to automate the ability of human learning by "improving the performance on future tasks after making observations about the world" (Russell & Norvig, 2020). Case-based reasoning (CBR) is a kind of machine learning (Weber, 2020, p. 35).

Similarity has always been important in pattern recognition, graphical pattern recognition, and machine learning (Milošević, Petrović, & Jeremi, 2017; Kantardzic, 2011) because as soon as we have created patterns, then we have to use similarity to match what was input to the systems and compare it with our patterns (Sun, 2023).

Albert Einstein said that the only source of knowledge is experience (Siegel, 2016, p. 4). Machine learning is about how to build computers and apps that improve automatically through experience (Jordan & Mitchell, pp. 255–260); that is, machine learning is a process of discovering intelligence from experience using computers and software. Therefore, machine learning is an experience-based Intelligence.

Machine learning is about how computers can use a model and algorithm to observe data about the world, adapt to new circumstances, detect, and extrapolate patterns (Russell & Norvig, 2020). Therefore, machine learning is a process of discovering intelligence from data, that is, machine learning is data intelligence, a process of discovering intelligence from data, because it is a process of using probabilistic models and algorithms on data to create intelligence through data (Sun, 2023).

One of the unsupervised machine learning is clustering (Milošević, Petrović, & Jeremi, 2017). How we calculate the similarity between two clusters or two objects is important for clustering (Aroraa, Lele, & Jindal, 2022, p. 277; Milošević, Petrović, & Jeremi, 2017; Kantardzic, 2011). There are several methodologies to calculate the similarity: for example, Min, Max, the distance between centroids, and other similarity metrics. Therefore, machine learning is similarity intelligence, a process for creating intelligence through similarity.

Overall, machine learning is an experience-based Intelligence, a process of discovering Intelligence through experience (Aroraa, Lele, & Jindal, 2022). Machine learning is data intelligence, a process of discovering intelligence from data (Sun, 2023). Machine learning is also similarity intelligence, a process for creating intelligence through similarity.

5.11.4 Deep Learning

AI has a larger and wider field that needs to be studied, knowledge representation, uncertainty processing, human-computer interaction, and many other areas (Russell & Norvig, 2020).

Deep learning is a set of machine-learning methods based on deep neural networks (Blatt, 2017, p. 52). Deep learning is a part of AI. The nature of deep learning today is based on probability statistics (Zhang & Song, 2019). Big data, computing power, and algorithms are three critical factors for successful market-oriented AI (Zhang & Song, 2019).

From an evolutionary viewpoint, AI has experienced two generations, the first generation is symbolic reasoning, and the second generation is the current probability learning (or deep learning; Zhang & Song, 2019), We are entering the third generation of AI which arms to establish AI theory and methods that are interpretable and robust to develop safe AI technology. At present, we have two roads, one is to combine with mathematics, and the other is to combine with brain science. It is necessary to combine data-driven and knowledge-driven intelligences because it is difficult to seek breakthroughs through mathematics and brain science.

The core of AI is knowledge representation and uncertainty reasoning (Zhang & Song, 2019), because they are the source of human wisdom. Knowledge, experience, and reasoning ability are the foundation of human reason. The AI systems that are now formed are very vulnerable, including being vulnerable to attack or deception. They require a large amount of data and are unexplained. There are serious defects in the AI systems. This defect is essential and caused by the method itself.

5.11.5 Expert Systems

An expert has profound and extensive domain knowledge in a special field, which can be collected by a knowledge-based system or an expert system (Sun

& Finnie, 2004). However, the special skill of an expert lies in his own heuristic rules that simplify and improve approaches to problem-solving. In particular, his skill of generalizing meta-knowledge and meta-cognition plays an important role in the domain areas. Expert systems are the most popular applied AI technology in AI history. An expert is a human being who has developed a high level of proficiency and insight in making judgments in a specific domain, for example, an education expert and a medical expert (Sharda, Delen, & Turba, 2018). An expert system is a computerized system that can imitate an expert's reasoning processes and knowledge in solving domain problems.

The classical expert systems include DENDRAL, MYCIN, XCON, and Watson Discovery Advisor.

- DENDRAL (Applied knowledge (i.e., rule-based reasoning) deduced likely molecular structure of compounds.

- MYCIN is a rule-based expert system for diagnosing and treating bacterial infections.

- XCON is a rule-based expert system for determining the optimal information systems configuration.

- Watson Discovery Advisor can understand the language of science, such as how chemical compounds interact, making it a uniquely powerful tool for researchers in life sciences and other industries. IBM announced significant advances in Watson's cognitive computing capabilities that can enable researchers to accelerate the pace of scientific breakthroughs by discovering previously unknown connections in big data (Medigration, 2014).

Theoretically speaking, ES = KB + IE, where ES = Expert Systems, KB = knowledge base, IE = inference engine. Graphically, the architecture of expert systems is illustrated in Figure 5.6.

From an engineering viewpoint (Sun & Finnie, 2004), an ES can be regarded as a process of the following sequential phases: knowledge acquisition, knowledge representation, knowledge matching, knowledge reasoning, knowledge explanation, knowledge utilization, and knowledge sharing, each of which has become a separate research field. For example, knowledge sharing is an important task for the social networking services provided by Facebook, YouTube, and WeChat.

Currently, an expert system has been embedded into a number of software and other computerized systems. For example, help in the

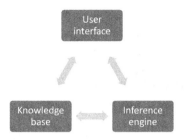

FIGURE 5.6   An architecture of ES.

computerized system is based on the architecture of expert system. In fact, search engines such as Chrome, Bing, and Baidu use the production rule of an expert system to provide help to the customers: that is, A, If A then B to help customers to search online. The current expert system has been renamed as knowledge-base system (Laudon & Laudon, 2020). Not only expert systems but also knowledge-base systems aim to discover knowledge intelligence from knowledge base. Therefore, we can call them knowledge intelligence system. The current development of expert systems and knowledge-base systems is also complemented with intelligent agents and multiagent systems

5.11.6 Intelligent Agents and Multiagent Systems

Intelligent agents and multiagent systems have become important technologies in AI and computer science. This section reviews intelligent agents and multiagent systems in some detail.

5.11.6.1 Intelligent Agents
Researchers in the agent world have offered a variety of definitions, for example, the following definitions are among them (Sun & Finnie, 2004):

1. An agent is anything that can be viewed as perceiving its environment through sensors and acting upon that environment through effectors

2. An agent is a self-contained program capable of controlling its own decision-making and acting, based on its perception of its environment, in pursuit of one or more objectives

3. An agent is a software program designed to perform a specific task based on its own knowledge and the message it received.

4. A software agent is a computer program that functions as a cooperating personal assistant to the user by performing tasks autonomously or

semi-autonomously as delegated by the user, with a common understanding agent more than a task perception and execution program

In this research, intelligent agents are considered autonomous and adaptive computer programs operating within software environments such as
databases or the Internet. They are the software counterparts of human
agents existing in business and society. Typical tasks performed by intelligent agents could include collecting, filtering, and processing information,
scheduling appointments, locating information, recommending, negotiat-
ing and alerting to commerce opportunities and making travel arrange-
ments, etc. For example, information agents filter and coherently organize
unrelated and scattered data. Autonomous agents can accomplish unsupervised actions. Another is why some people love TikTok. The reason is
that people can receive recommendations from the system recommender
on what they like to access next.

Individuals can handle these routine tasks and have been doing so for
years. But intelligent agent technology holds the promise of easing the
burdens on users by automating and augmenting such tasks. For detail,
see (Russell & Norvig, 2020; Sun & Finnie, 2004).

5.11.6.2 Multiagent Systems

Multiagent systems (MASs) have been studied for many decades, and
various types of such systems have been developed (Russell & Norvig,
2020; Sun & Finnie, 2004). MAS technology is now one of the most
important, exciting, and fast-moving areas of computing. This section
looks over the fundamentals of MASs.

From the viewpoint of distributed AI, a MAS is a loosely coupled network of problem-solver entities that work together to find answers to
problems that are beyond the individual capabilities or knowledge of each
entity. More recently, the term MAS has been given a more general meaning, and it is now used for all types of systems composed of multiple agents
showing the following characteristics:

- Each agent has incomplete capabilities to solve a problem.
- There is no global system control over agents.
- Data are decentralized.
- Computation is asynchronous.

One of the more important factors fostering MAS development is the increasing popularity of the Internet, which provides an open environment where agents interact with each other to reach their individual or shared goals.

Agent-based software engineering can significantly enhance the ability to model, design, and build complex and distributed MAS, more specifically,

- Agent-based decomposition is an effective way of partitioning the problem space of a complex system.

- The key abstractions of the agent-based mindset are a natural means of modeling complex systems.

- The agent-based philosophy for dealing with organizational relationships is appropriate for complex systems.

Coordination, cooperation, communication, and negotiation are important for any MASs:

- Communication forms the basis of the cooperation and is formed from the communication protocols and the resulting communication methods.

- Coordination is a property of a system of agents performing some activities in a shared environment. The degree of coordination is the extent to which they avoid extraneous activity by reducing resource contention, avoiding deadlock, and maintaining applicable safety conditions.

- Cooperation is coordination among nonantagonistic agents and arises as they plan and execute their actions in a coordinated way to achieve their goals.

- Negotiation means a compromise for both parties and causes a degradation of their results. All negotiation activities aim to permit constructive cooperation within the group of independently operating agents to reach their own goals.

For a single intelligent agent, these concepts need not be of importance, as it could do all the work on its own. However, their importance becomes evident in the MASs; standards-based mechanisms and means to communicate, coordinate, cooperate, and negotiate with all kinds of agents are the key for the MASs.

5.11.7 Case Based Reasoning

CBR is a reasoning paradigm based on previous experiences or cases (Sun, 2023). CBR is based on two principles about the nature of the world (Sun & Finnie, 2004): The types of problems an agent encounters tend to recur. Hence, future problems are likely to be similar to current problems. The world is regular: similar problems have similar solutions or similar causes bring similar effects (Sun & Finnie, 2004). Consequently, solutions to similar prior problems are a useful starting point for new problem-solving. The first principle implies that CBR is a kind of experience-based reasoning (EBR). The second principle is the guiding principle underlying most approaches to similarity-based reasoning (SBR) (Sun & Finnie, 2004). "Two cars with similar quality features have similar prices" is one application of the above-mentioned second principle, and also a popular experience principle summarizing many individual experiences of buying cars. The CBR system (CBRS) is an intelligent system based on CBR, which can be modeled as (Sun & Finnie, 2004):

$$CBRS = Case\ Base + CBRE \qquad (5.11)$$

where the case base (CB) is a set of cases, each of which consists of the previously encountered problem and its solution. CBRE is a CBR engine; it is the inference mechanism for performing CBR. The CBR can be formalized as:

$$\frac{P', P' \sim P\ P, \rightarrow Q}{\therefore Q'} \qquad (5.12)$$

where $P, P', Q,$ and Q' represent compound propositions, $P' \sim P$ means that if P' and P are similar, then Q and Q' are also similar. (5.12) is called *generalized modus ponens*, that is, (5.12) is one of the inference rules for performing modus ponens. Typical reasoning in CBR, known as the CBR cycle, consisting of (case) repartition, retrieve, reuse, revise, and retain (Sun & Finnie, 2004). Each of these five stages is a complex process. Similarity based reasoning or SBR dominates all these five stages (Sun, Finnie, & Weber, 2004). Therefore, CBR is a process for discovering similarity intelligence through SBR.

Therefore, CBR is experience-based intelligence, a process for discovering intelligence based on experience. Because case base is a kind of knowledge base (Bergmann, 2002), so that, CBR is also a knowledge-based intelligence (Sun, 2023).

Overall, data-based intelligence (Aroraa, Lele, & Jindal, 2022) and knowledge-based intelligence (Russell & Norvig, 2020) can provide constructive insights and decision supports for businesses and organizations.

5.11.8 Cloud Intelligence

Kevin Ashton introduced the Internet of Things (IoT) to describe a system where the Internet is connected to the physical world via ubiquitous sensors (Ashton, 2009). IDC defines the IOT as a network of networks of uniquely identifiable endpoints (or "things") that communicate without human interaction using IP connectivity (MacGillivray, Turner, & Shirer, 2015). It is important to note that autonomous connectivity is a key attribute within IDC's definition. IDC has also identified the IoT ecosystem as containing a complex mix of technologies including, but not limited to, modules/devices, connectivity, IoT purpose-built platforms, storage, servers, security, analytics software, IT services, and security.

The convergence of IoT, cloud, and big data creates new opportunities for self-service analytics. Everything will have a sensor that sends data and information back to the mothership. IoT generates massive volumes of structured and unstructured data, and an increasing share of this data is being deployed on cloud services (Tableau, 2021).

In IoT, things are devices that are endpoints of the network (Thompson & Rogers, 2017, pp. 22–24). One step up in the network is the IoT gateways: small computers and devices such as smartphones that collect signals and data from things. A company can use analytics to process the signals and data for improving business performance and making money. This company might belong to the automotive, healthcare, pharmaceutical, energy, security, telecommunications, and social media industries.

IoE intelligence is intelligence 2.0. IoE intelligence can be defined as:

$$\text{Intelligent IoE} = \text{Intelligent IoP} + \text{Intelligent IoT} + \text{Intelligent IoS}.$$

Furthermore, IoE intelligence can be defined as coefficient times IoT intelligence, IoP intelligence, and IoS intelligence, that is,

$$\text{IoE intelligence} = c \times \left(\text{IoT intelligence} + \text{IoP intelligence} + \text{IoS intelligence} \right).$$

where c is the coefficient connecting all the above intelligences.

The IoT extends intelligence to enhance the user experience. According to Vernon Turner of IDC, "the key for success in the field of the IoT doesn't lie in the scale of market opportunities, but in the matching degree between IT supplier solutions and the demands of the client. Can IT partners help clients transform into an information enterprise? Also, enterprises must face the impacts of the IoT within the global market context." (IDC, 2016).

5.11.9 AI-driven Smart Manufacturing

Driverless cars, related to computer vision and control, are AI-driven smart manufacturing.

AI-driven smart manufacturing is related to or underpinned by cloud computing, IoT, machine-to-machine communication, and cyber-physical systems. All these must be referred to and updated. The example, Nvidia (https://www.nvidia.com/) is one of the world leaders in AI Computing. NVIDIA invents the GPU and drives advances in AI, HPC, gaming, creative design, autonomous vehicles, and robotics. Because of the restriction of imports from the USA, Huawei has to develop a similar GPU to replace the products of NVIDIA. Some politicians should understand an easy truth, that is, if Mr. Jensen Huang (Yunxun), CEO of NVIDIA, an original Chinese, can develop NVIDIA products, Why Huawei cannot. If Taiwan Chinese of Semiconductor Manufacturing Company (TSMC) can develop chips, why cannot other Chinese in the Mainland?

From a more general viewpoint, autonomous vehicles, including cars, are experiencing a new generation of electrical cars controlled with chips connecting to cloud computing, IoT, machine-to-machine communication. Telsa is one of the leaders in the world. However, BYD is also another of the leaders in the world, and more Chinese car makers are challengers. Who will dominate the future of cars? Maybe Chinese-made cars will-- remembering the high-speed trains. This competition is very fierce. Finally, we will see the winner in another decade. Big data, AI and cloud computing, IoT are the driving factors for this completion. Wenjie of Huawei, with its Harmony OS, is the big challenger in this competition.

Look at AI's application in smartphones. Apple has its own OS, while Huawei has its OS. Both are directly competing in the Chinese market, while other Chinese smartphone makers, including Mi, Oppo, vivo, and Honor are also challengers in the world in competition with Apple and Samsung. Therefore, fierce pricing has not been launched to decide death and surviving the struggle. Certainly, big data, AI, cloud computing, and IoT will become the winners behind the EV (electric vehicle) cars and smartphone competition.

5.11.10 More Practical AI Applications

AI applications are also in the market, including driverless cars, related to computer vision and control, face recognition, machine translation voice and finger curve recognition, intelligent customer service robots, intelligent call service robots, intelligent voice sets, personal recommendation, medical image processing, image search, knowledge visualization, and AI chips (Tan, 2018). Intelligence as a product and service has been ubiquitous. One can search based on search online and get all the intelligent products and services anywhere and at any time. Even so, the AI market is still not mature, and far away from realizing a human being's intelligence, mind, and wisdom.

5.12 SUMMARY

This chapter looks at fundamentals of intelligence, including basic intelligence and how to calculate intelligence. Then it explores intelligence 1.0, intelligence 2.0, and meta AI with the six levels of intelligence. It examines multi-intelligence, artificial feet and artificial heads, and intelligence of the five senses and our bodies. This chapter provides a meta-approach to a hierarchy of data and intelligence, including meta (DIKIMW) and a meta-approach to intelligent systems. It provides an integrated framework of intelligence to a DIKIMW Intelligence. After reviewing intelligences in AI, this chapter explores wisdom and mind, from AI to artificial mind, cloud Intelligence, data intelligence, and similarity intelligence, and unveils the relationship among intelligence, mind, and wisdom. This section also explores system intelligence and unlearnability. This chapter also examines the age of meta-intelligence as competing in the digital world. The chapter provides the applications of AI including ML, CBR, intelligent agents and MAS, cloud intelligence and AI-driven manufacturing.

5.13 REVIEW QUESTIONS AND PROBLEMS

1. What is the relationship between metadata and meta-intelligence?

2. What is the difference between data mining and data analytics?

3. What has AI done for our intelligence?

4. Discuss ML as learning intelligence.

5. Discuss NLU as a kind of understanding of intelligence.

6. Argue that data mining is a kind of knowledge intelligence.

7. Discuss that CBR is a kind of experience intelligence or event intelligence.

8. Discuss that the term intelligence is fundamentally limited and misleading.

9. What is the relationship between human intelligence and ingenuity?

10. What is the relationship among curiosity, imagination, and association with human intelligence?

11. What is case-based reasoning?

12. What is cloud intelligence?

5.14 REFERENCES FOR FURTHER STUDY

1. Warren Parry (2015) Big Change, Best Path: Successfully Managing Organizational Change with Wisdom, Analytics, and Insight. Kindle Edition

2. Ali Intezari & David Pauleen (2018) Wisdom, Analytics and Wicked Problems: Integral Decision-making for the Data Age (The Practical Wisdom in Leadership and Organization Series). Gower.

3. Mike Grigsby (2018) Marketing Analytics: A Practical Guide to Improving Consumer Insights Using Data Techniques. Kogan Page

4. Thomas Davenport, Jeanne G. Harris (2017) Competing on Analytics: The New Science of Winning. Harvard Business Review Press.

5. Justice Royal, 2020, Meta Intelligence: Why it matters more than IQ or EQ.

6. Steven Simske, 2019, Meta-Analytics: Consensus Approaches and System Patterns for Data Analysis. Morgan Kaufmann

7. Danny A. J. Gómez Ramírez, 2020, Artificial Mathematical Intelligence: Cognitive, (Meta)mathematical, Physical and Philosophical Foundations. Springer.

8. Max Bennett, 2023, A Brief History of Intelligence: Evolution, AI, and the Five Breakthroughs That Made Our Brains, Mariner Books.

CHAPTER 6

Data Intelligence

Data intelligence dominates the digital age.

THIS RESEARCH INTRODUCES DATA intelligence by addressing the following research questions: What is data intelligence? What is the fundamental of data intelligence? What are the applications of data intelligence? After reviewing backgrounds and related Work, this chapter analyzes data as an element of intelligence and looks at data intelligence, and then information intelligence and knowledge Intelligence. This research presents the fundamentals, impacts, challenges, and opportunities of data intelligence, artificial mind and wisdom. This chapter also presents a unified framework for not only data intelligence. This research also looks at the age of metaintelligence for competing in the digital world. This chapter explores similarity intelligence, similarity computing, and analytics. This chapter proposes R^5 model for big data reasoning. There are at least three contributions to the academic communities. The research demonstrates that data intelligence is the basis for knowledge intelligence, which is a core of artificial intelligence. What are the impacts of data intelligence on knowledge intelligence? This research presents the fundamentals, impacts, challenges, and opportunities of data intelligence in the age of big data, AI, and data science. This research also presents a unified framework for not only data intelligence. The proposed approach in this chapter might facilitate research and development of data intelligence, bi data analytics, BI, artificial intelligence, and data science.

DOI: 10.1201/9781003450504-6

Learning objectives of this chapter:

- Define data intelligence.

- Recognize two applications of data intelligence.

- Explain big data intelligence.

- Gain familiarity with knowledge intelligence.

- Discuss similarity intelligence and its application in AI.

- Understand big data 4.0 and its relationship with intelligence.

- Explore big data reasoning.

- Understand the R^5 model of big data reasoning.

- Define DIKW intelligence.

- Identify the application of DIKW intelligence.

- Define meta-intelligence.

- Understand artificial intelligences.

- Contrast artificial mind and AI.

6.1 INTRODUCTION

Google search found about 8,130,000 results and a Google Scholar search found about 26,600 results for "data intelligence" (accessed on March 18, 2024). These demonstrate that data intelligence has drawn significant attention in industries and academia with the dramatic development of big data, data science, and AI. However, a deep analysis of the published section on data intelligence will find the following research issues: What are the foundations of data intelligence?

The Internet of Things (IoT) will be connected by more than 75 billion units worldwide by 2025 (Castrounis, 2020). The equipment will create an economic value of up to 11 trillion US dollars. The amount of data produced by connected devices and sensors is increasing. These data are very valuable for smart applications. Data intelligence is produced by this big data, IoT, IoP, and IoS.

This chapter will address these issues and look at data intelligence.

The rest of this chapter is organized as follows. Section 6.2 looks at the relationship between data intelligence and intelligence data. Section 6.3 looks at data as an element of intelligence. Section 6.3 discusses knowledge intelligence. Section 6.4 looks at AIS from AI. Section 6.5 proposes an integrated framework for DIKW intelligence. Section 6.6 explores intelligence, not only with data. Section 6.7 explores the artificial mind from AI. Sections 6.8 and 6.9 explore meta-intelligence and similarity intelligence. Section 6.10 proposes an R^5 model for big data reasoning. Section 6.11 explores big data 4.0 as a calculus between big data and big intelligence. The final section ends this chapter with concluding remarks.

6.2 INTELLIGENCE DATA ≠ DATA INTELLIGENCE

Intelligence data is not data intelligence although they are the same from a search engine viewpoint. However, in the physical world, intelligence data is data collected by persons or machines with their intelligence. For example, the staff member of the CIA who collected data and intelligence data. Data intelligence in this research is intelligence for human beings, machines, and systems based on BI, AI, and data science.

There are a few definitions of data intelligence. In the following, we analyze three of them.

1. Data intelligence is the analysis of various forms of data in such a way that it can be used by companies to expand their services or invest the future (Techopedia, 2021).

This definition implies that data intelligence is a special data analysis. The problem that arises is what is the relationship between intelligence and analysis. Therefore, this definition should be improved from a computing viewpoint. At least, data intelligence is not at the same level with data analysis. In other words, the definition for data intelligence has not yet passed the stage of theocratization, formalization, and scientification.

2. Data intelligence can be defined as "all the analytical tools and methods companies employ to form a better understanding of the information they collect to improve their services or investments" (Sisense, 2021).

This definition implies that data intelligence is "all the analytical tools and methods." The problem that arises is what is the relationship between intelligence and "analytical tools and methods." From a computing viewpoint, intelligence is not at the same level as analytical tools and methods. Further, it seems that only analysis and interaction are not enough to acquire intelligence to promote better decision-making in the future. The data technologies include those that organize, connect, and process data.

   3. Data intelligence is the ability to understand and use data (Collibra, 2020).

This definition is good, because "the ability" is used in the definition. This definition is more general than the first and second.

Based on the above analysis, we define data intelligence as the intelligence of human beings, machines, and systems to use intelligent data technologies, tools, and insights to optimize business processes and support decision-making for individuals and organizations. This definition incorporates the analysis of the first definition, the analytical tools and methods of the second definition, and the "skill and ability" of the third definition. Therefore, this definition is an integrated definition of data intelligence based on the above three definitions (Oxford, 2008). This definition is sounder or more rational than the above existing definitions.

Data intelligence is an important part of any organization's efforts to improve customer services (Sisense, 2021). One of the most common uses of data intelligence is to understand consumer behaviors and preferences using data mining techniques, because consumer behaviors and preferences are important parts of decision-making in e-commerce and web services. This use is also shared with data mining, data warehousing, and data analytics.

AI, machine learning, business performance analytics, data mining, online analytics, and event analytics are techniques of data intelligence for companies and organizations to process data and big data to make better decisions for improving business performance and competitive advantages (Techopedia, 2021). Data intelligence incorporates both AI and machine learning tools to obtain intelligence and its applications in business (Sisense, 2021).

Data intelligence aims to understand data, uncover alternative explanations, resolve issues, and identify future trends to improve the decisions of customers and organizations (Sisense, 2021).

6.3 DATA AS AN ELEMENT OF INTELLIGENCE

Data as an element of intelligence is the result of data technology, systems, and management in the past six decades. The booming data trade, data marketing, data industry, and data economy have expedited the research and development of data intelligence. AI used to be a kind of knowledge intelligence (Russell & Norvig, 2020) and now also includes data intelligence. In recent years, machine learning seems to have a similar role to AI in the market (Sun, 2023c). This implies that data intelligence is more important than knowledge intelligence in the market.

Data as an element of intelligence is also the result of data competing with information and knowledge. Information becomes an important term thanks to Shannon in 1954. Late information becomes an element of intelligence in the 1960s and in particular in the 1970s, because information economy and information highway were used as the national strategies at that time.

Knowledge became an element of intelligence 2000 years ago. In Confucius' time, knowledge had become important for developing intelligence. Since the ancient Greek philosophers, Socrates, Pluto, and Aristotle, knowledge has been influencing the development of human beings (Aristotle, 1801).

Knowledge became important in computer science in the later 1950s. Since then, knowledge has been a part of the research and development of ICT, aiming the liberation of human intelligence toward knowledge definition, knowledge processing, storage, manipulation, and sharing (Hawkins, 2021). Knowledge processing, knowledge management, and knowledge systems, knowledge engineering are important fields in this area, aiming to understand and develop knowledge intelligence, or knowledge-based intelligence (Sun, 2023c).

Now, data has become an element of data science, which is underpinned by data intelligence. Data science is separating from computer science and AI (ACM, 2020). In the near future, many universities will have Data Faculty, a Data School, and a Data Department. Data University will become an independent university. Some states have their own data departments as part of state governance.

6.4 BIG DATA INTELLIGENCE

Big data intelligence is the ability to use technologies, systems, and process intelligence to process or transform big data, make big data analytics actionable, and transform big data analytics into intelligence and insights.

Data intelligence is the basis for knowledge intelligence, which is a core of artificial intelligence. Big data intelligence is still an emerging research topic for data science and AI, compared with BI and artificial intelligence. Therefore, many fundamental issues are still open to the research and development of big data intelligence.

6.5 KNOWLEDGE INTELLIGENCE

Sherman Kent, a history professor who took a leave of absence from Yale to help found the US Central Intelligence Agency (CIA), titles the first research of his intelligence manifesto, "Intelligence is knowledge." (Powell, 2020). This is the key relationship between knowledge and intelligence. In other words, intelligence is from knowledge. From DIKIW viewpoint, intelligence is first a knowledge, and then intelligence covers data, information, and experience.

Data intelligence is the basis for knowledge intelligence; both are a core of artificial intelligence. CBR, expert systems, and knowledge-based systems are examples of knowledge intelligence, as mentioned in the previous chapter.

6.6 FROM AI TO AIS

Single word intelligence is fundamentally limited and misleading (Howard, 2012). This is not only for the theory of multiple intelligences. It is also correct for intelligence in AI. Therefore, from AI to AIs, intelligences are the real phenomena in the intelligence worlds, not only in human intelligences, but also in AIs.

AIs include data intelligence, knowledge intelligence, wisdom intelligence, experience intelligence, analytics intelligence, big data intelligence, understanding intelligence, learning intelligence, to name a few. For example, machine learning aims to develop learning intelligence. Expert systems aim to improve knowledge intelligence, big data analytics aims to provide analytics intelligence and insight to the organizations and individuals. In such a way, we can easily understand meta-intelligence as intelligence about intelligence.

Intelligences are also important from BI and BIs. We will discuss BIs from BI in Chapter 10.

6.7 DIKW INTELLIGENCE: AN INTEGRATED FRAMEWORK OF INTELLIGENCE

Data, information, knowledge, and wisdom (DIKW) form a hierarchical structure with a pyramid as a basis of intelligence (e.g., human intelligence, cognitive intelligence, AI, and machine intelligence (Sun & Finnie, 2005a; Rowley, 2007; Wang, 2015; Liew, 2013), as shown in Figure 6.1. DIKW is an extended form with the reverse pyramid of DIKW (Rowley, 2007; Wang, 2015; Liew, 2013).

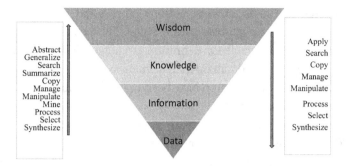

FIGURE 6.1   DIKW pyramid and generalization and specialization.

We have the following relationships among data, information, knowledge, and wisdom based on the above discussion (Johnsonbaugh, 2013).

$$\text{Data} \sqsubset \text{information} \sqsubset \text{knowledge} \sqsubset \text{widom} \qquad (6.1)$$

In the DIKW pyramid, information is defined in terms of data (Rowley, 2007), knowledge in terms of information and data (Sabherwal & Becerra-Fernandez, 2011), and wisdom in terms of knowledge, information, and data. DIKW can be considered as a dimension of enabling components or techniques to develop intelligence.

There are two transformations in this DIKW pyramid, as illustrated in Figure 6.1. The first is the data-to-information-to-knowledge-to-wisdom transformation, called bottom-up transformation. This transformation reflects operations such as abstract, generalize, mine, process, manipulate, select, copy, summarize, and search, to name a few, from data up to wisdom via information, and knowledge (Sun & Huo, 2020). For example, data mining is a data-to-information-to-knowledge technique that transforms data and information into knowledge (Kantardzic, 2011), because knowledge discovery from a database is the key task of data mining (Sun, Sun, & Strang, 2018). Search, select, and copy are fundamental transformations from data up to wisdom in the age of big data.

The second is the wisdom-to-knowledge-to-information-to-data transformation; it can be called top-down transformation. This transformation usually includes operations such as specify, process, manipulate, select, apply, and search, to name a few. For example, how to use Uber to book a car for traveling from the city mall to the university. One then needs to search and select the nearest Uber car to realize "service provision just as booked" using a smartphone.

The above-mentioned transformations correspond to a series of ICT techniques, models, algorithms, and methods. For example, the management of data includes database definition language (DDL) and structured query language (SQL) in database management systems (Coronel, Morris, & Rob, 2020). Search and selection have been realized through search engines like Google and Baidu.

It should be noted that establishing correspondences between these two bidirectional transformations (in Figure 6.1) and the ICT techniques, models, algorithms, and methods are the tasks of DIKW computing. DIKW computing covers almost all the activities of current ICT with applications.

We searched Amazon.com, and have not found a book on "wisdom science" or on "engineering of wisdom" or "wisdom engineering." There is one book on "management of wisdom" or "wisdom management," that is, Optimal Knowledge Management: Wisdom Management Systems Concepts and Applications (Thierauf & Hoctor, 2006). However, this book focuses on "the essentials of knowledge management, BI, and smart business systems" rather than wisdom management. This research demonstrates that wisdom computing in general, wisdom science, wisdom management, wisdom engineering in specific have not yet drawn much intention in academia and industries. However, some have tried to do so (McDonald, 2017). This section does not go into each of them because of the limitation of space and they are beyond the scope of this research.

6.8 INTELLIGENCE NOT ONLY WITH DATA

This section explores intelligence with not only data. More specifically, it reveals what the study of big data ignores in the trinity age of big data, analytics, and intelligence and looks at DIKW intelligence by presenting an integrated framework of intelligence. It then examines intelligence and wisdom algebra. It demonstrates that intelligence with not only data consists of information intelligence, knowledge intelligence, and wisdom intelligence.

6.8.1 Introduction

Intelligence with not only data reflects a social reality because most people live in an environment of intelligence with not only data, although they are living in the age of big data (Sun & Wang, 2017a). Big data is generated from various instruments, billions of calls, texts, tweets, phones, payment systems, cameras, sensors, Internet transactions, emails, videos, clickstreams, social networking services, and other sources (Henke & Bughin, 2016). Big data and its emerging technologies, including big data analytics and Hadoop (Coronel, Morris, & Rob, 2020), have been not only making dramatic changes in the way the business, e-commerce, and cloud services operate but also making traditional data analytics and business analytics bring new opportunities for academia, industry, and government (Sun, Sun, & Strang, 2018; Howson, Richardson, Sallam, & Kronz, 2019).

Big data intelligence (BDI) is intelligence driven by big data (Sun, Sun, & Strang, 2018). However, either AI or machine intelligence or BDI has technically ignored significant and fundamental questions on intelligence, that is,

1. What is intelligence without data?

2. What is the impact of intelligence with not only data on AI?

These questions are significant because people can live with not only data sometimes; people have intelligence with not only data sometimes. On the other hand, these questions are fundamental for AI and machine learning because if we can understand the above issues better; people need not explore deep learning using a waste of big data and oversupplied funds. People can enjoy the environment sometimes.

The remainder of this section is organized as follows: Subsection 6.8.2 explores intelligence with not only Data. Subsection 6.8.3 illustrates wisdom with not only data with an example. Subsection 6.8.4 looks at from Data Intelligence to Wisdom Intelligence. Subsection 6.8.5 ends this section with some concluding remarks and future work.

6.8.2 Intelligence with Not Only Data

As mentioned above, data is the raw material for computer processing. The processed data is information. Knowledge is the processed information with the help of experts (Laudon & Laudon, 2020). Wisdom can be defined as the collective and individual experience of applying knowledge, information, and data to solve problems (Laudon & Laudon, 2020). Wisdom is the integrated form of processed data, information, knowledge, and experience (Sun & Finnie, 2004). Therefore, the transformation from data to wisdom is a process of applying ICT to each of them. The corresponding ICT technologies consist of data processing and management, information processing and management, knowledge processing and management, experience processing and management, wisdom processing and management to obtain DIKW intelligence.

based on the discussion of meta in Chapter 2, we briefly have that.

$$O_d(\text{Data}) = \text{Information},$$

$$O_i(\text{Information}) = \text{Knowledge},$$

$$O_k(\text{Knowledge}) = \text{Wisdom}.$$

Therefore, we have

$$(O_d - i_d)(\text{Data}) = \text{Information with not only data},$$

$$(O_i - i_i)(\text{Information}) = \text{Knowledge with not only data},$$

$$(O_k - i_k)(\text{Knowledge}) = \text{Wisdom withnot only data}.$$

We can infer, based on set theory (Sun & Wang, 2017a), that.

$$\text{Information} = \left(\text{Information} - \text{data}\right) \cup \text{data},$$

$$\text{Knowledge} = \left(\text{Knowledge} - \text{data}\right) \cup \text{data},$$

$$\text{Wisdom} = \left(\text{wisdom} - \text{data}\right) \cup \text{data}.$$

In other words,

- Information is the union between a set of information with not only data and a set of data,
- Knowledge is the union between a set of knowledge with not only data and a set of data,
- Wisdom is the union between a set of wisdom with not only data and a set of data.

Integrating these discussions with what we mentioned in the previous section on DIKW, the following is valid.

- Information intelligence is the union between a set of information intelligence with not only data and a set of data intelligence.

- Knowledge intelligence is the union between a set of knowledge intelligence with not only data and a set of data intelligence.

- Wisdom intelligence is the union between a set of wisdom intelligence with not only data and a set of data intelligence.

Therefore, intelligence with not only data consists of information intelligence with not only data, knowledge intelligence with not only data, and wisdom intelligence with not only data.

6.8.3 Wisdom Intelligence with Not Only Data

The exemplar for wisdom intelligence is the theory of relativity developed by Albert Einstein. Einstein is best known for his mass–energy equivalence formula $E = mc^2$, which has been considered "the world's most famous equation" (Bodanis, 2000).

In 1905, Einstein published four groundbreaking sections, which contributed substantially to the foundation of modern physics and changed views on space, time, mass, and energy (Wikipedia-Annus, 2020). These four sections were written, Einstein did not have easy access to a complete set of scientific reference materials nor big data on physics, although he did regularly read and contribute reviews to *Annalen der Physik*. Additionally, scientific colleagues available to discuss his theories were few. The experimental confirmation of Einstein' theory of relativity could not be obtained until the time dilation experiments of Ives and Stilwell in 1938 and Rossi and Hall in 1941; Wikipedia-Annus, 2020). However, Einstein received the 1921 Nobel Prize in Physics.

It is obvious that Einstein's wisdom with not only data and thought experiment with not only data had played a decisive role in writing his theory of relativity.

6.8.4 From Data Intelligence to Wisdom Intelligence

Knowledge creation and production can be made as research publications in the form of books, book papers, journals, and conference papers, to name a few. It is a kind of intelligence. It is sometimes a kind of data intelligence because it is sometimes data-based. Many researchers have done data-based research. They said that how can they do research without data?

However, there are intelligences with not only data (Sun & Huo, 2020). Several research publications are not based on data. For example, Aristotle's Metaphysis is an extreme case without data.

Similarly, we can define information intelligence, knowledge intelligence, and wisdom intelligence. Many searchers have done information, knowledge, and wisdom-based research and published their research results. All these are information intelligence, knowledge intelligence, and wisdom intelligence, respectively. However, several research publications are not information, knowledge, and wisdom-based. Therefore, we have intelligence without information, intelligence without knowledge, and intelligence without wisdom.

In such a way, we can develop a continuum of intelligence. We can understand nature better through scientific investigation into the balance between intelligence with and without data, information, knowledge, and wisdom.

6.8.5 Summary

This section extended the DIKW hierarchy consisting of data, information, knowledge, and wisdom and proposed a novel perspective on data intelligence, information intelligence, knowledge intelligence, and wisdom intelligence. It demonstrated that intelligence with not only data consists of information intelligence with not only data, knowledge intelligence with not only data, and wisdom intelligence with not only data based on the proposed DIKW hierarchy and intelligence. Big data should incorporate intelligence with not only data to serve the world; at the same time, intelligence with not only data can enhance human intelligence and AI.

Intelligence can be extended to intelligence without information, intelligence without knowledge, and intelligence without wisdom.

6.9 FROM AI TO ARTIFICIAL MIND

This section examines AI and artificial mind from an evolutionary perspective. This includes intelligence, artificial mind, AI, and intelligent systems (IS) including expert systems, knowledge base systems, case-based reasoning (CBR), multiagent systems, and fuzzy logic, to name a few. The research demonstrates that AI aims to imitate, simulate, automate, and augment rational intelligence based on the market requirement. Artificial mind aims to imitate, simulate, automate, and augment cognitive intelligence, and irrational intelligence.

6.9.1 Introduction

AI is becoming a core business with analytic competency to transform business processes, reconfigure workforces, optimize infrastructure, and blend industries (Pettey & van der Meulen, 2018; Laney & Jain, 2017). The research questions are as follows:

- Why is mind more important than intelligence?

- What are the main objectives of artificial mind?

- How can we implement the main objectives of artificial mind?

6.9.2 Artificial Mind, AI, and Artificial Wisdom

The mind of human beings consists of rational intelligence, irrational intelligence and cognitive intelligence. It could be supposed that mathematically, mind = cogitative intelligence + rational intelligence. More specifically, artificial mind = artificial cogitative intelligence + artificial irrational intelligence + AI. In other words, the general objective of the artificial mind is to imitate, augment, and automate cogitative, irrational, and rational intelligence to enable individuals, society, and the world to have a beautiful future. One of the special objectives of the artificial mind is to 3D print a world-class artificial leader. The more general perspective is that artificial wisdom = artificial mind + AI, as illustrated in Figure 6.2. We do not go into this figure at the moment. Another big idea concerning the interrelationships among mind, intelligence, and wisdom is that mind = meta (intelligence), and wisdom = meta (mind). Then wisdom = meta² (intelligence). For example, from KBS's viewpoint, the key idea of current AI is as follows. Intelligence = Knowledge + Inference. Then we can have, the more knowledge, the more intelligence and the more inference, the more intelligence. A person with a brilliant mind might not have a big amount of knowledge nor a big number of inferences. For instance, a certain marshal has been recognized as one of the greatest marshals in history. However, he has not had the experience of studying at a military school nor leading any battle. Therefore, mind is at a higher level than intelligence, and wisdom is at the highest level. We are

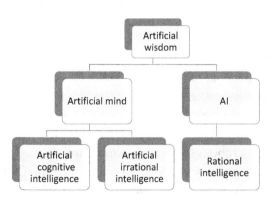

FIGURE 6.2   Artificial Wisdom = Artificial Mind + AI.

using techniques and research methods to treat mind, intelligence, and wisdom at the same level. This is the reason why we can predict that human intelligence cannot be defeated by AI, because we have not transferred ourselves from AI to artificial mind.

We are at a crucial juncture to cross the chasm from AI to artificial mind. The future development of an artificial mind will follow three stages for research and development:

Stage 1. Mimic, simulate, and augment a human mind with rules-based intelligent systems (RIS). The artificial mind learns to mimic and augment the simple functions of the human mind, which are rules-based.

Stage 2. Assist the human mind with experience-based IS. The artificial mind learns from prior experiences to replicate functions of the human mind, which are experience-based in nature. e.g. Deep learning, machine learning, and experience-based reasoning.

Stage 3. Cooperate with the human mind: The artificial mind learns to act with its discretion to cooperate with the functions of the human mind with RIS.

We are currently well-developed in Stages 1 and 2. We have not thought much about Stage 3. Stage 3 relates to RIS, big data analytics, knowledge-based IS, CBR, multiagent systems, and experience-based reasoning. Applying a systematic research methodology, we cover idiosyncratic behaviors of the human mind. While moving from Stage 2 to Stage 3, we need to better assess and understand the knowledge building and knowledge development process of the human mind to progress the development of the artificial mind.

6.9.3 Artificial Mind: Next Action

Cognitive Neuroscience, Psychology, Mathematics, and Technology in terms of mind and intelligence are vital for the artificial wisdom, mind, and intelligence. The next action is to realize artificial mind using the observation and thinking, systematic development, and scientific inquiry of artificial brains, robotics, robotic process automation, intelligent agents, cloud computing, social networking services, and online behaviors of customers in terms of cognitive psychology, cognitive science, artificial mind, and cognitive neuroscience based on analysis of EEGs using BESA systems (BESA, 2018), because everyone online can be considered as an intelligent agent, and a bot. To this end, a number of research projects and applications for research grants working together with global international research collaborators should be initiated.

There are two key ways to use EEG and BESA systems. The first way is to develop novel model, framework of artificial mind, and use the EEG device to collect sensor, source, and time-frequency data on autonomous nervous system (ANS) activity. Then The first way uses BESA systems to conduct cluster permutation statistics analysis for the collected data to verify the suggested model and framework. Another way is to develop a data-driven model and framework of an artificial mind. To this end, we first collect the sensor, source, and time-frequency data on ANS activity and literature and analyze the collected data using BESA systems.

6.9.4 Summary

This section provided an evolutionary investigation into AI to artificial mind. This includes intelligence, artificial wisdom, artificial mind, AI, intelligent systems including expert systems, knowledge base systems, CBR, multiagent systems, and fuzzy logic, intelligent big data analytics, to name a few. The research demonstrates that AI aims to imitate, simulate, automate, and augment rational intelligence based on the market requirement. Artificial mind aims to imitate, augment and automate cognitive intelligence, and irrational intelligence. The proposed approach in this section might facilitate the research and development of AI, artificial mind, big data analytics, BI, and business analytics, robotic process automation.

6.10 META-INTELLIGENCE

Meta-intelligence has drawn some attention in academia. Sternberg et al use a construct of meta-intelligence to encompass understanding, control, and coordination between these constructs and discusses the relations between creative, analytical, practical, and wisdom-based approaches as bases for solutions to problems (Sternberg, et al., 2021). Ruisel considers meta-intelligence to play an important role in the reflexes of intelligence. The latter is a mental process enabling the subjective representation of cognitive intelligence activity of individuals (Ruisel, 1994). Tarassov (1996) considers artificial meta-intelligence as a key to enterprise reengineering. All meta-intelligences are artificial.

Computational problems can be defined by traditional function execution, which implicitly holds the model of the problem to solve, and learning problems by the meta-methods that produce computational methods. Learning problems are then assimilated into computational methods that hold implicit meta-models. The process is repeated iteratively, each iteration named a kth-order intelligence. A second-order intelligence is interpreted as a first-order meta-intelligence (Arjonilla & Kobayashi, 2019). This kth order intelligence might be basically motivated by higher-order logic (Kleene, 1952) because higher-order logic is also part of computing, which I taught for postgraduate students two decades ago as a part of Logics for Computer Science and of another subject on Intelligent Computing a decade ago.

The above analysis demonstrates that meta-intelligence is an emerging area for data science, big data, and AI. The challenge is that most searched research publications lack the theoretical analysis and formalization of meta-intelligence. For example,

1. What are the fundamentals of meta-intelligence?

2. What are the relationships between meta-intelligence and AI as well as human intelligence?

3. What are the challenges and opportunities of meta-intelligence?

This research addresses these three research issues.

This selection discusses foundations, technologies, applications, challenges, and opportunities of meta-intelligence.

Meta-intelligence = intelligence about intelligence. It aims to understand intelligence, uncover alternative explanations, resolve issues, and identify future trends to improve decisions.

AI, machine learning, business performance analytics, data mining, online analytics, and event analytics are techniques of meta-intelligence for companies to process data and big data to make better decisions for improving business performance and competitive advantages (Techopedia, 2021). Meta-intelligence incorporates AI and machine learning tools to obtain intelligence and its applications in business (Sisense, 2021).

We have an inference engine and a search engine; we should develop an intelligence engine for realizing meta-intelligence. If the inference engine is the core of knowledge systems (Russell & Norvig, 2020), then intelligence engine is the core of intelligence systems for meta-intelligence.

Metauniverse is also motivated mathematics because the universe is a comprehensive set for discussion in a field. One example is below, when we discuss

1 + 2 = 3 = 2+1. This is in elementary mathematics.

If 1 + 2 = 2+1. Then 1+ 2 and 2+ 1 satisfy a commutative law. This is in metamathematics.

The meta-intelligence is a process of discovering knowledge, cognition, and intelligence with the five elements below (Bearman & Luckin, 2020):

1. Meta-knowing (knowing what knowledge is and how to use it).

2. Meta-cognition (knowing and directing our mental activity); meta-intelligence is a metacognitive capacity (Sternberg et al., 2021).

3. Meta-subjective intelligence (knowing and regulating our motivations and emotions).

4. Meta-contextual intelligence (knowing how our physicality interacts with our particular context); and

5. Perceived self-efficacy (judging how well our intelligence can equip us to succeed in particular situations).

There are many psychometric hierarchies of intelligence (Sternberg, et al., 2021). Meta is a special transformation with hierarchical characteristics. This is because data, information, knowledge, intelligence, mind, and wisdom are on different levels. Meta is an operation that transforms x on level x to y on level $x+1$.

However, as we know in data science or database systems (Coronel, Morris, & Rob, 2020), metadata is data about data. From a hierarchical viewpoint, intelligence is at level x, meta-intelligence is at level $x + 1$. In such a way, meta-intelligence is not a kind of knowledge, but it is a kind of wisdom, a higher-level intelligence.

This section addressed the following research questions: What is the fundamental of meta-intelligence? What are the technologies and applications of meta-intelligence? From an engineering viewpoint, meta-intelligence is a process of discovering knowledge, cognition, and intelligence with the mentioned five elements. Therefore, meta-intelligence will be an emerging frontier for paradigm, innovation, and creativity in the digital age.

6.11 SIMILARITY INTELLIGENCE

This section will explore similarity intelligence, similarity-based reasoning, similarity computing, similarity analytics, and a multiagent SBR system.

6.11.1 Introduction

Similarity, similarity relations, and similarity metrics has been playing an important role in computer science, AI, and data science (Minsky, 1985; Aroraa, Lele, & Jindal, 2022; Sun, 2022b; Ni & Zhang, 2022). Similarity has also played an important role in machine learning and case-based reasoning (CBR) (Milošević, Petrović, & Jeremi, 2017) and e-commerce (Sun & Finnie, 2004)

Intelligence has also been playing an important role in AI, business intelligence, machine learning, and CBR (Minsky, 1985; Russell & Norvig, 2020; Sun & Finnie, 2004; Laudon & Laudon, 2020). However, similarity intelligence has been ignored in these disciplines. More specifically, research issues in this direction are

1. Why is similarity intelligence important?

2. What are similarity computing and analytics and its impacts on similarity intelligence?

This section will explore similarity intelligence, similarity-based reasoning, similarity computing and analytics, and their relationships. To address the first issue, this section looks at the similarity intelligence and its impact on a few areas in the real-world. To address the second issue, this section examines similarity computing and analytics, and a multiagent SBR system. The main contributions of this section are 1. Similarity intelligence is discovered from experience-based intelligence consisting of data-based intelligence and knowledge-based intelligence. 2. Similarity-based reasoning, computing and analytics can be used to create similarity intelligence.

The rest of this section is organized as follows: Subsection 6.11.2 looks at Why similarity intelligence is important. Subsection 6.11.3 explores similarity-based reasoning, Subsection 6.11.4 examines similarity computing and analytics. Subsection 6.11.5 proposes a multiagent architecture for a SBR system, and Subsection 6.11.6 ends this section with some concluding remarks.

6.11.2 Why Is Similarity Intelligence Important?

Similarity has been playing an important role in mathematics, computer science, AI, and data science. Similarity has also played a significant role in fuzzy logic (Zadeh, 1971) and big data (Sun, 2022b). However, similarity intelligence has been ignored in these disciplines.

Similarity intelligence is a process for discovering intelligence from two or more objects or cases, using similarity algorithms and techniques. The Turing test (Turing, 1950) has already mentioned that the intelligence computing machinery is similar to that of human beings. This is a kind of similarity intelligence. Similarity intelligence includes similar relationships consisting of patterns and insights between the machines, human beings, and software apps (Turing, 1950; Sun, 2022b). In other words, similarity intelligence is not only from human beings, but also from machines or software or apps.

Similarity also plays an important role in ChatGPT, because similarity is crucial in natural language understanding and processing. Based on the research on analyzing 1000 texts produced by ChatGPT and found, on average, the similarity varies between 70 and 75% (Schwab, 2023). Therefore, one of the important tasks of ChatGPT (http://wwww.openAi.com) is to discover similarity intelligence from two or more objects, texts, and cases.

Similarity intelligence is important because it enables us to identify similarities and patterns from data sets, which can be used to make more informed decisions and predictions. By identifying similarities between different sets of data, objects, and cases (Sun, 2023c), we can better understand relationships and draw insights that might not be immediately apparent, at least similarity intelligence can allow us to select one from a similarity class as a representative and then we can analyze it as a characteristic of the similarity class (Sun, Finnie, & Weber, 2004). For example, in the field of customer relationship management (Laudon & Laudon, 2020), similarity intelligence can be used to identify patterns and preferences in consumer behaviors through similarity metrics. These patterns and preferences can then be used to develop targeted advertising and product recommendations that are more likely to appeal to specific groups of consumers.

Machine learning is an experience-based intelligence, a process of discovering intelligence through experience (Aroraa, Lele, & Jindal, 2022). Machine learning is data-based intelligence, a process of discovering intelligence from data. Machine learning is also similarity intelligence, a process for creating intelligence through similarity.

CBR is experience-based intelligence, a process for discovering intelligence based on experience (Sun, 2023c), because the case base is a kind of knowledge base (Bergmann, 2002; Sun & Finnie, 2004), so that, CBR is also a knowledge-based intelligence (Russell & Norvig, 2020).

Overall, similarity intelligence accompanying experience-based intelligence (Bergmann, 2002; Sun & Finnie, 2004), data-based intelligence (Aroraa, Lele, & Jindal, 2022) and knowledge-based intelligence (Russell & Norvig, 2020). to provide constructive insights and decision supports for businesses and organizations (Sun, 2023c).

Therefore, similarity intelligence is important not only for computer science, AI, big data, and data science, but also for businesses and organizations in a wide range of industries, enabling decision makers to obtain more informed decisions in an intelligent experience-based, knowledge-driven, and data-driven world.

6.11.3 Similarity-Based Reasoning

Similarity-based reasoning (SBR) has been studied by many researchers from different fields. For example, Sun (Sun, 1995) examined integration of rule-based and SBR from an AI viewpoint. He considered SBR as a reasoning-based similarity matching. Bogacz and Giraud-Carrier considered SBR as "reasons from similarity" from a neural network viewpoint (Bogacz & Giraud-Carrier, 2000). The relationship between CBR and SBR has drawn some attention (Sun, Finnie, & Weber, 2004). However, what is similarity-based reasoning? There is still no definition of it, to our knowledge. In fact, many methods of SBR seem to lack a sound theoretical or logical basis (Huellermeier, 2001). We need a relatively precise definition of SBR, in order to investigate similarity-based approaches to SBR.

Let P, P', Q, and Q' represent compound propositions, $P \rightarrow Q$ is a production rule, denoting if P then Q. A proposition can be inferred from propositions P and $P \rightarrow Q$, provided that P, and P' are similar ($P' \sim P$), and then Q and Q' are also similar; that is:

$$\frac{P', P' \sim P, P \rightarrow Q}{\therefore Q'} \tag{6.2}$$

Then, this reasoning paradigm is called similarity-based reasoning (SBR). The SBR reasoning is following the three similarity-based rules below.

6.11.3.1 Similarity-based Modus Ponens

In order to emphasize the importance of similarity between P and P', Q and Q' and show the difference of the inference rule of similarity-based reasoning (SBR) from the generalized modus ponens of fuzzy reasoning (Zimmermann, 2001), similarity-based modus ponens (SMP), can be defined as follows (Sun, 2023c):

$$\frac{P', P' \sim P, P \to Q, Q \approx Q'}{\therefore Q'} \tag{6.3}$$

Equation 6.3 is also a logical foundation for CBR (Sun & Finnie, 2004). SMP is one of the most important reasoning paradigms in many other disciplines, because it is the basic form of any similarity-based deductive reasoning paradigm (Bogacz & Giraud-Carrier, 2000; Huellermeier, 2001; Sun, 1995).

In a CBR customer support system, P' is the problem description of the customer, $P' \sim P$ means that P' and P are similar, $P \to Q$ is the case retrieved from the case base C based on a similarity-based retrieval algorithm. $Q \approx Q'$ means that Q and Q' are similar, and Q' is the satisfactory solution to the requirement of the customer.

While fuzzy reasoning is essentially a computational reasoning, SBR can be considered as both a symbolic reasoning and a computational reasoning (Sun & Finnie, 2004). If we regard SBR as a computational reasoning, then we can consider it as a special kind of fuzzy reasoning, to some extent, because similarity between P and $P', P \sim P'$, and similarity between Q and $Q', Q \approx Q'$, are replaced by the fuzziness between them in the context of fuzzy logic. This is the reason why we can use fuzzy reasoning to examine the similarity-based modus ponens in CBR (Sun & Finnie, 2004).

6.11.3.2 Similarity-Based Modus Tollens

Similarity-based modus tollens (SMT) is another inference rule for SBR. From a traditional viewpoint, we can consider SMT as an integration of SBR and modus tollens. The general form of SMT is as follows:

$$\frac{\neg Q', Q' \approx Q, Q \to P, P \to P'}{\therefore \neg P'} \tag{6.4}$$

Although fuzzy modus tollens has not been investigated in fuzzy logic (Zimmermann, 2001; Zadeh, 1965), this is the first time that similarity-based modus tollens is discussed (Sun, 2023c). With the increasing importance of similarity, SMT and its corresponding SBR will find their applications in business and mathematics.

Example 1. Similarity-based modus tollens. Let

- *RAT*: The applicant has a good credit rating.

- *REP*: The applicant has a good financial reputation.

- The loan officer has an experience rule, $RAT \rightarrow REP$: If the applicant has a good credit rating, then the applicant has a good financial reputation.

In this case, the loan officer knows the information from an applicant A, $\neg REP$: The applicant has an unsatisfactory financial reputation.

Because "a satisfactory financial reputation" is similar to "a good financial reputation", that is, $RAT \rightarrow REP$, therefore, the loan officer uses the above SMT to make the decision and obtain $\neg REP$: The applicant has an unsatisfactory credit rating, since "a good credit rating" is similar to "a satisfactory credit rating".

6.11.3.3 Similarity-Based Abduction

Abduction is an important reasoning paradigm in SBR. Similarity-based abductive reasoning (SAR) is a natural development of abductive reasoning (Baral, 2000), or an application of SBR in abductive reasoning. Its general form is as follows:

$$\frac{Q', Q' \approx Q, Q \rightarrow P, P \rightarrow P'}{\therefore P'} \tag{6.5}$$

Example 2. Similarity-based abductive reasoning. As in Example 1, let

- *RAT*: The applicant has a good credit rating,

- *REP*: The applicant has a good financial reputation,

- The loan officer has an experience rule, $RAT \rightarrow REP$: If the applicant has a good credit rating, then the applicant has a good financial reputation.

In this case, the loan officer knows the information from an applicant *A*, *REP'*: The applicant has a satisfactory financial reputation. Because "a satisfactory financial reputation" is similar to "a good financial reputation"; that is, *REP* ~ *REP'*, the loan officer uses the above similarity-based abductive reasoning to make the decision and obtain *REP'*: The applicant has a satisfactory credit rating, because "a good credit rating" is similar to "a satisfactory credit rating." It is obvious that "The applicant has a satisfactory credit rating" is an explanation for "The applicant has a satisfactory financial reputation." Therefore, similarity-based abductive reasoning can be also used for generations of explanation, as abductive reasoning does scientific discovery (Sun, 2023c).

6.11.4 Similarity Computing and Analytics

Similarity computing is a science, technology, system, and tools for determining the degree of similarity or dissimilarity between two or more objects to create similarity intelligence. That is, based on the research of Sun (Sun, 2023c),

$$
\begin{aligned}
\text{Similarity computing} = {}& \text{Similarity science} + \text{similarity engineering} \\
& + \text{similarity technology} + \text{similarity systems} \\
& + \text{similarity tools.}
\end{aligned}
\tag{6.6}
$$

Similarity relations, fuzzy similarity relations (Zadeh, 1971) and similarity metrics (Zimmermann, 2001) such as Cosine similarity, Jaccard similarity, Euclidean distance, and Pearson correlation coefficient, among others are fundamentals for realizing similarity or dissimilarity between two or more objects for similarity computing (Kantardzic, 2011).

Similarity analytics can be represented below (Sun, 2023c),

$$
\begin{aligned}
\text{Similarity analytics} = {}& \text{similarity science} + \text{similarity engineering} \\
& + \text{similarity technology} + \text{similarity intelligence} \\
& + \text{similarity systems} + \text{similarity tools.}
\end{aligned}
\tag{6.7}
$$

Basically, similarity analytics is a part of similarity computing to discover similarity intelligence in the domain (Sun, 2022a). Similarity computing and analytics can enable the analysis of large datasets, information-sets and knowledge-sets to identify and discover intelligence, patterns, knowledge and insights, and prediction of outcomes or cases. For example, in machine learning, similarity computing is used to find similarities between different data points, analytics is used to train models that enable predictions based on those similarities (Aroraa, Lele, & Jindal, 2022; Kantardzic, 2011; Sun, 2023c).

Although similarity science has not been proposed in academia, similarity engineering, similarity technology, similarity systems, and similarity tools based on similarity models, methods, and algorithms are well-known in the market (Zimmermann, 2001; Milošević, Petrović, & Jeremi, 2017; Iantovics, Kountchev, & Crisan, 2019).

Overall, similarity computing and analytics are science, technology, and systems in modern data, information, and knowledge analysis to enable researchers and practitioners to gain similarity intelligence, knowledge, and insights, and make predictions in various fields.

6.11.5 A Multiagent SBR Systems

This section proposes a multiagent SBR system as an example, which constitutes an important basis for developing any multiagent SBR systems (MSBRS).

6.11.5.1 A General Architecture of An SBR System

Similarity case base (SCB) is similar to a case base in a case base system (Sun & Finnie, 2004) illustrated in Figure 6.3. The SCB is a text case base in natural language processing systems (Aroraa, Lele, & Jindal, 2022), and an insight base in data mining systems and data analytics systems (Sun, 2022a). SCB consists of all the cases that the SBR System collects periodically. A user interface is used to interact with the SCB and MIE in the SBR System (see Section 6.11.5.3). The MIE is a multi-inference engine which consists of the mechanism for implementing three reasoning paradigms based on above-mentioned three similarity-based inference rules and their algorithms for SBR with manipulating the SCB to infer similarity-based problem solving and decision-making requested by the user. The

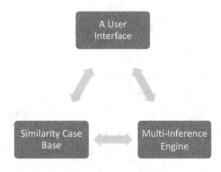

FIGURE 6.3   A general architecture for a SBR system.

remarkable difference between the mentioned SBRS and the traditional CBR system (CBRS) lies in that the latter's inference engine is based on a unique reasoning paradigm, while the MIE is based on many different reasoning paradigms. This implies that a CBRS is only a subsystem of the SBRS. Therefore, this SBR System is the extension of CBRS and similarity-based reasoning (Sun, 2017).

6.11.5.2 MABIE: A Multiagent Framework for a Similarity Based Inference Engine

As mentioned in the previous subsection, the MIE is a multi-inference engine for SBRS (Sun & Finnie, 2016). MIE could automatically adapt itself to the changing situation and perform one of the mentioned similarity-based inference rules for SBR, see Figure 6.4. However, any existing intelligent system has not reached such a high level (Sun & Finnie, 2005). The alternative strategy is to use multiagent technology to implement the MIE. Based on this idea, we propose a multiagent framework for a similarity-based inference engine (for short MABIE), which is a core part of a multiagent SBR system (MSBRS). In this framework, three rational agents (from SMP agent to SAR agent) are semiautonomous (Sun & Finnie, 2004). These three agents are mainly responsible for performing SBR corresponding to three similarity-based inference rules in the SBRS respectively. In what follows, we discuss each of them in some detail.

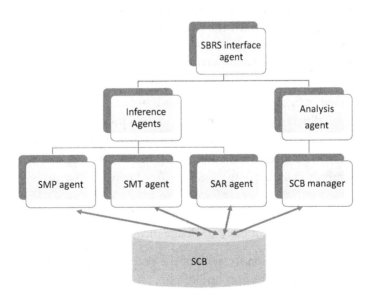

FIGURE 6.4   MIE and other agents in a MSBRS.

1. The SMP agent in the MABIE is responsible for manipulating the SCB based on similarity-based modus ponens and its algorithm to infer the similarity-based problems and solutions requested by the user. This agent can be considered as an agentization of an inference engine in a traditional CBR system. The function of the SMP agent can be extended to infer the cases in the SCB based on SMP (Sun & Finnie, 2005b; Wang, Zhang, & Zhang, 2023).

2. The SMT agent manipulates the SCB to infer the case requested by the user based on similarity-based modus tollens and its algorithms (see Section 5.3).

3. The SAR agent is responsible for manipulating the SCB to infer the case requested by the user based on similarity-based abductive reasoning and its algorithm. This agent can generate the explanation by the MABIE. This agent can be considered as an agentization of an inference engine in an abductive CBR system (Sun, Finnie, & Weber, 2005).

6.11.5.3 Some Other Agents in MSBRS

For the proposed MSBRS, there are some other intelligent agents, shown in Figure 6.4. These are an interface agent, an analysis assistant, and an SCB manager. In what follows, we will look at them in some depth (Sun & Finnie, 2016).

The SBRS interface agent is an advisor to help the MSBRS user to know which reasoning agent s/he should ask for help. Otherwise, the SBRS interface agent will forward the problem of the user to all agents in the MIE for further processing.

The output provided by the MIE can be considered as a suboutput. The final output as the solutions to the similarity-based problem of the user will be processed with the help of the Analysis agent, since different agents in the MIE use different inference rules, and then produce different, conflicting results with knowledge inconsistency. How to resolve such knowledge inconsistency is a critical issue for the MSBRS. This issue will be resolved by the Analysis assistant of the MSBRS. The Analysis assistant will

- Rank the degree of importance of the suboutputs from the MAMIE, taking into account the knowledge inconsistency,

- Give an explanation for each of the outputs from the MIE and how the different results are conflicting,

- Combine or vote to establish the best solutions,

- Forward them to the SBRS interface agent, who then forwards them to the user.

The SCB manager is responsible for administering the SCB. Its main tasks are SCB creation and maintenance, similarity case base evaluation, reuse, revision, and retention. Therefore, the roles of the SCB manager are an extended form of the functions of a CBR system (Sun & Finnie, 2004), because case base creation, case retrieval, reuse, revision, and retention are the main tasks of the CBR system (Sun, Finnie, & Weber, 2004).

6.11.5.4 Workflows of Agents in MSBRS

Now let us have a look at how the MSBRS works. The user, U, asks the SBRS interface agent to solve the problem, p. The SBRS interface agent asks U whether a special reasoning agent is needed (Sun & Finnie, 2016). U does not know. Thus, the SBRS interface agent forwards p (after formalizing it) to all agents in the MIE for further processing. The agent in the MIE manipulates the case in the SCB based on p, and the corresponding reasoning mechanism, and then obtains the solution, which is forwarded to the Analysis assistant. After the Analysis assistant receives all solutions to p, it will rank the degree of importance of the solutions, give an explanation for each of the solutions and how the results are conflicting or inconsistent, and then forward them (with p) to the SBRS interface agent, who would then forward them to U. If U accepts one of the solutions to the problem, then the MSBRS completes this mission. In this case, the SCB manager will look at whether this case is a new one. If yes, then it will add it to the SCB. Otherwise, it will keep some routine records to update the SCB. If U does not accept the solution provided, the SBRS interface agent will ask U to adjust some aspects of the problem p, which is changed into p', then the SBRS interface agent will once again forward the revised problem p' to the MIE for further processing.

6.11.6 Summary

AI has addressed experience-based intelligence and knowledge-based intelligence at their early stage. AI has been developing machine learning and deep learning to address data-based intelligence. In fact, similarity intelligence has been accompanying experience-based intelligence, knowledge-based intelligence, and data-based intelligence to play an important role in computer science, AI, and data science in general, and similarity computing and analytics in particular. The main contributions of this section are

1. It explored similarity intelligence. Similarity intelligence will be developed and created by many systems and algorithms in AI, computer science, and data science.

2. It explored similarity-based reasoning and proposed its three different rules, which constitute the fundamentals for all SBR paradigms.

3. It highlighted similarity-based reasoning, computing, and analytics to create similarity intelligence. As an example, the section also proposed a multiagent architecture for an SBR system (MSBRS).

Overall, similarity intelligence is discovered from big data, information, and knowledge using similarity relations, fuzzy similarity relations and metrics, SBR, similarity computing, and analytics.

6.12 R^5 MODEL FOR BIG DATA REASONING

Reasoning with big data and big data with reasons have drawn increasing attention in academia. This section will propose R^5 Model for big data reasoning. This R^5 Model consists of retrieval, reorganization, reuse, replication, retention, which are the main tasks for the reasoning process of big data, which is called big data reasoning, motivated by R^5 Model for case-based reasoning (Finnie & Sun, 2003). It argues that the proposed R^5 model is a new approach to big data reasoning to unify big data and therefore facilitates the development of big data with applications.

6.12.1 Big Data Retrieval

Big data retrieval is a technique that is used to retrieve the closest-matching cases stored in a cloud or system (Finnie & Sun, 2003).

Google scholar search "big data retrieval" found 738 results. These results include big data retrieval for heterogeneous multimedia, video big data retrieval, big data retrieval for transportation media, big data retrieval query scheduling, big data retrieval feature analysis, fast data retrieval, big data sharing, and so on.

Retrieving big data is challenging (Chen, Zhang, & Hu, 2017). It is difficult for the author to acquire real big data through big data retrieval, even though he has Google scholar, semantic scholar, and ResearchGate search as a public free search engine. This is also why we use big data driven small data retrieval in order to get the real information with less than 100 articles. This is also why the author uses research as a search, which is a process based on his curiosity, imagination, and association for any research topic. Furthermore, research is a process of search useful for every digital citizen.

Furthermore, big data search and retrieval are an iterative and incremental process, in particular in the practice.

As a scholar, the author searches and retrieves amazon.com and google books every six months using "big data," "cloud computing analytics," "big data analytics," "intelligent analytics," "intelligence wisdom," "cloud computing," "BI Analytics," "big data analytics," "artificial intelligence," "big data analytics," and more in order to find preferred books. He also uses Scopus, Google Scholar, Semantic Scholar, and ResearchGate to search and retrieve related papers to develop his own titles motivated by them.

6.12.2 Big Data Reorganization

Big data reorganization is a technique for data engineering, sometimes at the early stage for data preprocessing in a data system. For example, data reorganization of table structures is a normalization in database management systems (Coronel, Morris, & Rob, 2020).

How to reorganize big data for storage, for business, and trade is a big challenge. This is the business of big companies such as Google and Baidu. It is also a business for individuals. For the author, he must use the search engine of Google scholar, Scopus, Semantic Scholar, and Amazon to search related data or documents and then reorganize them based on the structure of this book.

6.12.3 Big Data Reuse

Big data as a case is reused to solve the problem (Finnie & Sun, 2003). Big data has been reused between two different companies in the name of strategic alliance. Big data has been reused for data trade between two different companies. Big data has been reused between individuals in the company. Big data has been reused on social media in the name of big data resharing, which also leads to information resharing, knowledge resharing, experience resharing, wisdom resharing.

The reuse of big data could be encouraged to realize Big Data benefits, including data trade (Custers & Uršič, 2016). The reuse of big data can promote preserving privacy, big data economics, and a beneficial society in the digital age.

6.12.4 Big Data Replication

Data Replication, also known as data synchronization, is a data integration system that can help add data and value to the business (Blatt, 2017). For example, data replication may build a complete view of a central data cube for access by multi-user and applications. Data replication may enhance relevant data access to a number of applications, along with databases and data warehouses.

Data synchronization has been used globally. For example, we have a smartwatch, which should be synchronized with your own smartphones, such as RedMi.

6.12.5 Big Data Retention

Big data retention is a part of data storage. Currently there are many databases, data warehouses, data lakes, and cloud databases, such as Oracle, cloud DB, and Hadoop, to retain big data (Finnie & Sun, 2003; Aroraa, Lele, & Jindal, 2022).

Google Drive, Microsoft OneDrive, and Dropbox are a personal cloud storage and file sharing platform as a big data retention center in the cloud (https://www.gartner.com/reviews/market, retrieved on 07 03 24). The author first used Dropbox and now uses Google Drive for teaching.

6.12.6 Summary

There are many reasoning paradigms for big data reasoning, one of them is the proposed R^5 Model for big data reasoning. This R^5 Model is a cyclic one for big data retrieval, big data reorganization, big data reuse, big data replication, and big data retention. Each of them has promoted the development of corresponding fields. Each of them will be challenging big data and developing new big data technology, systems, and tools.

6.13 SUMMARY

This chapter introduces data intelligence by addressing the following research questions: What is data intelligence? What are the fundamentals of data intelligence? What are the applications of data intelligence? After reviewing backgrounds and related Work, this chapter analyzes data as an element of intelligence, data intelligence, information intelligence, and knowledge Intelligence. This research presents the fundamentals, impacts, challenges, and opportunities of data intelligence, artificial mind, and wisdom. This chapter also presents a unified framework for intelligence with not only data.

This research also looks at metaintelligence and analyzes its relationship with data, mind, and wisdom. This chapter explores similarity intelligence, similarity computing, and analytics, and develops a multiagent similarity system. This chapter proposes R^5 model for big data reasoning. There are at least three contributions to the academic communities. 1. The research demonstrates that data intelligence is the basis for knowledge intelligence and a core of artificial intelligence. 2. Metaintelligence and Intelligences are more important than the intelligence of AI. 3. Similarity intelligence, similarity computing, and analytics will play a significant role in computer science and AI 3. R^5 model for big data reasoning will create a large number of analyticians in big data and AI, just as mathematics produces mathematicians in the history.

In future work, we will detail similarity intelligence, similarity computing, and analytics. we will extend R^5 model for big data reasoning by adding big data reduction, repartition, revision and redefinition, and restructure to create R^{10} model for big data reasoning.

6.14 REVIEW QUESTIONS AND PROBLEMS

1. What is data intelligence?

2. What is big data intelligence?

3. What is knowledge intelligence?

4. What is similarity Intelligence?

5. What is big data reasoning?

6. How can you understand the R^5 model of big data reasoning?

7. What is DIKW intelligence?

8. What is meta-intelligence?

9. How can you understand artificial mind from AI?

6.15 REFERENCES FOR FURTHER STUDY

1. Robert J. Sternberg, 2003, Wisdom, Intelligence, and Creativity Synthesized. Cambridge University Press.

2. Hanna Wallach, 2018, Computational social science ≠ computer science + social data, CACM 61 (3), Pages: 42–44.

3. Jack Reynolds, 2023, Microsoft Azure Data Engineering: The Big Reference Guide (The Data Engineering Series), Kindle Edition.

4. Robert J. Sternberg, James C. Kaufman, & Sareh Karami (eds), 2023, Intelligence, Creativity, and Wisdom: Exploring their Connections and Distinctions. Palgrave Macmillan.

5. Stephanie K. Ashenden (eds), 2021, The Era of Artificial Intelligence, Machine Learning, and Data Science in the Pharmaceutical Industry. Academic Press.

6. Joseph Sifakis, 2022, Understanding and Changing the World: From Information to Knowledge and Intelligence. Springer.

7. Timothy Powell, 2020, The Value of Knowledge: The Economics of Enterprise Knowledge and Intelligence (Knowledge Services). De Gruyter Saur.

CHAPTER 7

Data Analytics

All analytics are very important for ruling the world.

THIS CHAPTER FIRST DISCUSSES the fundamentals of data analytics. It explores the classification of data analytics and mathematical analytics. It looks at the Internet of analytics, big data analytics and advanced analytics platforms. The chapter explores analyticalizing as a process for developing analytics systems. The chapter examines big analytics, covering big information analytics, big knowledge analytics, big wisdom analytics, and big intelligence analytics. Then, this chapter discusses data science, covering database systems, data warehousing, data mining, data computing, and data analytics computing. This chapter will explore data analytics, and big data analytics. It proposes a workflow-driven big data analytics platform and a hierarchical life cycle of big data analytics. It also looks at cloud computing and examines the calculus of cloud computing. This chapter provides data analytics with applications in business, management, and decision making.

Learning objectives of this chapter:

- Define data analytics.

- Understand data analyticizing.

- Understand fundamentals of data analytics.

- Distinguish data analytics from data mining.

- Classify data analytics.

DOI: 10.1201/9781003450504-7

- Understand fundamentals of big data analytics.

- Understand the big data analytics platform.

- Understand visualization.

- Distinguish big data analytics from big analytics.

- Understand the hierarchical life of big data analytics.

- Define data science.

- Understand data engineering.

- Define cloud computing and identify three different cloud services.

- Understand the calculus of cloud computing.

7.1 INTRODUCTION

Data analytics might be the oldest among all types of analytics. Data analytics can be considered data-driven discoveries of knowledge, intelligence, and communications (Delena & Demirkanb, 2013). Data analytics mines the data from data sources such as data warehouses and data lakes for new knowledge and meaningful insights (Ghavami, 2020).

Data analytics is at the heart of business and decision-making (Sharda, Delen, & Turba, 2018), just as data analysis is at the heart of decision-making in almost real-world problem-solving (Azvine, Nauck, & Ho, 2003). Data analytics is used by businesses and management to analyze data and draw conclusions from the information, knowledge. and intelligence contained in the data or big data (Hurley, 2019, p. 163). Data analytics is used across various disciplines and domains, including industry, government, healthcare, medical science, physical sciences, and social sciences.

Although analytics has big impacts on data, organization, and society, data analytics is the most favored term used by most scholars and businessmen. Big data analytics services have created big market opportunities. Big data and its emerging technologies, including big data analytics, have revolutionized the way business operates and have pushed traditional data analytics and business analytics to bring new big opportunities for academia and enterprises (Brooks, 2022; McAfee & Brynjolfsson, 2012; Sun, 2023a). Big data analytics and intelligent big data analytics are emerging data science and technology and have become a mainstream market adopted broadly across industries, organizations, and geographic regions and among individuals to facilitate big data-driven decision-making for businesses and individuals to achieve desired business outcomes (Vesset, McDonough, Schubmehl, & Wardley, 2013; Sun & Wu, 2021).

The remainder of this section is organized as follows. Section 7.2 first discusses the fundamentals of data analytics. Section 7.3 explores mathematical analytics. Section 7.4 presents the classification of data analytics. Section 7.5 discusses the internet of analytics. Section 7.6 explores analyticalizing as a process of creating analytics. Section 7.7 look at big data analytics. Section 7.8 proposes a workflow-driven big data analytics platform. Section 7.9 inspects big data analytics with applications. Section 7.10 explores a hierarchical life cycle of big data analytics. Section 7.11 discusses could computing and provides a calculus of could computing. Final section ends this chapter with some concluding remarks decision-making.

7.2 FUNDAMENTALS OF DATA ANALYTICS

This section looks at data analytics.

7.2.1 What Is Data Analytics?

There are many perspectives on data analytics. For example, consider the four different definitions below.

Data analytics is a method or technique that uses data, information, and knowledge to learn, describe, and predict something.

Data analytics refers to "the whole KDD process" (Tsai, Lai, Chao, & Vasilakos, 2015). In other words, the data analytics process = the whole KDD process.

Data analytics is the science of using data to build models that lead to better decisions that in turn add value to individuals, companies, and institutions (Six Sigma Pro SMART, 2019)

Data analytics is the science and technology of examining, summarizing, and drawing conclusions from data to learn, describe, and predict something (Sun, 2019).

It is clear that we are far from an agreement on how to define data analytics. Even so, we will look at each of them in some detail in this chapter.

7.2.2 Data Analysis ≠ Data Analytics

Data analytics can be considered data-driven discoveries and communications (Delena & Demirkanb, 2013). Data analytics involves historical or current data and visualization (Turban & Volonino, 2011). This requires analytics to use data mining (DM) to discover knowledge from a large database or data warehouse (DW) or big data to assist decision-making (Turban & Volonino, 2011). DM employs advanced statistical tools to analyze big data now available through DWs and other sources to identify possible relationships, patterns, and anomalies and discover information or knowledge for rational decision-making (Coronel, Morris, & Rob, 2020). DM includes web mining and text mining (Laudon & Laudon, 2020). DW extracts or obtains its data from operational databases or external sources, providing a more comprehensive data pool, including historical or current data (Coronel, Morris, & Rob, 2020). Analytics is also required to use statistical modeling (SM) to learn something that can aid decision-making (Schneider, 2017, p. 183). Only these are not enough for decision-making in general, but business decision-making in specific, because a business decision maker such as CEO and CFO has not time to read discovered knowledge or patterns in long text. They hope to get succinct and vivid knowledge or patterns in the form of figures or tables presented by either PPT, spreadsheets, dashboards, scorecards, or barometers. They require analytics to use visualization techniques to make any information and knowledge patterns for decision-making in the form of figures or tables. In summary, analytics can use built-in analysis, modeling, visualization, and sharing technologies (Tableau, 2021) to facilitate business decision-making and realization of business objectives through analyzing current problems and future trends, creating predictive models to foresee future threats and opportunities, and analyzing/optimizing business processes based on involved historical or current data to enhance organizational performance (Delena & Demirkanb, 2013). Therefore, analytics can be succinctly represented below.

$$\text{Anylytics} = \text{DM} + \text{DW} + \text{SM} + \text{Visualization} + \text{sharing} \qquad (7.1)$$

When analytics is applied to data, we have

$$\text{Data Anylytics} = \text{Data analysis} + \text{DM} + \text{DW} + \text{SM} + \text{Visualization} + \text{sharing} \qquad (7.2)$$

Where DM is data mining; DW is data warehouse; SM is statistical modeling. Visualization has evolved in visual analytics, which combines reporting, data preparation, visual exploration, and dashboards in a single product. Visual analytics also provides the underpinnings of SAS solutions (prebuilt analytical applications). Visual Analytics is also a component of data science, visual data mining, and machine learning (Howson, Richardson, Sallam, & Kronz, 2019). Data can be manipulated while visualizing — such as when creating groups, bins, and new hierarchies. Dashboards are basic, without rich mapping. Business users like to scale and share visual explorations through visual-based data discovery with their stakeholders.

Overall, data analytics is a science and technology about analyzing, examining, summarizing, acquiring intelligence, and drawing conclusions from data to learn, describe, and predict something (Gandomi & Haider, 2015; Sun, 2019).

Summarizing the above discussion, we find that the processing of analytics as a system consists of examine + summarize + draw + learn + describe + predict.

7.2.3 DSS = Data Analytics?

Are decision support systems (DSS) similar to Data Analytics? They are not the same, but similar. For example, DSS is an information system (Laudon & Laudon, 2020). Data analytics has components of SM, DM, and DW. However, DSS can be made up of:

$$DSS = KB + DB + MB + IE + UI.$$

Where KB is knowledge base; DB = database; MB is model base; IE is inference engine; UI is user interface.

Intelligent data analytics can be made up of:

$$\text{Intelligent data analytics} = \text{data analysis} + DM + DW + SM + \text{visualization} + UI.$$

Therefore, DSS reflects the progress before the 1990s. Intelligent data analytics reflects the progress by the 2020s (Sun, 2023). Certainly, KB + DB + MB + IE will play an important role in developing intelligent data analytics. At the same time, DM + DW + SM + visualization will also impact the latest developments of DSS.

Finally, KB includes DDPP KB; DB includes DDPP DB; and MB includes DDPP MB in intelligent data analytics (see Section 4.9). This is the real difference between DSS and intelligent data analytics.

7.2.4 Difference between Data Mining and Data Analytics

This subsection will analyze the difference between data mining and data Analytics (Aroraa, Lele, & Jindal, 2022) and (Kantardzic, 2011).

$$\text{Data mining} = \text{data organization} + \text{data analysis} + \text{statistics} + \text{data visualization} + \text{intelligent techniques}$$

Therefore, there are intelligent techniques for data mining (Kantardzic, 2011).

Data analytics = data organization + data science + data analysis + data mining + data visualization (Aroraa, Lele, & Jindal, 2022).

Overall, these two books (Aroraa, Lele, & Jindal, 2022; Kantardzic, 2011) infer that

$$\text{data mining} \subset \text{data analytics.}$$

That is, data mining is a part of data analytics. In fact, this statement also consists with that in the previous section. Data mining is the basis of data analytics. In fact, one will find that data analytics is the successor of data mining when we look at the classification of data analytics in the latter section.

7.2.5 Statistics, Data Mining, and Analytics

This selection will explore Statistics, Data Mining, and Analytics and their relationships.

Statistics has descriptive statistics and predictive statistics. Data mining includes descriptive DM and predictive DM. Therefore, DM can be considered computerized statistics. Analytics has been classified as descriptive analytics, diagnostics analytics, predictive analytics, and predictive analytics. Therefore, DM is a part of analytics. In other words, analytics is an extension of DM.

1. Statistics aims to discover statistical facts and information from sample data because it is impossible to identify and collect all the

data for statistical analysis. DM aims to discover knowledge from a large database. Analytics aims to discover knowledge, insight, and intelligence from a large database and beyond. Therefore, all the three tasks of data analytics are knowledge-incomplete, driven information discovery, knowledge discovery, and intelligence discovery. From this perspective, statistics is the basis, DM is the development based on statistics, data analytics is the further development of statistics and DM.

2. Statistics is an applied mathematics, closely linked with probability. DM is a part of computer science and AI. Data analytics is a part of computer science, data science, and AI. Statistics is relatively close, DM is relatively open, analytics is completely open.

3. Statistics is close to mathematics. DM cannot be considered a part of mathematics. Analytics is far away from mathematics.

4. Statistics is a theoretical basis for data science. DM and analytics are a part of data science.

7.3 MATHEMATICAL ANALYTICS

Analytics has become the new queen of science and technology (Ghavami, 2020). Millions of analytics form a web of analytics around us based on a Google Scholar search. This section will present the definition of mathematical analytics. One can consider all the analytics in the web of analytics, such as data analytics, enterprise analytics, and organization analytics, as the special cases of the proposed definition (Sun, Pambel, & Wu, 2022).

Data analytics can be defined as the "art of examining, summarizing, and drawing conclusions from data". (Norusis, 1997). Let x be a variable, then, this definition of data analytics can be extended below (Sun & Stranieri, 2021).

x analytics can be defined as the "art of examining, summarizing, and drawing conclusions from x."

When x is information, knowledge, intelligence, and Google respectively, we have information analytics, knowledge analytics, intelligence analytics, and Google Analytics, at least from the definition level. For example, knowledge analytics can be defined as the "art of examining, summarizing, and drawing conclusions from knowledge."

Data analytics can also be referred to as a x method that "uses data to learn, describe, and predict something" (Turban & Volonino, 2011, p. 341). Let y be a variable, this definition of analytics can be extended below.

y analytics can also be defined as an x method that "uses y to learn, describe, and predict z. When y is information, knowledge, intelligence, and Google respectively, we have information analytics, knowledge analytics, intelligence analytics, and Google Analytics. For example, knowledge analytics can be referred to as an x method that "uses knowledge to learn, describe, and predict z".

In other words, y analytics can be defined as the x art of examining, summarizing, and drawing conclusions from y to learn, describe, and predict z, where y∈{data, information, knowledge, intelligence, and Google}. We have data analytics, information analytics, knowledge analytics, intelligence analytics, and Google Analytics. For example, intelligence analytics can be defined as the intelligence art of examining, summarizing, and drawing conclusions from intelligence to learn, describe, and predict z.

Therefore, data, information, knowledge, intelligence, and Google can be considered input for an analytics system y for processing. The processing of this analytics system is to examine, summarize, and draw conclusions from x. The analytics goal aims to learn, describe, and predict z. The z here is patterns, associations, knowledge, insights, and intelligence. This is the analytics as a process.

The above discussion demonstrates that data analytics is not all forms of analytics. Information analytics, knowledge analytics, intelligence analytics, and Google Analytics are extended forms of data analytics. In such a way, data analytics, information analytics, knowledge analytics, and intelligence analytics (for short, DIKI analytics) can be considered as the basic form of analytics (Sun & Huo, 2020). Briefly,

$$\text{Analytics} = \text{data analytics} + \text{information analytics} + \text{knowledge} \\ \text{analytics} + \text{intelligence analytics} \qquad (7.3)$$

In other words, analytics consists of data analytics, information analytics, knowledge analytics, and intelligence analytics, at a fundamental level. At a higher level, analytics can be a system of integrating a few analytics at the fundamental level. If we consider data analytics, information analytics, knowledge analytics, and intelligence analytics as the atomic level, then we have three levels of integrated analytics. The top (4th) level of analytics is the analytics system integrating data analytics, information analytics, knowledge analytics and intelligence analytics. From a Boolean structure viewpoint (Johnsonbaugh, 2013; Lang, 2002), there are 16 (2^4) different kinds of analytics based on equation (7.3).

7.4 DATA ANALYTICS: ONE CLASSIFICATION

As mentioned in Chapter 3, analytics can be classified differently. This section only classifies data analytics into four different categories: Descriptive analytics, diagnostic analytics, predictive analytics, and prescriptive analytics. All these four analytics are problem-oriented. That is, each of them will address the corresponding real-world problems. For example, descriptive analytics addresses the descriptive problem (Minelli, Chambers, & Dhiraj, 2013; Blatt, 2017), as shown in the following Table 7.1.

7.4.1 Descriptive Analytics

Descriptive analytics answers the question "What happened in the business?" It is looking at data and past event to describe the current business situation in a way that trends, patterns, and exceptions become apparent (Minelli, Chambers, & Dhiraj, 2013; Blatt, 2017). It focuses on discovering and explaining data characteristics and relationships based on existing data.

TABLE 7.1   Problem-Oriented Data Analytics

Analytics	Problems
Descriptive analytics	What and when did it happen? How much is impacted and how often does it happen? What is the problem? What happened?
Diagnostic analytics	Why happened? Why is something happening?
Predictive analytics	What is likely to happen? What if these trends continue? What if?
Prescriptive analytics	"So what"? and "Now what"? What is the best answer? What is the best outcome given uncertainty? What are significantly differing and better choices? What should happen? What event will occur, when it will occur, and why it will occur?

7.4.2 Diagnostic Analytics

Diagnostic analytics addresses why it happened by focusing on the processes and causes of the result (Blatt, 2017, p. 36). For example, diagnostic analytics is used to analyze the processes and causes of COVID-19 rather than the detailed symptoms of COVID-19. The processes and causes of COVID-19 can help us to analyze basic elements that lead to COVID-19. More generally, diagnostic analytics is used for system maintenance, clinic practice, and sports.

7.4.3 Predictive Analytics

Predictive analytics addresses the question "What is likely to happen in the business in the future?", which is a kind of forecasting. That is, predictive analytics is used for forecasting. It focuses on predicting future outcomes with a high degree of accuracy.

Predictive analytics is the branch of data mining that focuses on forecasting trends and estimating probabilities of future events (Coronel, Morris, & Rob, 2020). It employs mathematical and statistical algorithms, neural networks, AI, and other advanced modeling tools to create actionable predictive models based on available data. Predictive insights that draw on data to create forward-looking models and forecast future trends can help steer business decision-makers (Mittal, 2017).

For example, predictive analytics uses predictive modeling and algorithms to analyze the data and customer online behavior to know what the preferences of the customer in this class are; it will provide decisions on how to recommend further information and digital products to the customers in order to encourage the customers to buy. These ideas are based on the recommendations of Amazon's customers and TikTok's customers. This also implied that recommendations in e-commerce services, web services, and cloud services can be based on predictive analytics.

7.4.4 Prescriptive Analytics

Prescriptive analytics answers a combination of the previous questions to provide solutions to the "so what?" and the "now what?" questions, such as "what should I do to retain my key customers?" and "how do I improve my supply chain to enhance service levels while reducing my costs?" (Minelli, Chambers, & Dhiraj, 2013).

Prescriptive analytics is used to optimize and simulate the data and create a model for the future (Blatt, 2017, p. 34). The model is related to what event will occur, when it will occur and why it will occur? Prescriptive analytics provide a constructive insight for a decision for the future, for example, when using prescriptive analytics on the recent data on population in a suburb, and its recommendation for the future to develop new supermarket.

It should be noted that big data predictive and prescriptive analytics are used when "experimenting in the real world would be prohibitively expensive or overly risky, or take too much time" (Cramer, 2014).

7.4.5 MindSpot Analytics

MindSpot is an Australian app (https://app.mindspot.org.au/) supported by MQ Health, Macquarie University, and the Australian Government Department of Health and Aged Care (MindSpot, 2024). MindSpot has provided free mental health services to adults across Australia since 2012, including confidential psychological assessments and clinically proven treatments. MindSpot cares for Australian adults suffering from depression, anxiety stress, worry, panic, chronic pain, and distress due to chronic health conditions. More than 30,000 Australians register to use MindSpot each year. All MindSpot services are free.

MindSpot provides psychological assessments to the patients online or via telephone based on a questionnaire (MindSpot, 2024). Psychological screening assessments are designed to identify symptoms of different types of anxiety, depression, OCD, PTSD, chronic pain, and other conditions. After completing an assessment from the questionnaire, one will immediately receive an automated assessment report. The report consists of diagnostic analytics on one's generalized anxiety symptoms, depression symptoms, and social anxiety symptoms. Each has been classified as severe, moderate, mild, and healthy, with a certainty of numbers. The author used MindSpot to provide psychological assessments for one patient. The report for the patient's generalized anxiety symptoms, depression symptoms, and social anxiety symptoms is 3, 2, and 0 respectively. Thus, the patient is healthy for these three symptoms.

Therefore, MindSpot can be descriptive analytics and diagnostic analytics based on the generalized report for the patient. MindSpot also provides predictive analytics and prescriptive analytics to the patient because the diagnostic report also recommends that one schedule a meeting with a MindSpot therapist to discuss one' assessment and treatment options in the later stages.

7.5 THE INTERNET OF ANALYTICS

This section will look at all the kinds of analytics. We consider them as the web of analytics or the Internet of Analytics (IoA), corresponding to IoE, IoT, IoP and IoS in Chapter 5.

7.5.1 The Variety of Analytics

There are a great number of types of analytics, for example, sentiment analytics, software analytics, social media analytics, healthcare analytics, HR analytics, marketing analytics, academic analytics, learning analytics, business analytics, malware analytics, cyber-threats analytics, mining user logs analytics, reputation analytics, user choice analytics, branding analytics, utility proximity-search analytics, survey-based online asset analytics, online employment analytics, geology analytics, global climate analytics, remote learning analytics, homecare analytics, population growth and migration analytics, food-borne illness outbreaks analytics, ROI analytics, forecast analytics, scalable data analytics, big data analytics, deep data analytics, mass data analytics, predictive analytics, trust in data analytics, self-service analytics, pervasive analytics, social analytics, scalable analytics, real-time analytics, Google Analytics, location analytics, enterprise risk analytics, centralized analytics, federated analytics, and strategy analytics (Brooks, 2022; Holsapple, Lee-Post, & Pakath, 2014; Aroraa, Lele, & Jindal, 2022).

All of these have a hierarchical structure as illustrated in Figure 7.1.

This next section looks at several analytics in some detail.

FIGURE 7.1 A hierarchy of analytics.

7.5.2 Web Analytics

Web analytics consists of a set of techniques used to assess and improve the contribution of e-marketing for a business to a business, including reviewing traffic volume, referrals, clickstreams, online reach data, customer satisfaction surveys, leads, and sales (Chaffey, 2011).

Web analytics is a general form of website analytics, focusing on the collection, analysis, and reporting of internet data traffic or online customers' behaviors on a website by providing a business solution to address the question "what happens after they click" (Baltzan, 2013). Therefore, web analytics is a kind of descriptive analytics.

7.5.3 Text Analytics

Text analytics is about a set of linguistic, statistical, and machine learning techniques that model and structure the information content of textual sources for BI, exploratory data analysis, research, or investigation. It is roughly synonymous with text mining. In fact, Ronen Feldman modified "text mining" in 2004 to describe "text analytics." Text analytics is now used more frequently in business settings, while "text mining" is used in some of the earliest application areas, dating to the 1980s. The current success of text analytics is ChatGPT, which is an integration of large language models, reinforcement learning, and NLP.

Therefore, if web mining and text mining are applied data mining, then web analytics and text analytics are applied data analytics.

7.5.4 Watson Analytics

IBM Watson Analytics offers the benefits of advanced analytics without the complexity (Medigration, 2014). A smart data/knowledge discovery service available on the cloud, it guides data exploration, automates predictive analytics, and enables effortless dashboard and information graphic creation. One can get answers and insights to make confident decisions in minutes.

7.5.5 Digital Analytics

Digital analytics is a set of business and technical techniques that define, create, collect, verify, and transform digital data into reporting, research, analyses, recommendations, optimizations, predictions, and automations (Phillips, 2013).

Digital analytics is the analysis of qualitative and quantitative data from businesses and the competition to drive a continual improvement of the online experience that your customers and potential customers have which translates to your desired outcomes (both online and offline; Google, Oct 7, 2013).

7.5.6 Learning and Teaching Analytics

Learning analytics is a field of research that can be summarized as the collection, analysis, and application of data from educational communities (Larusson & White, 2014).

Learning analytics is defined as the measurement, collection, analysis, and reporting of data on students and their learning environment to better understand and optimize learning and environments for student's learning (Hoyos & Velásquez, 2020).

Learning analytics can also be defined as the application of data analysis techniques to understand the teaching-learning processes and make use of their results so that teachers can improve their teaching performance (Hoyos & Velásquez, 2020).

While learning analytics focuses on capturing data, facts, and evaluations of students to predict their performance and perform interventions to avoid negative outcomes such as dropping out, the teaching analytics focuses on capturing the actions of teachers in the instructional design and its deployment in the classroom or virtual environments to find elements that improve performance (Hoyos & Velásquez, 2020).

The teaching analytics differs from learning analytics in that the former is responsible for evaluating educational designs and deliveries by teachers to students (Hoyos & Velásquez, 2020).

Teaching analytics and learning analytics use data and analytical methods for treatment and study. The data for teaching analytics and learning analytics is generated simultaneously during the teaching-learning process. Their results are interrelated as they are dynamically affected by the actions of the actors in order to achieve better results during learning (Hoyos & Velásquez, 2020).

7.6 ANALYTICALIZING

Data analyticalizing is a process of creating and developing analytics system to provide analytics services with data intelligence. Data analyticalizing is a part of data analytics computing. This section presents a life cycle of analyticalizing covering data, information, and knowledge. Therefore,

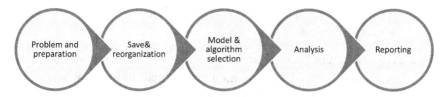

FIGURE 7.2   A system process of analyticalizing.

one can call it as data analyticalizing, information analyticalizing, knowledge analyticalizing, and intelligence analyticalizing.

Corresponding to a set of analytical methods, data analyticalizing as a
system process consists of saving, modeling and algorithm creation, analysis, and reporting, as illustrated in Figure 7.2.

From a most general perspective,

1. Problem-oriented task and preparation. For example, preparation of
   data (Thompson & Rogers, 2017), information, and knowledge.
   Problem-oriented task and preparation is a kind of project
   planning.

2. Save and reorganization are the first stage for a system process of
   analyticalizing. For example, data are saved in the database, data
   warehouse, and data lake (Coronel, Morris, & Rob, 2020). Information
   is saved in the information base. Knowledge is saved in the knowledge base (Laudon & Laudon, 2020).

3. Model is the result of modeling as a process, which was built to create models through modeling data, information and knowledge, and
   also system (Coronel, Morris, & Rob, 2020; Thompson & Rogers,
   2017). Information was saved in the information base. The data
   model, information model, and knowledge model are saved in
   corresponding model bases. Model bases are important for
   analyticalizing.

4. Algorithm selection also consists of algorithm analysis and creation.
   How to analyze data, information, knowledge, and intelligence, and
   process them is smartly based on corresponding algorithms. Then
   algorithms can be selected for processing data, information, knowledge and intelligence to address DDPP problems. In academia and
   some organizations, algorithm analysis and creation are important,

whereas algorithm selections will be used massively by most organizations and companies.

5. Analysis can be used for analytics, data analysis, information analysis, knowledge analysis, and intelligence analysis based on statistics, AI, machine learning, and other intelligent techniques.

6. Reporting is used for visualizing data, information, knowledge, intelligence, system and their reports to the stakeholders, including decision-makers and customers.

This analyticalizing process is iterative and incremental. Therefore, it is necessary to use agile methodology and mindset to develop the analytics systems (Thompson & Rogers, 2017, p. 27). In the next research, we will detail them.

Data modeling, data mining, are data warehousing are important for processing and managing data systems (Coronel, Morris, & Rob, 2020). We should also define analyticalizing (from analytics) rather than analyzing (from analysis), that is, the above process can be defined as an data analyticalizing. From there we will also have information analyticalizing, knowledge analyticalizing, and intelligence analyticalizing to create information analytics, knowledge analytics and intelligence analytics. Data analyticalizing will play the same role in data analytics, just as data mining in knowledge discovery. That is, data analyticalizing is an intelligence discovery from data whereas data mining is knowledge discovery.

Furthermore, data warehousing, data mining, and data analyticalizing are three different stages for processing data and creating data systems.

Data warehousing aims to extract, transform, and load data to an integrated data collection that is, data warehouse.

Data mining is to mine data to find new gold, knowledge, intelligence, and insights from the data warehouses, databases, and the web.

Data analyticalizing aims to analyticalize the knowledge, intelligence, insights, and wisdom from data and big data to meet the great expectations of customers and businessmen.

7.7 BIG DATA ANALYTICS

Big data analytics is an integrated form of data analytics and web analytics for big data (Sun, Sun, & Strang, 2018). Big data analytics is an emerging science and technology involving the multidisciplinary state-of-art information and communication technology (ICT), mathematics, operations research (OR), machine learning (ML), and decision sciences for big data (Chen & Zhang, 2014; Sun, Strang, & Firmin, 2017). This section looks at big data analytics. This section proposes two perspectives on big data analytics and an ontology of big data analytics. It also provides a classification of big data analytics based on the classification of data analytics.

7.7.1 Introduction

Big data analytics has impacted our thinking, working, and research, accompanied by the dramatic development of big data. However, big data analytics means different things to different people. For example, some consider big data analytics an enabler for digital technology, whereas others consider big data analytics a science and technology. This section presents two perspectives on big data analytics. The two perspectives focus on how to define big data analytics from a viewpoint of business, management, marketing, service, government, organization (enterprise), AI, computer science, mathematics, and philosophy respectively. One of the contributions of this section to big data communities is that it provides a general-purpose definition of big data analytics. One can use this general-purpose definition to easily define big data analytics from a strategic, tactical and operational viewpoint. The proposed approaches in this section might facilitate research and development of big data, business analytics, big data analytics, and AI.

7.7.2 Computer Science and AI-Oriented Perspective

Strategically, big data analytics can be defined as "Computer science for big data analytics." Big data analytics can be also defined as "AI for big data analytics," then big data analytics is a science and technology, like, mathematics and physics, taking into account big data as a background.

Tactically, big data analytics can be considered a scientific and technological integration of data warehouse, data mining, data management, data visualization, statistical modeling, and optimization.

Operationally, big data analytics can be referred to as the process of collecting, organizing, and analyzing big data to discover patterns, knowledge, intelligence, and other information within the big data (Gandomi & Haider, 2015). Similarly, big data analytics can be defined as techniques used to analyze and acquire knowledge and intelligence from big data (Gandomi & Haider, 2015).

The fundamentals for big data analytics include statistics, data mining, predictive modeling, machine learning, forecasting, simulation, constraint-based optimization, multiobjective optimization, and global optimization.

7.7.3 Business-Oriented Perspective

Strategically, big data analytics can be defined as "big data analytics for business." Big data analytics can also be defined as "big data analytics for management."

Tactically, big data analytics is technology for doing business and making money.

Operationally, big data analytics can be defined as "a set of big data technologies to support business decision-making to make money and improve the business performance by "big data analytics as a service."

Why does big data analytics matter for modern business organizations? The current big data analytics has embodied the state-of-the-art development of modern computing for business and management (Davis, 2014). Big data analytics has captured the attention of business and government leaders by decomposing big data analytics into text analytics, audio analytics, video analytics, social media analytics, and predictive analytics (Gandomi & Haider, 2015).

7.7.4 Classification of Big Data Analytics

The main components of big data analytics include big data descriptive analytics, big data diagnostic analytics, big data predictive analytics, and big data prescriptive analytics (Minelli, Chambers, & Dhiraj, 2013).

1 Big data descriptive analytics is descriptive analytics for big data. It is used to discover and explain the characteristics of entities and relationships among entities within the existing big data (Coronel, Morris, & Rob, 2020). It addresses the problems such as what happened, when, and what is happening. For example, web analytics for pay-per-click or email marketing data belongs to big data descriptive analytics (Cramer, 2014).

2 Big data diagnostic analytics is diagnostic analytics for big data. It addresses problems such as why something is happening. For example, Microsoft is an example of big data diagnostic analytics for its system services.

3 Big data predicative analytics is predicative analytics for big data, focusing on why something has happened (Blatt, 2017; Hurley, 2019).

Normally, big data predicative analytics looks for the processes and results using big data (Hurley, 2019).

4 Big data prescriptive analytics is prescriptive analytics for big data. It addresses problems such as what we should do, why we should do it, and what should happen with the best outcome under uncertainty (Minelli, Chambers, & Dhiraj, 2013). It also focuses on forecasting trends by addressing problems such as what will happen, what is likely to happen, and why it will happen (Demirkan & Delen, 2013; Turban & Volonino, 2011). Big data prescriptive analytics is used to create models to predict future outcomes or events based on the existing big data (Coronel, Morris, & Rob, 2020). For example, big data prescriptive analytics can be used to predict where might be the next attack target of terrorists. For example, big data prescriptive analytics can provide an optimal marketing strategy for an e-commerce company.

7.7.5 An Ontology of Data Analytics

Ontology has been important in computer science and AI (Gruber, 1995). A basic search in Google Scholar (i.e., section title and keywords) reveals that there are few publications titled "ontology of data analytics". We then explored it and put it as a part of this research by updating our early work on data analytics, and business analytics (Sun, Strang, & Firmin, 2017). We explore the interrelationship among data analytics, data diagnostic analytics, data descriptive analytics, data predictive analytics, and data prescriptive analytics using the proposed ontology. The results reported in this section on the ontology of data analytics is an extension and development of our early work. This is only the beginning of providing a relatively comprehensive ontology of data analytics. In this direction, we will investigate more academically reviewed sources as future work to develop an ontology of data analytics with three levels for each related analytics: big data, methods, and applications based on the method of Fan et al (Fan, Lau, & Zhao, 2015). Such an investigation would become an important guide for the research and development of data analytics.

An ontology is a formal naming and definition of a number of concepts and their interrelationships that really or fundamentally exist for a particular domain of discourse (Gruber, 1995). Then, an ontology of data analytics is an investigation into a number of concepts and their interrelationships that fundamentally exist for data analytics. Based on the above discussion, we propose an ontology of big data analytics, as illustrated in Figure 7.3. In this ontology, big data analytics is at the right side, while big data and data analytics are at the left side. Big data descriptive analytics, big data diagnostic analytics, big data predictive analytics, and big data prescriptive analytics are at the middle level as the core parts of any big data analytics.

In Figure 7.3, data analytics refers to a method or technique that uses data, information, and knowledge to learn, describe, and predict something (Turban & Volonino, 2011). In brief, data analytics can then be considered data-driven discoveries of knowledge, intelligence, and communications (Demirkan & Delen, 2013).

The fundamentals of big data analytics consist of mathematics, statistics, engineering, human interface, computer science, and information technology (Sun, Strang, & Firmin, 2017; Chen & Zhang, 2014). The techniques for big data analytics encompass a wide range of mathematical, statistical, and modeling techniques. Big data analytics always involves historical or current data and visualization. This requires big data analytics to use data mining (DM) to discover knowledge from a data warehouse (DW) or a big dataset in order to support decision-making, in particular in the text of big business and management (Turban & Volonino, 2011). DM employs advanced statistical tools to analyze the big data available through DWs and other sources to identify possible relationships, patterns, and anomalies and discover information or knowledge for rational decision-making (Coronel, Morris, & Rob, 2020). DW extracts or obtains its data from operational databases and external open sources, providing a more comprehensive data pool, including historical or current data (Coronel, Morris, & Rob, 2020). Big data analytics also uses statistical

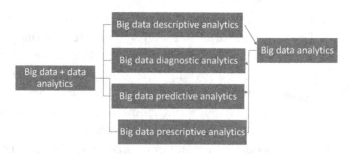

FIGURE 7.3   An ontology of big data analytics.

modeling (SM) to learn something that can support decision-making (Sun, Strang, & Firmin, 2017). Visualization techniques as an important part of big data analytics make knowledge patterns and information for decision-making in the form of figures, tables, and multimedia. In summary, big data analytics can facilitate business decision-making and realization of business objectives through analyzing current problems and future trends, creating predictive models to forecast future threats and opportunities, and analyzing/optimizing business processes based on involved historical or current data to enhance organizational performance using the mentioned techniques (Demirkan & Delen, 2013). Therefore, big data analytics can be represented below.

$$\text{Big data analytics} = \text{Big data} + \text{data analytics} + \text{DW} + \text{DM} + \text{SM} \\ + \text{ML} + \text{Visualization} + \text{optimization} \qquad (7.4)$$

Where + can be explained as "and". This representation reveals the fundamental relationship between big data, data analytics, and big data analytics, that is, big data analytics is based on big data and data analytics, as illustrated in Figure 7.3. It also shows that computer science and information technology play a dominant role in big data analytics by providing sophisticated techniques and tools of DM, DW, ML, and visualization (Sun, Strang, & Firmin, 2017). SM and optimization still play a fundamental role in the development of big data analytics (Minelli, Chambers, & Dhiraj, 2013).

It should be noted that the above equation is a concise representation of the technological components of big data analytics, and the proposed ontology of big data analytics in this Section is to look at what big data analytics constitutes at a relatively high level. We will consider the big data descriptive, diagnostic, predictive, and prescriptive analytics as one dimension, and the technological components of big data analytics as another.

So far, we examined analytics from a very general viewpoint, data analytics from not only data but also information, knowledge, and intelligence viewpoint, and big data analytics in this book. Analytics is a general concept, and it is related to organizations, and mathematics. Data analytics is limited to data; however, not only data includes information, knowledge, and others. that is, we have also information analytics, knowledge analytics and intelligence analytics. Big data analytics is analytics for big data. From this hierarchy, we can find the progress of big data analytics in this area.

7.8 A WORKFLOW-DRIVEN BIG DATA ANALYTICS PLATFORM

This section proposes a business process as a life cycle for a workflow-driven big data analytics platform.

7.8.1 Introduction

Big data analytics is a science with integrated technology for organizing big data, and analyzing and discovering knowledge, patterns, and intelligence from big data, visualizing and reporting the discovered knowledge, and insights for assisting decision-making (Strang & Sun, 2022).

Nowadays, data analytics have been classified into four different categories: 1) descriptive analytics, 2). diagnostic analytics, 3). predictive analytics, and 4) prescriptive analytics (Sun, 2019; Blatt, 2017; Hurley, 2019). However, there is no background knowledge behind this classification. This section addresses this issue and considers a business process as a life cycle for a workflow-driven big data analytics platform. However, we use the analytics engine at the middle level, knowledge, etc. at another level, and at the top level are all the business process analytics.

7.8.2 Two Stories

Peter feels unwell today. He visits Doctor Paul. Paul describes Peter's illness based on descriptive analytics. Peter's symptoms were diagnosed based on diagnostic analytics. Then Peter's illness was predicted based on predictive analytics. Finally, Paul prescribes tablets to ease Peter's illness based on prescriptive analytics.

ABBA is a global system company. Its enterprise system ASSA is well known in the big data industry. However, recently, the enterprise system has not run well. Then CEO of ABBA invites a global system service company (BAAB) for help. Then BAAB system engineer, Dr Weber, visits ABBA and investigates the enterprise system ASSA. Weber provides a description on ABBA's misfunction based on descriptive analytics. Weber diagnoses ASSA based on diagnostic analytics of BAAB. Then Weber provides a predication on ASSA's misfunction based on the predictive analytics of BAAB. Finally, Weber provides a prescription (solution) on how to solve ASSA's misfunction based on the prescriptive analytics of BAAB.

The two stories have a life cycle of the business workflow: description→ diagnosis→ prediction→ and prescription. We have the experience in clinics or hospitals. We have also experienced business workflow often. We have also encountered problem solving for system maintenance. This inspires us to present a lifecycle of analytics.

These two stories illustrate the basis for classifying data analytics into four categories: descriptive analytics, diagnostic analytics, predictive analytics, and prescriptive analytics.

7.8.3 A Workflow-Driven Analytics Platform

From a business perspective, many customers have multiple analytics and BI tools (Schlegel & Sun, 2023). A workflow of business-oriented problem-solving can consists of description, diagnosis, prognosis, and prescription. Therefore, a workflow-driven analytics platform consists of descriptive analytics, diagnostic analytics, predictive analytics, and prescriptive analytics. In order to manipulate and expedite the effectiveness and efficiency of all the mentioned analytics, the platform has a central mechanism, called an analytics engine.

Diagnosis is a process of recognizing an injury, condition, or disease from the signs and symptoms a patient displays (Talkinghealthtech, 2023). Diagnostics is a process of testing and other procedures, such as blood tests, to ascertain a diagnosis.

The lifecycle of analytics is illustrated in Figure 7.4.

In what follows, we explore this workflow-driven lifecycle of analytics from three different perspectives: a technological perspective, and a system perspective, and a source perspective.

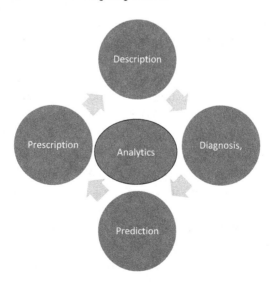

FIGURE 7.4   A lifecycle of analytics.

7.8.4 A Technological Perspective

From a technological perspective,

> Descriptive analytics is about description based on data analytics, information analytics, experience analytics, intelligent analytics, and wisdom analytics.

> Diagnostic analytics is about diagnostics based on data analytics, information analytics, experience analytics, intelligent analytics, intelligent analytics, and wisdom analytics.

> Predictive analytics is about prediction based on data analytics, information analytics, experience analytics, intelligent analytics, and wisdom analytics.

> Prescriptive analytics is about a prescription based on data analytics, information analytics, experience analytics, intelligent analytics, and wisdom analytics.

Furthermore, an intelligent analytics can be considered an intelligent system (Sun, 2019). An intelligent analytics can imitate, simulate, augment, and automate intelligent behaviors of human beings and solve problems that were heretofore solved by humans through generating representations, inference procedures, and learning strategies (Schalkoff, 2011; p. 2). Intelligent systems (IS) is made up of the principles, methodologies, techniques, and processes of applying AI to real-world problem-solving (Schalkoff, 2011). Intelligent systems are built based on the following intelligent techniques: knowledge representation (Schalkoff, 2011), expert systems and knowledge-based systems (Moutinho, Rita, & Li, 2006), case-based reasoning (CBR) (Sun & Finnie, 2004), genetic algorithms, swarm intelligence (Schalkoff, 2011), neural networks, fuzzy logic, intelligent agents and multiagent systems (Russell & Norvig, 2020), data mining and knowledge discovery from databases (KDD), decision support systems (DSS), and knowledge management (Moutinho, Rita, & Li, 2006), machine learning, to name a few.

Figure 7.5 is a system architecture of intelligent analytics. The input to the intelligent analytics system is the set of data, information, knowledge, experience, and wisdom. Each of them can be collected from human beings, the Web, sensors and databases, and other sources. All these inputs will be extracted, transformed, and loaded (based on extended ETL

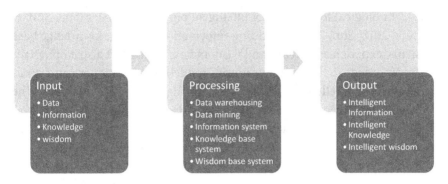

FIGURE 7.5   A system architecture of intelligent analytics.

techniques) to a central base like a central data warehouse. The intelligent processing of the intelligent analytics system includes data warehouse (DW), statistical modeling (SM), data mining (DM), information system (IS) (Laudon & Laudon, 2020), knowledge base system, and wisdom base system, based on AI-based analytical algorithms, modeling, techniques, and tools. The wisdom- based system as an intelligent system aims to transform wisdom into intelligent wisdom in an intelligent reporting form for business decision-making (Sun & Huo, 2020). The output of the intelligent analytics system is to use intelligent visualization to present intelligent information, intelligent knowledge, and intelligent wisdom in an intelligent reporting form. The information, knowledge, experience, and wisdom include knowledge patterns, relationships, and insights for business decision-making.

Intelligent big data analytics as an intelligent system can aid managers by extracting useful patterns of information, capturing and discovering knowledge, generating solutions to problems encountered in decision-making, delegating authority, and assigning responsibility (Sun & Firmin, 2012).

The relationships among intelligent systems, intelligent big data analytics, and intelligent analytics as follows can be summarized as:

Intelligent big data analytics ⊂ intelligent analytics ⊏ Intelligent Systems.

The above discussion demonstrates that the input of intelligent analytics as an intelligent system has extended the input of data analytics and intelligent big data analytics because the latter only considers data and big data as their input. The intelligent process of intelligent analytics has extended the technological foundation of intelligent big data analytics (Sun, Sun, & Strang, 2018; Sun, 2019) by adding information systems, knowledge base systems, experience systems, and wisdom base systems. It also emphasizes that AI-based analytical algorithms, modeling, techniques, and tools underpin the intelligent processing of intelligent big data analytics. The output of intelligent big data analytics has also extended that of data analytics and intelligent big data analytics by presenting intelligent information, knowledge, experience, and wisdom in an intelligent reporting form for decision-making.

7.8.5 A System Perspective

The workflow-driven analytics platform consisting of these four analytics can share the same data, information, knowledge, experience, and wisdom. Therefore, the workflow-driven analytics platform has a common data base, information base, knowledge base, experience base, and wisdom base, as shown in Figure 7.6.

The above discussion implies that analytics has penetrated any workflow of business or engineering (Schlegel & Sun, 2023; Sathi, 2013). Then, one stage of the workflow corresponds to analytics, just as in illustrated Figure 7.6.

7.8.6 A Resource Perspective

This section looks at vertical transformation and horizontal transformation of data, information, knowledge, experience, and wisdom. data,

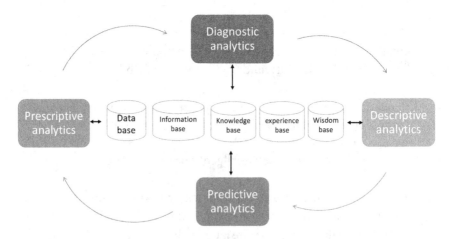

FIGURE 7.6   A system architecture of an integrated analytics.

information, knowledge (text, image, and video), experience, and wisdom as the input for computing machinery (e.g. computers, laptops, smartphones, database systems, and intelligent systems) are the resources. In this way, the resource can be classified into four different categories:

descriptive resource sets, diagnostic resource sets, predictive resource sets, and prescriptive resource sets.

For example, for data, the resource sets are datasets.

This classification raises two issues.

1. What are (historical and current) diagnostic datasets, descriptive datasets, predictive datasets, and prescriptive datasets?

2. How to develop descriptive datasets driving descriptive analytics, diagnostic datasets driving diagnostic analytics, predictive datasets driving predictive analytics, and prescriptive datasets driving prescriptive analytics?

For horizontal transformation, data is transformed into another data, T (data) = data. In computer science, this is data management and database management systems.

Information is transformed into another information, knowledge is transformed into another knowledge, experience is transformed into another experience, intelligence is transformed into another intelligence, and wisdom is transformed into another wisdom. Meta as an operation is a kind of transformation to transform data, information, knowledge, wisdom to intelligence. All these transformations correspond to data management, information management, knowledge management, management, intelligence management, and wisdom management, respectively.

For vertical transformation, data is transformed into information, data is transformed into knowledge, data is transformed into intelligence, information is transformed into knowledge, information is transformed into experience, information is transformed into intelligence, knowledge is transformed into intelligence, and intelligence is transformed into wisdom. All these vertical transformations correspond to data mining, information systems, knowledge systems, intelligent systems, and intelligent data analytics, respectively.

It should be noted that the original idea was developed when exploring big data analytics. However, the workflow driven data analytics platforms are also useful for analytics, data analytics, intelligent big data analytics, and business analytics.

7.9 A HIERARCHICAL LIFE CYCLE OF BIG DATA ANALYTICS

Data acquisition, processing, representation, and inferences (National Research Council, 2013) are in the lifecycle of big data analytics. Simulation is a part of the hierarchical life cycle of big data analytics. The following information addresses how to understand this life cycle, and at what level of implementation.

At least, there are three levels for the proposed life cycle of big data analytics. For example, at a high level, it consists of stages of descriptive big data analytics, diagnostic big data analytics, predictive big data analytics, and prescriptive big data analytics.

At a middle level, it consists of stages of acquiring (Holsapple, Lee-Post, & Pakath, 2014), generating (Holsapple, Lee-Post, & Pakath, 2014), assimilating (Holsapple, Lee-Post, & Pakath, 2014), selecting (Holsapple, Lee-Post, & Pakath, 2014), emitting knowledge relevant to making decisions, analysis, modeling, data mining, knowledge discovery, visualization, and simulation.

Modeling and simulation are a well-established enabler of theory and experimentation. Increased capability of modeling and simulation has historically enabled new science, and many fields increasingly rely on high-throughput computing (National Academies of Sciences, 2016).

At the bottom level are techniques and technologies for supporting the middle level. Data stream management, cloud, mobile, bandwidth, non-SQL databases, and new forms of data (Holsapple, Lee-Post, & Pakath, 2014) are all related to the technology of big data analytics.

7.10 CLOUD COMPUTING

Cloud computing is a computing paradigm in which scalable and elastic IT-enabled capabilities are delivered as a service using the internet technologies (Gartner, 2024a). 75% of organizations will adopt a digital transformation model predicated on the cloud as the fundamental underlying platform by 2026 (James & Duncan, 2023). This section will provide the foundations of cloud computing. It examines the calculus of cloud computing.

7.10.1 Introduction

Cloud computing has revolutionized our way of life and work, and our interacting and cooperating with data. Over the next 30 years, cloud-based computing has the potential to transform almost all cloud analytics adopted since the 2010s. A "multi-cloud" approach, whereby customers can choose to run an application in, and spanning, multiple cloud IaaS offerings (such as those of AWS and Microsoft Azure) is in its infancy. Qlik and SAP are among the first vendors to pursue this approach (Schlegel & Sun, 2023).

Big data, the Internet of things (IoT), and cloud computing have been hot areas for academia and industry and have entered an era of unprecedented change and innovation (Varghese & Buyya, 2019; Augustyn, 2016). Using ThoughtSpot, customers analyze more than 1 terabyte of data in memory from businesses to services, from health care to education (Augustyn, 2016).

There will be 100 billion devices connected to the Internet by 2045. These devices of IoT include almost all things, each of them related to digital, directly and indirectly, for example, mobile and wearable devices, appliances, medical devices, various sensors, cameras, various transportation means, clothing, and other technologies. People will use information, knowledge, and intelligence generated through big data and IoT to make more effective decisions and gain better lives (Augustyn, 2016). However, a big issue has not drawn significant attention in the scholarly peer-reviewed literature:

- What is a unified foundation of big data, IoT, and cloud computing?

Calculus is a branch of mathematics that "deals with rates of change" (Oxford, 2008). Calculus is also used for naming specific methods of calculation or notation, as well as some theories and operations (Date, 2004), such as relational calculus, propositional calculus, and process calculus. This section uses the latter annotation of calculus for this research. This section will address this issue by presenting a unified foundation of big data, IoT, and cloud computing. This unified foundation is based on the methodology of calculus.

The remainder of this section is organized as follows. Subsection 7.11.2 provides the foundations of cloud calculus. Subsection 7.11.3 proposes the calculus of cloud computing, which treats many aspects of cloud computing using mathematical methods and thought. Subsection 7.11.4 ends this section with some concluding remarks.

7.10.2 Foundations of Cloud Computing

First of all, we define cloud computing as 1 definition, 3 services, 4 deployments, and 5 characteristics as follows.

Cloud computing is defined as a model for enabling ubiquitous, convenient, on-demand network access to a shared pool of configurable computing resources (e.g., networks, servers, storage, applications, and services) that can be rapidly provisioned and released with minimal management effort or service provider interaction (NIST, 2018). This cloud model is composed of five three-service models, four deployment models, and five essential characteristics.

IaaS, PaaS, and SaaS are three main services in cloud computing, where I, P, S, and a are the abbreviated forms of infrastructure, platform, software, and as.

Amazon started offering AWS cloud services with its elastic compute cloud on July 11, 2006 (National Research Council, 2013). Goods can be rebundled in new ways in the economics of free, perfect, and instant (McAfee & Brynjolfsson, 2017, pp. 143–146). Massive bundles of information goods are often more profitable, proved by the profits of Amazon. This is also proved by the smashing and reassembling of wood mentioned in Chapter 1. Therefore, smashing, reassembling, and rebundling of digital goods are important for cloud services. The success of Amazon's cloud services encouraged the development of other cloud computing offerings. For example, Microsoft offers Azure cloud services, similar to those provided by Amazon.

Furthermore, cloud computing as a cloud service aims to provide cloud intelligence for industries and societies.

There are 4 deployment models (Wu, Buyya, & Ramamohana, 2016; NIST, 2018):

1. Public cloud,

2. Private cloud,

3. community cloud,

4. hybrid cloud.

Hybrid Cloud is a multi-cloud with a combination of public and private clouds or public and private IT infrastructure (Varghese & Buyya, 2019).

There are following 5 characteristics of cloud computing (NIST, 2018)

1. On-demand self-service,

2. Broad network access,

3. Resource pooling,

4. Rapid elasticity,

5. Measured service.

Rapid elasticity is capabilities that can be elastically provisioned and released, in some cases automatically, to scale rapidly outward and inward commensurate with demand. To the consumer, the capabilities available for provisioning often appear unlimited and can be appropriated in any quantity at any time.

7.10.3 A Calculus of Cloud Computing

This section proposes the calculus of cloud computing, which treats many aspects of cloud computing using mathematical methods and thoughts.

There are many definitions of cloud computing. For example, cloud computing can also be defined as a style of computing in which massively scalable and elastic IT-enabled capabilities are delivered as a service to external customers using Internet technologies (Gartner, 2024a).

The first definition given by the National Institute of Standards and Technology (NIST) considers cloud computing as a model for accessing computing resources. The second definition given by Gartner considers cloud computing as a style of computing in which capabilities are available as a service for customers.

Further, the essence of both definitions is that

$$Cloud\ computing = cloud + computing. \qquad (7.5)$$

Most generally, the cloud consists of the resources and services online, briefly

$$Cloud = online\ resources + online\ services. \qquad (7.6)$$

Online resources and online services are resources and services that can be accessed online.

The largest pool of online resources is from the Internet of Things (IoT). The largest pool of Internet services is the Internet of Services (IoS), where

IoS can be considered as web services. Therefore, mathematically, equation (7.6) can be represented as

$$Cloud = IoT + IoS. \tag{7.7}$$

Equation (7.7) is a new annotation for 5 characteristics of cloud computing in terms of resource pool (Buyya, Broberg, & Goscinski, 2010). This also implies that IoT is a part of the cloud.

Based on the ACM Computing Curriculum of 2020 (ACM, 2020), computing can be considered as a super-discipline, and represented as follows in a unified way,

$$
\begin{aligned}
Computing = {} & computing\ science + computing\ engineering \\
& + computing\ technology + computing\ systems \\
& + computing\ management + computing\ services.
\end{aligned} \tag{7.8}
$$

Cloud can be considered a mathematical operation if we know that the cloud has become a billion-level industry. Then applying cloud as an operation and its left distributive law to equation (7.8) and removing all occurrences of computing (this is an idempotent law in mathematics) from the right side, we have

$$
\begin{aligned}
Cloud\ computing = {} & cloud\ science + cloud\ engineering + cloud \\
& technology + cloud\ systems + cloud\ management \\
& + cloud\ services + cloud\ intelligence.
\end{aligned} \tag{7.9}
$$

Equation (7.9) is not only an in-depth analysis but also a mathematical foundation of cloud computing as a science, technology, engineering, system, service, and industry. This equation is also an application of the proposed approach for intelligent big data analytics (Sun & Huo, 2021).

From the equation (7.8), computing can be considered a mathematical operation. While one can apply this operation to other research fields of computing such as data computing and web computing, we use computing as an operation and its right distributive law to equation (7.6) and (7.7) and obtain (7.9) and (7.10) as follows.

$$Cloud\ computing = resources\ computing + services\ computing \tag{7.10}$$

$$\text{Cloud computing} = \text{IoT computing} + \text{IoS computing} \qquad (7.11)$$

Equation (7.10) reflects that the core of cloud computing is resources computing and services computing on the cloud. Equation (7.11) is a unified representation for integrating IoT and IoS with cloud computing.

Big data are strategic resources for organizations (Sun & Wang, 2017a). All resources and services online in general and all the IoT and IoS in particular can be considered as a part of big data, that is,

$$\left(\text{IoT} \cup \text{IoS}\right) \subseteq \text{big data} \qquad (7.12)$$

Therefore, combining equation (7.10) and (7.11), we have

$$\begin{aligned}
\text{Cloud computing} &= \text{IoT computing} + \text{IoS computing} \\
&\subseteq \text{big data computing}
\end{aligned} \qquad (7.13)$$

That is, cloud computing is a part of big data computing, this result is similar to that of the research of Wu et al (Wu, Buyya, & Ramamohana, 2016). Therefore, equation (7.13) exposes the close interrelationships among IoT, IoS, cloud computing, and big data computing. Equation (7.13) is a theoretical foundation for the proposed integrated approach to IoT, big data, and cloud computing.

Furthermore, as mentioned in the previous section, cloud computing is related to computer system resources or computing resources. IT resources have been used for the resources of cloud computing (Erl, Mahmood, & Puttini, 2013). Resources have been used to define cloud computing (Varghese & Buyya, 2019). This means that the resources of cloud computing should be either computer system resources, computing resources, or IT resources.

$$\text{IT} \subseteq \text{ICT} \subseteq \text{computing.} \qquad (7.14)$$

That is,

$$\text{IT resources} \subseteq \text{ICT resources} \subseteq \text{computing resources.} \qquad (7.15)$$

Computer system resources can be either IT resources or ICT resources. Therefore, it is a part of computing resources. The above mathematical analysis implies that IT resources is very limited in semantics. ICT is more general, and computing resources are most general and can be used as resources of cloud computing (Varghese & Buyya, 2019).

The above analysis leads to a new question: What are the resources of cloud computing? At least we know that the resources contain computer system resources, IT resources, ICT resources, computing resources, storage resources (Varghese & Buyya, 2019), etc.

Question 1: Can we consider all these resources in cloud computing as big data? If yes, then we have

$$\text{IT resources} \subseteq \text{ICT resources} \subseteq \text{computing} \\ \text{resources} \subseteq \text{big data}. \tag{7.16}$$

In such a way, big data is the strategic resource of cloud computing. Big data are the raw materials for resources and services processing in cloud computing. Then, we also have

$$\text{Cloud computing} \subseteq \text{big data computing} \tag{7.17}$$

Equation (7.17) reveals the relationship between cloud computing and big data computing once again.

How can we understand the types of cloud and cloud delivery?

Because cloud = resources + services, see the above formula, we have

$$\text{Public cloud} = \text{Public resources} + \text{Public services} \tag{7.18}$$

$$\text{Private cloud} = \text{Private resources} + \text{Private services} \tag{7.19}$$

$$\text{Community cloud} = \text{Community resources} \\ + \text{Community services} \tag{7.20}$$

$$\text{Hybrid cloud} = \text{Hybrid resources} + \text{Hybrid services} \tag{7.21}$$

Therefore, how to deliver computing resources and services to public, private, community, and hybrid cloud effectively, economically, and optimally is the core of cloud computing in terms of cloud delivery.

Cloud analytics is analytics that "support building, deployment, and management of analytics in the cloud, based on data stored both in the cloud and on-premises" (Richardson, Schlegel, Sallam, Kronz, & Sun, 2021).

Big data Analytics can be represented mathematically (Wu, Buyya, & Ramamohana, 2016).

$$\text{Big data Analytics} = \text{Machine learning} + \text{Cloud Computing} \quad (7.22)$$

Machine learning is a part of AI (Sun & Huo, 2021), that is machine learning $\subseteq$ AI. Then we can have

$$\text{Big data analytics} = \text{AI} + \text{Cloud Computing} \qquad (7.23)$$

As we know (Sun & Wang, 2017a; Sun & Stranieri, 2021),

$$\text{Big data analytics} = \text{big data} + \text{big data analysis} + \text{big DW} + \text{big DM} + \text{big SM} + \text{big ML} + \text{big visualization}$$

Where DW is data warehousing, DM is data mining, SM is statistical modeling, ML is machine learning. Then we have

$$\text{Cloud analytics} = \text{big data analytics} = \text{AI analytics} + \text{Cloud Computing analytics.} \qquad (7.24)$$

This implies that the above result is more inclusive than either (1) or (2). AI analytics refers to analytics based on AI, for example, AI analytics include intelligent data-based analytics and knowledge based analytics. Cloud Computing analytics can refer to analytics for cloud computing.

7.10.4 Summary

This section provides the foundations of cloud computing. It examines the calculus of cloud computing. The main contributions of this section consist of: 1. It presents a unified calculus of cloud computing. 2. It looks at the close interrelationships among IoT, resources and services, cloud computing, and big data computing. The proposed approach in this section will facilitate the research and development of cloud computing, intelligent analytics, business intelligence, and artificial intelligence.

7.11 BIG DATA ANALYTICS WITH APPLICATIONS

There are a great number of applications of big data analytics, for example, big data analytics based services innovation, big data analytics in business ecosystems, big data analytics with public and open data, Big data analytics and data markets, Big data analytics for e-commerce, Big data analytics in business decision-making, Big data analytics in healthcare, big data analytics in banking industry, big data analytics in social networking services, visualization analytics for big data, security and privacy issues in big data analytics, big data processing and management, and big data analytics for risk management. However, we will look at several applications of big data analytics.

7.11.1 Big Data Technology

Big data technology includes Hadoop, data discovery, open-source technology for big data analytics, cloud computing for big data, software as a service (SaaS), mobile analytics, mobile computing, crowdsourcing analytics, inter- and trans-firewall analytics, and data management of big data (Minelli, Chambers, & Dhiraj, 2013).

Apache Hadoop is a platform of big data analytics (Reddy, 2014). As an open-source platform, Hadoop stores and processes large datasets using clusters and commodity hardware. Hadoop can also scale up to hundreds and even thousands of nodes (Sun & Huo, 2021). The information stored in Hadoop will be effective (Blatt, 2017, p. 53).

The original creators of Hadoop were Doug Cutting (who used to be at Yahoo!) and Mike Cafarella (now working at the University of Michigan). Doug and Mike were building a project "Nutch" to create a large web index. They saw MapReduce and GFS sections from Google, which were relevant to the problem Nutch was trying to solve. They integrated the concepts from MapReduce and GFS into Nutch. Then later, these two components were pulled out to form the genesis of the Hadoop project. The name of Hadoop itself comes from Doug's son. Yahoo! Hired Doug and invested significant resources into growing the Hadoop project to store and index the web for Yahoo! Search. In 2008, recognizing the huge potential of Hadoop to transform data management across multiple industries, Amr left Yahoo! To co-found Cloudera with Mike and Jeff Hammerbacher. Doug followed in 2009 (Minelli, Chambers, & Dhiraj, 2013).

Hadoop is an open-source version of MapReduce (National Research Council, 2013). MapReduce is a style of distributed data analysis.

The software for big data analytics also includes SPSS, Microsoft Excel, and Power BI (Wade, 2020), SAS, Hadoop, R, Tableau, QlikView, and MATLAB.

7.11.2 Visualization

Data visualization plays an important part in combining data analytics (Sun, Sun, & Strang, 2018; Sharda, Delen, & Turba, 2018). This section looks at data visualization and its applications in data analytics and beyond.

Data visualization is the technique to help people understand the significance of data by organizing it virtually (Brooks, 2022). Data visualization enhances the user's ability to efficiently comprehend the meaning of the data and its mined knowledge and insights. The techniques of data visualization include (Aroraa, Lele, & Jindal, 2022; Brooks, 2022):

1. Pie charts and bar charts.

2. Line graphs.

3. Scatter plots.

4. Quantograms and typography.

5. Gantt charts.

6. Heat maps.

From them, people can easily recognize patterns, trends, associations, correlations, insights as knowledge and intelligence discovered from a database and warehouse (Brooks, 2022). Data visualization and data analytics deal with data (Aroraa, Lele, & Jindal, 2022). Data visualization helps data analytics to get better insights. Further, data visualization has been considered a visual subsystem in data analytics, visual analytics.

Visual analytics combines reporting, data preparation, visual exploration, and dashboards in a single product; it also provides the underpinnings of SAS solutions (prebuilt analytical applications). Visual analytics is also a component of data science, visual data mining, and machine learning (Howson, Richardson, Sallam, & Kronz, 2019).

Data can be manipulated while visualizing — such as when creating groups, bins, and new hierarchies.

Dashboards are basic, without rich mapping. Power BI provides data reporting using its visual analytics. Business users would like to scale and share visual explorations with more users. Virtualization is also important for cloud computing. Data virtualization, information virtualization, knowledge   virtualization,   algorithm   virtualization,   platform virtualization, system virtualization, and then, server virtualization of Amazon are all realized in visual analytics. Virtualization for everything is in the digital age.

Tableau has played an important role in data visualization. Tableau has a data visualization tool (Sharda, Delen, Turban, & King, 2018, p. 50). Data visualization aims to produce end-to-end reporting solutions and consulting for all internal business needs. Tableau sets the industry standard for user enablement with Meetup groups, roadshows, online tutorials, and the availability of skills in the market. Tableau 8.0 (http://www.tableausoftware. com/new-features/8.0) is not only a powerful data analytics tool but also for data visual analytics) for business and management.

7.12 SUMMARY

This chapter first discusses the fundamentals of data analytics. Then it explores mathematical analytics and presents the classification of data analytics. The chapter explores analyticalizing as a process for creating analytics. The chapter looks at the Internet of analytics, and examines big data analytics. The chapter proposes a workflow-driven big data analytics platform and a hierarchical life cycle of big data analytics. This chapter also discusses could computing and proposes a calculus of could computing. This chapter inspects big data analytics with applications in business, management, and decision-making. The main contributions in this chapter includes 1. a workflow-driven big data analytics platform and a hierarchical life cycle of big data analytics are important for big data analytics and business analytics. 2. analyticalizing as a process for developing analytics will play a significant rule in data analytics and business analytics, and 3. the calculus of computing will bridge big data, analytics, AI and the IoT.

In future work, we will delve into the analyticalizing as a process for creating analytics. we will also provide a workflow-driven big data analytics platform with applications.

7.13 REVIEW QUESTIONS AND PROBLEMS

1. What is data analytics?

2. How can you classify data analytics?

3. How can you understand the web of analytics?

4. What is visualization?

5. How can you understand the work-driven data analytics platform?

6. What is the relationship between data analysis and data analytics?

7. What is the difference between big data analytics and big analytics?

8. What is cloud computing?

9. List three popular big data systems.

10. What is the difference between data mining and data analytics?

11. What is the difference between data mining and statistics?

12. What is the largest database, information base, knowledge base, wisdom base?

13. How can we integrate intelligent analytics, augmented analytics, and modern analytics?

14. How can we understand resources in cloud computing?

7.14 REFERENCES FOR FURTHER STUDY

1. Philip M. Parker, 2022, The 2023–2028 World Outlook for Big Data Analytics, ICON Group International, Inc.

2. The Art of Service, 2023, Big Data And Analytics A Complete Guide. Big Data And Analytics Publishing.

3. Li M. Chen, Zhixun Su, Bo Jiang, 2015, Mathematical Problems in Data Science: Theoretical and Practical Methods, Springer.

4. Anil Maheshwari, 2024, Data Analytics Made Accessible: 2024 edition Kindle Edition.

5. Jonah Andersson, 2023, Learning Microsoft Azure: Cloud Computing and Development Fundamentals. O'Reilly Media.

6. Cathy Tanimura, 2021, SQL for Data Analysis: Advanced Techniques for Transforming Data into Insights. O'Reilly Media.

CHAPTER 8

Analytics Intelligence

Analytics intelligence plays a significant role in intelligent systems.

AنaLYTICS INTELLIGENCE IS ABOUT how to use analytics to win intelligence (Thompson & Rogers, 2017). Strategically, analytics intelligence is an intelligence that is derived from analytics systems. This chapter looks at analytics intelligence, intelligence analytics, DIKW analytics intelligence, big DIKW analytics intelligence, advanced computing, and quantum computing. This chapter also discusses Google Analytics as a data processing flow-oriented analytics and presents a unified approach to data processing flow-oriented big data analytics. This chapter discusses responsible big data and big data analytics and proposes applying responsible big data analytics to enhance responsible e-business services. Then this chapter looks over generative intelligence and explores analytical intelligence as the core of AI and generative intelligence. Analytical intelligence is underpinned by data analytics, big data analytics, and big analytics.

Learning objectives of this chapter:

- Contrast analytics intelligence and intelligence analytics.

- Explore 5 bigs of DIKI and analytics.

- Explain analytics intelligence.

- Define intelligence analytics.

- Understand DIKW analytics and intelligence.

DOI: 10.1201/9781003450504-8

- Explain generative AI.

- Identify Google Analytics as a data processing flow analytics.

- Learn about analytical intelligence and generative AI.

- Manage intelligent analytics.

- Define advanced computing.

- Understand responsible big data and big data analytics.

- Understand quantum computing.

8.1 INTRODUCTION

Analytics intelligence is intelligence on winning intelligence based on analytics (Thompson & Rogers, 2017). Strategically, analytics intelligence is an intelligence that is derived from analytics machines and systems. This chapter looks at analytics intelligence and intelligence analytics, as well as DIKW analytics intelligence and big DIKW analytics intelligence. This chapter also discusses Google Analytics as a data processing flow-oriented analytics and presents a unified approach to data processing flow-oriented big data analytics. This chapter discusses responsible big data and big data analytics and proposes applying responsible big data analytics to enhance responsible e-business services. It overviews generative intelligence. The chapter explores analytical intelligence as the core of AI and generative intelligence, not only in academia and the market. This is the analytical intelligence underpinned by data analytics, big data analytics, and big analytics. Therefore, we can work on intelligent data analytics and intelligent big data analytics, both used to develop analytical intelligence in terms of business and society. The chapter examines big data analytics intelligence with applications. Finally, the chapter discusses the spectrum of intelligent analytics.

The rest of this chapter is organized as follows: Sections 8.2 and 8.3 look at analytics intelligence and intelligence analytics. Section 4 proposes DIKW analytics intelligence. Sections 8.5 and 8.6 examine 5 Bigs of big DIKW intelligence and analytics and discuss how to manage DIKW techniques. Sections 8.7 and 8.8 discuss Google Analytics as a data processing flow-oriented analytics and presents a unified approach to data processing flow-oriented big data analytics. Sections 8.9 and 8.10 discuss responsible big data and big data analytics and propose applying responsible big data analytics to enhance responsible e-business services. Sections 8.11 and 8.12 review generative intelligence and explore analytical intelligence as the core of AI and generative intelligence. Section 8.13 discusses advanced computing. The final section ends this chapter with concluding remarks.

8.2 ANALYTICS INTELLIGENCE

Analytics intelligence is an intelligence that is derived from analytics systems. Analytics systems have been created by using analytics engineering and analytics technology like analyticizing.

Operationally, Analytics = analysis + SM + DM + DW + ML, and therefore using intelligence as the right operation to them, we have

Analytics intelligence = analysis intelligence + SM intelligence + DM intelligence + DW intelligence + ML intelligence.

Analysis intelligence is the most ordinary intelligence because any deep analysis will lead to intelligence, for example, data analysis will lead to data intelligence. Knowledge analysis will lead to knowledge intelligence. System analysis will also lead to system intelligence (see Chapter 5.5).

SM intelligence can be divided into statistical model intelligence and statistical algorithm intelligence. Statistical model intelligence is intelligence that is derived from the statistical model and its embedded system. Statistical algorithm intelligence is the intelligence that is derived from the statistical algorithm and its embedded system. The modeling and algorithm have brought about a model and algorithm industry. This is why model and algorithm intelligence is empowered by the model developers and algorithm engineers. One of the best algorithms is page rank, which underpins the foundation of Google as a search engine.

DM intelligence is the intelligence displayed from a DM system. Sometimes, we call DM an intelligent system or intelligent technology. The reason behind it is that DM will lead to data intelligence. That is, DM belongs to data intelligence.

DW intelligence is an intelligence demonstrated by a DW system. If DW is an important technology and tool for business systems, then DW as a technology and system will lead to data intelligence. That is, DW is data intelligence.

ML intelligence is intelligence displayed from an ML system. Traditionally, ML is a system that leads to knowledge-based intelligence (Russell & Norvig, 2020). Now, ML, in particular, deep learning is a system that leads to data-based intelligence. That is, ML intelligence consists of knowledge-based intelligence and data-based intelligence.

Therefore, analytics intelligence is an integrated intelligence. Analytics intelligence can be developed as an important part of big data computing (Wang, 2012). Incorporating data analytics intelligence with big data intelligence is one of big intelligences. Big intelligence has become the most vital part of enhancing BI and big intelligence (Sun, Sun, & Strang, 2018). Global free WIFI (Payton, 2015) is a kind of big intelligence, because it meets the big expectations of billions of people (Sun, Sun, & Strang, 2018).

8.3 INTELLIGENCE ANALYTICS

Intelligence analytics can be renamed intelligent analytics.

Intelligent analytics is an intelligent system that provides intelligence for its services or products to its customers.

Intelligent analytics consists of intelligent data analytics, intelligent big data analytics, intelligent information analytics, intelligent big information analytics; intelligent wisdom analytics, and intelligent big wisdom analytics. Each of them will be expressed as an analytics intelligence: data intelligence, information intelligence, knowledge intelligence, and wisdom intelligence respectively. Each of them has been mentioned in this book based on the context.

8.4 DIKW ANALYTICS INTELLIGENCE

As mentioned, DIKW is the accredited form of data, information, knowledge, and wisdom. Then we have:

DIKW analytics: = data analytics + information analytics + knowledge analytics + wisdom analytics.

Adding intelligence as an operation to both sides, we have

$$
\begin{aligned}
\text{DIKW analytics intelligence} := \; & \text{data analytics intelligence} \\
& + \text{information analytics intelligence} \\
& + \text{knowledge analytics intelligence} \\
& + \text{wisdom analytics intelligence.}
\end{aligned} \tag{8.1}
$$

Therefore, DIKW analytics intelligence is an integrated intelligence covering data analytics intelligence, information analytics intelligence, knowledge analytics intelligence, and wisdom analytics intelligence.

How to use analyticizing (see Section 7.6) as an engineering process to develop a DIKW analytics system to reflect DIKW analytics intelligence might be more difficult than creating a analytics system, see Section 7.8.

8.5 5 BIGS OF DIKI AND ANALYTICS

The previous section looked at big data in the name of 10 Bigs (Section 3.7). This section proposes and examines 5 Bigs of DIKI and analytics and their relationships.

8.5.1 Big Data

In the past decade, big data and its emerging technologies including big data analytics have been not only making big changes in the way the business operates but also making traditional data analytics and business analytics bring about new big opportunities for academia and enterprises (Gardner, 2023; Sun & Wang, 2017; Brooks, 2022).

8.5.2 Big Information

Big data has certainly ushered in the coming of big information because data and information have been used interchangeably (Sun, 2024). The dramatic development of the Internet and WWW since the middle of the 1990s has made huge amounts of information available to everyone in the world. The significant development of social media or social networking services such as Meta (formerly Facebook), Tweeter, QQ, and WeChat have produced not only big data but also big information (Sun, 2023).

8.5.3 Big Knowledge

Big data has also led to big knowledge that we are enjoying. As well-known, knowledge is power, knowledge can change a person's destiny; knowledge can also change the destiny of a country. Knowledge can change one country from a developing country into a developed one. Such knowledge is big knowledge! Many countries (including Australia) have been working hard to develop knowledge economies and knowledge societies (Sun, 2024). China is no exception. The Chinese dream makes China develop into a highly developed knowledge economy and knowledge society (Sun, 2023). Thus, mining big data for big knowledge is an important basis for realizing the Chinese dream of rejuvenation. Mining big data for big knowledge is also an important basis for keeping the USA as a continuous superpower in the world.

In computer science, discovering knowledge from a database (KDD), coined by Gregory Piatetsky-Shapiro in 1989, is the main task of knowledge discovery and data mining (EMC, 2015; Kantardzic, 2011). The research and development of KDD and data mining have also continued for over 40 years since Michael Lovell coined this term (Lovell, 1983). Now the combination of KDD and data mining with big data aims to promote further development of mining big data for big knowledge. At least, this is the task of intelligent big data analytics.

8.5.4 Big Intelligence

Intelligence has been not only a lasting topic for computer science under the flagship of AI and intelligence computing (Sun, 2023), but also an exciting topic for industries, organizations, and businesses under the flagship of BI (Gardner, 2023; Laudon & Laudon, 2020). AI has facilitated the development of intelligent services, intelligent manufacturing, and intelligent systems (Russell & Norvig, 2020; Sun, Pambel, & Wu, 2022). BI has promoted the improvement of competitiveness of business performance, supported management decision-making of organizations, and produced billionaire-level enterprises such as Google and Meta (Sabherwal & Becerra-Fernandez, 2011).

Big data intelligence (BDI) is a kind of intelligence driven by big data (Sun, Strang, & Li, 2018). In the big data world, big intelligence particularly refers to big data intelligence and big data analytics intelligence. Big data intelligence is big data-driven intelligence, which can be defined as a set of ideas, technologies, systems, and tools that can imitate, simulate, and augment human intelligence, machine intelligence, and system intelligence, and are related to big data management and processing (Sun, Strang, & Li, 2018). For example, intelligent methods for searching big data and visualizing knowledge mined from big data belong to big data technologies and systems.

Big intelligence has drawn increasing attention with the development of BI, big data analytics, and big data computing. Just as intelligence is a part of computing, big intelligence will be developed as an important part of big data computing (Wang, 2012; Gardner, 2023). Starlink satellites are an example of a big intelligence because they meet the big expectations of billions of people to receive Wi-Fi communications (Sun, Strang, & Li, 2018).

As well-known, big data is significant for innovation, competition, and productivity in the digital age (Manyika, Chui, & Bughin, 2011; Sun &

Huo, 2021). Big information, big knowledge, and big intelligence are also significant for effective management, decision-making, and innovation for the development of the economy, society, and even nations, because many governments and organizations have carried out a number of initiatives to develop big intelligence industry, knowledge economy (e.g. Australia), and wisdom cities (e.g. China).

8.5.5 Big Analytics

Big analytics is an emerging science and technology involving the multidisciplinary state-of-art information and communication technology (ICT), mathematics, operations research (OR), machine learning (ML), data sciences, and decision sciences for big data (Sun, Strang, & Firmin, 2017; Chen & Zhang, 2014; Sun & Stranieri, 2021). Augmented analytics platforms as an example of big analytics represent the mainstream market for data and analytics leaders in BI, data science, and machine learning (Howson, Richardson, Sallam, & Kronz, 2019).

In the world of big data, big analytics is a brief representation of big data analytics, big data-based analytics and big data-driven analytics (Minelli, Chambers, & Dhiraj, 2013; Sun, Sun, & Strang, 2018). However, big data analytics is not unique to big analytics. In fact, big analytics encompasses big data analytics, big information analytics, big knowledge analytics, and big intelligence analytics. Therefore, big analytics can be defined as the process of collecting, organizing, and analyzing big data, big information, big knowledge, and big intelligence to discover and visualize patterns, knowledge, insights, and intelligence within them for supporting decision-making.

Therefore, data, information, knowledge, and intelligence can be considered input for an analytics system for processing. The processing of this analytics system is to examine, summarize, and draw conclusions from the digital resources of big data, information, and knowledge. This analytics aims to learn, describe, and predict patterns, associations, knowledge, insights, and intelligence (Sun & Stranieri, 2021).

The above discussion demonstrates that data analytics is not all forms of analytics. Information analytics, knowledge analytics, and intelligence analytics are extended and advanced forms of data analytics. In such a way, data analytics, information analytics, knowledge analytics, and intelligence analytics (for short, DIKI analytics) can be considered as the basic form of analytics, taking into account DIKI [32, 28]. Based on natural deduction and association, we then have

Analytics: $=$ big data analytics $+$ big information analytics
$+$ big knowledge analytics $+$ big intelligence analytics   (8.2)

In other words, analytics consists of big data analytics, big information analytics, big knowledge analytics, and big intelligence analytics, at a fundamental level.

Adding big as an operation to both sides of DIKW analytics intelligence: = big data analytics intelligence + information analytics intelligence + knowledge analytics intelligence + wisdom analytics intelligence, we have

Big DIKW analytics intelligence : = big data analytics intelligence
$+$ big information analytics
intelligence $+$ big knowledge analytics
intelligence $+$ big wisdom analytics
intelligence.

(8.3)

Big analytics has been drawing increasing attention in the academia of computing, mathematics, operations research, decision sciences, business, management and industry of healthcare and medical science (Sun, 2024).

8.6 MANAGING DIKW TECHNIQUES

There are many methods and techniques useful for managing DIKI, for example, database and management (Coronel, Morris, & Rob, 2020), information base and management, knowledge base and management, and wisdom base and management (Sun & Huo, 2021), as shown in Figure 8.1. Data management (Laudon & Laudon, 2020), information management (Laudon & Laudon, 2020), and knowledge management (Sun & Finnie, 2005) are well-known in either information systems or intelligent systems (Turban & Volonino, 2011). We do not go into each of them. For details see other references such as (Coronel, Morris, & Rob, 2020) and (Laudon & Laudon, 2020).

In Figure 8.1, the data in the database can be classified into four different categories. Descriptive datasets, diagnostic datasets, predictive datasets, and prescriptive datasets. Descriptive datasets consist of historical descriptive datasets and current descriptive datasets. Diagnostic datasets consist of historical datasets and symptom datasets. Predictive datasets consist of historical predictive datasets and current predictive datasets. Predictive datasets consist of historical predictive datasets and current predictive datasets. Therefore, descriptive analytics is based on

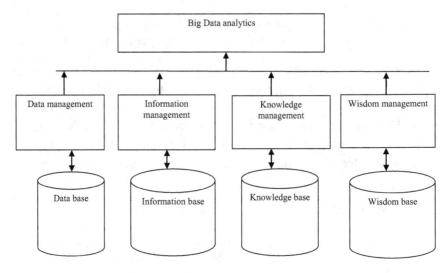

FIGURE 8.1   A model of management for DIKM base.

descriptive datasets, diagnostic analytics is based on diagnostic datasets, predictive analytics is based on predictive datasets, and prescriptive analytics is based on prescriptive datasets. Similarly, information (or knowledge or wisdom) can be classified into four categories, including diagnostic information sets which lead to diagnostic information (or knowledge or wisdom) management and analytics.

8.7 GOOGLE ANALYTICS AS DATA PROCESSING FLOW ORIENTED ANALYTICS

A data processing flow consists of four stages from left to right, from upstream to downstream (Penn, 2016), illustrated as in Figure 8.2. In what follows, we look at each stage of data processing flow and its corresponding Google Analytics services.

8.7.1 Store and Organize

The first stage consisting of "store and organize" is at the left of the data-processing flow. Google Analytics aims to store and organize website tags, which is accomplished by Google Tag Manager™. Tag Manager also allows for running website surveys and multivariate optimization tests, tracking social media audiences (Penn, 2016; Sun & Vajjhala, 2021). Tag Manager enables changes to the website without requiring editing the site itself.

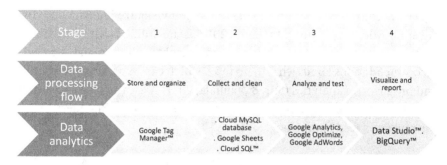

FIGURE 8.2   A model for data processing flow-oriented Google Analytics.

8.7.2 Collect and Clean

The second stage on the next left of the data processing flow consists of "collect and clean" (Sun & Vajjhala, 2021). Google Analytics aims to collect and clean data (Penn, 2016). All the analytics tools in this stage have their APIs, but some external data sources, like social media sites, require data collection separately. The Google Data Cloud gathers big data and prepares it for analysis and reporting. For example, we can collect social media engagement data from third-party vendors in a cloud MySQL database or Google Sheets. We can extract ad data from third-party advertising systems and store it in Cloud SQL™.

8.7.3 Analyze and Optimize

The next stage on the right of the data processing flow consists of "analyze and optimize" (Sun & Vajjhala, 2021). The corresponding Google Analytics are Google Optimize and Google AdWords aiming to analytically analyze big data and optimize the discovered value (Tableau, 2017), knowledge, and insights (Penn, 2016). Google Analytics tells us what is happening on our website, which is a kind of descriptive analytics. Google Optimize can test out a variety of assumptions to understand what works best on our sites. Google AdWords then enables us to market to the audiences that we prove effective with analytics and Optimize (Penn, 2016). Google Analytics alone used to be the star of the show, but now it is one of the Google Analytics platforms.

8.7.4 Visualize and Report

The farthest right stage of the data processing flow consists of "visualize and report" (Sun & Vajjhala, 2021). The corresponding Google Analytics is Data Studio™. Data Studio can assemble and visualize big data and discover knowledge and insights (Penn, 2016). Data Studio is where we transform our big data into analysis and insights, then make strategic recommendations about what to do next, which can be a part of predictive and prescriptive analytics (Sun & Vajjhala, 2021). We can make a basic but effective public relations reporting system out of Google BigQuery™ with the raw news feed from Google News.

8.8 DATA PROCESSING FLOW ORIENTED BIG DATA ANALYTICS: A UNIFIED APPROACH

The above discussion demonstrates that Google Analytics is flow-oriented data processing. Google develops analytics as systems and services for each stage of the mentioned data processing flow, from upstream to downstream.

With the dramatic development of big data and big data technology in the past decade, big data has become hundreds of billion-dollar industries (Statista, 2021). The data processing in the big data industry, generally consists of n stages of data processing flow from upstream to downstream, where n is a natural number, as follows.

$$DP1, DP2, \ldots, DPn, \tag{8.4}$$

Where DP is the abbreviation of data processing. Each of the above stages of the data processing flow corresponds to at least one intelligent analytics (Sun & Stranieri, 2021), that is,

$$DP1 \text{ analytics}, DP2 \text{ analytics}, \ldots, DPn \text{ analytics} \tag{8.5}$$

Every DPi ($i \in \{1, 2, \ldots, n\}$) analytics might be renamed properly.

The number n will be increased to very great and even to infinity (∞) with the further development of the big data industry. Therefore, more intelligent analytics and their services will be emerging (Schlegel & Sun, 2023). There are also more challenges for developing big data analytics and intelligent analytics as a system or service based on data processing flow. One of the challenges is the responsibility of these data processing flow-oriented big data analytics.

Data processing flow-oriented big data analytics should be responsible for every stage of the data processing flow. In other words, the responsibility of big data analytics should be divided into and aligned with every stage of the data processing flow. This is similar to the total quality control that should be carried out in every stage of a production line, rather than the final quality check before leaving for selling to the customers.

In addition, a full analytic workflow is from data preparation to visual exploration and insight generation (Richardson, Schlegel, Sallam, Kronz, & Sun, 2021). This corresponds to the proposed data processing flow. Then we have data processing flow-based analytics. One who controls the data processing flow-based analytics from upstream to downstream will dominate the data industry, just as Google has been doing.

8.9 RESPONSIBLE BIG DATA AND BIG DATA ANALYTICS

In 2015, the General Assembly of the United Nations (UN) adopted the 2030 Agenda for Sustainable Development, which includes 17 Sustainable Development Goals (SDGs) to realize that in 2030 all people enjoy peace and prosperity (UNDP, 2021). Responsible consumption and production are the 12th SDG of 17 SDGs. Big data analytics as a system and service is a part of responsible consumption and production. Therefore, responsible big data analytics and their services are significant for realizing the 12th SDG of the UN.

Responsible big data analytics has drawn some attention in academia. Fothergill et al. (2019) state that responsible data governance principles should include four responsible research and innovation features: anticipation, reflection, engagement, and responsiveness. These principles would consider future consequences, integrate mechanisms for fostering reflexivity, and enable stakeholder engagement. Responsible research innovation principles can ensure that research in technologies, including big data and artificial intelligence (AI), are socially acceptable and responsible (Stahl & Wright, 2018). The underlying guidance for responsible big data analytics research is based on the fact that most data impact people (Zook, Barocas, & Boyd, 2017). Privacy should be seen as contextual and depending on the nature of the data because privacy preferences differ across societies. Privacy is an important part of any responsible big data analytics as a service (Sun, Strang, & Pambel, 2020).

In the age of big data, analytics, and AI, big data and big data analytics should be responsible, because monetizing big data through the ever-increasing importance of global data trade and industry data trade using big data analytics can improve business performance. Selling internal data and big data analytics services to external consumers can be hundreds of billion-dollars profitable (Fattah, 2014; Tableau, 2017). Data monetization of Facebook (or Meta) and Google (or Alphabet) has become a miracle in the past decade. They have no traditional natural resources like the iron core. They have only two artificial resources; one is big data from artificial donation and aggressive collection using intelligent techniques based on intelligent algorithms. Another is big data analytics, which can transform big data into smart insights and big value (Richardson, Schlegel, Sallam, Kronz, & Sun, 2021; Sun, Pambel, & Wu, 2022). The question arises: are the big data and big data analytics of Google and Facebook responsible?

Gmail was launched in 2004; Google subsequently admitted that it has scanned private correspondence for personal information. In the same year, Facebook was founded, its business model is also based on the capture of and access to personal data and information (Kavenna, 2019).

Why does responsible data analytics matter to e-business services? There are many different answers to this question from researchers. Big data analytics uses predictive algorithms and mathematically calculates human behaviors. Then, data giants sell certainty to business customers who would like to know with certainty what we do. The best way to make the predictions desirable to customers is to ensure that they come true: "to tune and herd and shape and push us in the direction that creates the highest probability of their business success" (Kavenna, 2019).

In the Cambridge Analytica (CA) scandal (Hu, 2020) (also see Chapter 4), every aspect of CA's operations was simply mimicking a day in the life of a surveillance capitalist" (Kavenna, 2019). Trade of human futures using big data trade and big data analytics is irresponsible and illegal – like the slave trade was made illegal (Kavenna, 2019).

In what follows, this section looks at responsible big data and big data analytics based on the Cambridge Analytica case study.

Based on the Cambridge Dictionary (Cambridge, 1995), the term responsible means 1. "having control and authority over something or someone and the duty of taking care of it or them" 2. "Having good judgment and ability to act correctly and make decisions on your own". Therefore, big data analytics is responsible if it satisfies the following three conditions.

1. It has control and authority over something or someone.

2. It has the duty of taking care of it or them.

3. It has good judgment and the ability to act correctly and make decisions properly based on the existing laws and rules.

Briefly, responsible big data analytics is about human responsibility for developing and deploying big data analytics along fundamental human principles and values to ensure human flourishing and well-being in a sustainable world, based on the definition of responsible AI (Dignum, 2019, p. 119). Responsible big data and e-business services can be defined similarly. The responsibility of big data and big data analytics is relative to individuals, organizations, communities, societies, and the world. That is, for example, big data analytics should be responsible for individuals, organizations, people, communities, and countries based on the principle of international fairness. The following two cases will look at if the big data and big data analytics of Facebook are responsible for individuals, communities, and societies.

Cambridge Analytica (CA) was a British analytics firm that aimed to use big data to build detailed, and deeply personal, psychological profiles about people and then target them with what is essentially emotional manipulation in the form of ads (Wood, 2018). CA had an app that collected and exploited over 87 million Facebook users' data before the profiling was exposed (Hu, 2020; Isaac & Frenkel, 2018). CA could have created psychological profiles of 230 million Americans according to estimates. At that time, Facebook's platform did permit the apps to access the data from the users of the app and their friends, unless the friends explicitly prohibited the collection in their privacy settings (Wood, 2018).

In March 2018, CA was accused of engaging in enhanced micro-targeting and unethically using this information to support political campaigns in various countries (Hu, 2020). CA used behavioral micro-targeting through its massive dataset to deliver targeted messages supporting the Trump campaign in the 2016 US Elections (Wood, 2018). The Facebook-CA data and analytics case raised several ethical issues related to the responsible usage of big data by social networking sites, including user data collection and use practices (Hu, 2020; Wood, 2018).

Responsible big data and big data analytics are required at every stage along with the data processing flow from upstream and downstream, mentioned in Section 8.7. A new issue arises here: How to apply responsible big data and big data analytics to enhance responsible e-business services through monetization of big data and big data analytics as an e-business service? We will address it in the next section.

8.10 APPLYING RESPONSIBLE BIG DATA ANALYTICS TO ENHANCE RESPONSIBLE E-BUSINESS SERVICES

This section proposes four strategies for applying responsible big data analytics to enhance responsible e-business services.

Digital information sharing is indispensable for our work and lives in the digitalized society. Facebook is a digital giant with several e-business services that we rely on daily, just as we rely on foods for our daily survival. The question is: are the e-business services of Facebook responsible for banning news sharing to Australian people recently?

Making data available to external organizations is a key mechanism for business-to-business (B2B) e-business services in the age of big data (Fattah, 2014). Big data analytics has increased the use of this digital data exchange thanks to AI and cloud computing. This leads to open data initiatives, data marketplaces, and vendors who offer datasets emerging in every aspect of business and society. The core services of e-business giants, including Facebook, Google, Amazon, and Alibaba, are big data services and big data analytics services. Are their e-business services responsible? These issues require solutions to responsible e-business services. In what follows, we propose four strategies for applying responsible big data analytics to enhance responsible e-business services.

The first strategy is that big data analytics and its services should meet the basic ethical standard mentioned in the top nine ethical issues in AI (Bossmann, 2016; Bostrom & Yudkowsky, 2018), besides satisfying the three conditions mentioned in the definition of responsible big data analytics.

1. Unemployment. What happens after the end of jobs?

2. Inequality. How do we distribute the wealth created by AI machines?

3. Humanity. How do machines affect our behavior and interaction?

4. Artificial stupidity. How can we guard AI against mistakes?

5. Racist robots. How do we eliminate AI bias?

6. Security. How do we keep AI safe from adversaries?

7. Evil genies. How do we protect AI against unintended consequences?

8. Singularity. How do we stay in control of a complex intelligent system?

9. Robot rights. How do we define the humane treatment of AI?

Responsible big data analytics should provide a rational and satisfactory answer to each of the above for the world, taking into account the existing regulations and laws worldwide. For example, a rational and satisfactory answer can be below, because big data analytics is a part of AI (Sun & Vajjhala, 2021).

1. Unemployment. What happens after the adoption of big data analytics?

2. Inequality. How do we distribute the insights and wealth created by big data analytics?

3. Humanity. How do big data analytics affect our behavior and interaction?

4. Artificial stupidity. How can we guard big data analytics against mistakes and irresponsibility?

5. Racist robots. How do we eliminate the bias caused by using big data analytics?

6. Security. How do we keep big data analytics safe from adversaries?

7. Evil genies. How do we protect big data analytics against unintended consequences?

8. Singularity. How do we stay in control of complex intelligent analytics?

9. Robot rights. How do we define the humane treatment of intelligent analytics?

The second strategy is that big data analytics and its services should be accountable or explainable (Dignum, 2019), that is, every service of big data analytics should be explainable and auditable based on the new regulation of AI systems (Turek, 2020). In such a way, we could avoid the scandal of Facebook and Cambridge Analytica or similar (Wood, 2018). We can also use big data analytics and its services responsibly to enhance responsible e-business services.

Stoller claims that "Facebook was born, lives, and thrives in scandal"(Stoller, 2021). For example, Facebook's violations of privacy led to a Federal Trade Commission consent decree in 2012. Mr. Mark Zuckerberg was shown explicitly predatory in his business methods, supplemented by the Federal Trade Commission complaint filed in 2021. However, despite its years of lawlessness and recklessness, Facebook is still a globe-straddling monopoly over our information commons. The problem may not be Facebook, it might be a policy regime for monopolization, securities fraud, surveillance advertising, user data collection, and processing. This at least includes the opt-out policy used by the social media giant Facebook and other social media and internet advertising firms in the USA.

Opt-in is a personal collection policy in which the company collecting the information does not use the information for any other purpose (e.g., sell or rent the information or data) unless the customer specifically chooses to allow that use (Laudon & Laudon, 2020, p. 137).

Opt-out is a personal collection policy in which a business is allowed to collect personal information until the consumer specifically requests the data not to be collected.

Opt-in is the practice of EU countries. Opt-out is the practice of the USA. The opt-in model has appealed to privacy advocates and forced the data collection company to be responsible for the customer's interest and satisfaction. However, the opt-out model is very aggressive, and the data collection company's interest is a top priority. It is difficult for a data company to use the opt-out model to be responsible for customer's interests. Therefore, a new user data collection policy should be introduced to allow the responsibility of big data analytics to consider reasonably both the interests of data companies and customers. This implies that new policies and redevelopment of existing data collection policies are necessary for responsible big data and big data analytics. This is the third strategy for making big data analytics responsible.

The fourth strategy for responsible big data analytics is to look at the responsibility chain for data processing flow-oriented big data analytics mentioned in Section 8.8, every data processing flow stage corresponds to a big data analytics system. Every big data analytics corresponds to its responsibility. Different data processing flow stages and corresponding big data analytics have special responsibilities. Every stage of data processing flow needs to use responsible big data analytics because the responsibility chain results from the data processing flow-based big data analytics. Therefore, a responsibility chain should be developed for a data processing flow-oriented big data analytics system or platform (Dignum, 2019, p. 5).

8.11 GENERATIVE INTELLIGENCE

Generative AI is an intelligence that can learn from existing artifacts to generate new, realistic artifacts (at scale) that reflect the characteristics of the training data but don't repeat it (Gardner, 2024). Generative AI can produce a variety of novel content, such as images, video, music, speech, text, software code, and product designs. The current text content generation is ChatGPT.

ChatGPT of OpenAI has pushed the further development of generative intelligence in terms of transforming business and its impacts on business and society.

Generative AI uses several techniques, including prediction algorithms that continue to evolve (Gardner, 2024). For example, ChatGPT uses natural language translation, large language foundation models, and reinforcement learning models.

The benefits of generative AI include faster product development, enhanced customer experience, and improved employee productivity (Gardner, 2024). The risks of generative AI include the lack of transparency, accuracy, bias, intellectual property (IP) and copyright, cybersecurity and fraud, and sustainability. Therefore, China and Singapore have already promulgated new regulations regarding the use of generative AI (Gardner, 2024). From the author's viewpoint, this book and related contents are free from generative AI. Even so, some practical uses of generative AI today include: 1. Written content augmentation and creation, 2. Question answering and discovery, 3. Tone, 4. Summarization, 5. Simplification, 6. Classification of content for specific use cases, 7. Chatbot performance improvement, and software coding.

Generative AI provides new and disruptive opportunities to increase revenue, reduce costs, improve productivity, and better manage risk. It will shortly become a competitive advantage and differentiator (Gardner, 2024).

Industries that are most impacted by generative AI include pharmaceutical, manufacturing, media, architecture, interior design, engineering, automotive, aerospace, defense, medical, electronics, and energy. Gardner predicted that by 2025, more than 30% of new drugs and materials will be systematically discovered using generative AI techniques, up from zero today (Gardner, 2024). Gardner also predicted that by 2027, about 15% of new applications will be automatically generated by AI without a human in the loop. This is not happening at all today.

The major tech providers in the generative AI market include Salesforce and SAP, Microsoft, Google, Amazon Web Services (AWS) and IBM in the USA, and Baidu, Alibaba, Tencent, and Huawei in China.

Salesforce and SAP as Enterprise application providers are building LLM (Large language model) capabilities into their platforms (Gardner, 2024).

Google has two large language models, Palm, a multimodal model, and Bard, a pure language model. They are embedding their generative AI technology into their suite of workplace applications, which will benefit millions of people (Gardner, 2024).

Microsoft is embedding generative AI technology into its products, but it has the first-mover advantage and buzz of ChatGPT on its side (Gardner, 2024).

Amazon has partnered with Hugging Face, which has several LLMs available on an open-source basis, to build solutions. Amazon also has Bedrock, which provides access to generative AI on the cloud via AWS, with a set of AI models that create text and improve searches and personalization (Gardner, 2024).

IBM has multiple foundation models and a strong ability to fine-tune both its and third-party models by injecting data and retraining and employing the model (Gardner, 2024).

New risks are from generative intelligence. AI regulations and responsibilities are organized to address how can we coexist with AI, which is a big challenge for everyone in the digital world.

The author believes that generative intelligence is not the key to further development of AI. However, the key of AI is analytical intelligence. We will look at it in the next section.

8.12 ANALYTICAL INTELLIGENCE

The earlier analytical intelligence was from logical AI and symbolic AI (Russell & Norvig, 2020). This period has lasted until the inception of the Internet. However, big data has been booming since 2012 and onwards, and data analytics and big data analytics have become an important part of business analytics, and intelligent analytics. What is the key to data analytics? What is the key to AI? It is analytic, then how can we use analytic models, methods, and techniques to analyticize data and big data, to process information and big information, knowledge and big knowledge intelligently? This is the analytical intelligence. Analytical intelligence is the core of supporting generative intelligence.

Therefore, we can work on intelligent data analytics and intelligent big data analytics, both used to develop analytical intelligence in terms of business and society.

Analytical expertise, analytic consulting services, analytics reports, and visualizations, Watson, analytics platform, customer analytics, analytics professionals (Sharda, Delen, Turban, & King, 2018b, pp. 68–69), analytical methods, analytics and BI tools, analytical support, analytical systems, and analytical capabilities have been discussed in many textbooks (Sharda, Delen, Turban, & King, 2018b, pp. 28–42). All these lead to analytical intelligence. Therefore, analytical intelligence has been developed using analytical systems, including analytics, data analytics, and more analytics.

Customer relationship management (CRM) systems consist of operational CRM and analytical CRM systems. The analytical CRM system can analyze customer data output from operational CRM applications based on a customer data warehouse populated by operational CRM systems and customer touch points (Laudon & Laudon, 2020).

Developing analytical insights is the objective of any analytics system (Sharda, Delen, Turban, & King, 2018, p. 65). In fact, any analytics system aims to create analytical intelligence, including analytical insights.

The rule-based or symbolic approach to AI is now dormant. It seems unlikely to be revived outside a few narrow domains, and perhaps not even there (McAfee & Brynjolfsson, 2017, p. 85). However, all systems are based on models, rules, and algorithms. Everything behind the general customers is analytical. Rule-based systems have been embedded into almost every AI system, including analytics systems. All of these we can call analytical AI. Therefore, all analytical AI systems support generative AI.

8.13 ADVANCED COMPUTING

Advanced computing is defined as the advanced technical capabilities, including both computer systems and expert staff, that support research across the entire science and engineering spectrum and that are of a scale and cost so great that they are typically shared among multiple researchers, institutions, and applications (National Academies of Sciences, 2016). It also encompasses support for data-driven research as well as modeling and simulation. "Computing" should be read broadly as encompassing DIKI computing and DIKI analytics and other DIKI- intensive applications, as well as modeling and simulation and other analytically (numerically-intensive or symbolic) computing applications.

New technologies include Hadoop, NoSQL, with expertise in Bayesian approaches, neural networks, deep learning, and ensemble modeling. Data access and preparation, data management, data integration, visualization and presentation software, analytical tools including R and Python, and analytical workflow. All these can provide a solid foundation of analytic capabilities for new analytics ecosystems and platforms inside many companies and organizations. All can enable novel approaches to analytics, led by the chief analytics officer or chief data officer (Thompson & Rogers, 2017).

The advanced computing includes (Blatt, 2017; Sun, 2022)

1. In Memory computing,

2. Data lakes,

3. Cloud computing,

4. Deep Learning,

5. Hadoop,

6. NoSQL,

7. Quantum computing,

8. DDPP computing and analytics as a part of analytics technology,

9. 6G.

We have studied almost all of them in this book. In what follows, we will only look at Quantum computing briefly.

Quantum computing uses quantum science, technology, and engineering to solve complex problems that classical computers or supercomputers can't solve, or can't solve quickly enough (IBM, 2024).

Quantum science includes quantum mechanics covering quantum mechanical phenomena. The quantum theory was developed in the 1920s to explain the wave–particle duality observed at atomic scales (Wikipedia, 2024). The basic unit of information in quantum computing is the qubit, similar to the bit in traditional digital electronics. the qubit is the fundamental unit of quantum information. a qubit can exist in a superposition of its two "basis" states. The design of quantum algorithms involves creating procedures that allow a quantum computer to process qubits and their calculations efficiently and quickly (Wikipedia, 2024). Quantum algorithms provide speedup over conventional algorithms only for some tasks at the moment.

How to engineer high-quality qubits is challenging for quantum engineering. Scientists and engineers are exploring multiple technologies for quantum hardware and hope to develop scalable quantum architectures (Wikipedia, 2024). Over the years, small-scale quantum computers have been constructed by experimentalists to use trapped ions and superconductors.

At small scales, physical matter exhibits properties of both particles and waves, and quantum technology leverages this behavior, specifically quantum superposition, and entanglement, using specialized hardware that supports the preparation and manipulation of quantum states (Wikipedia, 2024).

Current quantum computing hardware generates only a limited amount of entanglement before getting overwhelmed by noise. IBM claimed that IBM Quantum leads the world in the hardware and software for quantum computing (IBM, 2024).

8.14 SUMMARY

Analytics intelligence is how to use analytics to win intelligence (Thompson & Rogers, 2017). Strategically, analytics intelligence is an intelligence that is derived from analytics systems. This chapter examines analytics intelligence and intelligence analytics, DIKW analytics intelligence, big DIKW analytics intelligence, advanced computing and quantum computing. This chapter also discusses Google Analytics as a data processing flow-oriented analytics and presents a unified approach to data processing flow-oriented big data analytics. This chapter discusses responsible big data and big data analytics and proposes applying responsible big data analytics to enhance responsible e-business services. Then this chapter overviews generative intelligence and explores analytical intelligence as the core of AI and generative intelligence. Analytical intelligence is underpinned by data analytics, big data analytics, and big analytics. The main contributions in this chapter are 1. DIKW analytics intelligence and 5 bigs of DIKI, and analytics will play a vital role in analytics intelligence. 2. Analytical intelligence is the core of AI and generative intelligence. 3. Analytical intelligence as the core of AI and generative intelligence, is underpinned by data analytics, big data analytics, big analytics, and intelligent big analytics.

Therefore, we can work on intelligent data analytics and intelligent big data analytics to develop analytical intelligence and promote generative intelligence in terms of business and society.

8.15 REVIEW QUESTIONS AND PROBLEMS

1. What is analytics intelligence?

2. What is intelligence analytics?

3. How can we understand DIKW analytics and intelligence?

4. What is generative AI?

5. What is the relationship between analytical intelligence and generative AI?

6. How to manage intelligent analytics?

7. What is advanced computing?

8. What is quantum computing?

8.16 REFERENCES FOR FURTHER STUDY

1. Mert Damlapinar, 2019, Analytics of Life: Making Sense of Data Analytics, Machine Learning & AI. Kindle Edition.

2. Bernard Marr, 2021, Data Strategy: How to Profit from a World of Big Data, Analytics and Artificial Intelligence. Kogan Page.

3. Gerardus Blokdyk, 2018, Analytics and Intelligence: A Complete Guide. 5STARCooks

4. Fernanda Aparecida Rocha Silva, 2018, Analytical intelligence in processes: Data science for business, IEEE Latin America Transactions, 16(8): 2240 – 2247.

5. Brian Paul, 2024, Ethics and Responsible AI: Guiding the Future of Artificial Intelligence with Integrity, Transparency, and Humanity, Independently published.

CHAPTER 9

Data, Analytics, and Intelligence

A Unified Approach

All data, big data, and analytics are for intelligence.

T HIS CHAPTER WILL EXPLORE data analytics intelligence and intelligent big data analytics with applications in business, management, and decision making. More specifically, this chapter looks at data analytics intelligence and big data analytics intelligence. It explores intelligent big data analytics systems, intelligent big data analytics ecosystems, and intelligent big data analytics as a management. It proposes big data 4.0 as the next frontier for revolutionizing the world and presents the calculus of intelligent analytics. This chapter examines intelligent big data analytics for enterprise systems. This chapter also explores insight computing after analyzing CACI computing.

Learning objectives of this chapter:

- Define data analytics intelligence.

- Understand big data 4.0 as the next frontier for revolutionizing the world.

- Explore big data 4.0 as the era of big intelligence.

DOI: 10.1201/9781003450504-9

- Discuss big data analytics intelligence to support decision-making.

- Understand a cyclic model for big data analytics intelligence.

- Understand intelligent big data analytics.

- Analyze the nature of intelligent analytics.

- Understand the calculus of intelligent analytics.

- Understand intelligent big data analytics for enterprise systems.

- Define and understand insight computing.

- Understand insight analytics.

- Identify applications of big intelligent analytics in healthcare, finance, and banking.

9.1 INTRODUCTION

Google Web and Google Scholar search and summarize its popularity for each of analytics on data, information, knowledge, and wisdom in Table 9.1. This is a kind of analytics on data, information, knowledge, and wisdom (retrieved on July 26, 2023).

On Figure 9.1, Google Scholar implies that data analytics and information analytics are similar in academia, while Google Web suggests that information analytics plays a more important role than data analytics in academia and industry, although data analytics are very popular in the big data and BI world (Sharda, Delen, & Turba, 2018; Sun & Stranieri, 2021). Knowledge analytics and wisdom analytics have also played an important role in academia and industry, although they are not popular in the BI world. This implies that not only data analytics but also information analytics, knowledge analytics, and wisdom analytics (or DIKW analytics) have played a critical role in computer science, AI, data science, business,

TABLE 9.1   Data Analytics, Information Analytics, Knowledge Analytics, and Wisdom Analytics

Analytics	Google Web	Google Scholar
Data Analytics	1,970,000,000	4,390,000
Information Analytics	2,630,000,000	4,560,000
knowledge Analytics	894,000,000	3,170,000
Wisdom Analytics	36,400,000	114,000

and management. Therefore, this chapter looks at data analytics intelligence, and big data analytics intelligence. It explores DIKW computing, analytics, and intelligence. The research presents a cyclic model for big data analytics and intelligence. The chapter provides the elements of intelligent data analytics: principles, techniques, and tools for business analytics and BI.

The rest of this chapter is organized as follows: Section 9.2 looks at data analytics intelligence. Section 9.3 discusses intelligent data Analytics as a system. Section 9.4 examines intelligent big analytics ecosystem. Section 9.5 intelligent big analytics as a management. Section 9.6 explores big data 4.0 as the next frontier for revolutionizing the World. Section 9.7 presents a calculus of intelligent analytics. Section 9.8 discusses intelligent big data analytics for enterprise Systems. Section 9.9 analyzes CACI computing. Section 9.10 examines insight computing.

9.2 DATA ANALYTICS INTELLIGENCE

Big data and analytics intelligence have significantly appealed to academia and industries. This section will examine big data analytics intelligence as an emerging frontier for big data analytics, business intelligence, and AI. More specifically, this section will provide the fundamentals of analytics intelligence based on the state-of-the-art research and development of academia and industries. Then, it looks at data analytics intelligence and big data analytics intelligence and their interrelationships. This section proposes an inclusive approach to big data analytics intelligence. Then, it presents a unified technological foundation of AI-driven big data analytics intelligence.

9.2.1 Data Intelligence and Big Data Intelligence

Data intelligence is "the use of various intelligent tools and methods to analyze and transform data or information to knowledge and intelligence or intelligent artifacts from which valuable insight can be drawn for supporting decision making," where intelligent artifacts include intelligent data insights (OmniSci, 2020).

The input of data using intelligent data input technology can be called intelligent data, which is a core component of intelligent analytics (Sun & Stranieri, 2021). Intelligent data input technology provides a strong data foundation. Data cleanses, restores, and enhances big datasets. Intelligent data processing is a core component of intelligent analytics as an intelligent system. It incorporates advanced analytics techniques to transform big data into big information, big knowledge, big insight, and big intelligence that supports informed decisions, (OmniSci, 2020; Sun & Stranieri, 2021). The intelligent outputs include intelligently visualized reports for informed decisions (Sun & Stranieri, 2021).

Enterprise data intelligence is used in business intelligence operations, analyzing sales, evaluating inventories, and building customer data intelligence (OmniSci, 2020).

Data intelligence platforms and data intelligence solutions are available from data intelligence companies such as data visualization intelligence, strategic data intelligence, and global data intelligence (OmniSci, 2020). For example, Google Analytics is a data intelligence platform and data intelligence solution.

Big data intelligence is data intelligence for big data. Furthermore, big data intelligence is realized by a set of intelligent techniques and tools that make big data analytics actionable and transform big data into big knowledge, big insights for supporting decision-making, and provide engagement capabilities for customers (OmniSci, 2020). In other words, big data intelligence is data intelligence for big data and intelligence driven from intelligent big data analytics (Sun & Huo, 2021).

Therefore, data intelligence and big data intelligence have a close relationship with data analytics intelligence and big data analytics intelligence.

9.2.2 Fundamentals of Analytics Intelligence and Big Data Analytics Intelligence

From the set theory, we have:

$$\text{Big data analytics intelligence} \subseteq \text{data analytics intelligence}$$
$$\subseteq \text{analytics intelligence} \tag{9.1}$$

Now we analyze analytics intelligence based on Google Scholar search and Google search respectively. The search results are listed in Table 9.2.

Google Scholar for "analytics intelligence" found about 932 results on April 2, 2024. The search demonstrates that few scholarly publications use "analytics intelligence" as a part of their titles, although analytics intelligence was introduced in scholarly publications in 2012 (Chen, Chiang, & Storey, 2012). Google Scholar for "data analytics intelligence" found about

130 results on April 2, 2024. The results demonstrate that "data analytics intelligence" as a keyword has not appeared in scholarly publications until 2017. Data analytics intelligence as a system appeared in scholarly publications in 2018. A Google Scholar search for "big data analytics intelligence" found about 69 results on April 2, 2024. The results demonstrate that few scholarly publications use "big data analytics intelligence" as a part of their titles. Therefore, both data analytics intelligence and big data analytics intelligence have not drawn much attention in academia. However, big data analytics has drawn significant attention in academia, industries, and governments.

Google search for "analytics intelligence", "data analytics intelligence" and "big data analytics intelligence" found about 117,000 results, 25,500 results, and 14,600 results respectively on 2 April 2024. This implies that analytics intelligence, data analytics intelligence, and big data analytics intelligence have drawn significant attention in industries. Now we delve into each of the top 20 found results and find that big data analytics intelligence was first mentioned by Mr. Jon Oltsik, a principal analyst at Enterprise Strategy Group ESG (Oltsik, 2012). He mentioned "The next-generation of security intelligence tools must provide big data analytics intelligence...." "Big data analytics, intelligence" often occurred in the found results.

Google defines analytics intelligence as a set of features, including algorithms used in Google Analytics, that use machine learning (ML) to help you better understand and act on your data" (Google Analytics Intelligence, 2020). This definition is based on Google Analytics intelligence because the latter is a powerful machine learning tool used by Google to help users better understand the analytics data (Rai, 2019).

Analytics intelligence functionality includes answers to questions, providing insights to user and conversion modeling (Google Analytics Intelligence, 2020). For example, you can ask Google Analytics Intelligence questions about your data in plain English and get fast answers (Rai, 2019). Auto-generated insights from Google Analytics provide alerts or

TABLE 9.2 Big Data Analytics Intelligence in Academia and Industries

Terms	Google Web (No.)	Google Scholar (No.)
Analytics intelligence	117,000	932
Data analytics intelligence	25,500	130
Big data analytics intelligence	14,600	69

notifications about the big changes happening on your website (Rai, 2019). User and conversion modeling features include smart goals, smart lists, session quality, and conversion probability, which use ML to model conversions and can be used in building audiences (Google Analytics Intelligence, 2020; Rai, 2019). Auto-generated insights and conversion modeling are characteristics of modern analytics, including augmented analytics (Howson, Richardson, Sallam, & Kronz, 2019).

Data analytics intelligence process generally consists of five stages: data preparation, data mining, result validation, result visualization, and explanation (OmniSci, 2020), where results include auto-generated insights.

9.2.3 A Cyclic Model for Big Data Analytics and Intelligence

This section provides an inclusive approach on a cyclic model for big data analytics intelligence, illustrated in Figure 9.1.

From Figure 9.1, big data analytics intelligence originated from big data, analytics, and intelligence. Briefly,

$$\text{big data analytics intelligence} := \text{big data} + \text{analytics} + \text{intelligence} \qquad (9.2)$$

Where + denotes add or integration. This is the simple representation of big data analytics intelligence. Considering integration as a system solution, we have

$$\text{Big data analytics intelligence} := \text{Big data analytics} \\ + \text{Big data intelligence} \qquad (9.3)$$

That is, big data analytics intelligence consists of big data analytics and big data intelligence. Big data analytics intelligence is an integration of big data analytics and big data intelligence. Integration of big data analytics

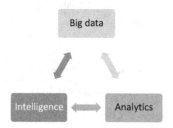

FIGURE 9.1   A cyclic model of big data analytics intelligence.

and big data intelligence is the current mainstream of both big data analytics and big data intelligence (Sun, 2019b).

Applying intelligence as an operation to both sides of (9.4),

$$\text{Big data analytics} = \text{big data} + \text{analytics} \qquad (9.4)$$

We have

$$\text{big data analytics intelligence} := \text{big data intelligence} \\ + \text{analytics intelligence} \qquad (9.5)$$

This is another perspective to (9.3). That is, big data analytics intelligence is an integrated system of big data intelligence and analytics intelligence (Sun & Huo, 2021).

Based on the above discussion, we have

$$\text{big data analytics intelligence} := \text{big data analytics} + \text{big data} \\ \text{intelligence} + \text{analytics intelligence} \qquad (9.6)$$

That is, from a system perspective, big data analytics intelligence is an integration of big data analytics, big data intelligence, and analytics intelligence. Therefore, equation (9.6) is a theoretical foundation of data analytics intelligence.

Big data intelligence, including data intelligence and big intelligence, has drawn increasing attention in academia and industry. Big intelligence plays a significant role in big data and big analytics.

Big intelligence here mainly includes big data intelligence and big analytics intelligence. They are about automating intelligence in general and human intelligence for processing big data and optimizing data analytics in specific and human intelligence for business and management (Sun, Strang, & Li, 2018). Big data and big analytics generate new big intelligence, big innovation, and big opportunities and challenges for the research and development of business, management, decision science, mathematics, and ICT, including machine learning and visualization techniques (Sharda, Delen, Turban, & King, 2018). Big data and big analytics with applications are changing the world and society. They are also changing how people and organizations are doing things and making decisions in the future (Sharda,

Delen, & Turba, 2018). Big data and big analytics are also changing business models, revenue models, management, and decision-making processes in companies and organizations, affecting resource schedules, including data in creating products and services.

9.2.4 Foundations of AI Driven Big Data Analytics Intelligence

This section looks at the foundation of AI-driven big data analytics intelligence as illustrated in Figure 9.2.

That is, the technological foundations of big data include 10 Vs, 10 Bigs, big needs, and so on (Sun, Strang, & Li, 2018).

The technological foundations of analytics include computer science, data science, statistical modeling, and operations research (Sun & Huo, 2021).

The technological foundations of intelligence include computer science, data science, statistics and mathematics, cognitive science, and operations research (Russell & Norvig, 2020).

All these will contribute the research and development of big data analytics intelligence.

9.2.5 Summary

This section provided the fundamentals of analytics intelligence and big data analytics intelligence based on the state-of-the-art research and

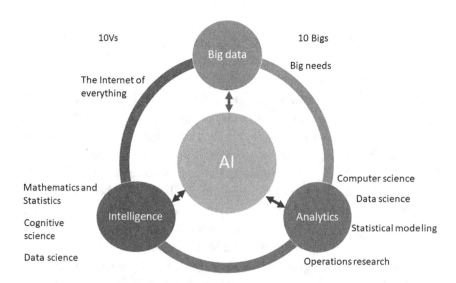

FIGURE 9.2 Foundations of big data analytics intelligence.

development of academia and industries. This section proposes an inclusive approach to big data analytics intelligence. Then it presents a unified foundation of AI-driven big data analytics intelligence. The main contributions of this section include: 1). Big data intelligence is data intelligence for big data, big data analytics, and intelligent big data analytics 2. Big data analytics intelligence is an integrated system of big data intelligence, big data analytics, and analytics intelligence. 3). All the mentioned technologies will contribute to the research and development of big data analytics intelligence.

In future work, we will apply data analyticalizing as a process to develop data analytics and big data analytics with data analytics intelligence.

9.3 INTELLIGENT DATA ANALYTICS AS A SYSTEM

Intelligent data analytics can be considered as an information system in general and an intelligent system in specific.

Intelligent systems (IS) encompass the principles, methodologies, techniques, and processes of applying AI to solve the real-world problems (Schalkoff, 2011). An IS is a system that can imitate, simulate, augment, and automate intelligent behaviors of human beings and solve problems that were heretofore solved by humans through generating representations, inference procedures, and learning strategies (Schalkoff, 2011; p. 2). IS are built based on the following intelligent techniques: knowledge representation (Schalkoff, 2011), expert systems, and knowledge-based systems (Moutinho, Rita, & Li, 2006), case-based reasoning (Sun & Finnie, 2004), genetic algorithms, swarm intelligence, neural networks, fuzzy logic, intelligent agents and multiagent systems (Russell & Norvig, 2020; Schalkoff, 2011; Zimmermann, 2001), data mining and knowledge discovery from databases (KDD) (Kantardzic, 2011), decision support systems (DSS) (Laudon & Laudon, 2020), and knowledge management (Moutinho, Rita, & Li, 2006), to name a few.

Intelligent big data analytics is designed and embedded in intelligent systems. This is an application form of intelligent big data analytics as an intelligent system. There are a number of intelligent big data analytics as the intelligent system in smart mobile phones, airplanes, supermarkets, and even in driverless cars. Intelligent big data analytics as an intelligent system has been accepted by businesses, markets, finance, banking, healthcare, and other industries (Howson, Sallam, & Richa, 2018).

Recently, Woolworths and Coles, and K-market in Australia have used intelligent machines with big data analytics. One scans what one is buying at the supermarket, then pays the bill there by clicks. No sales assistants work there anymore. Unmanned stores have become more and more popular in China nationwide. At airports, one can check in using an ID and get a boarding card automatically.

Intelligent big data analytics as an intelligent system can aid managers by extracting useful patterns of information, capturing and discovering knowledge, generating and visualizing solutions to problems encountered in decision-making, delegating authority, and assigning responsibility (Sun & Firmin, 2012).

Finally, the relationships among intelligent systems, intelligent big data analytics, and intelligent analytics can be summarized as

Intelligent big data analytics ⊂ Intelligent analytics ⊏ Intelligent systems.

The system architecture of a big data analytics is as follows: The system consists of three bases: knowledge base, data base, base, and intelligent algorithm base and analytics engine, illustrated as in Figure 9.3. All of them provide intelligent services to provide intelligent big data descriptive analytics, intelligent big data diagnostic analytics, intelligent big data predictive analytics, and intelligent big data prescriptive analytics. The output is the knowledge, intelligence, and insights from the intelligent big data analytics.

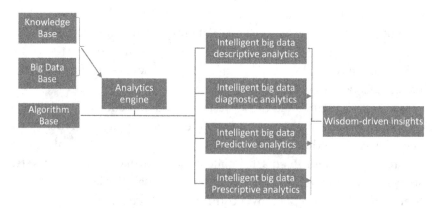

FIGURE 9.3   An architecture for intelligent big data analytics as system.

9.4 INTELLIGENT BIG DATA ECOSYSTEM

Intelligent big data ecosystem consists of data devices, data collectors and aggregators, data users, and buyers (Dietrich, 2013).

The fundamentals of big data analytics consist of data mining, statistics, mathematics, computer science, AI, machine learning, and data science (Dietrich, 2013).

The previous section has mentioned intelligent big data descriptive analytics, intelligent big data diagnostic analytics, intelligent big data predictive analytics, and intelligent big data prescriptive analytics. All of them can be integrated into an intelligent big data ecosystem, at least from a system viewpoint. One can use Sections 7.8 and 8.6 to detail this intelligent big data ecosystem.

9.5 INTELLIGENT BIG DATA ANALYTICS AS A MANAGEMENT

Management is the process of managers' coordinating and overseeing the work activities of others so that their activities are completed (Robbins, Bergman, Stagg, & Coulter, 2012). There are three levels of management: operational management, tactical management, and strategic management, which correspond to the activities of operational managers, middle managers, and top managers of organizations respectively (Robbins, Bergman, Stagg, & Coulter, 2012; pp. 14–19; Sun, 2019b). The main management functions or activities of a manager consist of planning, organizing, leading, and controlling (Terry, 1968; p.133; Robbins, Bergman, Stagg, & Coulter, 2012; pp. 14–19). Intelligent big data analytics as a management can be briefly represented as:

$$\text{Intelligent big data analytics as a management} = \text{Management of}$$
$$\text{intelligent big data analytics} + \text{intelligent big data analytics}$$
$$\text{for management} \tag{9.7}$$

The following subsections will look at the management of intelligent big data analytics and intelligent big data analytics for management in some detail.

9.5.1 Management of Intelligent Big Data Analytics

Many methods and techniques are useful for managing intelligent big data analytics, for example, data management, information management, and knowledge management (Sun, 2019b). These have played a significant role in big data analytics as an intelligent system because data, information, and knowledge are the foundation for intelligent systems and big data analytics (Sun & Finnie, 2004), as shown in Figure 9.4. Data management, information management (Laudon & Laudon, 2020), and knowledge management (KM) are well-known in either information systems (Sun, 2019b) or intelligent systems (Laudon & Laudon, 2020). We do not go into each of them, owing to space limitations. For details, see other references, such as (Sun & Finnie, 2004) and (Laudon & Laudon, 2020).

9.5.2 Intelligent Big Data Analytics for Management

Intelligent big data analytics should be applied to each of the main management functions in order to sustain business competitiveness, operate organizations more intelligently at all levels, and enhance management decision-making (Sun, 2019b), that is, it is important to look at intelligent big data analytics for planning, organizing, leading, and controlling, respectively. In what follows, we will look at each of these in detail.

9.5.2.1 Intelligent Big Data Analytics for Planning

Planning involves defining the organization's goals, establishing an overall strategy for achieving those goals, and developing a comprehensive set of plans to integrate and coordinate organizational work (Robbins, Bergman, Stagg, & Coulter, 2012, p. 294). In planning, managers define goals, establish strategies for achieving these goals, and develop plans to integrate and coordinate activities (Robbins, Bergman, Stagg, & Coulter, 2012, p. 14). To this end, the managers should define the nature and

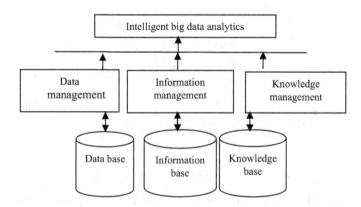

FIGURE 9.4   A model of management for intelligent big data analytics.

purpose of planning, classify the type of goals that organizations use, describe related types of plans that organizations use, describe project management, and discuss issues in planning. A comprehensive set of plans is the outcome of the planning process (Sun & Firmin, 2012).

Intelligent big data analytics for planning aims to imitate, simulate, augment, and automate some or all planning behaviors of managers of organizations, e.g., in corporate planning (Thierauf, 1982) and supply chain planning (Laudon & Laudon, 2020). More specifically, they should imitate and automate definition of goals, establishment of strategies for achieving these goals, and develop plans to integrate and coordinate activities (Sun & Firmin, 2012). To this end, data management, information management, and knowledge management should be the basis for any intelligent big data analytics for planning (Sun, 2019b). Data mining, business analytics, knowledge base systems (KBS), expert systems, and intelligent agents have been developed to aid planning. All these intelligent techniques are used as a decision-support tool for intelligent planning system. Case based systems as intelligent systems can also facilitate the intelligent big data analytics for planning (Sun & Finnie, 2004).

Intelligent big data analytics for planning can also be called intelligent planning analytics. Intelligent planning analytics has been used to automate planning, budgeting, forecasting, and analysis processes for an organization working with IBM® Planning Analytics (Cortell, 2017).

9.5.2.2 Intelligent Big Data Analytics for Organizing

Organizing aims to establish effective behavioral relationships among selected work, persons, and workplaces for the group to work together efficiently (Terry, 1968, p. 289). In other words, organizing means arranging and structuring work, persons, and workplaces to accomplish the organization's plans and goals (Robbins, Bergman, Stagg, & Coulter, 2012, p. 14). When organizing, managers determine what tasks need to get done, who is to do them, how the tasks are to be decomposed and grouped, who reports to whom, and at what level decisions are to be made. They also allocate and deploy organizational resources during the organizing process (Robbins, Bergman, Stagg, & Coulter, 2012, p. 368).

Intelligent big data analytics for organizing aims to imitate and automate all or some organizing behaviors of managers of organizations. More specifically, it should imitate and automate the decomposition of tasks, a grouping of persons who complete the decomposed task, allocation and deployment of organizational resources. Intelligent big data analytics for organizing also includes intelligent customer relationship analytics (CRA) software and intelligent supply chain analytics (SCA) software. CRA software uses intelligent technologies and big data analytics to organize business processes and marketing activities, including customer services and technical supports. The main CRA vendors are SAP (www.sap.com), oracle (www.oracle.com), and salesforce.com (CRM, 2012). SCA software as an intelligent system uses intelligent technology to organize supply activities, associated material, and information flows to organizations and marketing (Sun, 2016). SAP and Oracle are among the leading providers of SCA applications (Chaffey, 2011).

The intelligent big data analytics tools for organizing include spreadsheets and project management-specific applications. Spreadsheets are regularly used to assist managers in organizing information and data. Project management applications e.g. Microsoft Project, are also used to assist managers to organize activities, the planning and scheduling of activities. Tools such as Microsoft Project have intelligent capabilities evidenced through the automation and generation of management reports such as Gantt charts (Larson & Gray, 2011). Their functionality supports the organizational process to improve efficiencies and information quality (Caniels & Bakens, 2011).

9.5.2.3 Intelligent Big Data Analytics for Leading

Leading is to oversee and coordinate people to work so that organizational goals can be pursued and accomplished (Robbins, Bergman, Stagg, & Coulter, 2012, p. 467). When managers are leading, they motivate their subordinates, help resolve work group conflicts, influence individuals or work teams, select appropriate communication channels, or deal with individual or group behavior issues (Robbins, Bergman, Stagg, & Coulter, 2012, p. 14). Leading people involves understanding their attitudes, behaviors, personalities, and motivations as an individual, a group, or a community (Robbins, Bergman, Stagg, & Coulter, 2012, p. 469) and helping them to "achieve their respective essential goals as well as their maximum potentialities" (Terry, 1968, p. 451).

Intelligent big data analytics for leading aims to imitate and automate all or some leading behaviors of managers. More specifically, it should imitate and automate how to motivate subordinates, help resolve work group conflicts, influence individuals or work teams, select appropriate communication channels or deal with individual or group behavior issues, and understand attitudes, behaviors, personalities, and motivations of the individuals and teams (Sun & Firmin, 2012). However, understanding the attitudes, behaviors, personalities, and motivations of individuals and teams is still a big challenge for research and development of intelligent systems for leading (Sun, 2016). Although there is no special intelligent big data analytics for leading, there are intelligent analytics apps for assisting the leading of managers. For example, enterprise networking sites as limited online social networking services have been available in many large organizations for facilitating the leading of managers. Updated communication tools, including emails, have also facilitated the communications among the manager and his/her subordinates.

9.5.2.4 Intelligent Big Data Analytics for Controlling

Controlling is to determine what is being accomplished, that is, evaluate the performance and, if necessary, apply corrective measures so that the performance takes place according to plans (Terry, 1968, p. 544). In other words, a control mechanism has five basic elements: establish standards, supervise, monitor, compare, and correct work performance (Thierauf, 1982, p. 278). Controlling operations, processes, quantity, quality, time use, budget, and cost is the main job of a manager (Terry, 1968, p. 543; Sun, 2016). When managers are in the process of controlling, they must monitor and evaluate the activities to make sure they are being done as planned and correct any significant deviations (Robbins, Bergman, Stagg, & Coulter, 2012, p. 645). Therefore, a control process consists of measuring actual performance, comparing actual performance against the established standards, and taking managerial action, taking into account the goals and objectives of the organization (Sun & Firmin, 2012).

Intelligent big data analytics for controlling aims to imitate and automate all or some controlling behaviors of managers of organizations. More specifically, it should imitate and automate monitoring and evaluation of activities, measurement of actual performance, comparison of actual performance against the established standards and recommendations of managerial decisions (Sun & Firmin, 2012).

Intelligent big data analytics for controlling can also be called intelligent control analytics which has "the ability to comprehend, reason, and learn from processes, disturbances, and operating conditions" (Astrom & McAvoy, 1992). Intelligent control analytics has used intelligent techniques, including knowledge base systems, expert systems, neural networks, machine learning, multiagent systems, fuzzy logic (Astrom & McAvoy, 1992), and big data analytics, to process control and process automation.

Currently, digital surveillance CCTV (closed circuit TV) cameras and intelligent agents have been used to monitor and evaluate activities and recommendations of managerial decisions. The following proposed intelligent control analytics for controlling (ICA), shown in Figure 9.5, is based on the intelligent system for process control (Astrom & McAvoy, 1992; Sun, 2016), taking into account big data analytics as an intelligent system.

This ICA is a knowledge-based analytics for controlling. The knowledge base includes the performance knowledge of an entity that requires control, called controlee, and knowledge for supervision, monitoring, evaluation, and recommendation. The multiagent system includes multiple intelligent agents such as recommender, supervisor, monitor, and evaluator. The recommender will propose alternative strategies for adjusting the work of the controlee to the manager, and the manager will finally select one of the alternative strategies to ask the controlee to carry out (Sun, 2016).

We have examined intelligent big data analytics for planning, organizing, leading, and controlling respectively. In fact, many intelligent systems include not one but more than one function of the management functions. The most comprehensive intelligent big data analytics systems for enterprise management might be ERP (enterprise resource planning) systems which integrate all management facets of an enterprise, including accounting management, logistics management, manufacturing management, marketing management, planning management, project management, human resources management, SCM, CRM, and finance

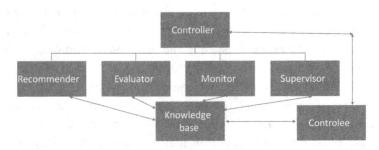

FIGURE 9.5   A system architecture of an intelligent control analytics.

management (Schneider, 2017; Laudon & Laudon, 2020). The two major ERP vendors are Oracle.com and SAP.com, as mentioned earlier (Sun, 2019b).

There are still few attempts toward unifying main management functions into intelligent big data analytics to automate planning, organizing, leading, and controlling at an organizational level. Any attempt in this direction is significant for the research and development of intelligent big data analytics.

9.6 BIG DATA 4.0: THE NEXT FRONTIER FOR REVOLUTIONIZING THE WORLD

9.6.1 Introduction

Albert Einstein once said, 'Wisdom is not a product of schooling but of the lifelong attempt to acquire it.' Google has been undertaking research on driverless cars for a few years. Google have also been launching a number of satellites to establish a global free WI-FI network. Facebook uses friending as a social operator and makes over two billion Facebook friends to share their happiness and hardness using Facebook as a social networking platform. Huawei has been working hard to provide networking equipment and relatively cheap smart phones for billions of poor and relatively poor people living in poor or relatively poor countries. All these are big wisdoms. These big wisdoms are beneficial to billions of people living in the world. These big wisdoms are certainly close to big data because Google is a big data company. Facebook is a big data company. Huawei is an emerging big data company. These motivate us to think about

1. What is the relationship between big data and big wisdom?

2. How can big data evolve to big wisdom?

To answer the question 1, we should first review the evolution from data to wisdom. To answer Question 2, we propose big data 4.0 as a next frontier for changing the world.

The rest of this section is organized as follows: Section 9.2 looks at analytics on data, information, knowledge, and wisdom. Section 9.3 explores DIKW Computing, Analytics, and Intelligence, and Section 9.4 proposes big data 4.0: The era of big intelligence.

9.6.2 Analytics on Data, Information, Knowledge and Wisdom

I will use Google Web and Google Scholar to summarize the popularity of each of them. This is a kind of analytics on data, information, knowledge, and wisdom (retrieved on April 2, 2024).

From Table 9.3, the results of Google Scholar and Google imply that

1. Data analytics are still a priority of importance in academia and industry. Information analytics, knowledge analytics, and wisdom analytics have played fewer roles in academia and industry.

2. Information analytics, knowledge analytics, and wisdom analytics have also drawn attention in academia and industry to welcome the new wave coming from big information, big knowledge, and big wisdom.

This analysis also implies that not only data analytics but also DIKW analytics have played a more important role in academia and industry for business, management, and decision-making.

9.6.3 DIKW Computing, Analytics, and Intelligence

As we know, computing as a super-discipline consists of computing science, computing engineering, computing technology, computing systems, and computing management (ACM, 2020) (Computing see Section 2.6). We will discuss DIKW computing. DIKW computing = Data computing + Information computing + Knowledge computing + Wisdom computing., Data computing constitutes data science, data technology, data engineering, data systems, data intelligence, and data management.

Information computing constitutes information science, information technology, information engineering, information systems, information intelligence, and information management.

TABLE 9.3   DIKW Analytics Searched by Google

DIKW Analytics	Google Web	Google Scholar
Data analytics	323,000,000	903,000
Information analytics	589,000	7,320
Knowledge analytics	52,000	2,100
Wisdom analytics	16,000	94

Knowledge computing constitutes knowledge science, knowledge technology, knowledge engineering, knowledge systems, knowledge intelligence, and knowledge management.

Wisdom computing constitutes wisdom science, wisdom technology, wisdom engineering, wisdom systems, wisdom intelligence, and wisdom management.

In such a way, data computing, information computing, knowledge computing, and wisdom computing are at a relatively higher level. This highest level is data industry, economy, and society.

From a data viewpoint, the relationship between data computing and the data industry, economy, and society is service and intelligence. That is, data computing provides services and intelligences to the data industry, economy, and society, where services consist of data science as a service with intelligence, data engineering as a service with intelligence, data systems as a service with intelligence, and data management as a service with intelligence. Further, the service also consists of data tools and techniques as a service with intelligence. Therefore, data computing underpins the development of the data industry, economy, and data society with service and intelligence.

Analytics is a part of computing.

Table 9.4 implies

$$DIKW\ Analytics := Data\ analytics + information\ analytics \\ + knowledge\ analytics + wisdom\ analytics.$$

Finally, analytics computing is illustrated as in Table 9.4. We we use computing as a science, engineering, technology, systems, intelligence, and management (see Section 2.6).

This analytics computing is the state-of-the-art analytics and computing in AI and computer science, except experience analytics computing. This is an important answer to not only data, big data, data analytics, and big data analytics but also data+, and data analytics+ as national policies and actions of some nations (e.g. China). Each of the cells in

Table 9.4 can find examples in the real-world although this is a theoretical model for analytics computing, I leave them to the readers.

Now, we discuss DIKW intelligence. that is, DIKW intelligence =

Data intelligence + information intelligence + knowledge intelligence + wisdom intelligence.

TABLE 9.4 Analytics Computing

Analytics	Science	Engineering	Technology	Systems	Intelligence	Management
Data analytics	Data analytics science	Data analytics engineering	Data analytics technology	Data analytics systems	Data analytics intelligence	Data analytics management
Information analytics	Information analytics science	Information analytics engineering	Information analytics technology	Data analytics systems	Information analytics intelligence	Information analytics management
Knowledge analytics	Knowledge analytics science	Knowledge analytics engineering	Knowledge analytics technology	Knowledge analytics systems	Knowledge analytics intelligence	Knowledge analytics management
Wisdom analytics	Wisdom analytics science	Wisdom analytics engineering	Wisdom analytics technology	Knowledge analytics systems	Wisdom analytics intelligence	Wisdom analytics management

From an engineering reviewpoint, DIKW engineering aims to use DIKW science and technology to create DIKW systems and products and services to acquire DIKW intelligence.

DIKW intelligence and cases will be used in next sections.

9.6.4 Big Data 4.0: The Era of Big Intelligence We Are Living in

Big data had a revolution that would transform and manage how we live, work, and think a decade ago (McAfee & Brynjolfsson, 2012; Mayer-Schoenberger & Cukier, 2013). We were in the trinity of big data, analytics, and AI (Henke & Bughin, 2016; Manyika, Chui, & Bughin, 2011). What is the future of big data? What era do we live in? This section argues that Big data 4.0 = meta^4 (big data) is the era of big intelligence we are living in, through exploring from big data 1.0 to big data 4.0.

9.6.4.1 Big Data 1.0 = Meta^0(Big Data)

Big data 1.0 = meta^0(big data) is the next frontier for innovation, competition, and productivity since 2011 (Manyika, Chui, & Bughin, 2011). Big data and big data analytics became a booming area for research and development globally that launched national strategies to develop big data and big data technology (Sun, Strang, & Li, 2018).

9.6.4.2 Big Data 2.0 = Meta (Big Data)

"Information is the oil of the 21st century, and analytics is the combustion engine" (Kumar, 2015). This means information and information analytics are the power for processing big information in the 21st century (Sun, 2024).

Big data 2.0 = meta (big data) = big information, implying that we are in the era of big information. Big information can be considered as the same time of big data 1.0, because data $\sqsubset$ information, from a set viewpoint. Many scholars and businesspeople have used big data and big information interchangeably. In fact, information exploration was more popular than big data a few decades ago (Beath, Becerra-Fernandez, Ross, & Short, 2012). Information computing consisting of information science, engineering, technology, systems, intelligence, industry, management, and services has still become an important field in academia and industry. For example, information technology and information systems are disciplines offered for postgraduate and postgraduate degree programs by many universities. However, most researchers and businesspeople have flattened big information with big data. For example, many public media, including books, have intentionally or technologically flattened big information with big data (Brooks, 2022; Aroraa, Lele, & Jindal, 2022). Data service and information service have been explored in an integrated way (Delena & Demirkanb, 2013). Therefore, this research also considers big information as big data.

9.6.4.3 Big Data 3.0 = Big Knowledge

The big data and its driven computing and economy will lead to knowledge revolutions in all sectors (Wang, 2012). These include knowledge computing, knowledge industry, knowledge services, and knowledge economy. The fundamental for all these knowledge revolutions is knowledge computing. Knowledge computing consists of knowledge science, knowledge technology, knowledge engineering, knowledge management, knowledge intelligence, and knowledge systems (Laudon & Laudon, 2020). All these provide techniques and methods for business and society, industry, and nations based on the knowledge revolutions in the fundamental areas in knowledge generation, dissemination, acquisition, utilization, representation, evaluation, and implementation, as well as knowledge understanding, sharing, discovery, modeling, reuse, transformation, dissemination, and visualization (Wang, 2012).

Meta^3 (big data) = meta^2 (big information) = meta (big knowledge) and big data $\sqsubset$ big information $\sqsubset$ big knowledge implies that we are also in the era of big knowledge. In fact, the knowledge economy and knowledge society used to be launched by many countries like Australia at the end of the last century. To develop a knowledge economy and knowledge society is still a dream of many developing countries. The era of big data has surpassed the era of big knowledge at the moment, although big knowledge should be becoming more important for the time being. We still believe that big knowledge can be the next step of big data in the time to come.

9.6.4.4 Big Data 4.0 = Big Intelligence

Big data 4.0 = Meta^4 (big data) = meta (big knowledge) = big intelligence, and big data $\sqsubset$ big information $\sqsubset$ big knowledge $\sqsubset$ big intelligence implies that we are in the era of big intelligence.

Generally speaking, big intelligence includes AI, BI, organizational intelligence, marketing intelligence (Chen, Chiang, & Storey, 2012), mobile intelligence, cloud intelligence, social networking intelligence, networking intelligence, web intelligence, and enterprise intelligence.

Big intelligence particularly refers to big data intelligence or big data-driven intelligence. It can be defined as an intelligence of human beings and machines to use a set of methods, technologies, systems, and tools that can manage and process big data (Sun & Wu, 2021). Big data analytics intelligence (BAI) can be defined as an intelligence of human beings and machines using a set of methods, systems, tools, and analytics that can manage and process big data. Big analytics intelligence, big data-driven intelligence, and big data intelligence have become the most important part of enhancing BI and big intelligence (Sun & Stranieri, 2021; Brooks, 2022).

Big Intelligence encompasses not only AI and other intelligences, but also big information intelligence, big knowledge intelligence, big data analytics intelligence, big information analytics intelligence, and big knowledge analytics intelligence. It also includes supply chain intelligence, customer intelligence, and more (Aroraa, Lele, & Jindal, 2022; Brooks, 2022). All these can be considered as the era of big intelligences, because only AI and BI are not enough. ChatGPT4.0, driverless cars, intelligent drones, intelligent big data analytics and other AI products encompass the era of big data 4.0; that is an era of big intelligences. We can find that all are big intelligence products and services around us: intelligent washing machines, cleaners, smart TV, smartphones, smart earphones, intelligent VR, intelligent IoT. We are immersed in the era of big intelligences. Therefore, we have entered the era of big intelligences, from big data 1.0 to big data 4.0.

Big intelligences have been supported by intelligent computing, which is formed as:

Intelligent computing: = intelligent science + intelligent engineering
+ intelligent technology + intelligent systems
+ intelligent management.

Intelligent business analytics aims to integrate AI, BI, business analytics, big analytics, data, information, knowledge, and intelligence using advanced ICT computing, digital technology, and DIKI computing to provide smart business services for improving business, management, and governance to create big intelligence to revolutionize our work, life, business, marketing, management, and organization, as well as healthcare, finance, e-commerce, and web services, in the setting of cloud computing, the Internet of Everything (IoE), and social networking computing (Laudon & Laudon, 2020).

More specifically, intelligent business analytics is science and technology about collecting, organizing, and analyzing big data, big information, big knowledge, and big intelligences to discover and visualize patterns, knowledge, insight, and intelligence within the big data, information, knowledge, and intelligence based on big business analytics, AI, and intelligent systems (Sun & Stranieri, 2021). Intelligent business analytics at least includes intelligent data analytics, intelligent information analytics, intelligent knowledge analytics, and intelligent intelligence analytics for business and business decision-making, all of them are underpinned by intelligent statistical modeling, machine learning, intelligent visualization, and intelligent optimization. Intelligent data analytics further includes big data, intelligent big data analytics, intelligent data analysis, intelligent data warehousing, intelligent data mining, and intelligent data visualization. Intelligent information analytics, and at least includes big information, intelligent information analysis, intelligent information warehousing, intelligent information retrieval, and intelligent information visualization.

Industry 4.0 motivated the systematic investigation of big data 4.0 and big analytics 4.0. This will let us enter society 4.0, that is,

Society 4.0 = Industry 4.0 + big data 4.0 + big analytics 4.0 + IoE 4.0.

What is a big wisdom? It is a wisdom that can benefit billions of people in the world. For example, SpaceX has launched is launching a space program in order to realize globally WIFI High-Speed Internet around the world Connecting at home or on the go (https://www.starlink.com/, on 14 November 2024). In such a way, everyone in the world can enjoy the WIFI if he or she can pay tens of dollars to buy a converter. Therefore, in the near future, we will find about 50% of the whole population in the world can enjoy the free WIFI globally. Meta (formerly Facebook) has over two billion people who can use its social networking platform to communicate with each other as Facebook friends.

What is big data 4.0? What is big analytics 4.0, What is IoE 4.0? They are big intelligence; they are big wisdom, the era we are entering.

However, there is still a long way to go for us to realize the true big data 4.0, big intelligence, and big wisdom, all of which will be harder than realizing Industry 4.0, because big data 4.0 consists of wisdom economy, wisdom industry, and wisdom services-centered society. What we are working toward is to transit from big data 1.0 to first Industry 4.0, then big data 4.0 and IoE 40, finally Society 4.0.

9.6.4.5 Summary

Data, knowledge, intelligence, and wisdom are elements of the research and development of computing over the past half of century (Liew A., 2013). Big data has become a strategic resource for organizations, industries, enterprises, businesses, and individuals, as well as national security. Big data is also a key enabler of exploring business insights and economics of services. This makes us wonder what's the next big thing in big data? One answer has already been provided, that is "Bigger Data." Our answer is big data 4.0. The objective of this research is to address two significant questions: What is the future of big data? What era do we live in? This section and this book address these two questions by looking at meta as an operation and argues that we are living in the era of big intelligence through analyzing from meta (big data) to big intelligence, using a power operation. The three main contributions in this research consist of 1. It analyzed Meta (DIKI) and revealed 5 bigs of DIKI consisting of big data, big information, big knowledge, big intelligence and big analytics. 2. Applying meta on 5 bigs of DIKI, this research inferred that big data 4.0 = meta^4 (big data) = big intelligence, where we are living, is supported by big data, big information, big knowledge, intelligent big analytics, and intelligent business analytics. 3. The calculus between big data 1.0 and big data 4.0 is big intelligence.

In future work, as an extension of future research directions, we will delve into real world cases such as cloud computing, IoT including the Internet of People (IoP) and the Internet of services (IoS), and ChatGPT to further verify the big intelligences which we are living in.

9.7 A CALCULUS OF INTELLIGENT ANALYTICS

Intelligent analytics is an emerging paradigm in the age of analytics. This section explores the calculus of intelligent analytics. More specifically, this research identifies the foundations, cores, and applications of intelligent big data analytics based on investigating the state-of-the-art scholars' publications and market analysis of advanced analytics. Then it presents technological foundations for intelligent big data analytics by examining intelligent big data analytics as an integration of AI and big data analytics. The research also presents a novel approach to extend intelligent big data analytics to intelligent analytics.

9.7.1 Introduction

Big data, analytics, AI, and their integration are at the frontier for revolutionizing our work, life, business, management, organization, healthcare, finance, e-commerce, and web services (Henke & Bughin, 2016; Lohr, 2012 February 11; John, 2013; Sun & Huo, 2021; Chen & Zhang, 2014; Laney & Jain, 2017; Russell & Norvig, 2020). Big data analytics has big market opportunities. For example, *the big data market is* forecasted to *experience an unprecedented growth rate with a market size from US$22.2 billion in 2023 to US$ 401 Billion by 2028 with a CAGR of 12.7% (2023-2028)* (Marketsandmarkets, 2022).

Intelligent big data analytics is an emerging science and technology based on AI (Russell & Norvig, 2020), becoming a mainstream market adopted broadly across industries, organizations, geographic regions, and among individuals to facilitate decision-making for businesses and individuals to achieve desired business outcomes (Laney & Jain, 2017; Sun, Sun, & Strang, 2018; Sun, 2019b; INFORMS, 2014). Intelligent big data analytics in particular and intelligent analytics in general have become a disruptive technology for effective innovation and decision-making in the digital age (Sun & Stranieri, 2021). However, the following issues have still been ignored to some extent in academia, industries, and governments.

1. What are the fundamentals of intelligent analytics?

2. What is the relationship between big data analytics and intelligent analytics?

3. How can we integrate big data analytics and AI?

This section will address these three issues by exploring the nature of intelligent analytics. More specifically, this section identifies the theoretical and technological foundations of intelligent big data analytics through an investigation into the state-of-the-art scholars' publications and market analysis of advanced analytics. Then it examines intelligent big data analytics as an integration of AI and big data analytics and technological foundations for intelligent big data analytics. The section extends intelligent big data analytics to intelligent analytics and looks at augmented analytics as intelligent analytics.

The remainder of this research is organized as follows: Sections 9.7.2 and 9.7.3 define intelligent as an operation and present a model for defining intelligent big data analytics, illustrated in Figure 9.6. Section 9.7.4 argues

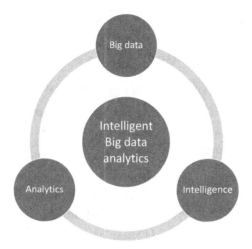

FIGURE 9.6   A model for Intelligent Big data analytics.

that intelligent big data analytics = big data analytics + AI. Section 9.7.5 proposes an ontology of intelligent big data analytics. Section 9.7.6 looks at technological foundations of intelligent big data analytics. Section 9.7.7 Section 9.6 presents an inclusive approach to intelligent analytics. Section 9.7 *examines augmented analytics as intelligent analytics.* Section 9.7.8 provides discussion and implications of this research. The final section ends this research with concluding remarks and suggestions for future work.

9.7.2 Intelligent as an Operation

Intelligent in this research is an operation. This operation can be understood in business like business operation, engineering like processing, technology like transformation, and mathematics like unary operation.

Let U be a universe of objects in the real-world. For example, U = {data analytics, data system} o is an intelligent operation. Then

$$o(\text{data analytics}) = \text{intelligent data analytics, and}$$
$$o(\text{data systems}) = \text{intelligent data systems.}$$

In other words, intelligent operation can be the abstract technology and tool that can change data analytics into intelligent data analytics, and data systems into intelligent data systems.

If AI has become an emerging market and industry, then it is useful for intelligent to be abstracted to an operation, at least from a meta level. That is, intelligent is a meta operation that can transform data analytics into intelligent data analytics, and data systems into intelligent data systems, because meta can change one from level i to level $i+1$ (see Section 2.9), and then from the ordinary level to intelligent level.

9.7.3 Representation of Intelligent Big Data Analytics

Big data analytics can be considered as a function (operator/operation) f.

Because big data analytics = big data + analytics + DM + SM + DW + visualization + optimization. Then

$$
\begin{aligned}
f\big(\text{Big data Analytics}\big) &= f(\text{big data} + \text{analytics} + DM + SM + DW \\
&\quad + \text{visualization} + \text{optimization}) \\
&= f\big(\text{big data}\big) + f(\text{analytics}) + f\big(DM\big) \\
&\quad + f\big(SM\big) + f\big(DW\big) + f(\text{visualization}) \\
&\quad + f(\text{optimization}).
\end{aligned}
$$

Intelligent is a kind of operation in ICT, cognitive science, and linguistics, for example, "intelligent" has transformed systems, technology, and tools into, intelligent technology, and intelligent tools respectively. Therefore,

Substituting f with intelligent as a function to both sides of the above equation, we have

$$
\begin{aligned}
\text{Intelligent}\big(\text{big data Analytics}\big) &= \text{intelligent big data analytics} \\
&= \text{Intelligent big data} + \text{intelligent analytics} \\
&\quad + \text{intelligent DM} + \text{intelligent SM} \\
&\quad + \text{intelligent DW} + \text{intelligent visualization} \\
&\quad + \text{intelligent optimization})
\end{aligned}
$$

This is a better form for better understanding intelligent big data analytics.

9.7.4 Intelligent Big Data Analytics = AI + Big Data Analytics

The interrelationship among big data, analytics, and AI has drawn increasing attention (Sun, 2019b). Intelligent big data analytics is similar to analytics intelligence (Wang, 2012). The difference between them is that the latter is limited to the data in cyberspace or the Web. The similarity between them is that incorporating AI into analytics is a huge global and social need in the near future (Wang, 2012).

9.7.5 Intelligent Big Data Analytics

Intelligent big data analytics is AI-driven big data analytics (Sun, Sun, & Strang, 2018; Sun, 2019b). Therefore, intelligent big data analytics can be represented as

$$\text{Intelligent big data analytics} = \text{Big data analytics} + \text{AI} \qquad (9.8)$$

Where + can be explained as "and". Equation (9.8) means that intelligent big data analytics includes big data analytics, AI, and their integration (Sun, 2019b).

As we know,

$$\begin{aligned}\text{Big data analytics} = \text{big data descriptive analytics} + \text{big data} \\ \text{diagnostic analytics} + \text{big data predictive} \\ \text{analytics} + \text{big data prescriptive analytics}\end{aligned} \qquad (9.9)$$

Intelligent big data analytics can be represented by extending Equation (9.8), applying intelligent as an operation to both sides of (9.9).

$$\begin{aligned}\text{Intelligent big data analytics} = \text{intelligent big descriptive data} \\ \text{analytics} + \text{intelligent big data diagnostic} \\ \text{analytics} + \text{intelligent big predictive data} \\ \text{analytics} + \text{intelligent big prescriptive} \\ \text{data analytics}\end{aligned}$$

$$(9.10)$$

Equation (9.10) shows that intelligent big data analytics consists of intelligent big data descriptive analytics, intelligent big data diagnostic analytics, intelligent big data predictive analytics, and intelligent big data prescriptive analytics. Equation (9.10) is an extension of existing data analytics (Delena & Demirkanb, 2013) by integrating AI with big data (Sun, 2019b).

Intelligent big data descriptive analytics is intelligent descriptive analytics for big data (Delena & Demirkanb, 2013; Kantardzic, 2011; Sun, Sun, & Strang, 2018). It is used to discover new, nontrivial information based on AI techniques (Kantardzic, 2011, p. 2), and to explain the characteristics of intelligent entities and relationships among intelligent entities within the existing big descriptive data (Coronel, Morris, & Rob, 2020). It addresses the problems such as what and when happened, and what is happening (Delena & Demirkanb, 2013; Kumar, 2015; Sun, 2019b; LaPlante, 2019). For example, intelligent business reports with dashboards for the global COVID-19 pandemic are the results from intelligent big data descriptive analytics on big data of the global COVID-19.

Intelligent big data diagnostic analytics is intelligent diagnostic analytics for big data (Sun, Sun, & Strang, 2018). It is used to examine data or content to answer the question, "Why did it happen?" (After one knows what happened, one wants to know why (LaPlante, 2019)), from the historical and current diagnostic data based on AI techniques, such as drill-down, data discovery, data mining, and correlations (Sun & Stranieri, 2021). For example, diagnostic analytics available on the cloud belongs to intelligent big data diagnostic analytics.

Intelligent big data predictive analytics is intelligent predictive analytics for big data (Sun, Sun, & Strang, 2018). It focuses on forecasting future trends by addressing the problems such as what will happen next. What is going to happen? and Why it will happen? based on historical and current big data (Kumar, 2015; Sun, 2019a, 2019b; LaPlante, 2019). Intelligent big data predictive analytics uses techniques of data mining (predictive mining), statistical modeling, mathematics, and AI to create intelligent models to predict future outcomes or events (Delena & Demirkanb, 2013; Coronel, Morris, & Rob, 2020; Sharda, Delen, & Turba, 2018). For example, intelligent big data predictive analytics can be used to predict smartly where the next attack target of terrorists might be (Sun, Sun, & Strang, 2018).

Intelligent big data prescriptive analytics is intelligent prescriptive analytics for big data (Sun, Sun, & Strang, 2018). It addresses the problems such as what we should do, why we should do, and what should happen with the best outcome under uncertainty (Minelli, Chambers, & Dhiraj, 2013; Delena & Demirkanb, 2013; LaPlante, 2019). Intelligent big data prescriptive analytics uses intelligent algorithms to determine optimal decisions for future actions (Delena & Demirkanb, 2013). For example, intelligent big data prescriptive analytics can be used to provide an optimal marketing strategy for an e-commerce company.

9.7.6 Technological Foundations of Intelligent Big Data Analytics

The fundamentals of intelligent big data analytics consist of AI and machine learning (ML), mathematics, statistics and data mining, human interface, computer science, operations research, data science, and systems (Chen & Zhang, 2014; INFORMS, 2014; Sun & Huo, 2021). The techniques for intelligent big data analytics encompass a wide range of mathematical, statistical, modeling, and algorithm techniques (Coronel, Morris, & Rob, 2020; Sun, 2018). Big data analytics always involves historical or current data, visualization (LaPlante, 2019) and workflow (Sathi, 2013). This requires big data analytics to use data mining (DM) to discover knowledge from a data warehouse (DW) or a big dataset to support decision-making (Holsapple, Lee-Post, & Pakath, 2014). DM employs advanced statistical and analytical tools to analyze the big data available through DWs and other sources to identify possible relationships, patterns, and anomalies and discover information or knowledge for business decision-making (Kantardzic, 2011; Delena & Demirkanb, 2013). In DM, regression and classification are usually used for prediction, predictive mining, and analytics, while clustering and association are used for description or descriptive mining, and analytics (Fan, Lau, & Zhao, 2015). DW extracts and obtains the data from operational databases and external open sources, providing a more comprehensive data pool (Holsapple, Lee-Post, & Pakath, 2014). Big data analytics also uses statistical modeling (SM) to discover knowledge through descriptive analysis that can support decision-making (Sun, Sun, & Strang, 2018). Visualization technologies, including display technologies as an important part of big data analytics, make knowledge patterns and information for decision-making in the form of figures, tables, or multimedia. In summary, big data analytics can facilitate business decision-making and realization of business objectives through analyzing existing data and future trends, creating predictive models to forecast future threats and opportunities, and optimizing business processes to enhance organizational performance using the mentioned techniques. Therefore, big data analytics can be represented technically below.

$$\text{Big data analytics} = \text{Big data} + \text{data analytics} + \text{DW} + \text{DM} + \text{SM}$$
$$+ \text{ML} + \text{visualization} + \text{optimization} \qquad (9.11)$$

Equation (9.11) reveals the fundamental relationship between big data, data analytics, and big data analytics, that is, big data analytics is based on big data and data analytics. It also shows that computer science, data science, AI, and statistics play a dominant role in big data analytics by providing the latest techniques and tools of DM, DW, ML, and visualization (Sun, 2018; Davis, 2014). SM and optimization still play a fundamental role in big data analytics (Minelli, Chambers, & Dhiraj, 2013; Sun & Huo, 2021).

Equations (9.9), (9.10), and (9.11) are a concise representation of the technological components of intelligent big data analytics. Figure 9.7 illustrates these equations on intelligent big data analytics and their interrelationships (Sun, Sun, & Strang, 2018).

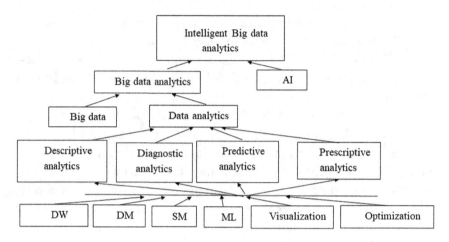

FIGURE 9.7   An ontology of intelligent big data analytics.

The currently leading DW includes Amazon's Redshift, Google's BigQuery, Microsoft's Azure SQL Data Warehouse, and Teradata (Tableau, 2020).

Apache Spark is one of the most popular big data analytics services. It is a big data analytics platform for several enterprises (Tableau, 2020). Spark provides dramatically increased large-scale data processing compared to Hadoop, and a NoSQL database for big data management (Coronel, Morris, & Rob, 2020; Reddy, 2014). Apache Spark has provided Goldman Sachs with excellent big-data analytics services (Tableau, 2020).

Applying intelligent as an operation to both sides of Equation (9.11) (Sun & Wang, 2017a), we have:

intelligent big data analytics = intelligent big data + intelligent data analytics + intelligent DW + intelligent DM + intelligent SM + intelligent ML + intelligent visualization + intelligent optimization

(9.12)

Where intelligent big data can be considered as big data, Equation (9.12) means that intelligent big data analytics at least includes big data, intelligent data analytics, intelligent data warehousing, data mining, intelligent statistical modeling, ML, intelligent visualization, and intelligent optimization (Delena & Demirkanb, 2013; Sun, Sun, & Strang, 2018; Sun & Stranieri, 2021), because data mining and ML are themselves intelligent techniques. Equation (9.12) demonstrates that AI plays a central role in transforming big data analytics into intelligent big data analytics by penetrating each component (Sun & Stranieri, 2021).

9.7.7 Intelligent Big Analytics: An Inclusive Perspective

This section extends intelligent big data analytics to intelligent analytics based on an inclusive approach.

Intelligent analytics is an emerging paradigm in the age of big data, analytics, and AI (Sun, 2019b). Incorporating AI into big data analytics has become a hotspot in many research fields, such as business, information systems, operations research, data science, and computer science (INFORMS, 2014; Sun, 2019b). However, the following issues are still significant for academia, industries, and governments.

1. Is intelligent big data analytics the unique form of intelligent analytics?

2. What are the fundamentals of intelligent analytics?

3. How can we apply mathematical methods and thinking to intelligent analytics?

This section will address these three issues.

Data analytics, big data analytics, and intelligent big data analytics have the following inclusion relationships (Sun, 2019b).

$$\text{Intelligent big data analytics} \sqsubset \text{big data analytics} \sqsubset \text{data analytics} \quad (9.13)$$

where $\sqsubset$ is an inclusion relation. The more specific form the analytics is, the more important it is for applications in academia, industries, and governments. For example, intelligent big data analytics is more important than data analytics nowadays, because it is an integration between AI and big data analytics (Sun & Stranieri, 2021).

As well-known, big data is significant for innovation, competition, and productivity in the digital age (Manyika, Chui, & Bughin, 2011; Sun & Huo, 2021), then big information, big knowledge, and big wisdom are also significant for effective management, decision-making, and innovation for the development of economy, society, and even nations, because many governments and organizations have carried out several initiatives on the development of the information industry (e.g. China, China has the Ministry of Information Industry), knowledge economy (e.g. Australia), and wisdom cities (e.g. China has launched many national projects for developing wisdom cities). Therefore, big information analytics, big knowledge analytics, and big wisdom analytics should have played the same significant role as big data analytics in the digital age. However, currently, some academia, industries, and governments have technically ignored them.

following (9.14), We already know that

$$\text{analytics} := \text{data analytics} + \text{information analytics} \\ + \text{knowledge analytics} + \text{wisdom analytics} \tag{9.14}$$

Therefore, applying big as an operation (Sun Z., 2019b) to both sides of equation (9.14),

following (9.14),

$$\text{Big analytics} := \text{big data analytics} + \text{big information analytics} \\ + \text{big knowledge analytics} \\ + \text{big wisdom analytics} \tag{9.15}$$

Equation (9.15) has extended the result on big analytics in which big analytics is a representation of big data analytics.

Now, let intelligent analytics be intelligent big analytics. Apply intelligent as an operation to both sides of Equation (9.15), we have

$$\text{Intelligent big analytics} = \text{Intelligent big data analytics} + \text{intelligent} \\ \text{big information analytics} + \text{intelligent big} \\ \text{knowledge analytics} + \text{intelligent big} \\ \text{wisdom analytics.} \tag{9.16}$$

Similarly, we can use Boolean structure to have 4 levels of integrated analytics and have 16 (2^4) different kinds of intelligent analytics based on equation (9.16).

Equations (9.15) to (9.16) form an inclusive approach to intelligent analytics. Intelligent big information (or knowledge or wisdom) analytics are not yet appealing to the mainstream in the analytics and BI market. However, data, information, knowledge, and wisdom have a very close relationship.

So far, we have also proved that analytics has experienced five stages from a computer science viewpoint, that is, analytics, data analytics, big data analytics, big analytics, and intelligent big analytics. All these form an analytics computing (Sun, 2022e), that is:

$$\text{Analytics computing} = \text{Analytics science} + \text{Analytics engineering} +$$
$$\text{Analytics technology} + \text{Analytics systems} +$$
$$\text{Analytics management} + \text{Analytics intelligence.}$$

(9.17)

However, data is only one element of at least five elements underpinning the digital age. The other elements at least include information, knowledge, intelligence, and wisdom. Therefore, only looking at intelligent big data analytics is not enough from a scientific viewpoint and from a practical viewpoint.

9.7.8 Augmented Analytics as Intelligent Analytics

This section will examine augmented analytics as intelligent analytics.

Augmented analytics is data analytics that uses "enabling technologies such as ML and AI to assist with data preparation, insight generation, and insight explanation to augment how people explore and analyze data in analytics and BI platforms" (Gartner-augmented analytics, 2020). It can be also defined as "a technology that automates the selection and preparation of data, the generation of insights, and the communication of those insights" (LaPlante, 2019, p. 5).

The features of augmented analytics include automated data preparation, automated insight generation and explanation, NLQ, and natural language narration, as well as content creation (Howson, Richardson, Sallam, & Kronz, 2019).

Augmented data preparation on multistructured data is the need to profile, enrich, and infer relationships (to automatically generate an analysis model), and to make recommendations to improve or enhance insights from data. It will stimulate differentiating innovations.

Insight generation is automated for identifying significant segments, clusters, drivers, outliers, and anomalies. Augmented alerting and anomaly detection are new trends in augmented analytics, although only a few smaller vendors offer these functions (Howson, Richardson, Sallam, & Kronz, 2019).

NLQ, NLP, NLG, natural language query, processing, and generation are used to access data and interpret findings (Howson, Richardson,

Sallam, & Kronz, 2019). With the use of voice- and search-based inter-faces, the query process (NLQ) changes from a primarily drag-and-drop query-building process into a more search-like experience. NLP includes conversational analytics that integrates chatbots and virtual assistants into the workflow for analytics. NLP allows nontechnical users to easily ask questions from source data (LaPlante, 2019, p. 6). NLG automates the process of translating complex data into text with intelligent recommen-dations, thereby accelerating analytic insights (LaPlante, 2019). NLG aims to generate explanations of charts, and insights enhance data literacy. NLG uses ML to explain findings that may have been either manually or automatically generated (Howson, Richardson, Sallam, & Kronz, 2019). Natural language narration includes narration of findings and prescrip-tive actions. These include an understanding of data distribution and cor-relations (Sun & Stranieri, 2021).

Content creation includes augmented data discovery, augmented alert-ing, search, and NLP for voice and text, as well as conversational analytics. Conversational analytics represents the convergence of several technolo-gies, including personal digital assistants, smartphones, bots, and ML (Howson, Richardson, Sallam, & Kronz, 2019). Virtual reality and aug-mented reality support for a broad range of content analytics and text ana-lytics for use on unstructured data.

Oracle Analytics has implemented augmented analytics capabilities across its platform (LaPlante, 2019). Augmentation is a kind of intelli-gence. Augmented analytics will be a dominant driver of new purchases of analytics and AI, data science, ML platforms, and embedded analytics in the years ahead (Howson, Richardson, Sallam, & Kronz, 2019).

Augmented analytics is a kind of intelligent big data analytics, because it has embedded AI and ML into the data analytics (LaPlante, 2019, p. 2) and also because it includes ML-enabled analytics, AI-driven analytics in all phases of the data workflow for analytics, from data preparation to data modeling, insight generation, and insight explanation. Augmented ana-lytics is a kind of intelligent data predictive analytics because it assists with insight generation and insight explanation (Kumar B., 2015; Sun & Stranieri, 2021). However, not only big data, but also big information, big knowledge, and big wisdom are required to generate and explain hind-sight, insight, and foresight for smart decision-making and business solu-tions. Therefore, how to manage and process big data, big information, big knowledge, and big wisdom based on AI is significant for the future of

ChatGPT, augmented analytics, and intelligent analytics. We will address it in future work.

Augmented analytics platforms as an example of big analytics representing the mainstream market for data and analytics leaders in the areas of BI, data science, and machine learning (Howson, Richardson, Sallam, & Kronz, 2019).

9.7.9 Discussions and Implications

Chen, et al., consider intelligent big data analytics as a big data system and use the collective intelligence model and multiagent paradigm to propose a collective intelligence framework to solve the system integration problem in the big data environment (Chen, Li, & Wang, 2015). However, few have discussed the fundamental problems of intelligent big data analytics nor provided an inclusive approach to intelligent analytics. This research identifies theoretical and technological foundations of intelligent big data analytics, based on investigating the state-of-the-art scholars' publications and market analysis of advanced analytics. It also presents the technological foundations for intelligent big data analytics by examining intelligent big data analytics as an integration of AI and big data analytics. This research demonstrates that intelligent big data analytics is not the unique form of intelligent analytics, which, in fact, consists of intelligent big data analytics, intelligent big information analytics, intelligent big knowledge analytics, and intelligent big wisdom analytics at a fundamental level.

Gartner uses advanced analytics, modern analytics, and augmented analytics to analyze AI and BI, big data, and analytics and their impacts (Laney & Jain, 2017; Howson, Richardson, Sallam, & Kronz, 2019). With the further development of analytics, either advanced analytics, modern analytics, augmented analytics, or intelligent analytics will be selected by the customers, because the general customers hope to use the simple concept to cover what they perceive, just as smartphones to intelligent phones are accepted in the world. Industries and governments also prefer simple terms to jargon words, just as they like big data rather than the massive data in the past decade.

From an evolutionary viewpoint, intelligent analytics is a more general form of data analytics (Kantardzic, 2011; Sun & Stranieri, 2021). Data analytics is an extension to data mining (Gandomi & Haider, 2015) because data analytics is considered as the whole data mining process or process of knowledge discovery in databases (KDD) (Tsai, Lai, Chao, & Vasilakos,

2015). Therefore, the relationships among data mining, intelligent big data analytics, and intelligent analytics can be represented as

Data mining $\subset$ intelligent big data analytics $\subset$ intelligent analytics.

This means that data mining as an intelligent technique is the foundation of intelligent analytics. However, the difference between intelligent analytics and data mining is that the former discovers AI-driven knowledge and wisdom not only from big data but also from big information, big knowledge, and big wisdom.

The theoretical implication of this research is that it provides an inclusive approach for understanding the interrelationship among big data, information, knowledge, wisdom, analytics, and AI and their integration. Intelligent analytics is not only intelligent big data analytics. Fundamentally, intelligent analytics consists of intelligent big data analytics, intelligent big information analytics, intelligent big knowledge analytics, and intelligent big wisdom analytics. This inclusive approach will pave a new way for developing intelligent analytics with applications.

The technical implication of this section is that the proposed approach to intelligent analytics in general and intelligent big data analytics, intelligent big information analytics, intelligent big knowledge analytics, and intelligent big wisdom analytics, in particular, can attract more researchers and practitioners to undertake the research and application of intelligent analytics, for more effective management decision-making in business workflow.

9.7.10 Summary

This section presents a calculus for intelligent analytics as an integration between analytics and AI. This research proposes an inclusive approach to intelligent analytics, which treats many aspects of intelligent analytics using mathematical methods and AI in a unified way. The main three contributions of this research to intelligent analytics with applications are 1). The calculus for intelligent analytics is the bridge between analytics and AI. 2). Intelligent analytics is a system integrating analytics and AI, taking into account big data, big information, big knowledge, and big wisdom and their close relationships. 3. Data, information, knowledge, intelligence, and wisdom are five elements in the digital age. Therefore, the proposed approach in this research might facilitate research and development of intelligent analytics, intelligent big data analytics, analytics intelligence, and AI.

9.8 INTELLIGENT BIG DATA ANALYTICS FOR ENTERPRISE SYSTEMS

This section looks at how to apply intelligent big data analytics for enterprise systems.

9.8.1 Enterprise Information Systems

Enterprise information systems (EIS) have drawn increasing attention in academia, organizations, and enterprises over the past few decades. EIS are also called enterprise systems (Laudon & Laudon, 2020). There are many different definitions of EIS. For example, EIS refers to

1. Systems that help managers and companies improve their performance by enabling them to seamlessly share data, information, and knowledge among departments and with external business partners (Turban & Volonino, 2011). These systems integrate functional systems such as accounting, finance, marketing, and operations.

2. Enterprise software based on a suite of integrated software modules and a common central database (Laudon & Laudon, 2020).

3. Information systems that support activities in multiple departments of an enterprise (Kroenke, Bunker, & Wilson, 2014, p. 605).

The first definition is self-contained for EIS and emphasizes sharing data, information, and knwoledge. The second stresses enterprise software with a common central database. The third is the most general definition. Combining these three definitions, we can define an EIS as an information system that has a common central database and supports activities in multiple departments of the enterprise through integrating the functional information systems (IS) such as accounting IS, finance IS, marketing IS and operations IS, and accessing the resources also available on the cloud. The support activities include helping managers and companies share experience and wisdom to improve their business performance and decision-making (Sun, Strang, & Firmin, 2017).

EIS mainly consists of ERP (enterprise resource planning) systems, SCM (supply chain management) systems, CRM (customer relationship management) systems, and knowledge management (KM) systems (Laudon & Laudon, 2020). The main EIS vendors, for example, SAP Business Suite, Oracle's e-Business Suite, and Microsoft's Dynamics Suite have used enterprise solutions and enterprise suites to make these EIS work closely with each other and link to systems of customers and suppliers based on web services, cloud services, and service-oriented architecture (SOA) (Laudon & Laudon, 2020).

9.8.2 SCM Systems

SCM systems enable better purchasing and scheduling decisions for the supply chain (Laudon & Laudon, 2020). SCM software is classified as software either for helping businesses plan their supply chains or for helping them execute the supply chain steps. The former are supply chain planning systems, whereas the latter are supply chain execution systems (Laudon & Laudon, 2020).

SCM use two different models: the push-based model and the pull-based model. In the push-based model, production master schedules are based on forecasts or estimates of the product's demands, and products are "pushed' to customers. In the pull-based model, also known as a demand-driven model or build-to-order, actual customer orders or purchases trigger events in the supply chain. Transactions to produce and deliver only what customers have ordered move up the supply chain from retailers to distributors to manufacturers, and eventually to suppliers. The pull-based model has been used by web-based SCM, whereas traditional SCM uses the push-based model. Walmart's continuous replenishment system is an example of using a pull-based model (Laudon & Laudon, 2020).

Therefore, supply chain analytics consists of supply chain planning analytics and supply chain execution analytics. Supply chain analytics helps to make sense of all the data by uncovering patterns and generating insights from big data sources (IBM, 2024c). These insights can help organizations and decision-makers improve quality, delivery, customer experience—and ultimately, profitability.

The supply chain planning solutions vendors include Oracle, Blue Yonder, and SAP (Gartner, 2023a).

9.8.3 CRM Systems

Customer relationship management (CRM) is a firm's most valuable asset (Laudon & Laudon, 2020). This is the result of the "customer is the God, and customer is always right," although some companies are still very greedy and have hubris, which is endemic in the corporate world. Even so, they still use CRM systems to improve customer relationships for their companies. A CRM system mainly consists of sales, marketing, and services (Laudon & Laudon, 2020, p. 379). This is also why CRM systems have been important for any firm, in particular, for big companies. The advanced CRM systems contain modules for partner relationship management and employee relationship management (Laudon & Laudon, 2020).

CRM analytics comprises all of the programming that analyzes customers' data and presents it to an organization for decision-making (Yasar & Kiwak, 2022). CRM analytics can be based on online analytical processing (OLAP) and data mining. CRM analytics systems can be classified as collaborative, operational, and analytical. A collaborative CRM system aims to streamline processes and workflows across various organizational structures. An operational CRM system automates numerous processes by providing a detailed picture of all customer interactions. An analytical CRM system works behind the scenes to analyze the sales data gathered by operational CRM apps.

Therefore, CRM analytics systems usually provide software and online tools for sales, customer service, and marketing (Laudon & Laudon, 2020). The major CRM system vendors include Zoho, Oracle, SAP, Salesforce.com, SAP CRM, and Microsoft Dynamics CRM (Gartner, 2024c).

9.8.4 Intelligent Big Data Analytics-Based EIS

As we know, standalone enterprise systems are becoming a thing of the past (Laudon & Laudon, 2020). The proposed analytics-based EIS is an integrated system consisting of SC planning analytics, SC execution analytics, CRM analytics, marketing analytics, sales analytics, service analytics, and big data analytics, as shown in Figure 9.8. In what follows, we describe this model in some detail.

A master enterprise warehouse mainly consists of big data related to sales, marketing, services, customers, SC (supply chain) planning, and SC execution flowing from the marketing, human resources, and other related departments. The enterprise knowledge base consists of data, information, and knowledge from the Web, call centers, direct mails, emails, retail stores, and clients and partners (Laudon & Laudon, 2020).

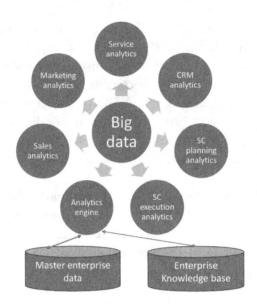

FIGURE 9.8 Intelligent big data analytics for EIS.

Big data analytics is based on a master enterprise warehouse and enterprise knowledge base, which provide related information and knowledge for sales analytics, marketing analytics, service analytics, CRM analytics, SC planning analytics, and SC execution analytics, as illustrated in Figure 9.8.

The analytics engine is a mechanism for managing and producing CRM analytics, SC planning analytics, SC planning analytics, marketing analytics, service analytics, big data analytics, and knowledge analytics. The analytics engine has OLAP, data mining, statistical modeling, visualization tools, and other data and knowledge analysis tools, including soft computing, fuzzy neuro-fuzzy NN, decision trees, and probabilistic models (Laudon & Laudon, 2020).

Discovering useful information, knowledge, patterns, and insights from big data has become the central topic for business operation, marketing, and EIS (Turban & Volonino, 2011). This is just the task of big data analytics (Sun, Strang, & Firmin, 2017).

Big data analytics allows enterprises to enhance business performance, efficiencies, and guiding decision processes (Kambatla, Kollias, Kumar, & Grama, 2014). Big data analytics also provides the most exciting opportunities and challenges for every field (Liebowitz, 2013, p. 65).

Furthermore, EIS is an important information system and knowledge-base system for improving the business performance and decision-making of CEOs and enterprises. Big data analytics is pivotal for developing EIS (Sun, Strang, & Firmin, 2017). From a technological viewpoint, big data analytics is a data-driven business-oriented technique that facilitates business decision-making and then improves EIS as a system component. From a data viewpoint, big data analytics relies on big data and data analytics. Big data have become a strategic resource for any organization and enterprise, in particular, for multinational organizations, as well as any EIS.

Currently, enterprises' development heavily relies on four cutting-edge technology pillars: cloud, mobile, big data, and social technologies. Each of these pillars corresponds to a special kind of web services, that is, cloud services, mobile services, big data services, and social networking service (Sun, Strang, & Firmin, 2017). Each of these services is becoming an inevitable component of any EIS. Each of these services has been supported by analytics services and technologies, as shown in Figure 9.8.

9.8.5 Summary

This section surveyed enterprise information systems, SCM systems, and CRM systems. Then it proposed analytics-oriented EIS, an integrated system consisting of SC planning analytics, SC execution analytics, CRM analytics, marketing analytics, sales analytics, service analytics, and big data analytics, supported by the master enterprise warehouse and analytics engine.

Analytics EIS is a data system processing data. It is also an information system transforming data to information. EIS is a knowledge base system transforming knowledge to intelligence and insights. Therefore, EIS can be used to process data, information, and knowledge to improve business performance and decision making. services and technologies have become an important emerging market, with big data services, cloud services, mobile services, and social networking services (Sun, Strang, & Firmin, 2017). All these four services and technologies shape the most important markets for IT, big data analytics, and EIS development (Sun, Strang, & Firmin, 2017; Sun, Demand-driven Services, 2023).

Analytics-based EIS will be applied in Section 10.11 for EIS and business analytics.

9.9 CRACI COMPUTING

Classification, regression, association, clustering, and insight rules have been discussed, not only in statistics, artificial neural networks, data mining, and analytics (Aroraa, Lele, & Jindal, 2022; Kantardzic, 2011; Sharda,

Delen, & Turba, 2018). The more generalized forms for them are: regression computing, classification computing, clustering computing, and association rules computing. Only in such a way, can we apply computing science, engineering, systems, intelligence, and management to develop their services and applications. That is:

CRACI Computing = classification computing + regression computing + association computing + clustering computing + insight computing.

Data mining and analytics aim to provide services on CRACI systems and services with data intelligence. However, they are only examples of CRACI Computing; only the latter can be used for covering more and changing data mining and analytics into an example based on the system generalization and specification (see Section 2.10).

Furthermore, we also have CRACI analytics = classification analytics, association analytics, clustering analytics, insight analytics.

In what follows, we look at insight computing and analytics.

9.10 INSIGHT COMPUTING AND ANALYTICS

9.10.1 Introduction

Google Scholar search "insight computing" found 48 results (February 31, 2024). Among them

1. No titles of the found results include "insight computing."

2. Insight computing was mentioned in 11 among the 48 results; 9 of the 15 are in English, whereas the other 2 results are in French, contributed from A Dubus, et. al, belonging to mathematics. Delving into these 8 out of 9 results listed in Table 9.5, we find that

However, no insight computing is mentioned in its abstract, presentation, and introduction in the 8 articles and presentations. This implies that insight computing has not drawn any attention in academia and industry so far, although insight generation and insight explanation have been mentioned and developed in some analytics systems (Howson, Richardson, Sallam, & Kronz, 2019). Even so, analyzing the data is important for actionable insights to make decisions on organizations (Hurley, 2019, p. 17).

TABLE 9.5　Insight Computing in Google Scholar

No.	Insight Computing	Authors	Remarks
1	To create deeper insights from the vast amount of data.	FD Hudson, EW Nichols. (downloaded)	Chapter 11: The internet of things and cognitive computing, 2016.
2	Discusses the insight computing of CCMP payload.	I Singh, KN Mishra, et al.	A novel privacy and security framework for the cloud network services, 2015.
3	Training from Steve Jones of Insight Computing.	M Evans, J Eyre 2004.	The Opportunities of a Lifetime: Model lifetime analysis of current British social policy.
4	Moving from observation to insight.	T Tran, 2016.	Evolution of machine learning: from expert to exploratory systems.
5	Discusses the insight computing of CCMP payload.	H Patel.	NC as a Security Services for Data Security in Cloud.
6	With all of the novel insight-computing.	R Naous – 2017.	Von Neumann and beyond: Memristor architectures: dissertation.
7	Discusses the insight computing of CCMP payload.	KN Mishra, 2018.	A novel mechanism for cloud data management in distributed environment.
8	A still unnamed "meeting insight computing system".	MJ Masoodi, N Abdelaal et al., 2021.	Workplace Surveillance and Remote Work.

9.10.2　Why Are Insights Important for Analytics?

Analytical insights: Strong C-level managers such as CTO, CDO, and CAO can help the CIO assess and implement the most effective technologies to support innovative, analytics-focused initiatives (Mittal, 2017).

What are emerging analytics capabilities? The IoT, big data modernization, cognitive computing, machine learning, and intelligent automation are all becoming core analytics capabilities (Mittal, 2017).

C-level executives try to understand the value of data analytics as a tool to generate insights and embed them in everyday decision-making processes (Mittal, 2017). Insight-oriented analytics generate insightful knowledge and wisdom. The top goal is above insight computing.

The entire analytics process is from what data to use, to how to represent the extracted knowledge, and exploit the insights to create economic and social value doe decision making. (https://www.i3e2021.com/, accessed March 18, 2021).

9.10.3 Insight Computing

Like physics and mathematics, intelligent big data analytics is a science and technology about collecting, organizing, and analyzing big data to discover patterns and relationships, knowledge, insight, intelligence and other information within the big data, and then visualize and communicate the discovered things.

Invaluable and valuable insights are keys to any decision-making (Thompson & Rogers, 2017).

The insight can be developed into insight computing.

Insight (Merriam-Webster, 2024) refers to as

1. The power or act of seeing into a situation,

2. The act or result of apprehending the inner nature of things or of seeing intuitively.

The first part of insight is penetration, while the second part of insight is apprehending. In other words, insight is penetration into and apprehending the essence of business, management, and decision-making. Therefore, insight is at an intelligent level rather than a knowledge level. Knowledge discovery is the aim of data mining, whereas insight discovery is the aim of data analytics. This is why data analytics, in particular intelligent data analytics, aims to discover insight for business, management, and decision-making.

Following a discussion on computing in the previous chapter, insight computing consists of insight science, insight technology, insight engineering, insight systems, insight management, and insight intelligence. An example of insight computing is data computing. An example of insight technology is data analytics, including predictive analytics which can generate predictive insights for business decision-making (Kingpin, 2024). An example of insight engineering is data analyticizing as a process. An example of insight systems is a data analytics system. An example of insight management is data analytics management. An example of insight intelligence is wisdom-oriented intelligence.

Data-driven insights are an example of big data analytics and intelligence directly towards data-driven analytics intelligence. Automated insights are the future of big data analytics and intelligence (Schlegel, Kurt; Sun, Julian, 2023).

9.11 SUMMARY

This chapter will explores data analytics intelligence and intelligent big data analytics with applications in business, management, and decision making. More specifically, this chapter looks at data analytics intelligence and big data analytics intelligence. It explores intelligent big data analytics systems, intelligent big data analytics ecosystems, and intelligent big data analytics as a management. It proposes big data 4.0 as the next frontier for revolutionizing the World and presents the calculus of intelligent analytics. This chapter examines intelligent big data analytics for enterprise systems. This chapter also explores insight computing after analyzing CACI computing. The main contributions include: 1 DIKW computing, analytics, and intelligence will play a significant role in big data 4.0 as the next frontier for revolutionizing the world. 2. Calculus of intelligent analytics is a bridge connecting big data analytics AI, BI, and other intelligent technologies. 3. Analytics-oriented EIS is an integrated system consisting of SC planning analytics, SC execution analytics, CRM analytics, marketing analytics, sales analytics, service analytics, and big data analytics, supported by the master enterprise warehouse and analytics engine 4. CACI computing and insight computing are new paradigms in computer science, AI, and data science.

Much of fundamental research in big data analytics remains to be done at the moment (National Research Council, 2013). In future work, we will provide a detailed analysis of CACI computing and analytics. we will delive into the calculus of intellient analytics with applications.

9.12 REVIEW QUESTIONS AND PROBLEMS

1. What is data analytics intelligence?

2. Why big data 4.0 is the next frontier for revolutionizing the world?

3. How can big data analytics intelligence be used for decision-making?

4. What is insight computing?

5. What is a cyclic model for big data analytics intelligence?

6. What is intelligent big data analytics?

7. How can you analyze the nature of intelligent analytics?

8. What is the calculus of intelligent analytics?

9. How can intelligent big data analytics be used for enterprise systems?

10. List applications of big intelligent analytics in healthcare, finance and banking.

9.13 REFERENCES FOR FURTHER STUDY

1. I. Almeida, 2023, Generative AI For Business Leaders: Collection (Byte-sized Learning). Now Next Later AI.

2. Jigar Tewar, 2023, Generative AI models 2023: Large language models (LLMs), Kindle Edition.

3. Joseph Sifakis, 2022, Understanding and Changing the World: From Information to Knowledge and Intelligence, Springer

4. Rob Pyne, 2021, Unlock: Leveraging the hidden intelligence in your leadership team, 2021, Xory Pty Ltd.

5. Jack Reynolds, 2023, Microsoft Azure Data Engineering: The Big Reference Guide (The Data Engineering Series) Kindle Edition.

6. Alex Holloway, 2024, Data Analysis in Microsoft Excel: Deliver Awesome Analytics in 3 Easy Steps Using VLOOKUPS, Pivot Tables, Charts And More, Kindle Edition.

7. R.L. Ackoff, 1989, From data to wisdom, Journal of applied systems analysis. Vol 16. pp.3–9.

CHAPTER 10

Business Intelligence

All data, analytics, and intelligence are for business intelligence.

THIS CHAPTER WILL EXPLORE business intelligence with applications based on data, analytics, intelligence, and their integrations. More specifically, this chapter analyzes BI, business analytics, eSMACS technologies and services, and intelligent business process analytics. This chapter explores business analytics and presents a calculus of intelligent business analytics. It looks at techniques for business analytics. This chapter provides six Ps as the elements of a generic framework for decision making in digital services and discusses decision analytics. It also proposes big data analytics services for enhancing BI and explores business analytics for enterprise information systems. It discusses cybersecurity intelligence and analytics, and explores platform engineering and economics. This chapter will provide six big trends in the era of big data-based AI and BI, and examines big data driven socioec-onomic development.

Learning objectives of this chapter:

- Understand intelligence in BI.

- Understand intelligent business process analytics.

- Explain business intelligences from BI.

- Identify BI as OI and MI.

- Define business analytics.

DOI: 10.1201/9781003450504-10

- Understand the calculus of intelligent business analytics.

- Familiarity with platform engineering and economics.

- Explore big data analytics services for enhancing BI.

- Understand business analytics for enterprise information systems.

- Explore GDDP to measure digital products and services for the digital economy and society.

- Discuss business analytics intelligence to empower intelligent business, management, and decision-making.

- Understand six big trends in the era of big data.

- Define decision analytics.

- Understand 6Ps for decision making.

- Explore big data-driven socio-economic development.

10.1 INTRODUCTION

Business intelligence (BI) was first introduced by an IBM researcher Mr. Luhn in 1958 (Luhn, 1958). Therefore, BI has a long and rich history. Decision support systems (DSS) and business performance management (BPM) integrated BI into business and management (Laudon & Laudon, 2020). Howard Dresner, a Research Fellow at Gartner Group, popularized "BI" as an umbrella term in 1989 to describe a set of concepts and methods to improve business decision-making based on fact-based support systems. BI has received increasing attention in academia, e-commerce business, and management since then (Lim, Chen, & Chen, 2013). BI has become not only an important technology for improving the business performance of enterprises but also an impetus for developing e-commerce and e-services (Laudon & Laudon, 2020).

Technological aspects of business analytics are rooted in the decision support systems (Holsapple, Lee-Post, & Pakath, 2014). However, business analytics has other roots, different from the technology, for example, operations research, because the data for business may be non-numeric, and their business solutions may rely on qualitative analysis, logic, reasoning, collaboration, negotiation, and deception because deception is a part of business negotiation. Therefore, business analytics is rooted in the theory, technologies, systems, and tools to support decision-making by providing powerful mechanisms for discovering, acquiring, generating, assimilating, selecting, sharing, and emitting information and knowledge (Holsapple, Lee-Post, & Pakath, 2014).

Since 2012, BI has evolved into data analytics and data science (Sharda, Delen, Turban, & King, 2018, p. 41). Now data analytics, big data analytics, and business analytics have moved BI and made BI into a blossom. That is not only BI but also other intelligences, including AI in business, management, and decision-making. All intelligent technologies, systems, and tools are used to find intelligences and insights in every transaction, activity of any business, management, and decision-making from big data, information, and knowledge sources.

However, BI is facing new challenges and opportunities because of the dramatic development of big data and big data technologies (Fan, Lau, & Zhao, 2015; Gandomi & Haider, 2015); that is, how to use big data analytics to enhance BI becomes a big issue for business, e-commerce, e-services, and information systems.

The above brief discussion and literature review imply a close relationship between big data analytics and BI. However, the following two important issues have not drawn significant attention in the scholarly peer-reviewed literature:

- What is the relationship between big data analytics and BI?

- How can big data analytics enhance BI?

This chapter will explore business intelligence with applications based on data, analytics, intelligence, and their integrations. More specifically, this chapter analyzes BI, business analytics, eSMACS technologies, and intelligent business process analytics. It explores business analytics and presents a calculus of intelligent business analytics. It looks at techniques for business analytics. It provides six Ps as the elements of a generic framework for decision making in digital services and discusses decision analytics. This chapter also proposes big data analytics services for enhancing BI and explores business analytics for enterprise information systems. It discusses cybersecurity intelligence and an-alytics, and explores platform engineering and economics. This chapter will provide six big trends in the era of big data- based AI and BI, and examines big data driven socioeconomic development.

The remainder of this chapter is structured as follows: Section 10.2 looks at fundamentals of BI. Section 10.3 considers BI as the combination of OI and MI. Section 10.4 discusses BI and eSMACS technologies. Section 10.5 explores business analytics. Section 10.6 proposes a calculus of intelligent business analytics. Section 10.7 looks at techniques for BI and business analytics. Sections 10.8 and 10.9 provides six Ps as the elements of a generic framework for decision making in digital services and discusses decision analytics. Section 10.10 examines big data analytics services for enhancing BI. Section 10.11 explores enterprise information systems and business analytics. Section 10.12 discusses cybersecurity intelligence and analytics. Section 10.13 explores platform engineering. Section 10.14 provides six big trends in the era of big data- based AI and BI. Section 10.15 examines big data driven socioeconomic development. The final section ends this chapter with some concluding remarks and future work.

10.2 FUNDAMENTALS OF BI

10.2.1 What is BI?

There are many definitions for BI. This section will analyze three of them, and then provide a unified definition of BI.

There are many different definitions on BI. For example,

1. "The process of BI is based on the transformation of data to information, then to decisions, and finally to actions"

(SHARDA, DELEN, TURBAN, & KING, 2018, P. 42).

However, business decision-makers need not only data but also information, knowledge, intelligence, and wisdom (or DIKIW). Because they need DIKIW, therefore, the process analytics, different from BI, as a system is based on the transformation of data to information, information to knowledge, knowledge to intelligence, and intelligence to wisdom incrementally, then to decisions, and finally to actions.

2. BI is defined as providing decision-makers with valuable information and knowledge by leveraging a variety of sources of data, as well as structured and unstructured information (Sabherwal & Becerra-Fernandez, 2011).

3. BI is a framework consisting of a set of concepts, theories, and methods to improve business decision-making based on fact-based support systems (Lim, Chen, & Chen, 2013).

The second definition of BI emphasizes information and knowledge for decision-makers. The last definition emphasizes "a set of concepts, theories, and methods to improve business decision-making," Based on the above analysis, BI can be defined as a set of theories, methodologies, architectures, systems, and technologies that support business decision-making with valuable data, information, and knowledge. This definition reflects the evolution of BI and its technologies from decision support systems (DSS) and its relations with data warehouses and executive information systems (Holsapple, Lee-Post, & Pakath, 2014).

This section will use BI as an intelligence for doing business or making money by human beings, machines, and systems using a comprehensive, cohesive, integrated set of systems, tools, apps, processes, and applications to capture, collect, integrate, store, and analyze data, information, knowledge, and wisdom to generate and present information, knowledge, insights, intelligences, and wisdom to support business decision-making. Even so, only a singular intelligence in business is not enough. We need more intelligences for doing business or making money by human beings, machines, and systems.

10.2.2 Intelligence in BI

There are many different perspectives on intelligence in BI.

The intelligence in the BI concept is related to the intelligence concept from Simon's classic decision-making process (intelligence, design, choice, and implementation). It does not originate from the AI field. Another origin is the intelligence concept in a military context.

In Simon's classic decision-making process, intelligence means that managers examine a situation and then identify and define the problem. It is the first stage of decision-making as a process (Turban & Volonino, 2011). Therefore, intelligence is motivated by Simon's model.

Big data analytics has brought a big challenge to BI, that is, some companies are abandoning BI. This makes us ask what Intelligence means in BI.

Therefore, the intelligence of BI has a close relation with that in AI. If intelligence in AI refers to emulating, simulating, and augmenting human intelligence and machine intelligence using ICT (Russell & Norvig, 2020), then the intelligence of BI is to emulate simulate, and augment human intelligence and machine intelligence in business using ICT.

We mentioned meta (knowledge) = intelligence. Does this intelligence belong to BI or AI? The answer is both. Furthermore,

1. The purpose of BI is to generate and present information to support business decision-making (Laudon & Laudon, 2020). This is an information intelligence.

2. Data modeling is an iterative and progressive process of creating a specific data model for a determined problem domain to support decision-making. This is a data intelligence.

3. Data warehousing is the progress of creating and managing data warehouses to support decision-making. This is also a data intelligence.

4. Data mining is the knowledge discovery from a large database. This is a kind of data intelligence and knowledge intelligence.

5. Analytics aims to discover insights for decision-makers. Therefore, insights are a kind of wisdom intelligence.

Therefore, BI at least includes intelligence in AI, data intelligence, knowledge intelligence, wisdom intelligence, or DIKW intelligence.

10.2.3 BI and Data Intelligence

According to (Sisense, 2021), BI focuses more on organizing data and presenting it in a way that makes it easier to understand and derive insights for business decision-making; however, data intelligence is more concerned with analyzing information. One problem arises here. What is the relationship between data and information? Data intelligence cannot focus on the analysis of information, because information is different from data, at least from a computing viewpoint.

Data intelligence = data + intelligence and BI= business + intelligence. On one side, data is an important element of business. That is, data is a part of business; data intelligence can facilitate BI. On the other side, both share intelligence, they have similar goals, methods, and technologies to obtain intelligence.

A family of techniques and intelligences from standard reports to advanced analytics has been examined under the roof of BI and AI.

In the history, reporting and dashboard are a presentation layer in BI to make or support decisions (Thompson & Rogers, 2017). DB and DW are a data storage layer. DM is an analysis layer. SM is an algorithm layer. Then we can use the system process of analytics to develop a system process of BI (Laudon & Laudon, 2020; Sharda, Delen, & Turba, 2018).

10.2.4 BI ≠Business Analytics

From a market and technological viewpoint, data analysis is a part of data analytics. Data mining can facilitate data analytics. Therefore, business organizations prefer to use business analytics rather than data mining, and data analytics.

Business analytics can cover more than data analytics and data mining, because there are many different business analytics (for example, SC analytics, customer analytics, and so on). Basically, we will have corresponding business analytics depending on how many BIs we have. Furthermore, BI is a more general concept for improving business performance and business decision-making. Business analytics is a pivotal part of developing BI, at least from a technological viewpoint. From a technological viewpoint, business analytics is a data-driven and business-oriented technique. It facilitates business decision-making and then improves BI. From a data viewpoint, business analysis relies on data analytics. Data has become a strategic source for any organization, but in particular, for multinational organizations. Discovering secrets such as patterns, knowledge and insights from databases, data warehouses, data marts, and the Web has become the No 1 priority topic for any business marketing operation.

10.2.5 From BI to Business Intelligences

The single word "intelligence" is fundamentally limited and misleading (Howard, 2012). This is not only for the theory of multiple intelligences (Howard, 1983). It is also right for intelligence in BI. In fact, only some indulge BI. Many already use BIs. That is, business consists of multiple intelligences, for example, BIs consists of financial intelligence, agile business intelligence, commercial intelligence, competitive intelligence, market intelligence, social intelligence, mobile business intelligence, retail intelligence, real-time intelligence, visual business intelligence, location intelligence, sales intelligence, product intelligence, and more (Brooks, 2022). In reality, every business action requires BIs to promote the business activities.

10.3 BI = OI + MI

Just as the steam engine drove the Industrial Revolution, big data and all the emerging technologies and applications have been dramatically revolutionizing our enterprises, organizations, industries, and societies (Betser & Belanger, 2013). BI can be seen as a specific information system, a cyclical informing process, a technology platform, or an information value chain (Skyrius, 2021). This concept is different from that of BI as a set of tools, techniques, and systems that support decision-making.

An organization like Google or Baidu can benefit from the big data analytics paradigm by providing its own data and analytics services to other organizations (Fattah, 2014).

As we know, BI= business + intelligence.

In other words, BI is the intelligence of doing business or making money. Therefore, BI is the science and technology of doing business or making money intelligently by human beings and machines, using a set of techniques, systems, and methods based on ICT.

Any business consists of internal parts and external parts; each part requires intelligences. The internal parts are about organization, whereas external parts concern the market.

Then BI can be considered organizational intelligence (OI) and market intelligence (MI).

Organizational intelligence can be defined as the capacity of an organization to create knowledge and use it to strategically adapt to its environment or marketplace (Halal, 1997).

Market intelligence is the intelligence derived by the organization from data and information about the market. It operates in or wants to help determine market segmentation, penetration, opportunity, and existing market metrics (Brooks, 2022, p. 41). Market intelligence is not the same as BI, but is a part of BI.

For short

$$BI = OI + MI$$

OI includes enterprise intelligence (EI). MI includes customer intelligence (CI). Then

$$BI = OI + MI = OI + EI + MI + CI$$

Where O = Organizational, M = Market, E = employee, C = customer.
Replacing analytics with intelligence in the above equation, we have

$$BI = OA + MA$$

These are the business analytics = Organizational analytics + Market analytics. Then we can have an extended business analytics:

$$BA = OA + MA = OA + EA + MA + CA$$

Where A = Analytics. This is the right operation to both sides of the equation.

In what follows, we look at organizational Analytics illustrated in Figure 10.1.

Organizational analytics can be defined as using advanced analytics techniques to design organizations to improve organizational intelligence. Organizational analytics consists of strategic analytics, tactic analytics, and operational analytics, which correspond to strategic management, tactic management, and operational management (Laudon & Laudon, 2020).

FIGURE 10.1   Organizational analytics.

Strategic analytics supports strategic decision-making for strategic managers, such as C-level managers. More generally, strategic analytics is used to generalize and discover strategic intelligence.

Tactic analytics supports tactic decision-making for managerial managers to generalize and discover tactic intelligence.

Operational analytics supports the operational decision-making of operational managers to generalize and discover operational intelligence.

Furthermore, one can use DDPP analytics to address DDPP problems at the strategic, tactic, and operational level.

SWOT analysis is a popular business method used to analyze and evaluate internal intelligence of strengths and weaknesses, and external intelligence of opportunities and threats for an organization and its rivalry (Schneider, 2017).

10.4 BI, ESMACS TECHNOLOGIES AND SERVICES

Currently, BI is based on six cutting-age technology pillars: electronic, cloud, mobile, big data, social, and security technologies (IDC, 2013), each of these pillars corresponds to a special kind of services, that is, electronic services, social networking services, cloud services, mobile services, big data services, and security services; all these constitute modern web services. Each of these services has been supported by analytics services and technologies (Sun, Strang, & Firmin, 2017). They are effectively supported by big data analytics services and technology with intelligence (Sun, 2018b), as shown in Figure 10.2.

It should be noted that for the-state-of-art web services, web services mainly consist of electronic services, social networking services, mobile services, analytics services, cloud services, and security services (Sun, 2023). In reality, each of them involves sophisticated ICT technologies. Then, technologies are added to electronic services, social networking services, mobile services, analytics services, cloud services, and security services (Sun, Strang, & Firmin, 2017). Here we emphasize big data analytics as a service and technology at the center to support electronic services and technologies, social networking services and technologies cloud services and technologies, mobile services and technologies, and security services and technologies to reflect big data and analytics as an emerging new service and technology with data intelligence and analytics intelligence.

Big data analytics as a service and technology has become an important emerging market, with electronic services, social networking services,

FIGURE 10.2   Interrelationship between big data analytics and eSMACS services.

cloud services, mobile services, and security services (Sun, Strang, & Firmin, 2017; Marketsandmarkets, 2022). All five of these services and the technologies shape the most important markets for e-commerce and e-services. In other words: modern web services = eSMACS services.

10.5 BUSINESS ANALYTICS

This section examines business analytics and its relationship with data analytics, information analytics, knowledge analytics, and intelligence analytics, which are four pillars of web analytics, business analytics, and analytics computing. It argues that analytics can be considered as a combination or integration of data mining, data warehouse, statistical modeling, and visualization, taking into account big data management.

10.5.1 Introduction

Business analytics are data-based applications of quantitative analysis methods used in business for decades (Williams, 2016, p. 27). Business analytics as an application of mathematical and statistical techniques has long been studied in operations research, management science, simulation analysis, econometrics, and financial analysis (Holsapple, Lee-Post, &

Pakath, 2014). Business analytics is an application of data analytics and big data analytics for business.

Business analytics can be applied to recommend next actions such as next purchases for online retailers, recognition of images for security and surveillance systems, real-time scoring of large volumes of streaming data such as for financial services firms, optimizing operating parameters in factories, and operating automated vehicles such as self-driving cars, trains, ships (Thompson & Rogers, 2017, pp. 28-29).

Business analytics emphasizes data-driven, statistical, and business decision-making, whereas big data analytics emphasizes business analytics mining from big data (Sharda, Delen, Turban, & King, 2018, p. 1).

10.5.2 Business Process Analytics

Business analytics cover numerous kinds of analytics, including revenue management analytics, trade promotion analytics, inventory management analytics, cost and financial analytics, supply chain and operations analytics (Williams, 2016, pp. 18–19), social media analytics, marketing analytics, location analytics, financial analytics, network analytics, search engine analytics, text analytics, marketing analytics, pricing analytics, retail analytics, management analytics, behavioral analytics, risk analytics, and supply chain analytics (Brooks, 2022). This implies that business analytics corresponds to business processes, transactions, applications, and industry. For example, health care is a business; thus, health care analytics is a business analytics. More generally, any business applications related to effective analysis of any datasets always require metrics and business analytics (Kambatla, Kollias, Kumar, & Grama, 2014).

Business process analytics is a process that can extract, interpret, and analyze processes for management and optimization. Business process analytics can be used to investigate complex systems and get insights relevant to decision-makers. The processes and information flow are important for identifying business process analytics. For example, DDPP analytics is based on a workflow and cyclic business process in Section 7.8.

10.5.3 Business Analytics and Intelligence

Business analytics provide the foundation of reality, truth, and understanding of all business processes and relationships based on data and big data (Thompson & Rogers, 2017, p. 8).

Furthermore, we have market intelligence and marketing analytics, retail intelligence, and retail analytics (Brooks, 2022). Then, using induction, if we have x intelligence, then we have x analytics, and vice versa, where x is a business transaction, activities, application, and industry. More generally, if $x \in$ {data, information, knowledge, wisdom}, then we also have x intelligence. This has been reflected in this book.

Finally, the relationship between analytics and intelligence is that analytics and intelligence are promoted to each other to develop business, management, and decision-making for people, machines, organizations, governments, and societies. Each of them must use analytics and intelligence to be in the competitive market globally. Otherwise, bankruptcy will come very soon. This is also the reason why we look at the following section. Overall, affordable cloud-based BI and analytics software can be affordable cloud-based solutions to organizations and individuals to get cloud services (Kingpin, 2024).

Furthermore, marketing and sales can use analytics and intelligence to acquire new customers and retain existing ones, to identify the most profitable customers and product opportunities, to learn from previous transactions how to structure prices, offers, products, and messages, to refine cross-selling, to determine the best times and channels to make offers and to calculate the best physical locations for new stores (Thompson & Rogers, 2017, pp. 104–105). Therefore, we have business analytics intelligence.

10.5.4 Intelligent Business Analytics

First of all, we address the question: what is *intelligent*? This is not a trivial question, because most individuals who use the term *intelligent* in their research have not really provided a basic answer to this question. Throughout this research, we use three perspectives on the term *intelligent*: First we use intelligent in AI (Russell & Norvig, 2020), that is, intelligent business analytics is an integration intelligence of integrating business analytics and AI, that is, the incorporation of the latest intelligent technologies in business analytics applications (Azvine, Nauck, & Ho, 2003). Second, we use intelligent in BI (Sun, Sun, & Strang, 2018), that is, intelligent business analytics is an integration intelligence of integrating business analytics and BI. Finally, we consider intelligent not only those in AI and BI. Intelligent covers more than those in AI and BI. For example, we consider intelligent a representation of what we are eagerly expecting. Intelligent is an operation of algebra, which is an abstraction of operations within an intelligent system (Sun & Wang, 2017a).

The intelligent business analytics platform consists of libraries of standard components for database connectivity, intelligent analysis routines, and advanced visualization components (Azvine, Nauck, & Ho, 2003), that is, (Sun & Stranieri, 2021).

$$
\begin{aligned}
\text{Intelligent business analytics} &= \text{intelligent techniques} + \text{DW} + \text{connection} \\
&\quad + \text{intelligent data analysis} + \text{visualization}
\end{aligned}
$$
(10.1)

$$
\begin{aligned}
\text{Intelligent big data analytics} &= \text{intelligent big data} + \text{intelligent} \\
&\quad \text{data analytics} + \text{intelligent DW} + \text{intelligent} \\
&\quad \text{DM} + \text{intelligent SM} + \text{intelligent ML} \\
&\quad + \text{intelligent visualization} + \text{intelligent} \\
&\quad \text{optimization}
\end{aligned}
$$
(10.2)

Intelligent data analysis methods have been used by Azwine et al. (Azvine, Nauck, & Ho, 2003). We use then the equation (10.2) (Sun & Stranieri, 2021), but based on a different perspective.

Intelligent business analytics can be considered as the integration of AI(AI) and business analytics, Briefly,

$$
\text{Intelligent business analytics} = \text{AI} + \text{business analytics} \tag{10.3}
$$

10.5.5 Intelligent Business Process Analytics

What are the core components of business? As a core component of business, business = marketing + operation + management. It should have corresponding analytics. That is, add analytics to both sides of the above formula and we have (Brookss, 2022):

$$
\begin{aligned}
\text{Business analytics} &= \text{marketing analytics} + \text{operation analytics} \\
&\quad + \text{management analytics.}
\end{aligned}
$$

Nine sets of activities in two categories are identified: primary and supporting (Krippendorff, 2019, pp. 103–104; Laudon & Laudon, 2020).

Primary activities include inbound logistics, outbound logistics, operations, marketing, sales, and services. Inbound logistics is about anything the organization does to take in materials, inputs, parts, or inventory to produce the product and service. Outbound logistics aims to store, move, and deliver the products and services to customers or end users.

Supporting activities consist of procurement, HR management, technology management, and Infrastructure. Procurement is related to how your company acquires what it needs to operate from external sources. Inbound logistics and procurement are also related to SCM. The products and services to customers or end users are parts of CRM.

Intelligent business is a process of creating intelligence for doing business. Adding intelligent as an operation to both sides of the above formula, we have

$$\text{Intelligent business} = \text{Intelligent marketing} + \text{intelligent operation} \\ + \text{intelligent management.}$$

Similarly, for analytics, we have

$$\text{Intelligent business analytics} = \text{Intelligent marketing analytics} + \\ \text{intelligent operation analytics} \\ + \text{intelligent management analytics.}$$

More generally, we have (Laudon & Laudon, 2020)

business = supply and procurement + production + operation + management + marketing + sales+ customer services+ human resources.

It should have corresponding intelligent analytics for each of them.

$$\text{Business analytics} = \text{supply and procurement analytics} \\ + \text{production analytics} + \text{operation} \\ \text{analytics} + \text{management analytics} \\ + \text{marketing analytics} + \text{sales analytics} \\ + \text{customer service analytics} \\ + \text{human resources analytics.} \qquad (10.4)$$

And

$$\text{Intelligent business analytics} = \text{Intelligent supply and} \\ \text{procurement analytics} + \text{intelligent} \\ \text{production analytics} + \text{intelligent operation} \\ \text{analytics} + \text{intelligent management analytics} \\ + \text{intelligent marketing analytics} \\ + \text{intelligent sales analytics} \\ + \text{intelligent customer service analytics} \\ + \text{human resources analytics.} \qquad (10.5)$$

The above Equation (10.4) has been studied in business analytics (Brooks, 2022). In what follows, this chapter will discuss Equation (10.5).

10.6 A CALCULUS OF INTELLIGENT BUSINESS ANALYTICS

This section will explore a calculus of intelligent business analytics by addressing the following research questions:

1. What are the elements, principles, technologies, and tools of intelligent business analytics and their interrelationships?

2. How can we incorporate the latest intelligent technologies into business analytics?

This research highlights three points and investigates each of them: First, not only big data but also big DIKIW are the most important elements for intelligent business analytics. Second, not only big data analytics and intelligent big data analytics but also big DIKIW and intelligent big DIKIW analytics are the foundation of intelligent business analytics. Third, the elements, principles, technologies, and tools of intelligent business analytics are emerging strategic sources for organizations and individuals in the ever-increasing competitive global environment. This research presents a framework for DIKIW-driven intelligent business analytics by incorporating DIKIW analytics into intelligent business analytics. The proposed approach in this research might facilitate research and development of intelligent business, intelligent analytics, big data analytics, business analytics, enterprise analytics, BI, AI, and data science.

10.6.1 Introduction

Intelligent business analytics has drawn increasing attention in industries. The Google search engine for "intelligent business analytics" shows about 35,300 results (retrieved on February 6, 2024). Some companies have used intelligent business analytics as their marketing mission. For example, Exigy has promoted intelligent business analytics as a cutting-edge technology that can digitally transform business and solve business challenges through providing "accurate insights, on-demand everywhere" (https://www.exigy.com/intelligent-business-analytics/).

AI and BI have been applied in business analytics for decades (Laudon & Laudon, 2020; Richardson, Schlegel, Sallam, Kronz, & Sun, 2021).

Furthermore, a Google Scholar search for "intelligent business analytics" (April 06, 2026) found only 196 results. This implies that intelligent business analytics is still an emerging research area in academia, although business analytics has been around for decades (Davenport, December

2013) and has drawn increasing attention in the past decade (Sun, 2020). The following are still pressing issues for the academia, industries, and governments:

1. What are the elements, principles, techniques, and tools of intelligent business analytics and their interrelationships?

2. What is the relationship between intelligent big data analytics and business analytics?

3. How can we incorporate the latest intelligent techniques into business analytics applications?

This research addresses the above-mentioned issues. More specifically, this research identifies and explores the elements, principles, technologies, and tools of intelligent business analytics by investigating the-state-of-the-art scholars' publications and market analysis of advanced analytics. It examines intelligent business analytics as integrating AI and business big data analytics. This research demonstrates that not only big data and big data analytics but also DIKIW (data, information, knowledge, intelligence, wisdom) and DIKIW analytics constitute the elements of intelligent business analytics. The research presents a framework for DIKIW-driven intelligent business analytics by incorporating DIKIW analytics into business analytics.

The remainder of this research is organized as follows: Subsection 10.6.2 identifies and looks at the elements of intelligent business analytics. Subsection 10.6.3 examines the principles of intelligent business analytics. Subsections 10.6.4 and 10.6.5 discuss the technologies and tools for intelligent business analytics. Subsection 10.6.6 provides discussion and implications as well as future research directions of this research. The final Sub section ends this research with some concluding remarks and suggestions for future work.

For research methodology, this research uses a multidisciplinary approach consisting of business, logical, algebraic, systematic methods, research as a search, and big data-driven small data analysis methods. For example, the backgrounds are based on the principle of "research as a search" and big data-driven small data analysis (Sun & Huo, 2021). This research uses Google Scholar-indexed publications search to reflect the state-of-the-art research publications on intelligent analytics and intelligent business analytics worldwide. It uses the market analysis provided by Gartner (Richardson, Schlegel, Sallam, Kronz, & Sun, 2021), which reflects the state-of-the-art research and development of the tools for intelligent business analytics. Both complement each other for understanding state-of-the-art intelligent big data analytics. This research also uses business, logical, and systemic approaches to examine intelligent business analytics incorporating KIDIW analytics with AI and to propose the technologies and tools for intelligent business analytics.

It should be noted that throughout this research, we use at least three perspectives on intelligent as a term: First, we use intelligent from an AI perspective (Russell & Norvig, 2020) to denote intelligent business analytics as integrating business analytics, business big data analytics, and AI-driven latest intelligent technologies (Sun & Stranieri, 2021; Russell & Norvig, 2020). Second, we use intelligent as a term from a BI perspective (Laudon & Laudon, 2020), to indicate that intelligent business analytics is about integrating business analytics and BI. Finally, we consider intelligent an entity that is not only used in AI and BI but can be applied elsewhere. For example, we consider intelligent a representation of what we eagerly expect. Intelligent can also be used as an operation of algebra, which is an abstraction of operations within an intelligent system (Sun & Wang, 2017b).

10.6.2 Elements of Intelligent Business Analytics

The elements of intelligent business analytics include data, data analytics, big data analytics, and intelligent big data analytics from a computing perspective. Correspondingly, from a business perspective, the elements of intelligent business analytics also include business data, business data analytics, business big data analytics, and business intelligent big data analytics. We will look at each of them below.

10.6.2.1 Data and Data Analytics

Data are raw, unorganized, and unprocessed materials such as facts, numbers, figures, signals, assertions, perceptions, or observations that represent the properties of objects and events (Rowley, 2007; Wang, 2015). Data usually lack meaning, context, content, and value (Sabherwal & Becerra-Fernandez, 2011). Data are considered the input of information systems, data analytics, and many other data systems (Coronel, Morris, & Rob, 2020).

Briefly, data analytics can be represented below:

$$\text{Data analytics} = \text{data} + \text{analytics} \qquad (10.6)$$

Hereafter, + can be explained as "and". From an algebraic viewpoint, data analytics is a system. Equation (10.6) implies that data is the set of the system; analytics is the operation performed over the dataset (Davenport, December 2013; Norusis, 1997).

10.6.2.2 Big Data and Big Data Analytics

Big data has become a strategic asset for organizations and nations (Sun & Stranieri, 2021). Big data analytics is a science and technology about organizing and analyzing big data, and discovering knowledge, insights, and intelligence from big data, visualizing and reporting the discovered expertise and insights for assisting decision-making (Sun, Sun, & Strang, 2018). Briefly, big data analytics can be represented below using big as an operation over both sides of (5)

$$\text{Big data analytics} = \text{Big data} + \text{Big analytics} \qquad (10.7)$$

Big data is the set of big data analytics as a system. Big analytics is the operation performed over the big data set (Davenport, December 2013).

Big data and big data analytics have become one of the most important research frontiers in academia and industries.

10.6.2.3 Intelligent Big Data Analytics

Intelligent big data analytics has become a disruptive technology for effective innovation and decision-making in the digital age (Sun, Pambel, & Wu, 2022). Intelligent big data analytics can aid managers by extracting useful patterns of information, capturing, and discovering knowledge, generating solutions to problems encountered in decision-making, delegating authority, and assigning responsibility (Sun & Huo, 2021).

Briefly, intelligent big data analytics can be represented as

$$\text{Intelligent big data analytics} = \text{Intelligent} + \text{Big data analytics} \qquad (10.8)$$

Intelligent in equation (10.8) means AI if one works in computing. It means BI, marketing intelligence, organization intelligence, and enterprise intelligence if one works in the corresponding fields. Therefore, intelligent as a term can be understood differently by different people. Even so, big data, analytics, AI, and their integration are at the frontier for revolutionizing our work, life, business, management, and organization (Sun, Pambel, & Wu, 2022).

Intelligent big data analytics can also be represented as

$$\text{Intelligent big data analytics} = \text{Intelligent} + \text{Big data} + \text{Analytics} \qquad (10.9)$$

Equation (10.9) at least means that intelligent big data analytics includes big data, analytics, and AI and their integration (Wang, 2012).

10.6.2.4 Business Analytics and Intelligent Business Analytics

We can define business analytics, business big data analytics, intelligent business big data analytics, and intelligent business analytics as follows.

Business data analytics is the art of examining, summarizing, and drawing conclusions from business data to learn, describe, and predict something. Business data are "flows of events or transactions captured by an organization's systems that are useful for transacting, but little else" (Laudon & Laudon, 2020, p. 455). Business data analytics and business analytics are used interchangeably.

Intelligent business analytics is the art of examining, summarizing, and drawing conclusions from business data and other sources to learn, describe, and predict something using AI and other intelligent techniques. Then

$$\text{Business analytics} = \text{Business} + \text{analytics} \qquad (10.10)$$

Apply intelligent to both sides of Equation (10.10) we have

$$\text{Intelligent Business analytics} = \text{intelligent business} + \text{intelligent analytics} \qquad (10.11)$$

In fact,

$$\text{Intelligent business analytics} = \text{Intelligent BI} + \text{Intelligent data analytics} \qquad (10.12)$$

Intelligent BI cover intelligent techniques such as SM, DM, DW, intelligent visualization, and optimization.

Based on the calculus of big data analytics and intelligent big data analytics in Section 9.7, we can extend the following formula of Intelligent business analytics.

$$\text{Intelligent Business analytics} = \text{BI} + \text{AI} + \text{Intelligent data analytics} \qquad (10.13)$$

$$\text{Intelligent analytics} = \text{BI} + \text{AI} + \text{big data analytics.} \quad (10.14)$$

And finally,

$$\begin{aligned}\text{Intelligent business analytics} = \text{BI} + \text{AI} + \text{other intelligent} \\ \text{techniques} + \text{Intelligent business} \\ \text{analytics} \quad (10.15)\end{aligned}$$

All digital things seem to be data, but much of it is not "data" outside the big data world (Williams, 2016, p. 34). In the age of big data, analytics, and AI (Minelli, Chambers, & Dhiraj, 2013), most people have flattened the hierarchical structure from data via information, knowledge, and intelligence up to wisdom to data level, so that wisdom as data, intelligence as data, knowledge as data, and information as data become popular in the digital world. In fact, information, knowledge, intelligence, and wisdom have played the same significant role as data in computing and ICT, business and management, and many other fields in the past few decades Figure 10.3 (Sun & Huo, 2020).

DIKIW forms a hierarchical structure (Liew A., 2013), as shown. DIKIW is an updated form with the reverse pyramid of DIKIW (Liew A., 2013) and DIKW (Sun & Huo, 2020).

$$\text{DIKIW} = \text{data} + \text{information} + \text{knowledge} + \text{intelligence} + \text{wisdom.} \quad (10.16)$$

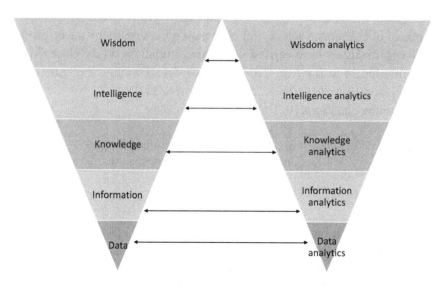

FIGURE 10.3   The pyramid of DIKIW and DIKIW analytics.

Apply analytics as an operation on both sides of equation (10.16), we have

$$
\begin{aligned}
\text{DIKIW analytics} = &\ \text{data analytics} + \text{information analytics} \\
&+ \text{knowledge analytics} + \text{intelligence analytics} \\
&+ \text{wisdom analytics}
\end{aligned}
\tag{10.17}
$$

From equations (10.17), analytics can be defined as DIKIW analytics consisting of data analytics, information analytics, knowledge analytics, and wisdom analytics, corresponding to data, information, knowledge, intelligence, and wisdom respectively, as shown in Figure 10.3.

DIKIW analytics are the important elements of intelligent business analytics, taking into account DIKIW and its implications on big data, data science, and AI (Sun & Huo, 2020; Weber, 2020). The above discussion demonstrates that data analytics is not a unique form of analytics. DIKIW analytics is a more inclusive representation of analytics.

Applying big as an operation (Sun & Wang, 2017b) to both sides of equation (10.16), we have

$$
\begin{aligned}
\text{Big DIKIW} = &\ \text{big data} + \text{big information} + \text{big knowledge} \\
&+ \text{big intelligence} + \text{big wisdom}
\end{aligned}
\tag{10.18}
$$

As well-known, big data is significant for innovation, competition, and productivity in the digital age (Manyika, Chui, & Bughin, 2011), then big information, big knowledge, big intelligence, and big wisdom are also vital for effective management, decision-making, and innovation for the development of economy, society, and even nation because many governments and organizations have carried out several initiatives on development of information industry (e.g. China), knowledge economy (e.g. Australia) and wisdom cities (e.g. China; Sun & Stranieri, 2021).

Combing equations (10.17) and (10.18), we have

$$
\begin{aligned}
\text{Big DIKIW analytics} = &\ \text{big data analytics} + \text{big information} \\
&\text{analytics} + \text{big knowledge analytics} \\
&+ \text{big intelligence analytics} \\
&+ \text{big wisdom analytics}
\end{aligned}
\tag{10.19}
$$

This implies that big DIKIW analytics should have played the same significant role as big data analytics; nevertheless, some academia, industries, and governments have technically ignored them.

Now, apply intelligent as an operation to both sides of Equation (10.19), we have

Intelligent big DIKIW analytics = Intelligent big data analytics
+ intelligent big information analytics
+ intelligent big knowledge analytics
+ intelligent big intelligence analytics
+ intelligent big wisdom analytics.

(10.20)

Equations (10.16) to (10.20) form a unified approach to integrate DIKIW, DIKIW analytics, big DIKIW, big DIKIW analytics, and intelligent big DIKIW analytics. This is an important complement to the current hotspots of big data, big data analytics, and intelligent big data analytics (Sun Z., 2019). DIKIW, DIKIW analytics, big DIKIW, big DIKIW analytics, and intelligent big DIKIW analytics are elements of intelligent business analytics because DIKIW is fundamental for business and management decision-making (Laudon & Laudon, 2020). Big DIKIW analytics and intelligent big DIKIW analytics can be represented as big analytics and intelligent big analytics respectively and

Intelligent analytics = intelligent DIKIW analytics
+ intelligent big DIKIW analytics

(10.21)

Based on (10.15 and 10.21), intelligent business analytics, as an application of intelligent analytics, at least includes intelligent business big data analytics, intelligent business information big analytics, intelligent business big knowledge analytics, and intelligent business big wisdom analytics.

Currently, intelligent business analytics can be classified into intelligent business descriptive analytics, intelligent business diagnostic analytics, intelligent business predictive analytics, and intelligent business prescriptive analytics for big data, information, knowledge, intelligence, and wisdom. Intelligent business big data analytics has made remarkable achievements thanks to the dramatic development of big data and big data analytics (Sun & Stranieri, 2021). Intelligent business big information/knowledge/wisdom analytics have not yet drawn significant attention in academia and industry, because some are still indulged in the age of big data. Big data is a foundation of big information, big knowledge, big intelligence, and big wisdom. Therefore, we are still at the foundational stage and look forward to the emerging age of big information, big knowledge, big intelligence, and big wisdom (Sun Z., 2023b).

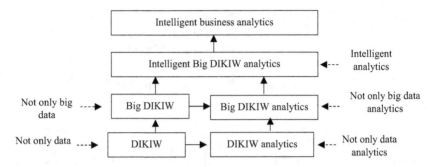

FIGURE 10.4   A framework for DIKIW-driven intelligent business analytics.

10.6.3 Principles of Intelligent Business Analytics

The principles of intelligent business analytics are laws, rules, models, and the theories that they are based on. Most parts of the previous section belong to the principles of calculus of intelligent business analytics. Even so, this section presents a framework for DIKIW-driven intelligent business analytics, as illustrated in Figure 10.4.

In Figure 10.4, DIKIW, big DIKIW, DIKIW analytics, and big DIKIW analytics are the solutions to that not only data, big data, data analytics, and big data analytics are important for intelligent business analytics. In other words, DIKIW, big DIKIW, DIKIW analytics, and big DIKIW analytics play a fundamentally vital role in developing intelligent business analytics.

Intelligent big DIKIW analytics is the further development of big DIKIW technology and big DIKIW analytics and the technological foundation for developing intelligent business analytics.

Therefore, Figure 10.4 is not only a framework for DIKIW-driven intelligent business analytics, it is also a spectrum of elements of intelligent business analytics (Sun & Huo, 2021).

10.6.4 Technologies for Intelligent Business Analytics

Technologies for intelligent business analytics include macro-technologies, meso-technologies, and micro-technologies, illustrated as in Figure 10.5. Macro-technologies will dominate a society of humans in a few decades. For example, eSMACS (electronic, social, mobile, analytics, cloud, and security) technologies have dominated our digital age with eSMACS products and services over the past decade. Meso-technologies work with other technologies to facilitate and promote the development of analytics to align with the market and social environment provided by the macro-technologies.

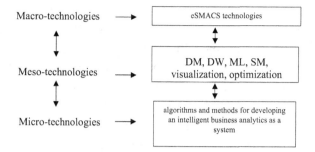

FIGURE 10.5 Macro, meso, and microtechnologies for intelligent business analytics.

Meso-technologies are also called techniques (Ghavami, 2020; Sharda, Delen, & Turba, 2018). Micro-technologies include all the algorithms and methods for developing intelligent business analytics as a system or service. This section only looks at meso-technologies for intelligent business analytics. Macro-technologies and other meso-technologies have been discussed in other chapters of this book.

The meso-technologies for intelligent big data analytics encompass a wide range of mathematical, statistical, modeling, and algorithm technologies (Coronel, Morris, & Rob, 2020; Sun Z., 2018b), and intelligent technologies such as soft computing, fuzzy logic, neuro-fuzzy systems, OLAP, neural networks, evolutionary computation, cloud computing, probabilistic computing, and statistical models. Intelligent big data analytics always involves historical or current data and data visualization (LaPlante, 2019). This requires intelligent big data analytics to use data mining (DM) to discover knowledge from a data warehouse (DW) to support decision-making (Ghavami, 2020). Therefore, we look at only three of them below in some detail.

Statistical modeling (SM) **and analysis**. Statistics is the science of collecting and organizing data and drawing meaningful and interpretable knowledge, intelligence, and wisdom from the datasets (Kantardzic, 2011, p. 140). Statistics includes statistical inference and statistical modeling. Statistical inference at least includes Bayesian inference, predictive regression, and logistic regression (Kantardzic, 2011). Statistical modeling aims to discover knowledge and insights through statistical analysis (Sun, Sun, & Strang, 2018). Statistical analysis includes descriptive analysis and predictive analysis. Descriptive analysis and predictive analysis lead to descriptive statistics, descriptive data mining, descriptive analytics, predictive statistics, predictive data mining, and predictive analytics (Kantardzic, 2011, p. 2; Ghavami, 2020, p. 97). More generally, not only statistical modeling technology, but other modeling technologies have a significant impact on big data, intelligence, and analytics with applications. For example, knowledge modeling technology includes decision trees and analytic hierarchy processes (Sharda, Delen, Turban, & King, 2018, p. 352).

Visualization is a technology for presenting results, generating insights, intelligence, and wisdom, typically in graphical dashboards, scorecards, and charts (Ghavami, 2020, p. 31). Visualization technologies at least include DIKIW visualization, for example, information visualization deals with abstract information such as text, hierarchies, and statistical data (Kantardzic, 2011, p. 450). In other words, data visualization is not a unique visualization technology. Visualization technologies including display technologies make knowledge patterns and information for decision-making in the form of figures, tables, or multimedia. Data visualization is an important part of business big data analytics and supports highly interactive dashboards, data exploration, and manipulation of chart images (Richardson, Schlegel, Sallam, Kronz, & Sun, 2021).

Optimization is a technology that enables effective decisions or predictions from database management, big data management, knowledge discovery, and intelligent systems. Historically, optimization technology is a part of operations research, which includes linear, nonlinear, and fuzzy programming models, and other mathematical programming models (Sharda, Delen, & Turba, 2018, pp. 362–370). The optimization principle is "everything can be improved" to meet the ever-increasing demands of humans, machines, platforms, and society. Optimization technology has been used in almost every discipline or area in academia and industry because finding a better solution or the best solution from a large number of alternatives using a step-by-step improvement process and intelligent business analytics is always a pressing demand from any decision-makers and organizations. Optimization technology can develop and improve intelligent business analytics as a system, metric, and service (Sun Z., 2019).

In summary, intelligent business analytics can facilitate business decision-making and improve the competitive advantages of an organization through analyzing existing DIKIW and future trends, creating predictive models to forecast future threats and opportunities, and optimizing business processes to enhance organizational performance using (Delena & Demirkanb, 2013; Sun & Stranieri, 2021).

10.6.5 Tools for Intelligent Business Analytics

There are various intelligent business analytics tools available in the market. The tools are not only for analytics developers but also for end-users. Gartner's magic quadrant for analytics and BI platforms (Richardson, Schlegel, Sallam, Kronz, & Sun, 2021) includes state-of-the-art tools for intelligent business analytics in the global market. These tools target businesspeople and data analysts, analytics developers, and other analytics consumers. This section explores the tools for intelligent business analytics in the market worldwide based on our early analysis and the latest research of Gartner (Richardson, Schlegel, Sallam, Kronz, & Sun, 2021; Schlegel & Sun, 2023).

Gartner's magic quadrant classifies the related data and analytics vendors into four categories: leaders, challengers, visionaries, and niche players, based on the following 12 critical capabilities, which have been updated to reflect areas of market change, differentiation, and customer demand (Richardson, Schlegel, Sallam, Kronz, & Sun, 2021; Schlegel & Sun, 2023):

1. Automated insights. It is a core attribute of augmented analytics. Automated insight is the ability to apply machine learning (ML) techniques to automatically generate insights for end users. Therefore, automated insights are intelligence or learning intelligence.

2. Analytics catalog. This refers to the product's ability to display analytic content to make it easy to find and consume. The catalog is searchable and makes recommendations to users.

3. Data preparation. This refers to support for drag-and-drop, a user-driven combination of data from different sources, and the creation of analytic models (such as user-defined measures, sets, groups, and hierarchies).

4. Data source connectivity. This refers to data source connectivity capabilities enabling users to connect to and ingest structured data contained in various types of storage platforms, both on-premises and in the cloud.

5. Data storytelling. This refers to the ability to combine interactive data visualization with narrative techniques to package and deliver insights in a compelling, easily understood form for presentation to decision-makers.

6. Data visualization. This refers to support for highly interactive and data exploration, with chart images. An array of visualization options include pie, bar, line charts, heat and tree maps, geographic maps, scatter plots, and other special-purpose visuals.

7. Governance. This refers to governance capabilities to track usage and manage how information is shared and promoted.

8. Natural language query. The natural language query capability enables users to ask questions about the data using terms typed into a search box or spoken.

9. Reporting. The reporting capability provides pixel-perfect, paginated reports that can be scheduled and bursted to a large user community.

10. Data science integration. Capabilities that enable augmented development and prototyping of composable data science and machine learning (DSML) models by citizen data scientists and data scientists with integration into the broader data science and machine learning ecosystem.

11. Metrics store. The ability to provide a virtualized layer allows users to create and define metrics as codes, govern those metrics from data warehouses, and service all downstream analytics, data science, and business applications. This also includes capabilities such as goal management.

12. Collaboration. Analytics collaboration is the application of collaboration capabilities to analytics workstreams for organizations that want to provide an environment where a broad spectrum of users can simultaneously co-produce an analytics project.

Remarks:

1. ChatGPT covers data storytelling, natural language query, and reporting.

2. Data science integration should be renamed because the ABI platform consists of many different analytics subsystems, from an analytics viewpoint (see the early chapters).

3. The metrics store should be renamed a metrics-base, just as database, model-base, and knowledge base have been integrated into the DSS

system. Different from the DSS system with three bases, any analytics has four bases consisting of metrics base, database, model-base, and knowledgebase. Metrics base can be replaced by algorithm base for analytics system. This also confirm that any analytics has metrics for business analytics systems.

The leaders of Gartner's magic quadrant must use analytics and BI platforms to support the needs of ICT, consumers, analysts, and data scientists. In 2023's magic quadrant, the leaders were Microsoft, Salesforce (Tableau), and Qlik (Schlegel & Sun, 2023). The challengers are MicroStrategy, Google, Alibaba Cloud, Amazon Web services, and Domo. In 2023's magic quadrant, the niche players are Incorta, GoodData, and Zoho; the visionaries encompass IBM, ORACLE, ThoughtSpot, Sisense, SAP, SAS, Tellius, and Pyramid Analytics. In what follows, we review the tools offered by the three leaders, Google, Amazon Web Services, and Alibaba Cloud in some detail (Sun, Pambel, & Wu, 2022) because Google, Amazon Web services, and Alibaba Cloud have become new challengers from 2021 to 2023 (Richardson, Schlegel, Sallam, Kronz, & Sun, 2021; Schlegel & Sun, 2023).

Alibaba Cloud is the largest public cloud platform provider in the Asia/Pacific market (Schlegel & Sun, 2023). Its product, Quick BI enables users to perform data analytics, data preparation and reporting, visual-based data discovery, interactive dashboards, and reports, as well as empowering enterprise users to view and explore data and make informed, data-driven decisions (Alibaba, 2024; Schlegel & Sun, 2023). Quick BI has extended its cloud roadmap from Alibaba Cloud to multiple cloud support that is compatible with Tencent Cloud, Microsoft Azure, and Huawei Cloud. Quick BI supports OLAP modeling of data sources, and converts data sources to multi-dimensional analytics models (Alibaba, 2024). Users can quickly access Quick BI analytics capabilities, such as digital workplace-oriented analytics and composable analytics (Schlegel & Sun, 2023).

Amazon Web Services (AWS) has its Amazon QuickSight and ML-powered natural language query capability (Schlegel & Sun, 2023). QuickSight is largely sold into the AWS customer ecosystem. AWS provides integrated global cloud service with Competitive pricing. Its serverless architecture can enable scale in terms of user volumes and concurrency for analytical complex use cases.

Google. Google Cloud's Looker is built on a developer-focused, code-centric virtualized semantic modeling layer (LookML). Looker is a cloud-architected ABI platform that offers highly governed analytics, including self-service visualizations and dashboards, and a code-first semantic modeling layer based on LookML (Schlegel & Sun, 2023). Looker Studio can operate in a self-service capacity entirely on its own, or it can connect to Looker if it wants to utilize the semantic layer to blend governed and ungoverned data. Looker's developer-focused analytics platform provides a version-controlled, collaborative framework to build internal BI and enable customers to build applications. Google Analytics and GA4 can improve your online sales by better understanding customer data and how customers interact with your website based on the acquisition, engagement, monetization, retention, custom behavior reporting, and lifecycle collection (Pittman, 2022, p. 9). Therefore, GA4 is good at screaming data and ensuring we don't have data overload (Pittman, 2022, p. 83).

Microsoft offers data preparation, visual-based data discovery, interactive dashboards, and augmented analytics in Power BI as an intelligent business analytics tool (Richardson, Schlegel, Sallam, Kronz, & Sun, 2021). Power BI is available as a SaaS option running in the Azure cloud or an on-premises option in the Power BI Report Server. The Power BI cloud service is extremely rich in its capabilities, including a set of augmented analytics and automated ML capabilities. Power BI Desktop can be a stand-alone, free personal analysis tool. Power BI offers AI-powered services such as text, sentiment, and image analytics.

Qlik. Qlik's lead solution to intelligent business analytics is Qlik. Qlik Sense Enterprise SaaS, which includes Qlik Sense, Qlik AutoML and Qlik Application Automation (Richardson, Schlegel, Sallam, Kronz, & Sun, 2021; Schlegel & Sun, 2023). Qlik Sense enables one to create interactive reports and dashboards with excellent charts and graphs (Qlik, 2021). It simplifies data analysis and helps one make effective decisions faster. Qlik Sense runs on the unique Qlik Associative Engine. Qlik's Cognitive Engine adds AI/ML-driven intelligent functionality to the product and works (Richardson, Schlegel, Sallam, Kronz, & Sun, 2021). Qlik's Associative Engine offers context-aware insight suggestions and augmentation of analysis. Qlik has built on its augmented analytics vision, with key elements based on its Cognitive Engine. It provides intelligent analytics services such as data preparation, search-based visual analytics, conversational analytics, associative insights, and accelerated creation. Composable analytics is one of the strengths of Qlik; that is, Qlik enables integrating analytics with business processes (Schlegel & Sun, 2023). Another strength of Qlik is that through acquisitions and organic development, Qlik has created a comprehensive set of technologies to support multiple business personas, including citizen data engineers and scientists, business analysts, and analytics developers.

Tableau Tableau's visual analytics platform transforms people to use data to solve problems (Tableau, 2024). It offers an intuitive, interactive, visual-based exploration experience that enables business users to access, prepare, analyze, and present findings in their data without technical skills or coding cloud-based analytic databases (Schlegel & Sun, 2023; Howson, Richardson, Sallam, & Kronz, 2019). CRM Analytics provides augmented analytics capabilities for analysts and citizen data scientists. Tableau's vision is to help business users and organizations be more data-driven, with contextualized insights (Tableau, 2024).

Overall, insights and automated insights generation have become intelligent services for business users. For example, Tableau enables composable analytics to bring insights into workflow with agility (Schlegel & Sun, 2023). Composable analytics is a relatively new analytics ability for business users and data developers. For example, Qlik enables integrating analytics with business processes (Schlegel & Sun, 2023). Analytics can be embedded into business applications. Application automation leverages a visual no-code approach to assemble automated flows that can be scheduled or event-driven.

However, all the above tools have not realized the business workflow of DDPP analytics. They still focus on data analytics and technically ignore the importance of information, knowledge, intelligence, wisdom and corresponding analytics, although the real focus of AI is how to transform knowledge into intelligence (Russell & Norvig, 2020). This is also the reason why we emphasize that not only data and data analytics play an ever-increasing role in developing intelligent business analytics and its services.

10.6.6 Discussions and Implications

This section will discuss the related work, based on the principle of research as a search and big data-driven analysis (Sun & Huo, 2021), and examine the theoretical and technical implications of this research, as well as limitations and future research directions.

10.6.6.1 Discussion

A Google search for "calculus" showed about 526,000,000 results (retrieved on February 9, 2023). This indicates that calculus has big interests in almost every discipline. However, a Google search for "calculus of intelligent business analytics" found no research results. This motivates us to develop a calculus of intelligent business analytics.

Gartner uses analytics and BI (or ABI) to do research and release an annual report on ABI platforms in the market (Richardson, Schlegel, Sallam, Kronz, & Sun, 2021; Schlegel & Sun, 2023). The difference between ABI and intelligent business analytics is that the former is a loose and simple collection of analytics and BI without scientific and systemic investigation; the latter is a logical and systemic treatment based on intelligent analytics, DIKIW analytics, and their applications in business. Therefore, intelligent business analytics is a more scientific term for analytics, big data, intelligence, and intelligent business.

10.6.6.2 Theoretical and Technical Implications

The theoretical implication of this research is that it provides a unified solution so that 1. not only data, big data, data analytics, big data analytics, and intelligent big data analytics underpin the development of intelligent business analytics. 2. AI-driven intelligent techniques have played a significant role in intelligent business analytics. The research demonstrated that intelligent business analytics consists of intelligent business big data analytics, intelligent business big information analytics, intelligent business big knowledge analytics, and intelligent business big wisdom analytics. This approach will pave a new way for developing intelligent business analytics with principles, technologies, tools, and applications.

The technical implication of this research is that the proposed approach on intelligent business analytics in general and intelligent business DIKIW analytics in specific can appeal to more researchers and practitioners to undertake the application of intelligent business analytics for more effective decision-making, taking into account the proposed DIKIW framework for intelligent business analytics.

10.6.6.3 Future Research Directions

Intelligent business analytics is an application of intelligent analytics for businesses to promote intelligent business, improve business performance, and support business decision-making. Intelligent business analytics is an analytics paradigm of integrating big DIKIW, AI, and other intelligent technologies, analytics intelligence, and intelligent analytics. Therefore, one of the future research directions is to address systems integration among intelligent analytics, modern analytics, and intelligent business to realize intelligent business analytics for supporting decision-making (Howson, Richardson, Sallam, & Kronz, 2019).

As mentioned earlier, intelligent business analytics is an emerging frontier for intelligent business. Many fundamental theoretical, technological, and managerial issues surrounding the development and implementation of intelligent business analytics remain unsolved. For example, how can we apply intelligent business analytics to improve intelligent business, healthcare, mobile commerce, web services, cloud services, and digital transformation? What are the implications of intelligent business analytics on intelligent business and management, IoT, blockchain, service, and society? These should be addressed as a future research direction to meet the social, economic, marketing, managerial, scientific, and technological demands from different parties or individuals for intelligent business analytics with applications.

10.6.7 Summary

This research explored the calculus of intelligent business analytics, which mainly consists of the elements, principles, technologies, techniques, and tools, from analytics, data analytics, big data analytics to intelligent analytics, of intelligent business analytics. This research highlights 1). not only data, big data, data analytics, and big data analytics underpin the development of intelligent business analytics. 2). not only AI-driven intelligent techniques have played a significant role in intelligent business analytics. The main three contributions of this research are 1). Intelligent business analytics is a science and technology of digitally transforming data and big data into big information, knowledge, intelligence, and wisdom for enhancing business performance and decision-making. 2). DIKIW, big DIKIW, DIKIW analytics, and big DIKIW analytics as elements will play a significant role in intelligent business analytics. 3). AI and other intelligent technologies are promoting the development of intelligent business analytics. Therefore, intelligent business analytics is an emerging paradigm that analytically transforms a business into intelligent business, big data into big wisdom, and decision-making into intelligent decision-making under the ever-increasing complexity of businesses and business processes for developing intelligent business, improving business performance, and supporting decision-making. The proposed approach in this research might facilitate research and development of intelligent business, big data analytics, business analytics, enterprise analytics, BI, AI, and data science.

10.7 TECHNIQUES FOR BI AND BUSINESS ANALYTICS

Technologies and tools have been discussed in this Chapter and other chapters. This section will look at the technologies and tools for BI and business analytics.

10.7.1 ERP

Enterprise resource planning (ERP) is an enterprise system that integrates business processes in manufacturing and production, finance and accounting, sales and marketing, and human resources into a single software system (Laudon & Laudon, 2020). In other words, improving HR management with AI and big data has been an important part of ERP development (Strang & Sun, 2022). A big challenge is how to use AI, machine learning, and big data to improve HR management and the HR functions of ERP. The final goal of incorporating AI and big data analytics within HR management is to automate the recruitment processes and liberate the repetitive and time-consuming recruitment process, including interviewing several human applicants for any jobs.

10.7.2 BI Tools

The principal tools for BI include software for database query and reporting (e.g., SAP ERP, Oracle ERP, etc.), tools for multidimensional data analysis (e.g., OLAP), and DM (e.g., predictive analysis, text mining, web mining (Laudon & Laudon, 2020)). Data warehousing is a foundation of BI (Lim, Chen, & Chen, 2013).

Dashboards show key business performance indicators in a single integrated view. Therefore, dashboards monitor business activity with business performance.

Portals can integrate information using web browsers from multiple sources into a single webpage.

10.7.3 Designing Business Analytics for BI

Different companies and organizations require different analytics tools (Schneider, 2017). For example, it is enough for a small company to use Microsoft Excel to do business analytics. For middle-sized companies, Microsoft Excel, and IBM SPSS are suitable tools for organizing business analytics. Google Analytics is always important for online business. This implicates that it is necessary to analyze the analytics tools and their applicability to different companies. All ABI (or analytics and BI) tools, including Microsoft, Qlik, and Tableau, are useful for global companies (Schlegel & Sun, 2023).

10.8 6PS: A GENERIC FRAMEWORK FOR DECISION MAKING IN DIGITAL SERVICES

Decision-making is a process of exploring available alternatives until an acceptable threshold is reached (Krippendorff, 2019, p. 113). Decision-making aims is to look for a good enough one rather than an optimal solution. This section proposes 6Ps: a generic framework for decision-making in digital services, which integrates the environment (6 Ps) of decision-making for decision-makers.

10.8.1 Introduction

A decision is a choice in which one selects between two or more alternatives after thinking carefully (Sun, Meredith, & Stranieri, 2012). Decision-making in digital services has drawn increasing attention in the web service community over recent years. For example, Yao et al. (2006) discuss flexible DM strategies for web service negotiation. Denning and Hayes-Roth (2006) look at DM in very large networks and conclude that decision-makers should learn how to share situation information and to make decisions locally through market-like mechanisms that focus resources on high-value activities. DM in web services refers to a decision maker who chooses one from the alternative recommended web services provided by a web service support agent.

This section proposed a P^6 model for decision-making in digital services, which reflects what a decision-maker examines within the environment for making decisions in digital services including web services, as shown in Figure 10.6.

In this proposed P^6 model: The core is the decision-making in general and customer decision-making (CDM) in special in digital services. The P^6 model consists of 6Ps: product, price, people, place, process, and promotion (Schneider, 2017).

The above 6 Ps (or some of them) have been, to some extent, described in many textbooks on marketing and e-commerce (Chaffey, 2011; Schneider, 2017). Most companies use a particular combination of these 6 Ps or 4 Ps as a marketing mix or marketing strategy to achieve their goals for selling or promoting their products and services (Schneider, 2017).

FIGURE 10.6   The P⁶ model for decision-making in digital services where Dam is decision making.

From a system perspective, marketing is the environment where the customers or service requesters live and look around. The above-mentioned 6 Ps reflect the system environment through which the customers can eye or examine whenever making decisions on web services, as illustrated in the proposed model, shown in Figure 10.6. In what follows, we will look at each of the existing 6 Ps from the customer's perspective.

10.8.2 Product

The product can be defined as physical goods or services that a company sells in e-business and web services (Schneider, 2017). For example, books sold by fishpond.com.au are physical goods. E-journal articles provided by Elsevier.com are digital services. When deciding on purchasing a product, the customer always looks at the quality, features, branding, associated customer service, warranty, reliability, and integrity of the product (Sun, Meredith, & Stranieri, 2012). In the digital era, researchers tend not to read many journal articles in hard copy form; they tend to read journal articles online as digital service products. In contrast to traditional services, one of the characteristics of web services is that the product presented online is available globally to billions of digital users, without the limitations of time and distance. Therefore, the global transparency of a product dramatically increases the choice space for a customer to make decisions in web services.

10.8.3 Price

The price is the amount the customer pays for the product or service (Schneider, 2017). Once the customer intends to buy a product or service, the next step is to make a decision based on the price of the product or service; how much can the customer pay to purchase the product or service? Internet technologies have significantly increased the diversity of prices. For example, in the past, a customer would purchase an air ticket for a flight from Sydney to Melbourne at a very high price. Now, he can buy an air ticket at a very low price by quickly accessing different flight vendors online and comparing prices. Further, the global price transparency in e-business and web services greatly helps a customer to select a good or service at a relatively low price. For example, in the majority of cases, the price for a book on business analytics or artificial intelligence from amazon.com is much higher than that from Australasia's biggest online store, http://www.fishpond.com.au/Books, in particular from the perspective of an Australian customer. Therefore, the Australian customer will first visit http://www.fishpond.com.au/Books to buy a book online to enjoy the price advantage. Further, the pricing of web services or e-commerce differs with the market, and the type of customer (Sun, Meredith, & Stranieri, 2012). For example, the search engines provide an individual customer with free search, translation, and readings of books.

10.8.4 People

People involved in digital services mainly include service providers, service requesters, and service brokers. More generally, all business agents and intelligent agents that help deliver services from service providers to service requesters (customers) are related to the customer for his decision-making in digital services (Chaffey, 2011). The intelligent agents include auto-responders, e-mail notifications, frequently asked questions ns (FAQs), online search engines, and virtual assistants such as infomediaries and credit card information receivers (Sun, Meredith, & Stranieri, 2012). Customers can see and interact with physical people to make decisions. The customer can also interact with the intelligent agents to make decisions in web services to buy the goods and services. With the development of digital technology, more and more intelligent agents involved in digital services help customers to make decisions and facilitate customers to buy goods and services online. Customers now look for product reviews from past customers and clients via blogs, forums, and social media. Social networks and media play an important role in customer decision-making in web services.

10.8.5 Place

Place involves distributing products or services to customers in line with demand and minimizing the costs for inventory, transport, and storage (Chaffey, 2011). The Internet has a great implication for place in the context of customer decision-making in web services. For example, in the past, an academic staff member had to visit the University library to read journal articles. In this digital age, the academic simply sits in his office to access the e-journals. Therefore, the distance between the office and the product or service provider becomes almost zero. Online presence of the goods or services also shortens the physical distance between the customer location and the place where goods or services are provided. For some goods or services such as digital journals and computer games, the customer can get what he sees on the website where the goods or services are present.

10.8.6 Process

From a company perspective, the process involves the methods and procedures that companies use to achieve all marketing functions (Chaffey, 2011). From a customer perspective, the process involves all the stages that a good and service can transfer from the providers to the customer. The stages in the process include the access of the good or service presence, the good or service request submission and processing, the payment and confirmation for purchasing the good or service, and the delivery of the good or service to the customer. Whenever deciding to purchase a good or service, the customer is concerned about the efficiency and effectiveness of the process involved in the good and service delivery.

10.8.7 Promotion

Promotion includes spreading information about the product and service (Schneider, 2017). Promotion involves communication with customers and other stakeholders to inform them about the product and the organization (Chaffey, 2011). From the perspective of companies, promotion in e-business usually follows the AIDA (attention, interest, desire, and action; Sun, Meredith, & Stranieri, 2012), that is, the first step of promotion is to attract the attention of the prospective customers to the good or service.

The interest phase is the next step, which involves encouraging a customer's interest in the good or service available on the websites. Building a desire for action from customers is the third step. The final decision for buying the good or service is action. From a customer's perspective, whenever making a decision, a customer might doubt any promotion from the service providers and therefore usually collects promotion information for similar services from different providers and examines the collected information.

10.8.8 Summary

This section proposes 6Ps: a generic framework for decision-making in digital services, which integrates the environment (6 Ps) of decision-making for decision-makers.

The further framework examines interrelationships among the 6 Ps, 6 Cs, and another 6Ps, and their influences on decision-making in digital services and unifies what the decision makers can "eye" or see (the above-mentioned 6Ps), should "think" (the above-mentioned another 6 Ps) and "act" (6 Cs), and whenever making decisions in digital services. For detail see (Sun, Meredith, & Stranieri, 2012).

10.9 DECISION ANALYTICS

Business analytics use data, models, and algorithms to expedite decision-making process to solve various kinds of decision problems, for example, DDPP problems. DDPP analytics are used to solve not only one problem but also DDPP problems in a business process and a workflow of the business, as we mentioned in Section 4.9. In fact, any business analytics mentioned in this chapter aims to solve problems and decision-making problems.

The steps of the decision-making processes consist of 1). Identify the decision problem and size, 2). Get data, information, knowledge, and intelligence, 3). Identify alternatives, 4). Choose one among alternatives, 5). Take action, and 6). Review the decision (Brooks, 2022, p. 193).

More generally, decision analytics is an integrated system consisting of product analytics, price analytics, people analytics, place analytics, process analytics, and promotion analytics. That is:

$$
\begin{aligned}
\text{Decision analytics} = \ & \text{product analytics} + \text{price analytics} \\
& + \text{people analytics} + \text{place analytics} \\
& + \text{process analytics} + \text{promotion analytics}.
\end{aligned}
$$

Adding intelligence as an operation to both sides of the above equation, we have:

Decision analytics intelligence = product analytics intelligence + price analytics intelligence + people analytics intelligence + place analytics intelligence + process analytics intelligence + promotion analytics intelligence.

Therefore, decision analytics intelligence is a discipline that includes a wide range of decision-making analytics intelligences, AI, BI, and complex applications (Panetta, 2021).

Decision analytics engineering is a process of creating and managing decision analytics and its services to acquire decision analytics intelligence.

Skills, trust, and access to decision analytics are important triads for any decision-making. In order to meet this triad, it is necessary to rely on the traditional triads of people, process, and technology. By balancing investments across these three areas: people, process, and technology, rather than, for example, putting all resources into technology, organizations can build reliability and trustworthiness in their data services and analytics services that will draw users in and enable them to rely on the big data and business analytics to do their jobs and business (Thomas, 2013).

Decision analytics aims to automate decisions. In fact, 100% automatic decisions are all around us. Amazon estimates that 35% of its sales are from cross-selling activities such as recommendation items (McAfee & Brynjolfsson, 2017, p. 47).

10.10 BIG DATA ANALYTICS SERVICES FOR ENHANCING BI

AI and BI have penetrated modern analytics, including augmented analytics, embedded analytics, mobile analytics, and cloud analytics (Eiloart, 2018; Howson, Richardson, Sallam, & Kronz, 2019; Schlegel & Sun, 2023). Amazon QuickSight is a cloud analytics and BI services for performing ad hoc analysis and publishing interactive dashboards (Howson, Richardson, Sallam, & Kronz, 2019). This section looks at how to apply big data analytics services to enhance BI in some detail.

10.10.1 Introduction

This is the era of big data (Sun, Sun, & Strang, 2018). Big data and big data analytics have revolutionized innovation, research, and development (Sun, Pambel, & Wu, 2022). Big data analytics services have created big market opportunities (Sun, Sun, & Strang, 2018). Big data analytics is an emerging big data technology, and has become a mainstream market adopted broadly across industries, organizations, and geographic regions and among individuals to facilitate big data-driven decision-making for businesses and individuals to achieve desired business outcomes (Schlegel & Sun, 2023).

Business intelligence (BI) has become not only an important technology intelligence for improving the business performance of enterprises but also is a marketing brand for developing business, e-commerce, and e-services (Sun, Sun, & Strang, 2018). It is also the momentum for developing organizational intelligence, enterprise intelligence, management intelligence, customer intelligence, and market intelligence (Brooks, 2022). However, BI is facing new big challenges because of the dramatic development of big data and big data technologies (Fan, Lau, & Zhao, 2015; Gandomi & Haider, 2015); that is, how to use big data analytics services to enhance BI becomes a big issue for business, e-commerce, e-services, and information systems (Sun, Sun, & Strang, 2018; Schlegel & Sun, 2023).

This section looks at the ontology of big data analytics. This section also examines big data analytics as a technology and service for enhancing BI by examining the relationship between big data analytics and BI. This section then reviews a big data analytics service-oriented architecture (BASOA), in which we also explore how to apply big data analytics services to enhance BI, where we show that the proposed BASOA is viable for enhancing BI based on our surveyed data analysis.

The remainder of this paper is organized as follows. Subsections 10.10.2 and 10.10.3 looks at the ontology of big data analytics and the ontology of business analytics. Subsection 10.10.4 presents BASOA, a big data analytics services-oriented architecture. Subsection 10.10.5 applies the proposed BASOA to enhance BI. Subsection 10.10.6 discusses SAP and BASOA. The final subsection ends this section with some concluding remarks and future work.

10.10.2 An Ontology of Big Data Analytics

This subsection proposes an ontology of big data analytics and looks at the interrelationship between big data analytics and data analytics.

As we know, from a workflow perspective, big data analytics can be classified as follows (Section 7.8):

$$
\begin{aligned}
\text{Big data analytics} = \ & \text{big descriptive data analytics} \\
& + \text{Big data diagnostic analytics} \\
& + \text{big predictive dataanalytics} \\
& + \text{big prescriptive data analytics} \quad (10.22)
\end{aligned}
$$

Where + can be explained as "and". Equation (10.22) indicates that big data analytics consists of big descriptive data analytics, big data diagnostic analytics, big predictive data analytics, and big prescriptive data analytics, also see Figure 10.7.

1. Big data descriptive analytics is descriptive analytics for big data.

2. Big data diagnostic analytics is diagnostic analytics for big data

3. Big data predictive analytics is predictive analytics for big data.

4. Big data prescriptive analytics is prescriptive analytics for big data

An ontology is a formal naming and definition of a number of concepts and their interrelationships that really or fundamentally exist for a

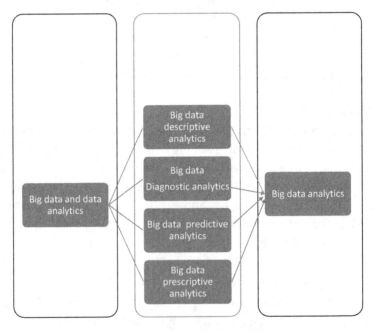

FIGURE 10.7   An ontology of big data and data analytics.

particular domain of discourse (Sun, Sun, & Strang, 2018). Then, an ontology of big data analytics is an investigation into several concepts and their interrelationships that fundamentally exist for big data analytics, as illustrated in Figure 10.7. In this ontology, big data analytics is at the right side, while big data and data analytics are at the left side. Big data descriptive analytics, big data diagnostic analytics, big data predictive analytics, and big data prescriptive analytics are below the big data analytics as its components.

10.10.3 An Ontology of Business Analytics

We have looked at data analytics, web analytics, information analytics, knowledge analytics, big data analytics, and business analytics in Section 10.5. The relationship of all these analytics can be summarized in the ontology of business analytics, as illustrated in Figure 10.8. In Figure 10.8, a directed arrow from A to B represents a generalization relationship from A to B, that is, B is generalized from A, where A and B represent analytics, data analytics, and so on respectively. For example, data analytics is generalized from analytics by emphasizing the applications of sophisticated techniques, and tools of DM, DW, SM, and visualization based on the fundamental theory and methods of analytics. In other words, data analytics is generalized from analytics and is more powerful than data analysis. The generalization relationship here is similar to that among subclass, class, and superclass used in object-oriented technology (Pressman & Maxim, 2014). For example, we can consider big data analytics as a superclass of data analytics.

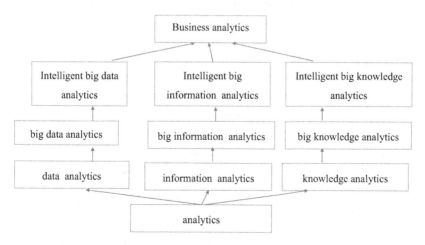

FIGURE 10.8   An ontology of business analytics.

In the ontology, business analytics is at the top while analytics is at the bottom. analytics is the most general concept that directly generalizes data analytics. In other words, analytics is a part of data analytics. All the other analytics, including big data analytics, can be considered as the generalized and applied form of data analytics and support business analytics (Sun, Strang, & Firmin, 2017).

Furthermore, data, information, and knowledge have close interrelationships in business and IT (Chaffey, 2011; Sun, Strang, & Firmin, 2017). Information analytics is generalized from information and analytics, while knowledge analytics is also generalized from knowledge and analytics. Big data analytics can be generalized from data analytics, taking into account that big data as one of the dominated resources (Sun, Strang, & Firmin, 2017), as shown in Figure 10.8.

Business analytics is an extended form of all analytics, including big data analytics in business. Business analytics consists of descriptive, diagnostic, prescriptive, and predicative analytics for business. But this is not enough, more analytics will belong to business analytics in Figure 10. 7 and Figure 10.8.

The business data may be non-numeric, and their business solutions may rely on qualitative analysis, logic, reasoning, collaboration, and negotiation. Therefore, business analytics is also rooted in the theory, technologies, systems, and tools to support decision-making by providing powerful mechanisms for discovering, acquiring, generating, assimilating, selecting, and emitting data, information (corresponding to information analytics) and knowledge (corresponding to knowledge analytics; Holsapple, Lee-Post, & Pakath, 2014; Sun, Strang, & Firmin, 2017).

For any business activities, we can detail big data analytics into big data descriptive analytics, big data diagnostic analytics, big data predictive analytics, and big data prescriptive analytics at the workflow-based business process. Similarly, we can use detail intelligent big data analytics in intelligent big data descriptive analytics, intelligent big data diagnostic analytics, intelligent big data predictive analytics, and intelligent big data prescriptive analytics.

Similarly, we can detail big knowledge analytics in big knowledge descriptive analytics, big knowledge diagnostic analytics, big knowledge predictive analytics, and big knowledge prescriptive analytics at the workflow-based business process or processed intelligently.

It should be noted that many authors call business analytics digital analytics, which is a set of business and technical activities that define, create,

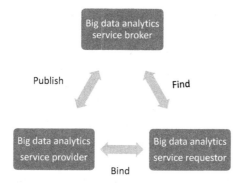

FIGURE 10.9   BASOA: A big data analytics SOA.

collect, verify and transform digital data into reporting, research, analyses, recommendations, optimizations, predictions, and automation (Phillips, 2013). In fact, digital analytics could be a more general form of analytics applied in all computing activities because the latter is ubiquitous in the current digital society. Therefore, digital analytics can include business analytics, covering all data analytics, information analytics, knowledge analytics, and big data analytics, as illustrated in Figure 10.8.

10.10.4 BASOA: Main Players

Data analytics as a service was discussed in the previous section. This section proposes a big data analytics service-oriented architecture (BASOA) and examines each of the main players in the BASOA. Unlike the traditional SOA (Papazoglou, 2008), the proposed BASOA specifies general services to big data analytics services, as illustrated in Figure 10.9. We use BA in this architecture, BASOA, to represent big data analytics, which implies that big analytics (BA) can represent big data analytics briefly.

This BASOA consists of three main players: big data analytics service provider, big data analytics service requestor, and big data analytics service broker. In what follows, we will look at each of these in some detail, taking into account BI.

Big data analytics service requestors include organizations, governments, and all-level business decision makers, such as C-level managers like CEO, CIO, and CFO. Big data analytics service requestors also include business information systems and e-commerce systems. Big data analytics service requestors require big data analytics services, including information analytics services, knowledge analytics services, and business analytics services with visualization techniques to provide knowledge patterns and information for decision-making in a form of figures or tables or reports (Kauffman, Srivastava, & Vayghan, 2012). More generally, big data analytics service requestors include people who like to make decisions or acquire information based on analytical reports provided by big data analytics service providers (Sun, Strang, & Firmin, 2017). Therefore, a person with a smartphone receiving analytics services is also a big data analytics service requestor (Demirkan & Delen, 2013).

Big data analytics service brokers are all the entities that facilitate the development of big data analytics services, which include popular presses, traditional media and social media, consulting companies, scholars and university students, and so on (Sun, Strang, & Firmin, 2017). All these use a variety of methods and techniques to improve the understanding of big data analytics services in general and data analytics, business analytics, web analytics, and their services in particular (Sun, Strang, & Firmin, 2017); all these have been offered to university students as course material or content in business and computing areas to some extent in recent years. McKinsey Consulting (http://www.mckinsey.com/), Boston Consulting Group (BCG), and IDC as big data analytics service brokers have played a significant role in pushing big data analytics in businesses and enterprises. Gartner and Forrester are also famous big data analytics service brokers in the world (Sun, Sun, & Strang, 2018; Schlegel & Sun, 2023).

Big data analytics service providers include analytics developers, analytics vendors, analytics systems or software, and other intermediaries that can provide analytics services. Recently, web analytics service (WAS) providers have been important big data analytics service providers. A WAS provider, for example, Adobe Marketing Cloud (http://www.adobe.com/au/solutions/digital-marketing.html), aggregates and analyses blog data about the online behaviors of users who visited the client's website, then evaluates a variety of analytical reports concerning the client's customer online behaviors that the client wishes to understand. This can facilitate strategic business decision-making (Park, Kim, & Koh, 2010). Application service providers (ASPs) can also provide web analytics in a hosted ASP model with quicker implementation and lower administrative costs (Park, Kim, & Koh, 2010). Analytics developers provide analytic tools with extensive data extraction, analytics, and reporting functionality such as Piwik, and CrawlTrack (Laudon & Laudon, 2020). Google is not only a search engine provider, but also a WAS vendor, because Google provides Google Analytics (http://www.google.com/analytics/), big data analytics, with good tracking tools. Most hosting websites, like Baidu and

Tencent, also provide these similar big data analytics services. A mobile phone company can provide big data analytics services to customers with a smartphone (Demirkan & Delen, 2013). For example, mobile App Analytics (http://www.google.com/analytics/mobile/), a part of Google Analytics, is also a mobile big data analytics services provider that helps the smartphone customers discover new and relevant users through traffic source reports. Mobile App Analytics plays a role of integration in getting engaged through event tracking and flow visualization and sets and tracks the goal conversions one wants most: purchases, clicks, or simply time spent on the app. More generally, many information systems have contained an analytics app as a system component to generate tables, diagrams, or reports. All these kinds of information systems can be considered big data analytics service providers. The big data analytics services providers include Amazon, Alibaba, Baidu, Huawei, Google, Microsoft, Tencent, and Pinduoduo (Schlegel & Sun, 2023; Sun, Strang, & Firmin, 2017).

10.10.5 Applying BASOA to Enhance BI

BAaaS (Big data analytics as a service) means that an individual or organization or information system or software agent uses a wide range of analytics tools or apps wherever they may be located (Demirkan & Delen, 2013). BAaaS can turn a general analytic platform into a shared utility for an enterprise or organization with visualized analytic services (Demirkan & Delen, 2013). A big data analytics service can be available on the Web or smartphones (Sun, Sun, & Strang, 2018). Therefore, big data analytics services include e-analytics services or web analytics services (WAS) and Amazon Web Services (AWS). Furthermore, big data analytics services also include business analytics services, marketing analytics services, organizational analytics services, security analytics services, and predictive analytics services (Roche, 2016). Big data analytics services are gaining popularity rapidly in business, e-commerce, e-service, and management in recent years. For example, the big data analytics services model has been adopted by many famous web companies such as Amazon, Microsoft, and eBay (Demirkan & Delen, 2013). The key reason behind this is that the traditional hub-and-spoke architectures cannot meet the demands driven by increasingly complex business analytics (Demirkan & Delen, 2013). BAaaS promises to provide decision-makers with visualization of much-needed big data (Sun, Sun, & Strang, 2018). Cloud analytics is an emerging alternative solution for big data analytics.

As previously defined, BI is a set of theories, methodologies, architectures, systems, and technologies that support business decision-making with valuable data, information and knowledge". BASOA is an architecture for supporting business decision-making with big data analytics services. The theory of big data analytics providers, brokers, and requestors of the BASOA can facilitate the understanding and development of BI and business decision-making. For example, from an in-depth study of the BASOA, an enterprise and its CEO can know who are the best big data analytics providers and brokers to improve his organization, business, market performance, and global competitiveness.

10.10.6 SAP and BASOA

SAP, one of the leading vendors of ERP (Elragal, 2014), has introduced its enterprise service-oriented architecture (Laudon & Laudon, 2020). SAP's architecture specifies general services to enterprise services, whereas our BASOA model specifies general services to big data analytics services. Big data analytics services should be a part of state-of-the-art e-commerce services. Then, the proposed BASOA can be considered as a concrete application for the enterprise service-oriented architecture of SAP. However, SAP's enterprise systems focus on key applications in finance, logistics, procurement, and human resources management as an ERP system. our BASOA will be incorporated into the next generation enterprise systems integrating SCM, CRM, and KM systems, and e-commerce systems. This is also the motivation of our proposed BASOA.

10.10.7 Summary

This section looked at big data analytics' importance for modern business organizations and proposed an ontology of big data analytics. This section also presented a big data analytics service-oriented architecture (BASOA). The preliminary analysis of the collected data shows that this proposed BASOA is viable for facilitating the development of BI (Sun, Sun, & Strang, 2018). The proposed approach in this section might facilitate research and development of big data analytics, business analytics, BI, e-commerce, and e-services.

In future work, we will analyze the collected data vigorously and explore the enterprise and e-commerce acceptability of BASOA for BI. We will also explore big data analytics and its applications in e-commerce and cloud services, and realize BASOA using intelligent agents' technology, where we will also look at some implementation-related issues such as how to collect, store, and process big data – by whom, for what, access rights, and many more.

10.11 ENTERPRISE INFORMATION SYSTEMS AND BUSINESS ANALYTICS

Big data analytics and business analytics are disruptive technology and innovative solutions for enterprise development. However, these are still big issues: what is the relationship between business analytics, big data analytics, and enterprise information systems (EIS)? How can business analytics enhance the development of EIS? How can we incorporate analytics into EIS? This section addresses these three issues by presenting an analytics services-oriented architecture (ASOA), and applying ASOA to EIS. This section then examines the incorporation of business analytics into EIS by proposing a model for business analytics services-based EIS, or ASEIS for short, taking into account intelligent agents.

10.11.1 Introduction

Enterprise information systems (EIS) have been implemented or adopted in many firms in general, and Fortune 500 companies in particular, to achieve performance excellence and enhance decision-making over the past few decades (Laudon & Laudon, 2020; Sun, Strang, & Firmin, 2017). EIS is based on organization-wide data and big data beyond the enterprise, including that from the Web. How to use big data and big data analytics to improve EIS has become a big challenge for enterprises and the development of EIS, recently.

The following important issues have not been drawing significant attention in the scholarly peer-reviewed literature:

- What is the relationship between big data analytics and EIS?

- How can big data analytics be incorporated into EIS?

This section addresses these two issues by proposing business analytics and EIS. It presents an analytics service-oriented architecture (ASOA). It examines the incorporation of big analytics into EIS by proposing a model for big data analytics services-based EIS (for short, ASEIS), taking into account intelligent agents.

The remainder of this section is structured as follows. Subsection 10.11.2 discusses business analytics and EIS. Subsection 10.11.3 presents an analytics service-oriented architecture (ASOA). Subsection 10.11.4 applies the proposed ASOA to EIS. Subsection 10.11.5 proposes a model for business analytics services-based EIS, for short ASEIS. The final Subsection ends this section with some concluding remarks and suggestions for future work.

10.11.2 Business Analytics and EIS

Based on the previous subsection's discussion, data analytics can facilitate the development of EIS, because it can support business decision-making with valuable data, information, and knowledge (Sun, Strang, & Firmin, 2017). Both EIS and data analytics are common in emphasizing the data, information, and knowledge as a strategic resources for enterprises (Azvine, Nauck, & Ho, 2003), in particular, for global enterprises. EIS involves interactive visualization for data exploration and discovery (Brust, 2013), which can be considered a part of big data analytics (Schlegel & Sun, 2023). EIS includes analytical tools for using data captured by the system to evaluate the business and marketing performance (Sun, Strang, & Firmin, 2017). The analytical tools are a fundamental part of any business analytics system. This implies that EIS and business analytics share some common tools and functions to support business decision-making and improve the business performance of enterprises.

As mentioned in chapter 9, enterprises' development heavily relies on four cutting-age technology pillars: cloud, mobile, big data, and social technologies. Each of these pillars corresponds to a special kind of web services, that is, cloud services, mobile services, big data services, and social networking services (Sun, Strang, & Firmin, 2017). Each of these services has been supported by intelligent data analytics services and technologies supported by AI and BI, as shown in Figure 10.10.

In Figure 10.10, web searches belong to cloud services and technologies. The big data and business analytics services rely on the Internet

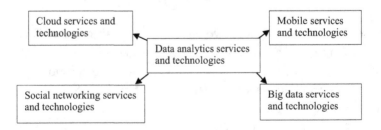

FIGURE 10.10   Analytics services support EIS.

infrastructure if they are related to the Web; otherwise, they rely on hardware and information systems. For example, the CCTV (Closed-circuit television) of a metropolis collects real-time big data on traffic, security, and other social events of the city, which will be processed by information systems and analytics to provide big data services to help maintain the surveillance and security of the city and safety of residents.

Furthermore, business analytics is a pivotal part of developing EIS (Sun, Strang, & Firmin, 2017). From a technological viewpoint, business analytics is a data-driven business-oriented technique that facilitates business decision-making and improves EIS as a system component. From a data viewpoint, business analytics relies on data analytics; data and big data have become strategic resources for organizations and enterprises, in particular, for multinational organizations and EIS. Discovering useful information, knowledge, patterns, and insights from databases, data warehouses, data marts, and the Web has become the central topics both for business operations and EIS (Turban & Volonino, 2011). This is just the task of business analytics.

10.11.3 Analytics Service-Oriented Architecture

This section proposes an analytics service-oriented architecture (ASOA) and then examines each of the main players in the ASOA. One of the major challenges in big data analytics is to specify overall system architecture (National Research Council, 2013). ASOA is one addressing this challenge.

The service-oriented architecture (SOA) is fundamental for web services (Papazoglou, 2008). SOA includes three players and three fundamental operations for any web services. The three players are service provider, service requestor, and service broker (Sun Z., 2023b). The service provider is the owner of the web service. The service requestor is the customer or consumer of the web service. The service broker is an intermediary that facilitates the discovery, selection, composition, consultation, recommendation, transfer, or delivery of web services from the service provider to the service requestor (Tabein, Moghadasi, & Khoshkbarforoushha, 2008). The three fundamental operations are publish, find, and bind (Sun, Strang, & Firmin, 2017).

- Publish operation: The service provider publishes the web service to the service broker.

- Find operation: The service requestor finds web services from the service broker.

- Bind operation: The service requestor invokes the found web services from the service provider.

As an application of the SOA, the rest of this section proposes an ASOA by specializing general services as analytics services, as illustrated in Figure 10.11.

Unlike the extended SOA of (Papazoglou & Georgakopoulos, 2003), the SOA is extended by adding the players to the SOA, taking into account eSMACS services. In this ASOA, the service provider is an analytics service provider. The service requestor is an analytics service requestor. The service broker is an analytics service broker. In what follows, we will look at each of these in some detail, taking into account BI and EIS.

Analytics service requestors require data analytics services, big data analytics services, information analytics services, knowledge analytics services, business analytics services with visualization techniques to make any knowledge patterns and information for decision-making in a form of a figure or table or report (Kauffman, Srivastava, & Vayghan, 2012).

McKinsey Consulting (http://www.mckinsey.com/) and Boston Consulting Group (BCG), as analytics service brokers, have played an important role in pushing analytics in businesses and enterprises, just as they promote big data. Gartner, Forrester, McKinsey, and IDC are also famous analytics service brokers in the world (Demirkan & Delen, 2013).

Analytics service providers include analytics developers, analytics vendors, analytics systems or software, and other intermediaries that can

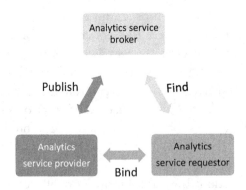

FIGURE 10.11   ASOA: An analytics SOA.

provide analytics services (Sun, Strang, & Firmin, 2017). More generally, many information systems including EIS have contained an analytics App as a system component to generate table, diagram, or report. All these kinds of information systems can be considered as analytics service providers. For example, predicative analytics is a component of web mining systems that sifts through data to identify patterns of e-customer behaviors that predict which offers customers might respond to in the future or which customers the company may be in danger of losing in the near future (Turban & Volonino, 2011). The big data analytics services providers on the Web include Amazon, Google, and Microsoft, and Alibaba (Sun, Strang, & Firmin, 2017).

10.11.4 Applying ASOA to EIS

This section addresses how to apply the proposed ASOA to EIS in some detail, taking into account a model for applying ASOA to EIS (Sun, Strang, & Firmin, 2017), as shown in Figure 10.12.

As previously defined, EIS support business decision-making with valuable data, information, and knowledge. ASOA is an architecture for supporting business decision-making with analytics services. The theory of analytics providers, analytics brokers, and analytics requestors of the ASOA can facilitate the understanding and development of EIS and business decision-making. For example, from a deep analysis of the ASOA, an enterprise and its CEO can know who are the best analytics providers and brokers to improve his business, market performance, and competition (Sun, Strang, & Firmin, 2017).

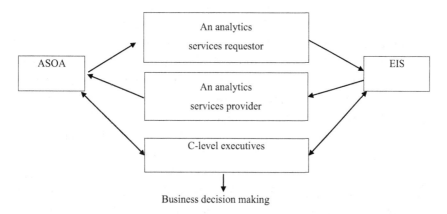

FIGURE 10.12   Applying ASOA to EIS.

An EIS can be considered as an analytics services' requestor of the ASOA in order to improve its performance, on the one hand. For example, big data analytics might be incorporated into an existing EIS to meet the enterprise requirement for the business analytics and big data analytics (Sun, Strang, & Firmin, 2017). In this way, the upgraded EIS will have more powerful performance for the enterprise's data processing and support ability for business decision-making. On the other hand, an EIS can be considered as an analytics service provider of the ASOA, because an advanced EIS can provide analytics services to enterprises and its C-level executives for business decision-making. The analytics services might include a weekly/monthly/quarterly visualized market trend report, online customer comments summary, and analysis report (Lau, Li, & Liao, 2014).

Business analytics as a system component in an EIS can monitor data generated in business operations so as to analyze performance based on key indicators and present the analysis results to a wide range of users in a visual way (Azvine, Nauck, & Ho, 2003). The incorporation of business analytics into the existing EIS can allow CEOs and other managers of the enterprise to use the output of business analytics, as a service, to make decisions in the corresponding business processes, such as marketing, SCM, CRM, and so on (Azvine, Nauck, & Ho, 2003).

10.11.5 ASEIS: An Analytics Services-Based EIS

As an application of ASOA to EIS, this section proposes a model for analytics services-based EIS, or ASEIS for short. The ASEIS is the answer to the previous question: How can big data analytics be incorporated into EIS?

As we know, standalone enterprise systems are becoming a thing of the past (Laudon & Laudon, 2020). The proposed ASEIS will incorporate analytics services into an integrated EIS that consists of main functions of SCM systems, CRM systems, and KM systems, as shown in Figure 10.13. In what follows, we will examine this model in some detail.

SCM systems are classified as either SC (supply chain) planning systems or SC execution systems (Laudon & Laudon, 2020). Then SC planning and SC execution are main functions of any SCM systems. CRM systems mainly consist of sales, marketing, and services (Laudon & Laudon, 2020). A knowledge management system mainly consists of create, capture, refine, store, manage, disseminate, and share knowledge (Turban & Volonino, 2011). Therefore, our ASEIS, as an analytics

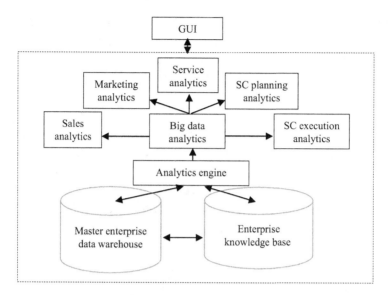

FIGURE 10.13   A model for analytics-based EIS.

platform, includes SC planning analytics, SC execution analytics, marketing analytics, sales analytics, service analytics, and big data analytics, taking into account knowledge analytics.

Master enterprise data warehouse (MEDW) mainly consists of data related to sales, marketing, services, customers, SC (supply chain) planning, and SC execution flowing from department of marketing, human resources, and other data related to departments. All these can be considered as structured data. Enterprise knowledge base (EKB) consists of information and knowledge from the Web, call center, direct mails, emails, retail store, client, and partner (Laudon & Laudon, 2020). All these data of EKB are mainly either semi-structured or unstructured data.

Big data analytics is based on MEDW and EKB and provides related knowledge and information for sales analytics, marketing analytics, service analytics, SC planning analytics, and SC execution analytics.

Big data analytics is based on MEDW and EKB and provides related knowledge and information services for sales analytics, marketing analytics, service analytics, SC planning analytics, and SC execution analytics.

An analytics engine is a mechanism for managing and producing SC planning analytics, SC planning analytics, marketing analytics, service analytics, customer analytics, and big data analytics, as well as knowledge analytics. The analytics engine has OLAP, data mining, statistical modeling, optimization, visualization tools, and other data and knowledge analysis tools based on the techniques, including soft computing, machine learning, fuzzy neural networks, decision trees, and probabilistic models (Laudon & Laudon, 2020; Sun, Strang, & Firmin, 2017).

10.11.6 Summary

This section looked at business analytics as a technology for supporting EIS. This section presented an analytics service-oriented architecture (ASOA) and discussed how to apply the ASOA to EIS and then propose a model of ASEIS: An Analytics Services-Based EIS, by looking at business analytics as a technology and service for supporting EIS. ASEIS integrates external data with internal organizational data of enterprises, which is one of the significant issues for successful adoption of EIS in enterprises. The discussion of the ASEIS and the work of SAP implies that the ASEIS is useful for developing the next generation of EIS in the big data era. The preliminary analysis on the collected data shows that this proposed ASOA is viable for facilitating the development of EIS (Sun, Strang, & Firmin, 2017)

In future work, we will also explore how to design and implement ASEIS based on big data analytics derived from the following questions: How the components of the enterprise can be analyzed by the analytics services? What should the main functions of these EIS be based on analytics? How can we develop analytics services-centered EIS in order to integrate the above mentioned EIS?

10.12 CYBERSECURITY INTELLIGENCE AND ANALYTICS

Cybersecurity analytics and metrics have been studied and have become a vital power in big data analytics and BI (Weber, 2020, p. 134). We have mentioned security as a service when we discussed eSMACS services. Now we look at cybersecurity intelligence and analytics.

Cybersecurity is a part of computer and information security (Laudon & Laudon, 2020). Cybersecurity deals with the availability, integrity, and confidentiality of the data and prevents the sensitive data from the end-user released wrongly (Weber, 2020). Cybersecurity can be used to assist in risk management to improve cybersecurity intelligence. Cybersecurity intelligence is intelligence that uses cybersecurity technology, engineering, and systems to prevent and act against cyber threats. Cybersecurity intelligence is also a cyber threat intelligence used to gather and analyze relevant data and information about cyber threats to prevent computing systems from hacking and to enhance cybersecurity.

The most common cybersecurity threats include computer viruses, trojan horses, spyware, ransomware, computer worms, phishing attacks, crypto-jacking, IoT attacks, and third-party risks, people as a cybersecurity threat (Weber, 2020; Laudon & Laudon, 2020).

Cybersecurity technology is used to keep cybersecurity at bay, nowadays. These technologies are composed of computer systems, the internet, software programs, apps, hardware verification, user-conduct analytics, information technology security, cloud technology, blockchain cybersecurity technology, and cybersecurity analytics (Weber, 2020; Laudon & Laudon, 2020).

User-conduct analytics uses big data to check on user behaviors. Whenever the malevolent behavior of a user occurs, user-conduct analytics will figure out that behavior (Weber, 2020).

Cybersecurity analytics is a technology and system that can aggregate data for collecting evidence, building timelines, and analyzing capabilities to design and perform a proactive cybersecurity strategy that detects, analyzes, and mitigates cyber threats (Fortinet, 2024).

Cybersecurity analytics uses big data analytics technologies and behavioral analytics to monitor the network, spot changes in how resources or the traffic on the network and the cloud are used, and enable the individual and organization to address threats immediately (Fortinet, 2024).

Some of the typical use cases for cybersecurity analytics include (Fortinet, 2024):

1. Analyzing traffic to identify patterns that may indicate attacks.

2. Monitoring user behaviors.

3. Detecting threats.

4. Monitoring the activities of remote and internal employees.

5. Identifying insider threats.

Therefore, cybersecurity analytics can help one understand what is happening within one's company and help one act when needed most to improve cybersecurity intelligence (Van Rijmenam, 2020, p. 28).

More generally, cybersecurity analytics can be extended to

$$
\begin{aligned}
\text{Cybersecurity computing} = {}& \text{cybersecurity science} + \text{cybersecurity} \\
& \text{engineering} + \text{cybersecurity technology} \\
& + \text{cybersecurity systems} + \text{cybersecurity} \\
& \text{intelligence} + \text{cybersecurity management} \\
& + \text{cybersecurity service.}
\end{aligned}
$$

Cybersecurity science is about understanding, developing, and practicing cybersecurity using scientific experimentation, inquiry, and methods (Dykstra, 2015). Scientific experimentation and inquiry reveal opportunities to optimize and create more secure cyber solutions in cybersecurity science. The scientific method contains five essential elements in cybersecurity science: ask a good question, formulate hypotheses, make predictions, experimentally test the predictions, and analyze the result.

Cybersecurity engineering is a process of creating and managing cybersecurity systems and platforms to provide cybersecurity services with cybersecurity intelligence.

Cybersecurity engineering involves creating and managing hardware, software, and security policies for protecting digital systems, networks, and data (HCU, 2024). Some typical daily tasks performed by cybersecurity engineers may include:

1. Addressing any network or system security breaches or viruses.

2. Using appropriate security controls to protect the organization's digital files and infrastructure.

3. Planning, implementing, managing, monitoring, and upgrading measures for protecting cybersecurity systems, networks, and data.

4. Using various management tasks, reporting, and communication with other departments.

5. Performing penetration testing and identifying cybersecurity system and network vulnerabilities.

The vendors of cybersecurity analytics and systems include Fortinet, IBM, and Splunk, to name a few.

10.13 PLATFORM ENGINEERING

This section looks at platform engineering.

A platform normally consists of many subsystems as an integrated system. For example, a platform is an integrated system of operating system

(OS) and the kind of hardware CPU and GPU it runs on. Therefore, from a system viewpoint, platform = meta(system).

Platforms are online environments that take advantage of the economics of free, perfect, and instant. It can be also defined as a digital environment with the near-zero marginal cost of access, reproduction, and distribution. The Internet is the platform most familiar to most of us (McAfee & Brynjolfsson, 2017, pp. 137-142).

Platform engineering can be defined as an emerging technology approach that can accelerate the delivery of applications and the pace at which they produce business value (Perri, 2023). Platform engineering can also improve developer experience and productivity by providing self-service capabilities with automated infrastructure operations.

A mobile operating system (OS) is an OS used for smartphones, tablets, smartwatches, smart glasses, or other non-laptop personal mobile computing devices. Android is one of the most popular mobile OSs, Android takes about 53.32% of the above-mentioned mobile systems. Android and iOS currently dominate 80% of the market share of mobile OS worldwide (Wikipedia-OS, 2024).

In 2005, Google bought Android, a startup, for about $50 million (McAfee & Brynjolfsson, 2017). Android has become the world's most popular mobile OS (McAfee & Brynjolfsson, 2017, pp. 166–167).

Android is the first revolutionary OS to stop Windows' development. It seems that Android is unbeatable in the global OS market. However, thanks to the sanctions of the US government, Harmony OS has become one of the OSs used in Huawei 60 Pro, which can connect all the IoT devices, including auto-driving systems, smartphones, tablets, smartwatches, and laptops. Harmony OS has become an open system; it treats different smart devices as a single super device (https://www.harmonyos.com/en/).

Digital platforms have been rapidly spreading into industries like exercise, transportation, lodging, and banking that deal in physical goods and services (McAfee & Brynjolfsson, 2017, pp. 191–197). These are sometimes called O2O (Online-to-Offline) (Schneider, 2017). China is the world's most fertile territory for mobile O2O platforms. For example, Tencent, Alibaba, TikTok, and Pingduoduo.

Uber is a tech company that connects the physical and digital worlds to help moving happen at the tap of a button. Uber's mission is "Movement is what we power. It's our lifeblood. It runs through our veins" (Uber, 2024). Uber is a two-sided network, the increase in demand doesn't just affect the consumers who use its ride-hailing app; it also increases demand for drivers who use rider-finding apps. In fact, as the number and thus density of riders increases, each driver will have less downtime and make more money per hour (McAfee & Brynjolfsson, 2017, pp. 218–224). Residents, tourists, and business travelers all have the same goal when they want to go somewhere in a city: to get there quickly, safely, and cheaply. Platforms can capture much, or even all of the value as they spread throughout an industry. It succeeds at capturing and creating value in part because it reduces information asymmetries that previously kept some beneficial transactions from happening. The key to many platforms is the power of two-sided networks, where decisions on which one set of customers and products can profoundly affect demand by a different set of customers for a different set of products. Platforms with two-sided networks can become multisided networks, amplifying the role of cross-elasticities.

Uber was born on a snowy night in Paris in 2008. Uber has grown into a global platform powering flexible earnings and the movement of people and things in ever-expanding ways (Uber, 2024).

More generally, platform engineering should be extended to platform computing, that is,

$$
\begin{aligned}
\text{Platform computing} = \ &\text{platform science} + \text{platform} \\
&\text{engineering} + \text{platform technology} \\
&+ \text{platform systems} + \text{platform} \\
&\text{intelligence} + \text{platform management} \\
&+ \text{platform service.}
\end{aligned}
$$

The author leaves the investigation to the readers for detailing each of them, based on computing.

10.14 SIX BIG TRENDS IN THE ERA OF BIG DATA BASED AI AND BI

This section reveals six big trends in the era of big data and discusses their interrelationships from three different viewpoints: data science, big data, and AI. These six big trends consist of the informatization of big data, mining big data for big knowledge, mining big data for big intelligence, networking of big data, socialization of big data, and commercialization of big data. The research demonstrates that big data are the raw materials that will be transformed into information, knowledge, intelligence, networking, society, and big markets, using ICT and digital technology, data science, AI, and big data analytics. These six big trends will bring about big industries, smarter cities, smarter societies, and smarter countries (Sun & Stranieri, 2021).

10.14.1 Introduction

We are in the era of big data, AI, and analytics. Countries around the world have drawn increasing attention to their research and development and big impacts on the economy and society since 2012. Big data have become a strategic resource for organizations, industries, enterprises, businesses, and individuals, as well as national security (Sun, Sun, & Strang, 2018). Big data, AI, and analytics are also key enablers in exploring business insights and economics of services. China and the USA have developed their national big data development plan, and many universities in China and the USA have offered programs for big data, AI, and data science. Big data, AI, and analytics have become one of the most important research frontiers for innovation, research, and development (Sun & Stranieri, 2021; Sun, Pambel, & Wu, 2022).

It should be noted that the proposed six big trends of big data are directly translated from Chinese (Sun & Wang, 2021). In Chinese, these six big trends of big data are the informatization of big data, knowledge *hua* of big data, intelligence *hua* of big data, networking *hua* of big data, socialization of big data, and commercialization of big data (Sun & Wang, 2021). Hua (or tion) is a process of research and development as well as applications targeting a special but big goal at a social, national, or global level. To the knowledge of the author, we have not a counterpart for knowledge *hua*, intelligence *hua*, networking *hua* respectively, although informatization, socialization, and commercialization can be considered as the counterparts of information *hua*, social *hua*, and goods *hua*. Therefore, we use similar concepts or clauses, from big data to big knowledge, from big data to big intelligence, and networking of big data, to represent knowledge *hua*, intelligence *hua*, networking *hua* respectively, as follows.

To this end, this section is organized as follows: Subsection 10.14.2 explores the informatization of big data. Subsection 10.14.3 looks at mining big data for big knowledge. Subsection 10.14.4 explores mining big data for big Intelligence. Subsection 10.14.5 discusses the networking of big data. Subsection 10.14.6 looks at the socialization of big data. Subsection 10.14.7 discusses the commercialization of big data. The final subsection ends this research with some concluding remarks and future research directions.

10.14.2 Informatization of Big Data

The main task of information systems is to transform data into information (Laudon & Laudon, 2020; Sun Z., 2023b). The research and development of database systems and information systems have existed for at least 60 years. Now, integrating big data within information systems is for promoting the further development of informatization of big data. China's national development of informatization belongs to this category. Informatization of big data will also become more and more important, and the value of information is becoming more and more important (Sun & Wang, 2017b).

10.14.3 Mining Big Data for Big Knowledge

Discovering knowledge from a database (KDD) is the main task of knowledge discovery and data mining (Sun Z., 2023b). Now the combination of KDD and data mining with big data aims to promote further development of mining big data for big knowledge. The further development is to mine big knowledge for big intelligence and big wisdom, using knowledge science and engineering and AI (Russell & Norvig, 2020).

10.14.4 Mining Big Data for Big Intelligence

The main task of data-based AI is to discover intelligence from big data (Sun Z., 2023b). This is also an important task and direction of market-based AI. This can be called data intelligence. The advances of driverless cars, drones, and ChatGPT are examples of this trend. The perseverance of human beings in liberating their intelligence is an important basis for the development of mining big data for big intelligence. No one likes to be stupid. Everyone wants to be smart, intelligent, and more intelligent than others. Intelligent chips, intelligent machines, AI machines, and intelligent systems are already ubiquitous in the market. Therefore, China has promulgated a national plan for the development of AI. Research and development of smart or smart cities, smart societies, and smart countries have become an important development direction. Mining big data for big intelligence is not only important for China's future, it is also the direction of the efforts of all other countries in the world. In the next few decades, more and more countries and individuals will struggle for and benefit from mining big data for big intelligence, mining big knowledge for big intelligence, and mining big intelligence for big wisdom. Automated insights provided by advanced analytics, big data analytics, and intelligent big data analytics are pointing in this direction (Schlegel & Sun, 2023).

10.14.5 Networking of Big Data

The inception of the Internet in the world in the middle 1990s has led to the booming of e-commerce and electronic services. Amazon, the first online bookseller, is now an empire for selling almost everything. Alibaba is also a big winner in e-commerce and electronic services. China is still springing up in this area and developing its e-commerce and e-services in every corner of its countryside. JD.com, Pinduoduo, TikTok, and Tencent have also become intentional companies and provide e-services and cloud services globally.

In recent years, the Internet of everything (IoE), the Internet of Things (IoT), the Internet of Peoples (IoP), and the Internet of Services (IoS) have flourished globally. All these show that the networking of data and intelligent networking are becoming more and more important. In the near future, everything we have (furniture, electrical appliances, cars, drones, health, smart phones) will be connected to the Internet. Our brain and many parts of our body will be automatically connected to the Internet, all these parts are underpinned by the intelligent networking of big data as an infrastructure. Therefore, the intelligent networking of big data is the basis of mining big data for big intelligence, mining big data for everything, and is also an important infrastructure for smart communities, smart cities, and smart countries.

10.14.6 Socialization of Big Data

In the current age of the Internet and the era of IoT, everyone is interacting with the Internet; most people are shopping from the Internet and obtaining a variety of services. Everyone is busy using WeChat, ChatGPT, and WhatsApp to communicate with friends, and share data, information, knowledge, experience, and wisdom. Friends exchange through sending messages, photos, and tweets, transferring information, knowledge, experience, and intelligence. As a result, everyone contributes to data, everyone is contributing to big data, everyone is a selfless voluntary devotee of big data, and everyone is a must-have consumer of big data, whether it is paid or free.

In China's cities, the most humane and legal way to punish a person is to prevent her/him from using WeChat for a month. One cannot be alive without using WeChat for one day! Therefore, the socialization of big data is the foundation of modern society.

Of course, we cannot forget that at least 45% of the world's population still can't connect to the Internet or cloud (UNDP, 2022). They can't use any online social networking sites like we can. Therefore, we still have a long way to go in socializing data, information, knowledge, and experience.

10.14.7 Commercialization of Big Data

The direct consequence of the above "five hua" of big data is the commercialization of big data. The resources of China's Baidu, Alibaba, TikTok, Tencent (ABT) are big data, only big data! The big data of Baidu, Alibaba, and Tencent are sold and exchanged in the data trade market. Their huge profits come from the commercialization of big data. Similarly, in the United States, Meta, Google, and Amazon have huge profits directly from the commodification of big data, data trade.

The socialization of big data will produce more and more data. In the 21st Century, big data has not yet brought the same sized industry of big data processing as the petrochemical industry of the last century. In today's big data kingdom, only a few data companies are buying, grabbing money from people all over the world, no matter how much one has. Therefore, the commercialization of big data is a big world, and there is much to do here!

The six *hua* mentioned above are also processes for transformation, processing, mining, exploration, and development. This growth needs another 50 years of questing. This process brings together the coordinated development of science, technology, engineering, management, systems, and tools, and the resulting progress of the country and society. Therefore, we have to pay attention to these six major trends mentioned above and work hard for them, because they together constitute the global competitiveness of the country, your country, and the inevitable or necessary way for each country to become a developed country or a brighter country from a developed country. Finally, one has to recognize that the real competition between China and the USA is big data rather than others put forward in the name of the national interest.

10.14.8 Summary

This section reveals six big trends in the era of big data and discusses their interrelationships from three different viewpoints: data science, big data, and AI. These six big trends consist of the informatization of big data, mining big data for big knowledge, mining big data for big intelligence, networking of big data, socialization of big data, and commercialization of big data. The research demonstrates that big data are the raw materials that will be transformed into information, knowledge, intelligence, networking, society, and big markets using ICT and digital technology, data science, and AI. These six big trends will bring about big industries, smarter cities, smarter societies, and smarter countries. The proposed approach in this section might facilitate the research and development of big data, IoT, cloud computing, AI, big data analytics, and BI.

10.15 BIG DATA DRIVEN SOCIOECONOMIC DEVELOPMENT

Big data technology, including big data analytics, has revolutionized our work, lifestyles, economies, and societies (Sun & Wu, 2021). Big data analytics has become a mainstream market adopted broadly across industries, organizations, geographic regions, and among individuals to facilitate big data-driven decision-making for individuals, organizations, and governments (Schlegel & Sun, 2023). This section will examine big data-driven socioeconomic development from an interdisciplinary approach. More specifically, this section explores ESMACS goods and services that have played an important role in digital trade and economy. This section presents a GDDP (gross domestic data products) as a GDP-like data metric for measuring economic performance and social progress. This research presents a strategic model for big data-driven socioeconomic development, which consists of two levels: The first level is big data-centered, including big data-driven technologies, services, economies, and societies. The second level consists of big data-driven eSMACS technology, service, economy, and society as the example of the first level. This research demonstrates that big data-driven SMACS (i.e., social, mobile, analytics, cloud, and service) technologies, services, economies, and societies underpin big data-driven socioeconomic development.

10.15.1 Introduction

Big data has become one of the most important frontiers for research and development in academia and industries (Sun & Wu, 2021). Big data and big data analytics have increasingly become critical elements for nearly all industries and keys to successful digital businesses and intelligent businesses, based on the following three predictions from Gartner researchers (Peters & Duncan, 2020, 1). 30% of organizations would exceed data and analytics ROI (return on investment) by governing the least amount of data that matters most to their strategic goals by 2023, 2). In 2023, 90% of the world's top 500 companies would have converged analytics governance into broader data and analytics governance initiatives.

Socioeconomic development has drawn increasing attention in academia, industries, and governments. For example, Miladinov looks at the relationship between socioeconomic development and life expectancy based on the evidence from the EU accession candidate countries (Miladinov, 2020). The UN has used the Human Development Index (HDI) to measure annually the socioeconomic development of all nations in the world (UNDP, 2022). The relationship between big data and socioeconomic development has drawn attention in academia. For example, Pappalardo, et al. use big data to study the relationship between human mobility and socioeconomic development (Pappalardo, Pedreschi, Smoreda, & Giannotti, 2015). However, the following research issues have not drawn much attention in academia and industries.

1. What is the relationship between big data and socioeconomic development?

2. How can big data contribute to socioeconomic development?

This section will address both of them. To address the first research issue, this section looks at socioeconomic development and its relationships with the HDI of the UN. It presents a GDDP (gross domestic data products) as a GDP-like data metric for measuring economic performance and social progress. To address the second research issue, this section presents a strategic model for big data-driven socioeconomic development.

The remainder of this section is organized as follows. Subsection 10.15.2.14.2 looks at socioeconomic development and presents the GDDP as a GDP-like data metric for measuring economic performance and social progress. Subsection 10.15.3 proposes a strategic model for big data-driven smart socioeconomic development and exemplifies it with big data-driven eSMACS technologies, services, economies, and societies. The final Subsection ends with some concluding remarks and future work.

10.15.2 GDDP as a Data Metric for Measuring Economic Performance and Social Progress

This subsection looks at socioeconomic development and its relationships with the human development of the UN. It will present GDDP as a

GDP-like data metric for measuring economic performance and social progress to facilitate big data-driven socioeconomic development.

Socioeconomic development is the process of social and economic development in a society (UNDP, 2022; Stiglitz, Fitoussi, & Durand, 2018). The output of socioeconomic development is economic performance and social progress, measured by GDP and HDI, etc., (Stiglitz, Fitoussi, & Durand, 2018).

GDP (Gross Domestic Product) is a measurement of a country's economy using expenditures, production, services, or incomes. The world economy consists of 212 economies (World Population Review, 2024). The GDP rankings for the countries or economies in the world are released annually by the International Monetary Fund (IMF) (IMF, 2023), the World Bank (World Bank, 2022), and the UN (UNstats, 2022).

HDI (Human Development Index) consists of three indices for measuring a healthy life, knowledge, and a decent standard of living (UNDP, 2022). The United Nations Development Program (UNDP) has published a series of annual Human Development Reports since 1990 (Sagar & Najam, 1998). HDI and their rankings for the economies in the world are available online (UNDP, 2022). The HDI has become an important alternative to the GDP to measure socioeconomic development.

The above analysis shows that GDP and HDI are the metrics for measuring socioeconomic development. However, GDP and HDI are the classic metrics for measuring socioeconomic development in the agriculture and industry economy and society. The digital age where we live requires new metrics for measuring digital socioeconomic development.

In what follows, this subsection proposes GDDP as a GDP-like data metric for measuring economic performance and social progress. GDDP is the abbreviation of gross domestic data products. It covers data products and services and their consumption in a country or an economy. For example, how many GBs of data have been uploaded for the individual to the Internet for a certain time? The answer is the data product contributed by the individual at this time. Furthermore, how many GBs of data have been downloaded from the Internet by the individual for a certain time? The answer is the data product consumed by the individual at this time. Therefore, everyone is both a data producer and data consumer in the big data era. More strictly, the following holds:

Assume p_i as an individual, $i = \{1, 2, \ldots, n, \ldots\}$. U_{p_i} is the data that has been uploaded to the Internet by p_i for a certain time in GB. D_{p_i} is the data that has been downloaded from the Internet by p_i for a certain time in GB. Then, a GDDP for a country or an economy is

$$GDDP = c. \sum_{i=1}^{N} \left(U_{p_i} + D_{p_i} \right) \tag{10.23}$$

Where, c is the money per GB based on the big statistics of the world (Howdle D., 2024). N is the number of people in the country or an economy. For example, China has 1.4 billion. Then equation (10.23) becomes below.

$$China's\ GDDP = c. \sum_{i=1}^{1.4\ billion} \left(U_{p_i} + D_{p_i} \right) \tag{10.24}$$

For *GDDP* per capita, we have

$$GDDP\ per\ capita = c. \frac{\sum_{j=1}^{N} \left(U_{p_i} + D_{p_i} \right)}{N} \tag{10.25}$$

Therefore, GDDP can be considered a GDP-like data metric for measuring economic performance and social progress in the digital age. In what follows, this section justifies the viability for applying GDDP for a country's economic performance and social progress.

What is the standard of a country for data production and data consumption? The data exchange means the data upload and download. Furthermore, data communication like at Facebook or WeChat has also audio, video, and text communication; all these can be considered as data uploads and data downloads. Every data upload or download can be considered a data business transaction.

Dan Howdle provides worldwide mobile data pricing in 2024, the cost of 1GB of mobile data in 237 countries or economies (Howdle, 2024). For example, the cost of 1GB of mobile data in China, the USA, Australia, Japan, and South Korea (in US$) is 0.38, 6.0, 0.70, 3.48, and 5.1 respectively (Howdle, 2024). This is the basis for one's cost in using mobile data. Further, one must pay the connection plan fee for connecting to the internet or WIFI. One likes to chat using social networking platforms such as

Facebook and WeChat. One likes to download digital movies to watch. One likes to publish media online (photos, blogs, microblogs), and so on. All these are measured as uploaded and downloaded data. Finally, one will contribute to the GDDP and GDDP per capita. The GDDP might imply that the lower the price for mobile data in a country, the more a person contributes to the GDDP (Sun & Wu, 2021). This is worth further investigation.

GDDP is a metric for measuring economic performance and social progress besides GDP, GNI, and HDI (Stiglitz, Fitoussi, & Durand, 2018). This is because the digital economy and big data-driven economy have become an important economic performance for a country. This is also because social progress has been underpinned by big data and big data technology. Big data has formed a big market for big data trade, services, and consumption (Statista, 2021). In fact, GDDP is a well-being metric. One who enjoys 4G and 5G Wi-Fi becomes richer and socially sufficient in most countries or economies. Big data has become one of the most critical key indicators for monitoring economic performance and social progress. Most countries or economies have promulgated their strategies for developing big data and big data technology to get national interest and advances from the international competition in the market. Big data has become a key determinant of economic growth in some countries or economies, such as the USA and China (Statista, 2021). Therefore, GDDP is a GDP-like data metric for measuring the socioeconomic development of a country or an economy. The GDDP can also be considered a complement to HDI or a part of the existing HDI for a country.

Remark: GDDP was introduced in GB in 2021 (Sun & Wu, 2021). The coefficient c was introduced to multiple GB with c, then GDDP is a GDP-like data metric.

10.15.3 A Strategic Model for Big Data Driven Socioeconomic Development

The 10 Bigs of big data discussed in Chapter 2 lead to a strategic model for big data-driven socioeconomic development, as shown in Figure 10.14. Strategically, this model consists of big data with 10 Bigs, big data-driven technologies, services, economies, and societies, all these have been expediating the socioeconomic development of most countries in the past decade (Sun & Wu, 2021).

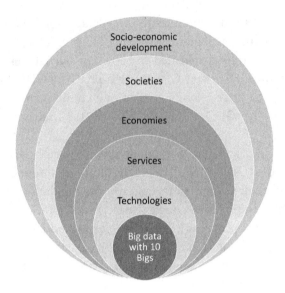

FIGURE 10.14   A strategic model for big data-driven socioeconomic development.

This strategic model shows that big data with 10 Bigs are the foundation of big data-driven technologies, services, economies, and societies in the big data-driven socioeconomic development.

Big data-driven technologies. Big data-driven technologies are technologies based on or supported by big data and the Internet of things (IoT) and AI. Big data is ubiquitous. Therefore, big data-driven technologies have drawn increasing attention in many fields (Sun & Wu, 2021). Big data-driven technologies are shaping markets and business patterns and refashioning considerably the sectors of healthcare, manufacturing, logistics, supply chain management, energy, agriculture, and e-commerce. Big data-driven technologies have been utilized to process and analyze the large amounts of data collected from the sensory devices (Yaqoob, 2000). They are instrumental in developing smart cities because they have become the norm in transportation systems (Baker & Schwanen, 2021).

Big data-driven services. Big data-driven services are services based on or underpinned by big data, IoT, AI, and intelligent analytics (Sun & Stranieri, 2021). Big data services and big data analytics services belong to this category. Big data-driven services have been used for developing smart environments, smart homes, smart cities, and smart planets (Sun & Wu, 2021).

Big data-driven economies. Big data-driven economies are based on or underpinned by big data, IoT, AI, and intelligent analytics (Sun & Stranieri, 2021). This has been exemplified by the rise of driverless cars, the dramatic development of AI, augmented realities, facial recognition technologies, tracking our behaviors anywhere, and sharing properties, services, and information globally (Sun & Wu, 2021).

Big data-driven societies. Big data-driven societies are big data societies or societies based on or underpinned by big data, IoT, AI, and intelligent analytics (Sun & Stranieri, 2021).

In fact, big data-driven technologies, services, economies, and societies are underpinned by eSMACS (electronic, social (networking), mobile, analytics, cloud, and service) technologies, services, economies, and societies. In the rest of this section, we will briefly examine each of them with an example in some detail, as illustrated in Table 10.1.

In Table 10.1, the first column denotes SMACS. The second column lists the detailed SMACS technologies with an example for each; that is, social networking technology with Meta as an example, mobile technology with iPhone as an example, analytics technology with Qlik as an example, cloud technology with Alibaba Cloud (www.alibabacloud.com/) as an example, security technology with Nozomi as an example. Similarly, the third column lists SMACS services with an example for each; that is, social networking services with Meta as an example, mobile services with WeChat Pay (www.wechat.com) as an example, analytics services with Google Analytics (analytics.google.com) as an example, cloud services with Google Mail as an example. Security services with Huawei as an example. The fourth column lists SMACS economies with an example for each, that is, social networking economy with Uber (www.uber.com) as an example, mobile economy with Samsung smartphone as an example, analytics economy with Google Analytics as an example (Penn, 2016), cloud economy with Microsoft Azure (azure.microsoft.com) as an example, Security economy with cyber security economy as an example. The last column lists SMACS societies with an example for each, that is, social networking society with WeChat as an example, the mobile society with China Mobile (www.10086.cn) as an example, analytics society with Google Analytics as an example, cloud society with Microsoft Azure as an example, Security society with the 5G society as an example.

eSMACS technologies, services, economies, and societies can be also considered examples of big data-driven technologies, services, economies,

TABLE 10.1 Big Data-Driven e-SMACS Technologies, Services, Economies, and Societies

SMACS	Technologies	Services	Economies	Societies
Social networking.	Social networking technology (Meta).	Social networking services (Meta).	social networking economy (Uber).	Social networking society (WeChat).
Mobile.	Mobile technology, (iPhone).	Mobile services (WeChat Pay).	Mobile economy (Samsung smartphone).	Mobile society (China Mobile).
Analytics.	Analytics technology (QLIK).	Analytics services (Google Analytics).	Analytics economy (Google Analytics).	Analytics society (Google Analytics).
Cloud.	Cloud technology (Alibaba).	Cloud services (Gmail).	Cloud economy (Microsoft Azure).	Cloud society (Microsoft Azure).
Security Service.	Security technology (Nozomi).	Security services (Huawei).	Security economy (cyber security).	Security society (5G society).

and societies. We do not go into each of the mentioned examples here anymore because of space limitations.

E-business has experienced significant development since 1995 (Schneider, 2017). In about the past three decades, e-business has been transited from business online to e-business services, which have evolved into e-commerce, e-services, social (online) networking services, mobile services, analytics services, cloud services, and security services (Schneider, 2017; Sun & Vajjhala, 2021). All these can be considered eSMACS services (Sun & Wu, 2021; Ghavami, 2020, p. 1). The eSMACS services can be called digital services supported by digital computing and technologies (Sun & Vajjhala, 2021). Almost all traditional services, such as FREG (foods, resources, energy, and goods) services, are fully or partially replaced by eSMACS services or digital services. In what follows, we will briefly look at each of them in some detail.

10.15.3.1 E-services

E-services are electronic services, corresponding to the e-commerce introduced in the middle 1990s (Schneider, 2017). Generally, every service online is an e-service. Therefore, e-commerce services are one of the most important e-services. Other e-services are free services online (Sun & Vajjhala, 2021). For example, many of us enjoy Gmail as a free service. Most of us are expecting free Wi-Fi services.

10.15.3.2 Social Networking Services

Social networking services (SNS) correspond to social commerce and can be called social commerce services (Schneider, 2017). Social networking services include social media services (Ghavami, 2020). Meta's services, WeChat services, and TikTok services belong to this category (Sun & Vajjhala, 2021).

10.15.3.3 Mobile Services

Mobile services correspond to mobile business and can be called mobile business services (Sun & Vajjhala, 2021). Mobile services include location-based services and mobile banking services (Laudon & Laudon, 2020). Mobile services have evolved rapidly over the past two decades (Sun & Wu, 2021). The most popular mobile services include mobile financial or banking services, mobile commerce services (e.g. Weixin pay and AliPay), mobile SNS, and the Internet of Services (IoS) (Sun & Vajjhala, 2021).

10.15.3.4 Analytics Services

Digital analytics has emerged as a disruptive technology and innovative solution to the global economy. This means that analytics services have become an important emerging market, together with cloud services, mobile services, and social services. All the four services and the technologies shaped the most important markets for IT in 2014 (IDC, 2013).

Big data analytics services and technologies have become an important emerging market, together with big data services, cloud services, mobile services, and social networking services (Sun, Strang, & Firmin, 2017). All these four services and the technologies have shaped the most important market for IT and EIS development.

IBM SPSS Modeler is a high-performance data mining and text analytics workbench that helps build predictive models quickly and intuitively and creates predictive analytics for data-driven decision-making (IBM, 2013). IBM SPSS predictive analytics includes analytics services below:

- Predictive customer Analytics: acquire, extend (grow), retain.
- Predictive operational Analytics: manage, maintain, maximize.
- Predictive threat and fraud Analytics: monitor, detect, and control.

All these are related to data collection, CCI, statistics, modeler, and decision management.

10.15.3.5 Cloud Services

A cloud service is any service provided in the cloud (Sun & Vajjhala, 2021). More specifically, cloud services are designed to provide flexible, scalable applications, resources, and services, and are fully managed by a cloud services provider, based on a free or "pay-as-you-go" model (Coronel, Morris, & Rob, 2020). Cloud services mainly comprise four different types of services: Infrastructure as a Service (IaaS), Platform as a Service (PaaS), Software as a Service (SaaS), and storage as a service (StaaS) (NIST, 2018; Buyya, Broberg, & Goscinski, 2010). The Internet of services (IOS), together with the Internet of people (IOP), and the Internet of things (IOT) are three important components of the Internet of Everything (IoE) (Sun & Stranieri, 2021). Amazon Web Services are well-known cloud services. IoP are enjoying IoT and IoS services (Sun & Wu, 2021).

10.15.3.6 Security as a Service

Security as a service is supported by security computing and technologies. Managed security service providers include Cisco (https://tools.cisco.com), IBM (https://www.ibm.com/), Huawei https://www.huawei.com/en/ and Alibaba (https://www.alibaba.com).

Each of the above-mentioned services can be classified further, for example, as a kind of e-services. E-business services include e-commerce services, e-supply chain services, e-marketing services, e-procurement services, and e-banking services. All these services can be considered digital services.

A Google search and Google Scholar search for "eSMACS services" and "e-business service" have been summarized in Table 10.2 (retrieved on October 31, 23). The Google search result reflects the participation, attention, and penetration of industries, individuals, and societies. The Google

TABLE 10.2   The Summary of Google Search and Google Scholar Search for e-SMACS Services and Digital Services

e-SMACS Services	Google (all) Search (M)	Google Scholar Search (N)
E-service	15,950,000,000	238,000
Social networking service	678,000,000	4,670,000
Mobile service	16,600,000,000	8,460,000
Analytics service	7,060,000,000	3,890,000
Cloud service	3,030,000,000	5,380,000
Security service	6,860,000,000	5,370,000
Digital service	6,350,000,000	7,980,000
e-business service	7,530,000,000	734,000

Scholar search results reflect the participation, attention, and penetration of academia.

M and N in the parentheses are the found results of searches (retrieved on October 31, 2023). The searched results in Table 10.2 demonstrate that:

1. Based on the search number of Google (all) and Google Scholar, e-services and mobile services are the most popular in society, while mobile services and digital services are the most popular in academia.

2. Social networking services are the least popular in society, and e-business service is least popular in academia.

3. As modern e-business services, eSMACS services become the most popular and inclusive in both society and academia. They are the most influential services of digital services.

All the services mentioned in Table 10.2 can be considered as e-services and digital services. The above preliminary statistical analysis holds:

$$e - \text{business services} \subseteq \text{eSMACS services} \subset \text{digital services} \qquad (10.26)$$

In other words, eSMACS services are modern e-business services, and they are an important part of digital services. That is,

$$\text{eSMACS services} + e - \text{business services} \subseteq \text{Digital services} \qquad (10.27)$$

10.15.4 Summary

This section provided a strategic perspective on big data-driven socioeconomic development. More specifically, this section presented GDDP as a GDP-like data metric for measuring economic performance and social progress in the digital age. The main contributions of this section, at least, include 1). The presented GDDP can be developed into a GDP-like metric for measuring economic performance and social progress in particular and human development and socioeconomic development in general. GDDP can be considered a representative metric in the digital age, while the existing GDP and HDI are the classic metrics in the agriculture society and industrial society. 2. The proposed strategic model for big data-driven socioeconomic development is the abstraction of current big data and big data technology and their implications for the global economy and social development. 3. The big data-driven SMACS technologies, services, economies, and societies will further underpin the big data-driven socioeconomic development.

Developing GDDP as a viable GDP-like metric system requires at least 100 indices to characterize big data in terms of big data transactions, big data business, big data economy, and big data society, etc. Therefore, future work will study this research issue deeply.

Learning to extend GDDP to measure digital products and services is important for the digital economy and society, which is another topic for future study.

10.16 SUMMARY

This chapter explored business intelligence with applications based on data, analytics, intelligence, and their integrations. More specifically, this chapter analyzed BI, business analytics, eSMACS technologies, and intelligent business process analytics. This chapter presented a calculus of intelligent business analytics and examined techniques for business analytics. This chapter also proposes big data analytics services for enhancing BI and business analytics for enterprise information systems. It explores platform engineering and economics. It discussed big data driven socioeconomic development, BI analytics, decision analytics, cybersecurity intelligence, and analytics. The main contributions of this chapter include: 1) It proposed big data analytics services for enhancing BI and business analytics for enterprise information systems. 2) It explored a calculus of intelligent business analytics. 3) It provided six big trends in the era of big data-based AI and BI and discussed big data driven socioeconomic development. 4) The GDDP can be developed into a GDP-like metric for measuring economic performance and social progress in particular and human development and socioeconomic development in general.

In future work, we will delve into platform engineering and economics and the calculus of intelligent business analytics to analyze the challenges of BI and business analytics in the digital age.

10.17 REVIEW QUESTIONS AND PROBLEMS

1. What does intelligence mean in BI?

2. What is intelligent business process analytics?

3. How can we understand business intelligences from BI?

4. What is BI = OI + MI?

5. What is business analytics?

6. How can you understand the calculus of intelligent business analytics?

7. What are platform engineering and economics?

8. How can you use big data analytics services for enhancing BI?

9. How can we use business analytics for enterprise information systems?

10. In what way is how to extend GDDP to measure digital products and services important for digital economy and society?

11. How can you use business analytics intelligence to empower intelligent business, management, and decision-making?

10.18 REFERENCES FOR FURTHER STUDY

1. Barry Devlin, 2013, Business unIntelligence: Insight and Innovation beyond Analytics and Big Data, Technics Publications, LLC.

2. Demirkan H., Delen D. 2013, Leveraging the capabilities of service-oriented decision support systems: Putting analytics and big data in cloud. Decision Support Systems 55(1): 412-421.

3. Nils J. Nilsson, 2014, Principles of artificial intelligence, Morgan Kaufmann Publishers Inc., San Francisco, CA 1980 &.

4. Nils J. Nilsson, 2010, The Quest for AI (Illustrated Edition), Cambridge University Press.

5. James R. Evans, 2016, Business Analytics: Methods, Models, and Decisions, 2nd Ed.

   Francesco Corea. Big data Analytics: A Management Perspective, Kindle Edition

6. Information Resources Management Association. Big Data: Concepts, Methodologies, Tools, and Applications. IGI 2016.

CHAPTER 11

Conclusion

All Data, analytics, and intelligence are for the people.

ATA, ANALYTICS, AND INTELLIGENCE have impacted us heavily over decades. AI, data management, data warehousing, data mining, data analytics, and BI, have evolved rapidly over the past 70 years. This book not only highlights data but also information, knowledge, intelligence, and wisdom (or DIKIW). This book also looks at DIKIW computing, analytics, services, and intelligence with applications.

We are in the digital era. Therefore, this book not only look at DIKIW and eSMACS services but also DIKIW and eSMACS computing, science, technology, systems, services, and intelligence.

Engineering is a part of any computing. This book looks at not only data engineering, analytics engineering, and intelligence engineering, but also demonstrates that data engineering aims to use data science and technology to develop and manage data systems and services with data intelligence. This is also valid for information engineering, knowledge engineering, analytics engineering, and intelligence engineering. All these are processes of engineering in this book. This engineering idea has been realized in data modeling, data mining, data warehousing, and, in particular, analyticizing. The reasoning is because the key of data mining and data warehousing belongs to an engineering category. Different from other books, this book uses analyticalizing to change analytics into an engineering paradigm, that is, data analyticalizing, information analyticalizing, knowledge analyticalizing, intelligence analyticalizing, and wisdom analyticalizing. All of them will create and develop data analytics, information analytics, intelligence analytics, wisdom analytics, business analytics, and more, respectively. All these have been augmenting our intelligence, wisdom, and our workstyle. We hope you enjoy the journey of data, analytics, and intelligence, and will meet you in the future in an unknown world.

This book demonstrates that data analyses, data management, data infrastructure, and information delivery are basic technological and economic elements of BI and analytics. This book also demonstrates that, originating from statistics and developed by data mining, big data, and AI, analytics, data analytics, big data analytics, intelligent big data analytics, and intelligent big analytics are foundation of business analytics and business intelligence.

In the coming decade, billions of brains and trillions of devices will be connected to the Internet, in the age of the IoE, IOE = IoT + IOP + IOS, not only gaining access to the collective knowledge, experience, intelligence, and wisdom of our humanity, but also contributing to it. More and more knowledge, experience, intelligence, and wisdom will be accessed and shared by human beings, machines, and software agents in H2H (human to human), H2M (or human to machine) or M2M (machine to machine) way. The intelligence of IOE = intelligence of IoT + intelligence of IOP + intelligence of IOS will impact all the other intelligences (DIKIW intelligence, eSMACS intelligence, analytics intelligence, and more around us.

This book describes the three rebalancing centers of this digital era: data, analytics, intelligence, and their relationships: data and intelligence, data and analytics, analytics and intelligence, data and intelligence, and their integrations as three dimensions. Although important elements and principles are important for this book, our research finds several formulas derived from calculus A calculus for searching big data, a calculus of intelligent analytics, and a calculus of intelligent business analytics form a calculus paradigm. Then this book can be renamed as a calculus of data, analytics, and intelligence. All of them will provide computing (DIKIW) as science, engineering, technologies, systems, services, and intelligence to make better decisions in an increasing variety of fields.

There are at least ten following contributions in this book.

1. The Boolean structure dominates this book.

2. Meta computing, science, engineering, technology, systems, and intelligence are important methods for this book.

3. Data engineering also dominates this book.

4. The cycle of business workflow for description, diagnosis, prognosis, and prescription leads to DDPP problems, analytics, and computing.

5. Problem-driven computing and analytics are also the key to developing this book.

6. Big data 4.0: = big intelligence is a calculus bridging the big data, AI, and BI.

7. The calculus for searching big data, the calculus of intelligent analytics, and the calculus of intelligent business analytics form a calculus paradigm. Thus, this book can be renamed as a calculus of data, analytics, and intelligence.

8. Data analyticalizing, as data engineering, is a process of creating and managing data analytics for data intelligence.

9. Insight computing and insight science as a state of the art will lead to the future of big data analytics, intelligent analytics computing, and business analytics because automated insights have been the key function of current data and business analytics platforms and systems (Schlegel & Sun, 2023).

10. Big data, big information, big knowledge, big intelligence, and big wisdom are the future for any data, analytics, and intelligence.

11. Analytics, data analytics, big data analytics, intelligent big data analytics, intelligent big analytics, and intelligent business analytics have been a hierarchy derived from data computing, analytics computing, and intelligence computing.

Taking a Boolean approach, this book presents crucial topics in data, analytics, and intelligence, including computing, multi-industry applications, techniques, and methods for exploring data, information, knowledge, wisdom, analytics, and intelligence. The essential research is emphasized in the fields of AI, data science, computer science, information systems, and technology. This book highlights that computing science, engineering, systems, intelligence, services, and intelligence with applications penetrate every chapter of the book. Therefore, this book is an ideal source for data analysts, computing professionals, researchers, and academics.

Smart and intelligent are still the expectations of human beings in the things and environments around us. You can find smart homes, smart cities, and smart everything (Van Rijmenam, 2020, p. 95). AI and AIs have been ubiquitous in the global market in terms of chips (Nvidia), smartphones (Huawei), drones (Dajiang, https://www.dji.com/global), and more, to name a few, different from other AI waves in the past. Therefore, how can we use AIs, BIs and other intelligent techniques to turn our organizations into intelligent ones, and how to change ourselves into smart people (Van Rijmenam, 2020, p. 138)? There are at least three strategies in the digital age. One of the strategies is to datafy one's organization; that is, datafication is a process of making a business data-driven, by transforming business and action into quantified data and information. It involves collecting (new) data from various sources and processes using IoT devices and/or creating detailed customer profiles based on all digital customer touchpoints (Van Rijmenam, 2020, p. 140).

Another of the strategies is to analyticize data, information, knowledge, experience, and wisdom to provide intelligences for individuals and organizations.

The last strategy is to intelligentize the organization, individual, society, and nation to change them into smart and intelligent entities.

Finally, data, analytics, and intelligence are elements of the digital economy, technology, and society. Embedding these elements into digital wisdom, networks, products, and services will make people, organizations, and societies smarter and more intelligent. Let us embrace data, analytics, intelligence, and their embedded products and services to welcome the new digital future as a new digital citizen.

11.1 REVIEW QUESTIONS AND PROBLEMS

1. What is TEA as a generic framework for decision-making in digital services? See (Sun, Meredith, & Stranieri, 2012)?

2. What is the relationship between datafy, analyticize, and intelligentize?

3. How can we understand that intelligence of IOE = intelligence of IoT + intelligence of IOP + intelligence of IOS will impact all the other intelligences?

4. Do you agree that this book can be renamed as a calculus of data, analytics, and intelligence? Why, write a short thesis with 200 words to argue it.

ACKNOWLEDGMENT

This research is supported partially by the Papua New Guinea Science and Technology Secretariat (PNGSTS) under the project grant No. 1-3962 PNGSTS.

References

3pillarglobal. (2021, August 29). *The Evolution of Big Data Analytics Market.* Retrieved from 3pillarglobal: https://www.3pillarglobal.com/insights/the-evolution-of-big-data-analytics-market/

Ackoff, R. L. (1989). From data to wisdom. *Journal of Applied Systems Analysis, 16,* 3–9.

Ackoff, R. (1992). *From Data to Wisdom.* Retrieved August 31, 2017, from Ackoff, R. L. Ackoff's Best. New York: John Wiley & Sons, pp 170–172. http://faculty.ung.edu/kmelton/Documents/DataWisdom.pdf

ACM. (2020). *Computing Curricula 2020.* Retrieved May 12, 2022, from ACM: https://www.acm.org/binaries/content/assets/education/curricula-recommendations/cc2020.pdf

Alibaba. (2024). *Quick BI.* Retrieved from https://www.alibabacloud.com/product/quickbi

Aristotle. (1801). *The Metaphysics of Aritotle.* (T. Taylor, Trans.) London: Davis, Wilks and Taylor, Chancery-Lane.

Arjonilla, F. J., & Kobayashi, Y. (2019). k-th Order Intelligences: Learning To Learn To Do. *33rd National Conference on Artificial Intelligence (*人工知能学会全国大会論文集*).* Japan: The Japanese Society for Artificial Intelligence. Retrieved from https://www.jst.ge.jst.go.jp/article/pjsai/JSAI2019/0/JSAI2019_2K3E104/_article/-char/ja/

Aroraa, G., Lele, C., & Jindal, M. (2022). *Data analytics: Principles, tools and Practices.* New Dalhi, India: BPB.

Ashton, K. (2009). "That 'Internet of Things' Thing. in the real world, things matter more than ideas." *RFID Journal,* 22 June.

Astrom, K. J., & McAvoy, T. J. (1992). Intelligent control. *Journal of Process Control, 2*(3), 115–126.

Augustyn, J. (2016). *Emerging Science and Technology Trends: 2016–2045: A Synthesis of Leading Forecasts.* Retrieved March 17, 2019, from Office of the Deputy Assistant Secretary of the Army (Research & Technology): https://www.csiam.org.cn/Uploads/Editor/2017–07–21/5971a7aa26e97.pdf

Azvine, B., Nauck, D., & Ho, C. (2003). Intelligent business analytics — A tool to build decision-support systems for eBusinesses. *BT Technology Journal, 21*(4), pp.65–71.

Bajec, M., & Krisper, M. (2001). Managing business rules in enterprises. *Elektrotehniski vestnik, 68*(4), 236–241.

Bajić-Bizumić, B., Rychkova, I., & Wegmann, A. (2013). Simulation-driven approach for business rules discovery. In Franch X., Soffer P. (eds) *Advanced Information Systems Engineering Workshops. CAiSE 2013. Lecture Notes in Business Information Processing* (Vol. 148, pp. 111–123). Berlin, Heidelberg: Springer.

Baker, S. (2018, May 9). *Cambridge Analytica Won't Be Revived Under New Company Name.* Retrieved from Bloomberg: https://www.bloomberg.com/news/articles/2018–05–08/cambridge-analytica-won-t-be-revived-under-new-company-name

Baker, L., & Schwanen, T. (2021). *Big Data Driven Transport Planning and Governing in the Postcolonial 'Smart City': A Case Study of Bangalore.* Retrieved July 14, 2021, from https://www.peak-urban.org/project/big-data-driven-transport-planning-and-governing-postcolonial-smart-city-case-study.

Baltzan, P. (2013). *Business Driven Information Systems.* Sydney: McGraw Hill Australia.

Baral, C. (2000). Abductive reasoning through filtering. *Artificial Intelligence, 120,* 1–28.

Bearman, M., & Luckin, R. (2020). Preparing University Assessment for a World with AI: Tasks for Human Intelligence. In M. Bearman, P. Dawson, R. Ajjawi, & J. Tai (Eds.), *Re-imagining University Assessment in a Digital World. The Enabling Power of Assess* (pp. 49–63).

Beath, C., Becerra-Fernandez, I., Ross, J., & Short, J. (2012, June). Finding value in the information explosion. *MIT Sloan Management Review, 53*(4), 18–20.

Bergmann, R. (2002). *Experience Management: Foundations, Development Methodology and Internet-Based Applicaions.* Berlin: Springer.

BESA. (2018). *BESA.* Retrieved September 16, 2018, from http://www.besa.de/products/besa-epilepsy/besa-epilepsy-overview/.

Betser, J., & Belanger, D. (2013). Architecting the enterprise with big data analytics. In J. Liebowitz, *Big Data and Business Analytics* (pp. 1–20). Boca Raton, FL: CRC Press.

Blatt, T. J. (2017). *Analytics: Business Intelligence, Algorithms and Statistical Analysis* (5th Edition). Orlando, FL: Todd Blatt.

Bodanis, D. (2000). *E = mc2: A Biography of the World's Most Famous Equation.* New York: Walker.

Bogacz, R., & Giraud-Carrier, C. (2000). A Nowel modular neural architecture for rule-base and similarlity-base reasoning. Retrieved from http://www.math.princeton.edu/~rbogacz/papers/Springer00.pdf.

Borne, K. (2014, April). *Top 10 Big Data Challenges – A Serious Look at 10 Big Data V's*. Retrieved from https://web.archive.org/web/20180831134659/https://mapr.com/blog/top-10-big-data-challenges-serious-look-10-big-data-vs/.

Bossmann, J. (2016, October 21). *Top 9 Ethical Issues in Artificial Intelligence*. Retrieved March 5, 2021, from World Economic Forum: https://www.weforum.org/agenda/2016/10/top-10-ethical-issues-in-artificial-intelligence/

Bostrom, N., & Yudkowsky., E. (2018). The Ethics of Artificial Intelligence. In K. Frankish, & W. Ramsey, *Cambridge Handbook of Artificial Intelligence*. New York: Cambridge University Press.

Brooks, R. A. (1991). Intelligence without representation. *Artificial Intelligence* 47(1–3), 139–159.

Brooks, S. (2022). *Business Intelligence and Analytics: Concepts, Techniques and Applications*. New York, NY: Murphy & Moore Publishing.

Brown, S., Gandhi, D., & Herring, L. (2019, September). *The analytics academy: Bridging the gap between human and artificial intelligence*. Retrieved April 8, 2020, from McKinsey: https://www.mckinsey.com/business-functions/mckinsey-analytics/our-insights/the-analytics-academy-bridging-the-gap-between-human-and-artificial-intelligence.

Brust, A. (2013). *Gartner releases 2013 BI Magic Quadrant*. Retrieved February 14, 2014, from http://www.zdnet.com/gartner-releases-2013-bi-magic-quadrant-7000011264/.

Buyya, R., Broberg, J., & Goscinski, A. M. (2010). *Cloud Computing Principles and Paradigms*. Hoboken: John Wiley & Sons, Inc.

Cambridge. (1995). *Cambridge International Dictionary of English*. Bath, UK: Bath Press.

Caniels, M., & Bakens, R. (2011). The effects of project management information systems on decision making in a mulit project enviroment. *International Journal of Project Management*, 30(2), 162–175.

Cao, H. (2022, August 31). *DEPA could be a digital WTO. (*曹和平*:DEPA可能是数字版WTO，中国力争尽早加入)*. Retrieved August 31, 2022, from https://www.guancha.cn/CaoHePing/2022_08_31_655899.shtml.

Castrounis, A. (2020, May 15). *Data science, machine learning and AI*. Retrieved May 16, 2020, from 每日頭條: https://kknews.cc/tech/9vj8gg8.html.

Chaffey, D. (2011). *E-Business and E-Commerce Management: Strategy, Implementation and Practice* (5th Edition). Harlow England: Prentice Hall.

Chen, P. P. (1976). The entity-relationship model-toward a unified view of data. *ACM Transactions on Database Systems*, 1(1), 9–36.

Chen, H., Chiang, R., & Storey, V. (2012). Business intelligence and analytics: From big data to big imppact. *MIS Quarterly*, 36(4), 1165–1188.

Chen, K., Li, X., & Wang, H. (2015). On the model design of integrated intelligent big data analytics systems. *Industrial Management & Data Systems*, 115(9), 1666–1682.

Chen, C. P., & Zhang, C.-Y. (2014). Data-intensive applications, challenges, techniques and technologies: A survey on Big Data. *Information Sciences*, 275, 314–347.

Chen, Z., Zhang, W., & Hu, B. (2017). Retrieving objects by partitioning. *IEEE Transactions on Big Data, 3*(1), 44–54.

Cheng, X., & Li, G. (2020). Data science and computing intelligence: Concept, paradigm, and opportunities. *Bulletin of Chinese Academy of Sciences, 35*(12), 1470–1481.

Chowdhary, K. (2020). *Fundamentals of Artificial Intelligence*. New York, NY: Springer International Publishing.

Clissa, L. (2022, February 20). *Survey of Big Data sizes in 2021*. Retrieved March 11, 2022, from arxiv: https://arxiv.org/abs/2202.07659.

Codd, E. F. (1970). A relational model of data for large shared data banks. *The Communications of ACM, 13*(6), 377–387.

Collibra. (2020, October 16). *What is Data Intelligence?* Retrieved October 27, 2021, from https://www.collibra.com/blog/what-is-data-intelligence.

Conover, W. J. (1999). *Practical Nonparametric Statistics* (3rd Edition). New York: Wiley & Sons, Inc.

Console, L., Theseider Dupre, D., & Torasso, P. (1991). On the relationship between abduction and deduction. *Journal of Logic and Computation, 1*(5), 661–690.

Coronel, C., Morris, S., & Rob, P. (2020). *Database Systems: Design, Implementation, and Management* (14th Edition). Boston: Course Technology, Cengage Learning.

Cortell. (2017). *IBM Planning Analytics*. Retrieved July 29, 2018, from http://www.cortell.co.za/our-partners/ibm-planning-analytics/.

Cramer, C. (2014, May 19). *How Descriptive Analytics Are Changing Marketing*. Retrieved September 6, 2015, from http://www.miprofs.com/wp/descriptive-analytics-changing-marketing/.

CRM. (2012, October). *CRM*. Retrieved January 8, 2013, from Wikipedia: http://en.wikipedia.org/wiki/Customer_relationship_management

Custers, B., & Uršič, H. (2016). Big data and data reuse: A taxonomy of data reuse for balancing big data benefits and personal data protection. *International Data Privacy Law, 6*(1), 4–15.

Da, S. (2023, April 3). *AI and the Wisdom of the Human Beings (*大宗师: 人工智能 *vs* 人类智慧*)*. Retrieved April 5, 2023, from https://blog.creaders.net/u/523/202304/459290.html.

Danyluk, A., & Leidig, P. (2021). *Computing Competencies for Undergraduate Data Science Curricula: ACM Data Science Task Force*. ACM. Retrieved from https://dl.acm.org/doi/pdf/10.1145/3453538

Date, C. J. (2004). *An Introduction to Database Systems* (8th Edition). Addison Wesley.

Davenport, T. H. (2013, December). Analytics 3.0. *Harvard Business Review*, 65–72.

Davis, C. K. (2014). Viewpoint beyond data and analytics – Why business analytics and big data really matter for modern business organizations. *CACM, 57*(8), 39–41.

Delena, D., & Demirkanb, H. (2013). Data, information and analytics as services. *Decision Support Systems, 55*(1), 359–363.

Demirkan, H., & Delen, D. (2013). Leveraging the capabilities of service-oriented decision support systems: Putting analytics and big data in cloud. *Decision Support Systems, 55*(1), 412–421.

Denning, P. J., & Hayes-Roth, R. (2006). Decision Making in Very Large Networks. *Communications of the ACM, 49*(11), 19–23.

Descartes, R. (1637). *Discourse on the Methods*. GlobalGrey 2018. Retrieved from https://www.globalgreybooks.com/index.html.

Desjardins, J. (2019, June 21). *A Visual History of the Largest Companies by Market Cap (1999-Today)*. Retrieved April 8, 2020, from Visual Capitalist: https://www.visualcapitalist.com/a-visual-history-of-the-largest-companies-by-market-cap-1999-today/

Dietrich, D. (2013). *Big Data Analytics*. Retrieved February 3, 2014, from EMC Academic Alliance: https://www.youtube.com/watch?v=d1PHKCc1fog

Dignum, V. (2019). *Responsible Artificial Intelligence: How to Develop and Use AI in a Responsible Way*. Cham, Switzherland: Springer.

Donoho, D. L. (2017). 50 years of data science. *Journal of Computational and Graphical Statistics 26*(4).

Dykstra, J. (2015). *Essential Cybersecurity Science*. O' oreilly. Retrieved April 11, 2024, from O'Reilly learning platform: https://www.oreilly.com/library/view/essential-cybersecurity-science/9781491921050/ch01.html.

Eiloart, J. (2018, December 2). *Top five business analytics intelligence trends for 2019*. Retrieved from https://www.information-age.com/business-analytics-intelligence-123477004/.

Elragal, A. (2014). ERP and Big Data: The Inept couple. *Procedia Technology, 16,* 242–249.

EM360 Tech. (2020, September 18). *Top 10 Cloud Data Warehouse Solution Providers*. Retrieved August 25, 2021, from https://em360tech.com/data_management/tech-features-featuredtech-news/top-10-cloud-data-warehouse-solution-providers.

Epp, S. S. (1995). *Discrete Mathematics with Applications*. Brooks/Cole Publishing Company Pacific Grove. Retrieved from file:///C:/AA%20New%20Ideas%20Papers/Materials/discrete_mathematics_with_applications-EPP.pdf.

Erickson, G. S., & Rothberg, H. N. (2013). Competitors, intelligence, and big data. In J. (Liebowitz.

Erl, T., Mahmood, Z., & Puttini, R. (2013). *Cloud Computing: Concepts, Technology & Architecture*. Pearson.

Fan, S., Lau, R. Y., & Zhao, J. L. (2015). Demystifying Big Data analytics for business intelligence through the lens of marketing mix. *Big DataResearch, 2,* 28–32.

Fattah, A. (2014, March 21). *Going Beyond Data Science Toward an Analytics Ecosystem*. Retrieved February 18, 2021, from IBM: https://www.ibmbigdatahub.com/blog/going-beyond-data-science-toward-analytics-ecosystem-part-3

Finnie, G., & Sun, Z. (2003). R5 model of case-based reasoning. *Knowledge-Based Systems, 16*(1), 59–65.

Fortinet. (2024). *What is Cybersecurity Analytics?* Retrieved February 20, 2024, from https://www.fortinet.com/resources/cyberglossary/cybersecurity-analytics.

Fothergill, B. T., Knight, W., Stahl, B. C., & Ulnicane, I. (2019). Responsible Data Governance of Neuroscience Big Data. *Frontiers in Neuroinformatics, 13*(28), doi:10.3389/fninf.2019.00028.

Gailly, F., & Geerts, G. L. (2013). Ontology-driven business rule specification. *Journal of Information Systems, 27*(1), 79–104.

Gandomi, A., & Haider, M. (2015). Beyond the hype: Big data concepts, methods, and analytics. *International Journal of Information Management, 35*, 137–144.

Gao, J., Koronios, A., Kennett, S., & Scott, H. (2010). Business rule discovery through data mining methods. In Amadi-Echendu, J., *Definitions, Concepts and Scope of Engineering Asset Management. Engineering Asset Management, Engineering Asset Management Review* (Vol. 1, pp. 159–172). London, Scott: Springer. doi:https://doi.org/10.1007/978-1-84996-178-3_9.

Gardner. (2024). *Big Data*. Retrieved October 16, 2017, from https://www.gartner.com/it-glossary/big-data.

Gartner. (2023a). *Gartner Magic Quadrant for Supply Chain Planning Solutions*. Retrieved 2024, from https://www.gartner.com/en/documents/4321599.

Gartner. (2023b). *Products In Analytics and Business Intelligence Platforms Market*. Retrieved June 12, 2023, from Gartner: https://www.gartner.com/reviews/market/analytics-business-intelligence-platforms.

Gartner. (2024a). *Cloud Computing*. Retrieved from Gartner Glossary: https://www.gartner.com/en/information-technology/.

Gartner. (2024b). *CRM Customer Engagement Center*. Retrieved April 4, 2024, from https://www.gartner.com/reviews/market.

Gartner. (2024c). *Diagnostic Analytics*. Retrieved from Gartner Glossary: https://www.gartner.com/en/information-technology/glossary/.

Gartner. (2024d). *Gartner Experts Answer the Top Generative AI Questions for Your Enterprise*. Retrieved January 29, 2024, from Gartner: https://www.gartner.com/en/topics/generative-ai.

Gartner-augmented analytics. (2020). *Augmented Analytics*. Retrieved August 13, 2020, from Gartner Glossary: https://www.gartner.com/en/information-technology/glossary/augmented-analytics.

Ghavami, P. (2020). *Big Data Analytics Methods: Analytics Techniques in Data Mining, Deep Learning and Natural Language Processing* (2nd Edition). Boston/Berlin: de Gruyter.

Goes, P. B. (2014). Big Data and IS research. *MIS Quarterly, 38*(3), iii–viii.

Google. (2013, October 7). *Digital Analytics Fundamentals - Lesson 2.1 The Importance of Digital Analytics*. Retrieved March 12, 2014, from Google analytics: https://www.youtube.com/watch?v=JbXNS3NjIfM.

Google. (2024). *What Is a Data Lake?* Retrieved March 21, 2024, from Google Cloud: https://cloud.google.com/learn/.

Google Analytics Intelligence. (2020). *About Analytics Intelligence*. Retrieved September 3, 2020, from Google: https://support.google.com/analytics/answer/7411707?hl=en.

Gruber, T. (1995). Toward principles for the design of ontologies used for knowledge sharing. *International Journal of Human-Computer Studies, 43*(5–6), 907–928.

GTAI. (2014). *Industrie 4.0 Smart Manufacturing for the Future.* Retrieved August 13, 2016, from Germany Trade & Invest: http://www.gtai.de/GTAI/Content/EN/Invest/_SharedDocs/Downloads/GTAI/Brochures/Industries/industrie4.0-smart-manufacturing-for-the-future-en.pdf.

Halal, W. E. (1997). Organizational Intelligence. *strategy+business - a PwC publication, Fourth Quarter* (9). Retrieved from https://www.strategy-business.com/article/12644.

Halevy, A., Norvig, P., & Pereira, F. (2009). The unreasonable effectiveness of data. *IEEE Intelligent Systems, May,* 8–12.

Hardin, J. M. (2013). *What Is Business Analytics?* Retrieved March 11, 2014, from https://www.youtube.com/watch?v=QTLF4xYY41U.

Hawkins, J. (2021). *A Thousand Brains: A New Theory of Intelligence.* New York, NY: Basic Books.

HCU. (2024). *What is Cybersecurity?* Retrieved April 11, 2024, from Hoston Christian University: https://hc.edu/articles/.

Henke, N., & Bughin, J. (2016, December). *The Age of Analytics: Competing in a Data Driven World.* Retrieved from McKinsey Global Institute.

Holmstedt, M., & Dahlin, P. (2021). The end of business intelligence and business analytics. In P. Ekman, P. Dahlin, & C. Keller (Eds.), *Management and Information Technology after Digital Transformation (Chapter 17)* (p. 10). London: Routledge.

Holsapple, C., Lee-Post, A., & Pakath, R. (2014). A unified foundation for business analytics. *Decision Support Systems, 64,* 130–141. doi:10.1016/j.dss.2014.05.013.

Howard, G. (1983). *Frames of Mind: Theory of Multiple Intelligences.* New York: Basic Books. Retrieved from Gardner, Howard (1983), Frames of Mind: The Theory of Multiple Intelligences.

Howard, G. (1999). *Intelligence Reframed: Multiple Intelligences for the 21st Century.* New York: Basic Books.

Howard, G. (2012, June). *The Theory of Multiple Intelligences: As Psychology, As Education, As Social Science.* Retrieved October 21, 2023, from https://howardgardner01.files.wordpress.com/2012/06/473-madrid-oct-22-2011.pdf.

Howarth, J. (2022, December 12). *30+ Incredible Big Data Statistics (2023).* Retrieved May 3, 2023, from https://explodingtopics.com/blog/big-data-stats#top-big-data-stats.

Howarth, J. (2023). *80+ Amazing IoT Statistics (2024–2030).* Retrieved from https://explodingtopics.com/blog/iot-stats.

Howdle, D. (2024). *Worldwide mobile data pricing 2024.* Retrieved July 11, 2021, from https://www.cable.co.uk/mobiles/worldwide-data-pricing/.

Howson, C., Richardson, J., Sallam, R., & Kronz, A. (2019, February 11). *Magic Quadrant for Analytics and Business Intelligence Platforms*. Retrieved July 7, 2019, from Gartner: https://cadran-analytics.nl/wp-content/uploads/2019/02/2019-Gartner-Magic-Quadrant-for-Analytics-and-Business-Intelligence-Platforms.pdf.

Howson, C., Sallam, R. L., & Richa, J. L. (2018, February 26). *Magic Quadrant for Analytics and Business Intelligence Platforms*. Retrieved August 16, 2018, from Gartner: www.gartner.com

Hoyos, A. A., & Velásquez, J. D. (2020). Teaching analytics: Current challenges and future development. *IEEE Revista Iberoamericana De Tecnologias Del Aprendizaje, 15*(1), 1–9.

Hu, M. (2020). Cambridge Analytica's black box. *Big Data & Society, 7*(2), 1–6.

Hu, W. C., & Kaabouch, N. (2014). *Big data management, technologies, and applications*. IGI Global.

Hu, S., Liu, Y., & Wang, S. (2020). Teaching exploration of case-based data modeling optimization for database system. *Open Journal of Social Sciences, 8*, 514–521.

Huellermeier, E. (2001). Similarity-based inference as evidential reasoning. *International Journal of Approximate Reasoning, 26*, 67–100.

Hurley, R. (2019). *Data Science: A Comprehensive Guide to Data Science, Data Analytics, Data Mining, Artificial Intelligence. Machine Learning, and Big Data*. Middletown, DE: Hurley.

Hussein, A. (2020). Fifty-six Big Data V's characteristics and proposed strategies to overcome security and privacy challenges (BD2). *Journal of Information Security, 11*(4), 304–328. doi:10.4236/jis.2020.114019.

Iantovics, L. B., Kountchev, R. K., & Crisan, G. C. (2019). ExtrIntDetect—A new universal method for the identification of intelligent cooperative multiagent systems with extreme intelligence. *Symmetry, 11*(9), 1–22.

IBM. (2013). *Introduction to Predictive Analytics with SPSS Modeler*. Retrieved March 12, 2014, from https://www.youtube.com/watch?v=uOj4_xHZ2C4.

IBM. (2023). *Prescriptive Analytics*. Retrieved June 26, 2023, from IBM: https://www.ibm.com/prescriptive-analytics.

IBM. (2024a). *Natural Language Processing*. Retrieved March 29, 2024, from IBM: https://www.ibm.com/topics/.

IBM. (2024b). *Quantum Computing*. Retrieved April 1, 2024, from https://www.ibm.com/topics/.

IBM. (2024c). *What Is Supply Chain Analytics?* Retrieved April 5, 2024, from IBM: https://www.ibm.com/topics/.

IDC. (2013, December). *IDC Predictions 2014: Battles for Dominance — and Survival — on the 3rd Platform*. Retrieved February 13, 2014, from http://www.idc.com/getdoc.jsp?containerId=244606.

IDC. (2016, April 14). *Large Scale Digital Transformation: Innovation Process in the New Era*. Retrieved from http://www.idc.com/getdoc.jsp?containerId=prCHE41190916.

IDC. (2019, April 4). *IDC Forecasts Revenues for Big Data and Business Analytics Solutions will Reach $189.1 Billion This Year with Double-Digit Annual Growth Through 2022*. Retrieved January 23, 2020, from IDC: https://www.idc.com/getdoc.jsp?containerId=prUS44998419.

IDC. (2022). *Beyond Digital Transformation: What Comes Next?* IDC. Retrieved from https://info.idc.com/rs/081-ATC-910/images/.

IDC. (2024). *Expert Guidance on the Digital-First Strategies*. Retrieved February 17, 2024, from https://www.idc.com/promo/future-of-x.

IMF. (2023). *World Economic Outlook database: October*. Retrieved February 18, 2024, from INTERNATIONAL MONETARY FUND: https://www.imf.org/en/Publications/WEO/weo-database/2023/.

INFORMS. (2014). Defining analytics a conceptual framework. *ORMS Today*, *43*(3). Retrieved August 12, 2020, from INFORMS: https://www.informs.org/ORMS-Today/Public-Articles/June-Volume-43-Number-3/Defining-analytics-a-conceptual-framework.

Ingle, P. (2023). *Top Data warehousing tools in 2023*. Retrieved July 26, 2023, from MarktechpostMediaInc:https://www.marktechpost.com/2023/07/23/top-data-warehousing-tools-in-2022/.

Inmon, B. (1992, 2005). *Building the data warehouse* (4th Edition). Wiley.

Isaac, M., & Frenkel, S. (2018, September 28). *Facebook Security Breach Exposes Accounts of 50 Million Users*. Retrieved March 13, 2021, from The New York Times: https://www.nytimes.com/2018/09/28/technology/facebook-hack-data-breach.html.

James, S., & Duncan, A. D. (2023, April 24). *Over 100 Data and Analytics Predictions Through 2028*. Retrieved December 22, 2023, from Gartner Research: https://emt.gartnerweb.com/ngw/globalassets/en/doc/documents/.

Jech, T. (2003). *Set Theory: The Third Millennium Edition, Revised and Expanded*. Springer. Retrieved from Wikipedia: https://en.wikipedia.org/wiki/Cardinality_of_the_continuum.

Jenkins, C., Lopresti, D., & Mitchell, M. (2020). *Next Wave Artificial Intelligence: Robust, Explainable, Adaptable, Ethical, and Accountable*. Retrieved January 12, 2021, from https://cra.org/ccc/resources/ccc-led-whitepapers/#2020-quadrennial-papers.

John, G. (2013). *The Age of Artificial Intelligence*. Retrieved from TEDxLondonBusinessSchool: https://www.youtube.com/watch?v=0qOf7SX2CS4.

Johnsonbaugh, R. (2013). *Discrete Mathematics* (7th Edition). Pearson Education Limited.

Johnson-Laird, P. N., Khemlani, S. S., & Goodwin, G. P. (2015). Logic, probability, and human reasoning. *Trends in Cognitive Sciences*, *19*(4), 201–214.

Jordan, M. I., & Mitchell, T. M. (2015). Machine learning: Trends, perspectives, and prospects. *Science*, *349*(6245), 255–260.

Judson, T. W. (2013). *Abstract Algebra: Theory and Applications*. USA: GNU Free Documentation License.

Kambatla, K., Kollias, G., Kumar, V., & Grama, A. (2014). Trends in big data analytics. *Journal of Parallel and Distributed Computing, 74*(7), 2561–2573.

Kantardzic, M. (2011). *Data Mining: Concepts, Models, Methods, and Algorithms.* Hoboken, NJ: Wiley & IEEE Press.

Kauffman, R. J., Srivastava, J., & Vayghan, J. (2012). Business and data analytics: New innovations for the management of e-commerce. *Electronic Commerce Research and Applications, 11*, 85–88.

Kavenna, J. (2019, October 4). *Shoshana Zuboff: Surveillance capitalism is an assault on human autonomy.* Retrieved February 28, 2021, from https://www.theguardian.com/books/2019/oct/04/shoshana-zuboff-surveillance-capitalism-assault-human-automomy-digital-privacy.

Kindler, H., Densow, D., Fischer, B., & Fliedner, T. (1995). Mapping laboratory medicine onto the select and test model to facilitate knowledge-based report generation in laboratory medicine. In P. E. Barahona, *LNAI 934.* Berlin: Springer.

Kingpin. (2024, January 9). *Global Business Intelligence and Analytics Software Market Research Report 2024.* Retrieved February 25, 2024, from kingpin-marketresearch: https://www.kingpinmarketresearch.com/global-business-intelligence-and-analytics-software-market-26510637.

Kleene, S. C. (1952). *Introduction to Metamathematics.* Ishi Press International.

Koorn, R., et al. (2015). Big Data analytics & privacy: How to resolve this paradox? *Compact, 4*, 1–10.

Krippendorff, K. (2019). *Driving Innovation Within: A Guide for International Enterpreneurs.* New York: Columbia University Press.

Krishnamurthi, S., & Fisler, K. (2020). Data-centricity: A challenge and opportunity for computing education. *Communications of the ACM, 63*(8), 24–26.

Kroenke, D., Bunker, D., & Wilson, D. (2014). *Exerperiencing MIS* (3rd Edition). Australia: Person.

Kumar, B. (2015). An encyclopedic overview of 'big data' analytics. *International Journal of Applied Engineering Research, 10*(3), 5681–5705.

Kumar, M. (2019, April 4). *IDC Forecasts Revenues for Big Data and Business Analytics Solutions.* Retrieved April 7, 2020, from IDC: https://www.idc.com/getdoc.jsp?containerId=prUS44998419.

Kumara, B. T., et al. (2015). Ontology-Based Workflow Generation for Intelligent Big Data Analytics. *2015 IEEE International Conference on Web Services, ICWS 2015, 27 June 2015 to 2 July* (pp. 495–502). New York; United States: IEEE.

Laney, D. (2001). *3D data management: controlling data volume, velocity, and variety, META Group, Tech. Rep. (949).* Retrieved October 27, 2015, from http://blogs.gartner.com/doug-laney/files/2012/01/ad949-3D-Data-Management-Controlling-Data-Volume-Velocity-and-Variety.pdf.

Laney, D., & Jain, A. (2017, June 20). *100 Data and Analytics Predictions Through*. Retrieved August 4, 2018, from Gartner: https://www.gartner.com/events-na/data-analytics/wp-content/uploads/sites/5/2017/10/Data-and-Analytics-Predictions.pdf.

Lang, S. (2002). *Algebra, Graduate Texts in Mathematics 211* (Revised 3rd Edition). New York: Springer-Verlag.

LaPlante, A. (2019). *What Is Augmented Analytics? Powering Your Data with AI*. Boston: O' Realy. Retrieved from https://go.oracle.com/LP=84622.

Larson, E. K., & Gray, C. F. (2011). *Project Management: The Managerial Process* (5th Edition). New York: McGraw-Hill.

Lau, R. Y., Li, C., & Liao, S. S. (2014). Social analytics: Learning fuzzy product ontologies for aspect-oriented sentiment analytics. *Decision Support Systems, 65*, 80–94. http://doi.org/10.1016/j.dss2014.05.005.

Laudon, K. G., & Laudon, K. C. (2020). *Management Information Systems: Managing the Digital Firm* (16th Edition). Harlow, England: Pearson.

Leake, D. B. (1993). Focusing construction and selection of abductive hypotheses. *Proceedings of the 11th Interational Joint Conference on Artificial Intelligence* (pp. 24–29).

Liebowitz, J. (2013). *Big Data and Business Analytics*. Hoboken: CRC Press.

Liebowitz, J. (2014, May 28). Business analytics and decision-making: The years ahead. *The World Financial Review*. Retrieved from http://www.worldfinancialreview.com/?p=1904.

Liew, A. (2013). DIKIW: Data, Knowledge, Intelligence, Wisdom and their inter-relationships. *Business Management Dynamics, 2*(10), 49–62.

Lim, E., Chen, H., & Chen, G. (2013). Business intelligence and analytics: Research directions. *ACM Transactions on Management Information Systems, 3*(4, Article 17), 1–10.

Lohr, S. (2012 February 11). The age of Big Data. *The New York Times*, 1–5.

Loshin, D. (2013). *Big Data Analytics: From Strategic Planning to Enterprise Integration woth Tools, Techniques, NoSQL and Graph*. Amsterdam: Elsevier.

Lovell, M. C. (1983). Data mining. *The Review of Economics and Statistics, 65*(1), 1–12.

Lu, X. (2023, April 27). *With the rise of the "fourth industry", have we found the "explosion point" of the new technological revolution? (吕欣:"第四产业"兴起，我们找到了新科技革命的"爆发点"?)*. Retrieved April 27, 2023, from Observer (Guancha): https://www.guancha.cn/lvxin/2023_04_27_690134_s.shtml.

Luhn, H. P. (1958). A business intelligence system. *IBM Journal of Research and Development 2*(4), 314–319.

Ma, Y. (2016, October 13). *Jack Ma: The future is driven by wisdom and data (马云: 未来是智慧驱动 与数据驱动)*. Retrieved July 5, 2023, from People net 赵越、杨波 (eds): http://it.people.com.cn/n1/2016/1024/c1009-28801537.html.

MacGillivray, C., Turner, V., & Shirer, M. (2015, June 2). *Explosive Internet of Things Spending to Reach $1.7 Trillion in 2020, According to IDC*. Retrieved from IDC: http://www.idc.com/getdoc.jsp?containerId=prUS25658015.

Macmillan. (2007). *Macmillan English Dictionary for Advanced Learners*. London: Macmillan.

Magnani, L. (2001). *Abduction, Reason, and Science, Processes of Discovery and Explanation*. New York: Kluwer Academic/Plenum Publishers.

Manyika, J., Chui, M., & Bughin, J. E. (2011, May). *Big data: The next frontier for innovation, competition, and productivity*. Retrieved from McKinsey Global Institute: http://www.mckinsey.com/business-functions/business-technology/our-insights/big-data-the-next-frontier-for-innovation.

Marketsandmarkets. (2022). *big data market (2023–2028)*. Retrieved March 13, 2024, from marketsandmarkets: https://www.marketsandmarkets.com/.

Mayer-Schoenberger, V., & Cukier, K. (2013). *Big Data: A Revolution that Will Transform How We Live, Work, and Think*. Houghton Mifflin Harcourt Publishing Company.

McAfee, A., & Brynjolfsson, E. (2012). Big data: The management revolution. *Harvard Business Review*, 61–68.

McAfee, A., & Brynjolfsson, E. (2017). *Machine, Platform, Crowd: Harnessing Our Digital Future*. W. W. Norton & Company.

McDonald, D. (2017). *The Golden Passport: Harvard Business School, the Limits of Capitalism, and the Moral Failure of the MBA Elite*. New York: Harper Collins Publishers.

Medigration. (2014, September 4). *IBM Watson ushers in a new era of data-driven discoveries*. Retrieved March 29, 2024, from https://healthcare-in-europe.com/en/news/.

Merriam-Webster. (2022). *Merriam-Webster Dictionary*. Retrieved May 11, 2022, from https://www.merriam-webster.com/dictionary/computing.

Merriam-Webster. (2023a, December 21). *Algorithm*. Retrieved December 21, 2023, from https://www.merriam-webster.com/dictionary/algorithm.

Merriam-Webster. (2023b). *Analysis*. Retrieved April 22, 2022, from Merriam-Webster Dictionary: https://www.merriam-webster.com/.

Merriam-Webster. (2023c, October 30). *Meta*. Retrieved November 6, 2023, from Merriam-Webster dictionary: (https://www.merriam-webster.com/dictionary/meta).

Merriam-Webster. (2024a). *Induction*. https://www.merriam-webster.com/dictionary/induction.

Merriam-Webster. (2024b, Feburary 1). *insight*. Retrieved December 21, 2023, from Merriam-webster: https://www.merriam-webster.com/dictionary/insight.

Mike, K., & Hazzan, O. (2023). What is data science? *CACM*, 66(2), 12–13.

Miladinov, G. (2020). Socioeconomic development and life expectancy relationship: Evidence from the EU accession candidate countries. *Genus*, 76(2). doi:10.1186/s41118-019-0071-0.

Milošević, P., Petrović, B., & Jeremi, V. (2017). IFS-IBA similarity measure in machine learning algorithms. *Expert Systems with Applications, 89,* 296–305.

MindSpot. (2024). *MindSpot.* Retrieved Feburary 1, 2024, from https://www.mindspot.org.au/

Minelli, M., Chambers, M., & Dhiraj, A. (2013). *Big Data, Big Analytics: Emerging Business Intelligence and Analytic Trends for Today's Businesses.* Wiley & Sons.

Minsky, M. (1985). *The Society of Mind.* London: Heinemann.

Mittal, N. (2017, March 20). *Building Effective Analytics Ecosystems: CIO Insights and Analysis from Deloitte.* Retrieved February 17, 2021, from The Wall Street Journal: https://deloitte.wsj.com/cio/2017/03/20/building-effective-analytics-ecosystems/.

Moutinho, L., Rita, P., & Li, S. (2006). Strategic diagnostics and management decision making: A hybrid knowledge-based approach. *Intelligent Systems in Accounting, Finance and Management, 14,* 129–155.

Mueller, V. (2016). *Fundamental Issues of Artificial Intelligence.* New York, NY: Springer International Publishing.

National Academies of Sciences, E. M. (2016). *Future Directions for NSF Advanced Computing Infrastructure to Support U.S. Science and Engineering in 2017–2020.* Washington, DC: The National Academies Press.

National Research Council. (2013). *Frontiers in Massive Data Analysis.* Washington, DC: The National Research Press.

Negnevitsky, M. (2005). *Artificial Intelligence: A Guide to Intelligent Systems* (2nd Edition). Harlow: Addison-Wesley.

Ni, C., & Zhang, J. (2022). A kind of novel edge computing architecture based on adaptive stratified sampling. *Computer Communications, 183,* 121–135. doi:10.1016/j.comcom.2021.11.012.

Nilsson, N. J. (1998). *Artificial Intelligence: A New Synthesis.* San Francisco, California: Morgan Kaufmann Publishers, Inc.

NIST. (2018, January 8). *Final Version of NIST Cloud Computing Definition Published.* Retrieved February 20, 2019, from https://www.nist.gov/news-events/news/2011/10/final-version-nist-cloud-computing-definition-published.

Norusis, M. J. (1997). *SPSS: SPSS 7.5 Guide to Data Analytics.* Upper Saddle River, NJ: Prentice Hall.

NZ. (2020). *Digital Economy Partnership Agreement (DEPA).* Retrieved October 3, 2022, from https://www.mfat.govt.nz/en/trade/free-trade-agreements/free-trade-agreements-in-force/digital-economy-partnership-agreement-depa.

Oltsik, J. (2012, February 14). *The Intersection of Security Intelligence and Big Data Analytics.* Retrieved September 4, 2020, from https://www.csoonline.com/article/2221688/the-intersection-of-security-intelligence-and-big-data-analytics.html.

OmniSci. (2020). *Data Intelligence.* Retrieved September 3, 2020, from OmniSci: https://www.omnisci.com/technical-glossary/data-intelligence.

OpenAI. (2023). *Introducing ChatGPT*. Retrieved April 16, 2023, from https://openai.com/blog/chatgpt.

Oxford. (2008). *Oxford Advanced Learner's English Dictionary* (7th Edition). Oxford University Press.

Panetta, K. (2021, March 15). *Gartner Top 10 Data and Analytics Trends for 2021*. Retrieved February 17, 2022, from Gartner: https://www.gartner.com/smarterwithgartner/gartner-top-10-data-and-analytics-trends-for-2021.

Papazoglou, M. P. (2008). *Web Services: Principles and Technology*. Harlow, England: Pearson Prentice Hall.

Papazoglou, M. P., & Georgakopoulos, D. (2003). Service-orented computing. *Communications of the ACM, 46*(10), 25–28.

Pappalardo, L., Pedreschi, D., Smoreda, Z., & Giannotti, F. (2015). Using big data to study the link between human mobility and socio-economic development. *2015 IEEE International Conference on Big Data* (pp. 871–878).

Park, J., Kim, J., & Koh, J. (2010). Determinants of continuous usage intention in web analytics services. *Electronic Commerce Research and Applications, 9*(1), 61–72.

Patil, R. (2014, March 8). *Big data is like crude oil*. Retrieved April 5, 2020, from Dataconomy: https://dataconomy.com/2014/03/big-data-is-like-crude-oil-4/.

Payton, M. (2015, June 25). *Google wants to bring free wifi to the world and its starting now*. Retrieved August 12, 2016, from Metro.co.uk: http://metro.co.uk/2015/06/25/google-wants-to-bring-free-wifi-to-the-world-and-its-starting-now-5265352/.

Penn, C. S. (2016, October 4). *Understanding the Google Analytics Ecosystem*. Retrieved February 17, 2021, from https://www.christopherspenn.com/2016/10/understanding-the-google-analytics-ecosystem/.

Perri, L. (2023). *What Is Platform Engineering?* Retrieved March 17, 2024, from Gartner: https://www.gartner.com/en/articles/.

Peters, G., & Duncan, A. D. (2020). *100 Data and Analytics Predictions Through 2024*. Retrieved March 4, 2021, from https://emtemp.gcom.cloud/ngw/globalassets/en/doc/documents/721868-100-data-and-analytics-predictions-through-2024.pdf.

Pettey, C., & van der Meulen, R. (2018, April 25). *Gartner Says Global Artificial Intelligence Business Value to Reach $1.2 Trillion in 2018*. Retrieved August 4, 2018, from Gartner: https://www.gartner.com/newsroom/id/3872933.

Pfleeger, C. P., & Pfleeger, S. L. (2006). *Security in Computing* (4th Edition). Prentice Hall.

Phillips, J. (2013). *Building a Digital Analytics Organization: Create Value by Integrating Analytical Processes, Technology, and People into Business Operations*. Upper Saddle River, New Jersey, US: Financial Times Press. pp. 7–8.

Pittman, C. (2022). *Google Analytics and GA4: Improve your online sales by better understanding customer data and how customers interact with your website*. Kingsport, Tennessee: SMP Publishing.

Plato & Jowett (Translator), B. (2022). *The Republic*. Independently Published.

PNG Government. (2022, July 26). *PNG Digital Government Plan 2023–2027*. Retrieved August 22, 2022, from https://www.ict.gov.pg/.

Powell, T. W. (2020). *The Value of Knowledge: The Economics of Enterprise Knowledge and Intelligence (Knowledge Services)*. K G Saur Verlag Gmbh & Co.

Pressman, R., & Maxim, B. (2014). *Software Engineering: A Practitioner's Approach* (8th Edition). McGraw-Hill Education.

Qlik. (2021). *Qlik*. Retrieved August 28, 2021, from https://www.qlik.com/us.

Rai, S. (2019, August 1). *What Is Google Analytics Intelligence?* Retrieved September 3, 2020, from https://www.monsterinsights.com/what-is-google-analytics-intelligence-beginners-guide/.

Reddy, C. K. (2014). A survey of platforms for big data analytics. *Journal of Big Data (Springer), 1*(8), 1–20.

Reeves, S., & Clarke, M. (1990). *Logic for Computer Science*. Wokingham, England: Addison-Wesley Publishing.

ResearchAndMarkets. (2022, August 15). *The Worldwide Big Data & Analytics Industry is Expected to Reach $146 Billion by 2027*. Retrieved May 14, 2023, from ResearchAndMarkets.com: https://www.businesswire.com/news/home/20220815005342/en/The-Worldwide-Big-Data-Analytics-Industry-is-Expected-to-Reach-146-Billion-by-2027---ResearchAndMarkets.com#:~:text=The%20Global%20Big%20Data%20%26%20Analytics%20Market%20size,9.96%25%20to%20reach%2.

Rich, E., & Knight, K. (1991). *Artificial Intelligence* (2nd Edition). New York: McGraw-Hill.

Richardson, J., Schlegel, K., Sallam, R., Kronz, A., & Sun, J. (2021, February 15). *Magic Quadrant for Analytics and Business Intelligence Platforms*. Retrieved March 6, 2021, from Gartner: https://www.gartner.com/doc/reprints?id=1-254T1IQX&ct=210202&st=sb.

Robbins, S., Bergman, R., Stagg, I., & Coulter, M. (2012). *Management 6*. Frenchs Forest: Pearson Australia.

Roche, S. (2016, April 21). *IDC Reveals 53% of Organizations in the APEJ Region Consider Big Data and Analytics Important for Business*. Retrieved from IDC: http://www.idc.com/getdoc.jsp?containerId=prAP41208316.

Rowley, J. (2007). The wisdom hierarchy: Representations of the DIKW hierarchy. *Journal of Information and Communication Science, 33*(2), 163–180.

Ruisel, I. (1994). From academic and personal intelligence to wisdom. *Studia Psychologica, 36*(3), 137.

Russell, B. (1967). *History of Western Philosophy*. UK: Simon & Schuster/Touchstone.

Russell, S., & Norvig, P. (2020). *Artificial Intelligence: A Modern Approach* (4th Edition). Upper Saddle River: Prentice Hall.

Sabherwal, R., & Becerra-Fernandez, I. (2011). *Business Intelligence: Practices, Technologies, and Management*. Hoboken, NJ: John Wiley & Sons, Inc.

Sagar, A. D., & Najam, A. (1998). The human development index: A critical review. *Ecological Economics*, 25(3), 249–264.

Sathi, A. (2013). *Big Data Analytics: Disruptive Technologies for Changing the Game*. Boise, ID, USA: MC Press: IBM Corporation.

Schalkoff, R. J. (2011). *Intelligent Systems: Principles, Paradigms, and Pragmatics*. Boston: Jones and Bartlett Publishers.

Schlegel, K., & Sun, J. (2023). *Magic Quadrant for Analytics and Business Intelligence Platforms*. Gartner. Retrieved July 21, 2023, from https://www.gartner.com/doc/reprints?id=1-2955ETOT&ct=220215&st=sb?ocid=lp_pg398450_gdc_comm_az.

Schneider, G. P. (2017). *Electornic Commerce* (12th Edition). Cengage Learning.

Schwab, P.-N. (2023, February 16). *ChatGPT: 1000 texts analyzed and up to 75,3% similarity*. Retrieved March 17, 2023, from intotheminds: https://www.intotheminds.com/blog/en/chatgpt-similarity-with-plan/.

Sharda, R., Delen, D., & Turba, E. (2018). *Business Intelligence and Analytics: Systems for Decision Support* (10th Edition). Boston, MA: Pearson.

Sharda, R., Delen, D., Turban, E., & King, D. (2018). *Business Intelligence, Analytics, and Data Science: A Managerial Perspective* (4th Edition). Pearson.

Siegel, E. (2016). *Predictive Analytics: The Power to Predict Who Will Click, Buy, Lie, or Die*. Hoboken, NJ: Wiley & Sons.

Sisense. (2021). *Data Intelligence*. Retrieved October 27, 2021, from Sisense: https://www.sisense.com/glossary/data-intelligence/.

Six Sigma Pro SMART. (2019, January 3). *Data Analytics for Beginners: Analytics Lifecycle*. Retrieved May 12, 2020, from youtube: https://www.youtube.com/watch?v=1QH7iukKZgg.

Skyrius, R. (2021). Business intelligence definition and problem space. In R. Skyrius, *Progress in IS, in: Business Intelligence, chapter 0* (pp. 7–26). Berlin: Springer.

Sommerville, I. (2010). *Software Engineering* (9th Edition). Harlow, England: Pearson Education.

Stahl, B. C., & Wright, D. (2018). Ethics and privacy in AI and Big Data: Implementing responsible research and innovation. *IEEE Security & Privacy*, 16(3), 26–33. doi:10.1109/MSP.2018.2701164.

State Council, China. (2016, April). *Made in China 2025*. Retrieved August 13, 2016, from http://baike.baidu.com/item/%E4%B8%AD%E5%9B%BD%E5%88%B6%E9%80%A02025.

Statista. (2021). *Revenue from Big Data and Business Analytics Worldwide from 2015 to 2022 (In Billion U.S. Dollars)*. Retrieved July 7, 2021, from https://www.statista.com/statistics/551501/worldwide-big-data-business-analytics-revenue/.

Sternberg, R. J., Glaveanu, V., Karami, S., Kaufman, J. C., Phillipson, S. N., & Preiss, D. D. (2021). Meta-Intelligence: Understanding, Control, and Interactivity between Creative, Analytical, Practical, and Wisdom-Based Approaches in Problem Solving. *Journal of Intelligence*, 9(2), 19 (1–22).

Stiglitz, J. E., Fitoussi, J.-P., & Durand, M. (2018). *OECD: Beyond GDP Measuring What Counts for Economic and social Performance and For Good Measure Advancing Research on Well-being Metrics Beyond GDP*. Paris, France: OECD Publishing. Retrieved from https://www.oecd.org/statistics/measuring-economic-social-progress/HLEG-reports.pdf.

Stodden, V. (2020). The data science life cycle: A disciplined approach to advancing data science as a science. *Communications of the ACM, 63*(7), 58–66.

Stoller, M. (2021, October 26). *Facebook was Born, Lives and Thrives in Scandal. It's Been Lawless for Years*. Retrieved November 5, 2021, from The Guardian: https://www.theguardian.com/commentisfree/2021/oct/26/facebook-scandal-mark-zuckerberg-frances-haugen.

Strang, K., & Sun, Z. (2022). ERP staff versus AI recruiters using employment real-time Big Data. *Discover Artificial Intelligence, 2*(21). https://doi.org/10.1007/s44163-022-00037-1.

Sun, R. (1995). Robust reasoning: Integrating rule-based and similarity-based reasoning. *Artificial Intelligence, 75*, 241–295.

Sun, Z. (2016). A framework for developing management intelligent systems. *International Journal of Systems and Service Oriented Engineering, 6*(1), 37–53.

Sun, Z. (2017). A logical approach to experience-based reasoning. *Journal of New Mathematics and Natural Computation, 13*(1), 21–40. doi:10.1142/S1793005716002939.

Sun, Z. (2018a). 10 bigs: Big Data and its ten big characteristics. *PNG UoT BAIS, 3*(1), 1–10. doi:10.13140/RG.2.2.31449.62566.

Sun, Z. (2018b). Intelligent Big Data analytics: Foundations and applications. *PNG UoT BAIS, 3*(4), 1–8. doi:10.13140/RG.2.2.11037.41441.

Sun, Z. (2019a). Intelligent Big Data analytics: A managerial perspective. In Z. Sun, *Managerial Perspectives on Intelligent Big Data Analytics* (pp. 1–19). USA: IGI-Global.

Sun, Z. (2019b). *Managerial Perspectives on Intelligent Big Data Analytics*. IGI-Global.

Sun, Z. (2020a). Big data analytics thinking and big data analytics intelligence. *PNG UoT BAIS, 5*(6), 1–11. Retrieved from https://www.researchgate.net/publication.

Sun, Z. (2020b). *Business Analytics Intelligence: An Emerging Frontier for Innovation and Productivity*. Retrieved February 3, 2021, from https://www.researchgate.net/profile/Zhaohao_Sun/publication/343876626_Business_Analytics_Intelligence_An_Emerging_Frontier_for_Innovation_and_Productivity.

Sun, Z. (2020c). Digital computing and eSMACS computing. *PNG UoT BAIS, 5*(7), 1–9. doi:10.13140/RG.2.2.19412.83846.

Sun, Z. (2021). The age of metaintelligence: Competing in the digital world. *PNG UoT BAIS, 6*(8), 1–11. https://www.researchgate.net/publication/355788448_The_Age_of_Metaintellidoi:10.13140/RG.2.2.23279.97449.

Sun, Z. (2022a). A mathematical theory of big data. *Journal of Computer Science Research, 4*(2), 13–23. https://doi.org/10.30564/jcsr.v4i2.4646.

Sun, Z. (2022b). Problem-based computing and analytics. *International Journal of Future Computer and Communication, 11*(3), 52–60.

Sun, Z. (2022c–8). *A Hierarchy of Data and Intelligence: A Meta Approach.* Retrieved from PNG UoT BAIS 7(2): 1–9: https://www.researchgate.net/publication/360298286_Hierarchy_of_Data_and_Intelligence_A_Meta_Approach.

Sun, Z. (2023a). Data, analytics, and intelligence. *Journal of Computer Science Research, 5*(4), 43–57.

Sun, Z. (2023b). Demand-driven Services. In F. Gallouj, C. Gallouj, & M.-C. Monno (Eds.), *Encyclopedia of Services* (pp. 74–77). Cheltenham, UK: Edward Elgar Encyclopedia Publishing, www.elgaronline.com

Sun, Z. (2023c). Similarity intelligence: Similarity based reasoning, computing, and analytics. *Journal of Computer Science Research, 5*(3), 14–23.

Sun, Z. (2024). Big Data 4.0: The Era of Big Intelligence. *Journal of Computer Science Research, 6*(1), 1–15.

Sun, Z., & Finnie, G. (2003). Brain-like architecture and experience-based reasoning. *Proceedings of the 7th Joint Conf on Information Sciences (JCIS), September 26–30, 2003* (pp. 1735–1738). Cary, North Carolina.

Sun, Z., & Finnie, G. (2004). *Intelligent Techniques in E–Commerce: A Case–based Reasoning Perspective.* Heidelberg Berlin: Springer–Verlag.

Sun, Z., & Finnie, G. (2005a). Experience management in knowledge management. *LNAI 3681, Berlin Heidelberg: Springer–Verlag*, 979–986.

Sun, Z., & Finnie, G. (2005b). MEBRS: A multiagent architecture for an experience based reasoning system LNAI, ISSN: 0302–9743, Vol. 3681. (pp. 972–978). Germany: Springer.

Sun, Z., & Finnie, G. (2007). A fuzzy logic approach to experience based reasoning. *International Journal of Intelligent Systems, 22*, 867–889.

Sun, Z., & Finnie, G. (2016). *A Similarity based Approach to Experience Based Reasoning (Prepprint).* Retrieved from University of Wollongong: ro.uow.edu.au.

Sun, Z., Finnie, G., & Weber, K. (2004). Case base building with similarity Relations. *Information Sciences (Elsevier), 165*(1–2), 21–43.

Sun, Z., Finnie, G., & Weber, K. (2005). Abductive case based reasoning. *International Journal of Intelligent Systems, 20*(9), 957–983.

Sun, Z., & Firmin, S. (2012). A strategic perspective on management intelligent systems. In J. Casillas et al, *Management Intelligent Systems, AISC 171* (pp. 3–14). Springer.

Sun, Z., Han, J., & Dong, D. (2008). Five perspectives on case based reasoning. LNAI 5227. *ICIC2008, Shanghai* (pp. 410–419). Berlin: Springer.

Sun, Z., & Huo, Y. (2020). Intelligence without Data. *Global Journal of Computer Science and Technology C, 20*(1), 25–35.

Sun, Z., & Huo, Y. (2021). The spectrum of Big Data analytics. *Journal of Computer Information Systems, 61*(2), 154–162. doi:10.1080/08874417.2019.1571456.

Sun, Z., Li, A., Liu, K., & Jie, J. (2008). Correspondence relationships among algebra, logic and intelligent systems. *4th National Conference of Logic System, Intelligent Science and Information Science (CLSIST2008)*. Guizhou: see CNKI at http://cpfd.cnki.com.cn/Article/CPFDTOTAL-GZLJ200800001003.htm.

Sun, Z., Meredith, G., & Stranieri, A. (2012). TEA: A generic framework for decision making in web services. *International Journal of Systems and Service Oriented Engineering*, 3(3), 41–63.

Sun, Z., Pambel, F., & Wu, Z. (2022). The elements of intelligent business analytics: Principles, techniques, and tools. In Z. Sun & Z. Wu, *Handbook of Research on Foundations and Applications of Intelligent Business Analytics* (pp. 1–20).

Sun, Z., Pinjik, P., & Pambel, F. (2021). Business case mining and E-R modeling optimization. *Studies in Engineering and Technology*, 8(1), 53–66.

Sun, Z., Strang, K., & Firmin, S. (2017). Business analytics-based enterprise information systems. *Journal of Computer Information Systems (JCIS)*, 57(2), 169–178. http://doi.org/10.1145/2684200.2684358.

Sun, Z., Strang, K., & Li, R. (2018). Big data with ten big characteristics. *Proceedings of 2018 The 2nd Intl Conf. on Big Data Research (ICBDR 2018), October 27–29* (pp. 56–61). Weihai, China: ACM.

Sun, Z., Strang, K. D., & Pambel, F. (2020). Privacy and security in the Big Data paradigm. *Journal of Computer Information Systems*, 60(2), 146–155.

Sun, Z., Strang, K., & Wu, Z. (2022). Driving Digital Services with Big Data Analytics. *The 6th International Conference on Big Data Research (ICBDR 2022), Harbin, China, Aug. 10–12* (pp. 42–47). New York: ACM Proceedings.

Sun, Z., & Stranieri, A. (2021). The nature of intelligent analytics. In Z. Sun, *Intelligent Analytics with Advanced Multi-industry Applications* (pp. 1–22). Hershey: IGI-Global.

Sun, Z., Sun, L., & Strang, K. (2018). Big Data analytics services for enhancing business intelligence. *Journal of Computer Information Systems (JCIS)*, 58(2), 162–169. doi:10.1080/08874417.2016.1220239.

Sun, Z., & Vajjhala, N. R. (2021). Responsible Big Data Analytics for e-Business Services. *The 5th Intl Conf on Big Data Research (ICBDR)* (pp. 28–34). Tokyo Japan, September 25–27: ACM.

Sun, Z., & Wang, P. P. (2017a). A mathematical foundation of Big Data. *Journal of New Mathematics and Natural Computation*, 13(2), 8–24.

Sun, Z., & Wang, P. P. (2017b). Big Data, analytics and intelligence: An editorial perspective. *Journal of New Mathematics and Natural Computation*, 13(2), 75–81.

Sun, Z., & Wang, P. P. (2021). *The Scientification of China*. UK: Cambridge Scholars Publishing.

Sun, Z., & Wu, Z. (2021). A Strategic Perspective on Big Data Driven Socioeconomic Development. *The 5th International Conference on Big Data Research (ICBDR), September 25–27* (pp. 35–41). Tokyo, Japan: ACM.

Swami, D., & Sahoo, B. (2016). Service delivery model for Big Data as a service. *International Journal of Data Mining and Knowledge Engineering, 8*. Retrieved from https://www.researchgate.net/publication/305040380_SERVICE_ DELIVERY_MODEL_FOR_BIG_DATA_AS_A_SERVICE.

Sweeney, D. J., Williams, & Anderson, D. (2011). *Fundamentals of Business Statistics* (6th Edition). Natorp Boulevard, OH: South-Western Cengage Learning.

Szabo, M. E. (1969). *The Collected Papers on Gerhard Gentzen*. Amsterdam: North-Holland Publishing Company.

Tabein, R., Moghadasi, M., & Khoshkbarforoushha, A. (2008). Broker-based Web service selection using learning automata. *2008 International Conference on Service Systems and Service Management, June July 2008* (pp.1–6).

Tableau. (2017). *Top 10 Big Data Trends*. Retrieved July 06, 2021, from https:// www.tableau.com/resource/top-10-big-data-trends-2017.

Tableau. (2020). *Top 8 Trends for 2016: Big Data*. Retrieved from www.tableau. com/Big-Data.

Tableau. (2021). *Top Ten Big Data Trends*. Retrieved February 17, 2022, from Tableau: https://www.tableau.com/sites/default/files/whitepapers/849188_ big_data_trends__slideshare_v2_0.pdf.

Tableau. (2024, August 25). *Tableau*. Retrieved August 25, 2021, from https:// www.tableau.com/why-tableau/what-is-tableau.

Taherdoost, H., & Madanchian, M. (2023). Artificial Intelligence and knowledge management: Impacts, benefits, and implementation. *Computers (MDPI)*, 12, 72. https://doi.org/10.3390/computers1204007.

Talkinghealthtech. (2023). *What is Diagnostics Versus Diagnosis?* Retrieved July 21, 2023, from Talking HealthTech Pty Ltd: https://www.talkinghealthtech. com/glossary/diagnostics-versus-diagnosis.

Tan, T. (2018, May 29). AI: Angel or Devil (谭铁牛: 人工智能:天使还是魔鬼). *The 19th Academician Conference of the Chinese Academy of Sciences (第十 九次中科院院士大会)*. Retrieved July 18, 2018, from www.cnic.cas.cn/ kxcb/kpwz/202106/t20210629_6118883.html.

Tarassov, V. B. (1996). Artificial Meta-Intelligence: A Key to Enterprise Reengineering. In *Proceedings of the Second Joint Conference on Knowledge Based Software Engineering* (JCKBSE'96, Sozopol, Bulgaria, September 1996). Sofia: BAAI, pp. 15–24.

Taylor, T. (1801). *The Metaphysics of Aristotle, Translated from Greek, Digitized by Google*. UK, London: Davis, Wilks, and Taylor, Chancery-Lane.

Techopedia. (2018, September 10). *Big Data as a Service (BDaaS)*. Retrieved April 2, 2020, from Techopedia: https://www.techopedia.com/definition/29399/ big-data-as-a-service-bdaas.

Techopedia. (2021). *Data Intelligence*. Retrieved October 26, 2021, from Techopedia: https://www.techopedia.com/definition/28799/data-intelligence.

Techopedia. (2022). *Social Computing*. Retrieved May 17, 2022, from https://www. techopedia.com/definition/13852/social-computing.

Techtarget. (2022). *Mobile Computing*. Retrieved May 17, 2022, from https://www. techtarget.com/searchmobilecomputing/definition/nomadic-computing.

Teradata. (2023). *What Is Big Data?* Retrieved from https://www.teradata.com/glossary/what-is-big-data.

Terry, G. R. (1968). *Principles of Management* (5th Edition). Homewood, IL: Richard D. Irwin, Inc.

Thalheim, B. (2000). *Entity-Relationship Modeling Foundations of Database Technology*. Berlin: Springer.

Thierauf, R. J. (1982). *Decision Support Systems for Effective Planning and Control: A Case Study Approach*. Englewood Cliffs, NJ: Prentice Hall.

Thierauf, R. J., & Hoctor, J. J. (2006). *Optimal Knowledge Management: Wisdom Management Systems Concepts and Applications*. Hershey, PA: Idea Group Inc.

Thomas, I. (2013). Putting big data at the heart of the decision kaning process. In J. Liebowitz, *Big Data and Business Analytics*. Hoboken: CRC Press. (pp. 153–170).

Thompson, J. K., & Rogers, S. P. (2017). *Analytics: How to Win with Intelligence*. Basking Ridge, NJ: Technics Publications.

Torasso, P., Console, L., Portinale, L., & Theseider, D. (1995). On the role of abduction. *ACM Computing Surveys, 27*(3), 353–355.

Tsai, C., Lai, C., Chao, H., & Vasilakos, A. (2015). Big data analytics: A survey. *Journal of Big Data, 2*, 31–62.

Tsinghua University & CAAI. (2019). *Report of AI Development*. Beijing: Qinhua University & CAAI.

Turban, E., & Volonino, L. (2011). *Information Technology for Management: Improving Performance in the Digital Economy* (8th Edition). Hoboken, NJ: John Wiley & Sons.

Turek, M. (2020). *Explainable Artificial Intelligence (XAI)*. Retrieved November 13, 2020, from DARPA: https://www.darpa.mil/program/explainable-artificial-intelligence.

Turing, A. (1950). Computing machinery and intelligence. *Mind, 49*, 433–460.

Uber. (2024). *About Uber*. Retrieved April 11, 2024, from Uber: https://www.uber.com/au/en/about.

UNDP. (2021). *The SDGS in Action*. Retrieved November 18, 2021, from United Nations Development Programme (UNDP): https://www.undp.org/sustainable-development-goals.

UNDP. (2022). *Human Development Report 2021–22*. New York, NY: The United Nations Development Programme. Retrieved July 10, 2021, from https://hdr.undp.org/content/human-development-report-2021-22

UNstats. (2022). *Basic Data Selection*. Retrieved February 18, 2024, from https://unstats.un.org/unsd/snaama/Basic.

Vaidya, D. (2023). *Business Functions*. Retrieved June 23, 2023, from Wallstreetmojo Team: https://www.wallstreetmojo.com/business-functions/.

Van Rijmenam, M. (2020). *The Organisation of Tomorrow: How AI, Blockchain and Analytics turn your business into a data organisation*. London and New York: Routledge.

Vardi, M. Y. (2016). The moral imperative of Artificial Intelligence. *Communications of the ACM, 59*(5), 5.

Varghese, B., & Buyya, R. (2019). Next generation cloud computing: New trends and research directions. *Future Generation Computer Systems 79*, 849–861.

Vesset, D., McDonough, B., Schubmehl, D., & Wardley, M. (2013, June). *Worldwide Business Analytics Software 2013–2017 Forecast and 2012 Vendor Shares (Doc # 241689)*. Retrieved June 28, 2014, from http://www.idc.com/getdoc. jsp?containerId=241689.

Wade, R. (2020). *Advanded Analytics in Power BI with R and python*. New York: Apress.

Wang, F.-Y. (2012). A big-data perspective on AI: Newton, Merton, and Analytics Intelligence. *IEEE Intelligent Systems, Sept/Oct, 27*(5), 2–4.

Wang, Y. (2015, June). Formal cognitive models of data, information, knowledge, and intelligence. *WSEAS Transactions on Computers, 14*, 770–781.

Wang, W., Zhang, J., & Zhang, T. (2023). Novel edge caching approach based on multi-agent deep reinforcement learning for Internet of vehicles. *IEEE Transactions on Intelligent Transportation Systems, 24*(6), 1–16. doi:10.1109/ TITS.2023. 3264553.

Weber, H. (2020). *Big Data and Artificial Intelligence: Complete Guide to Data Science, AI, Big Data, and Machine Learning*. USA: ICGtesting.

Wikipedia. (2024a). *Mobile Operating System*. Retrieved April 11, 2024, from https://en.wikipedia.org/wiki/Mobile_operating_system.

Wikipedia. (2024b). *Quantum Computing*. Retrieved April 1, 2024, from wikipedia: https://en.wikipedia.org/wiki.

Wikipedia. (2024c, January 18). *Train*. Retrieved October 5, 2018, from https:// en.wikipedia.org/wiki/Train.

Wikipedia-Annus. (2020, May 28). *Annus Mirabilis Papers*. Retrieved May 30, 2020, from Wikipedia: https://en.wikipedia.org/wiki/Annus_Mirabilis_ papers.

Wikipedia-Bicycle. (2024). *Bicycle*. Retrieved October 5, 2018, from https:// en.wikipedia.org/wiki/Bicycle.

Wikipedia-Car. (2024, January 18). *Car*. Retrieved from Wikipedia: https:// en.wikipedia.org/wiki/Car.

Wikipedia-Digital signal. (2024). *Digital Signal*. Retrieved October 5, 2018, from Wikipedia: https://en.wikipedia.org/wiki/Digital_signal.

Wikipedia-Sammuel. (2024, April). *Machine Learning*. Retrieved April 27, 2024, from https://en.wikipedia.org/wiki/Machine_learning.

Wikipedia-speaker. (2024). *Loudspeaker*. Retrieved October 9, 2018, from wikipedia: https://en.wikipedia.org/wiki/Loudspeaker.

Wikipedia-Transport. (2024). *Transport*. Retrieved October 9, 2018, from Wikipedia: https://en.wikipedia.org/wiki/Transport.

Williams, S. (2016). *Business Intelligence Strategy and Big Data Analytics: A General Management Perspective*. Amsterdam: Morgan Kaufmann.

Wood, M. (2018, March 19). *Cambridge Analytica, Facebook and the new data war*. Retrieved November 3, 2018, from https://www.marketplace.org/2018/03/19/ tech/cambridge-analytica-facebook-and-new-data-war.

World Bank. (2022). *DGP (Current US$) in 2022*. Retrieved February 18, 2024, from https://data.worldbank.org/indicator/.

World Population Review. (2024). *GDP Ranked by Country 2024*. Retrieved February 18, 2024, from https://worldpopulationreview.com/countries/countries-by-gdp.

Wu, C., Buyya, R., & Ramamohana, K. (2016). *Big Data Analytics = Machine Learning + Cloud Computing*. Retrieved July 20, 2018, from https://arxiv.org/ftp/arxiv/papers/1601/1601.03115.pdf.

Xinhua, E., & Han, J. (2013). Big Data-as-a-Service: Definition and architecture. *15th IEEE International Conference on Communication Technology*. IEEE.

Yao, Y., Yang, F., & Su, S. (2006). Flexible decision making in web services negotiation. In J. Euzenat & J. Domingue (Eds). AIMSA 2006, *LNAI 4183* (pp. 108–117).

Yaqoob, I. E. (2000). Blockchain for digital twins: Recent advances and future research challenges. *IEEE Network*, 34(5), 290–298.

Yasar, K., & Kiwak, K. (2022). *TechTarget*. Retrieved April 5, 2024, from CRM-analytics: https://www.techtarget.com/searchcustomerexperience/definition/.

Zadeh, L. A. (1965). Fuzzy sets. *Information and Control*, 8(3), 338–353.

Zadeh, L. A. (1971). Similarity relations and fuzzy orderings. *Information Sciece (Elsever)*, 3, 177–200.

Zhang, B., & Song, D. (2019, May 26). *The miracle of AI is difficult to reproduce in the short term, and the potential of deep learning technology has reached its ceiling*. 张钹; 宋笛: *AI奇迹短期难再现，深度学习技术潜力已近天花板*. Retrieved June 8, 2019, from Economic Observer (经济观察报): https://finance.sina.com.cn/roll/2019-05-26/doc-ihvhiews4638601.shtml.

Zimmermann, H. J. (2001). *Fuzzy Set Theory and Its Application* (4th Edition). Boston/Dordrecht/London: Kluwer Academic Publishers.

Zook, M., Barocas, S., & Boyd, D. E. (2017). Ten simple rules for responsible big data research. *PLOS Computational Biology*, 13(3), e1005399. Retrieved from Ten simple rules for responsible big data research. PLOS Computational Biology, 13 (3). e1005399.

Index

Pages in *italics* refer to figures and pages in **bold** refer to tables.

Printed in the United States
by Baker & Taylor Publisher Services